SCRAM FROM KENYA!

James Franks first visited Kenya in 1947, as a young subaltern in the Royal Engineers. The experience made such an impression on him that he planned to settle in the country once he had qualified in England as a chartered surveyor.

In the event it was to be 40 years before he returned. On that visit he read an interview with the self-styled Field Marshal Mwariama, a Mau Mau leader, which became the catalyst for further research in Kenya and elsewhere, and which led to the writing of *Scram from Kenya!*

He is the author of four other books and numerous articles and occasional papers.

Scram from Kenya!

from colony to republic

James Franks

In 1989 Eliud Waweru, our Kikuyu driver in Kenya, shared with us his experiences and his copies of *Daily Nation*. One issue of the newspaper contained an article about the veteran Mau Mau leader Mwariama and his execution of a British soldier. It was Eliud who suggested that an objective and balanced account of the post-war years leading to Kenya's independence had yet to be written. *Scram from Kenya!* is an attempt to fill the gap he saw . . .

© 2004 James Franks
James Franks reserves the moral right to be identified as the author of this work

ISBN 0-9542587-4-6

British Library Cataloguing-in-Publication Data
A catalogue record for this book is available from the British Library

Published by Pomegranate Press
Dolphin House, 51 St Nicholas Lane, Lewes, Sussex UK BN7 2JZ
email: pomegranatepress@aol.com

Printed by Viscan Graphics, 40 Mimosa Road, Singapore 808002

Contents

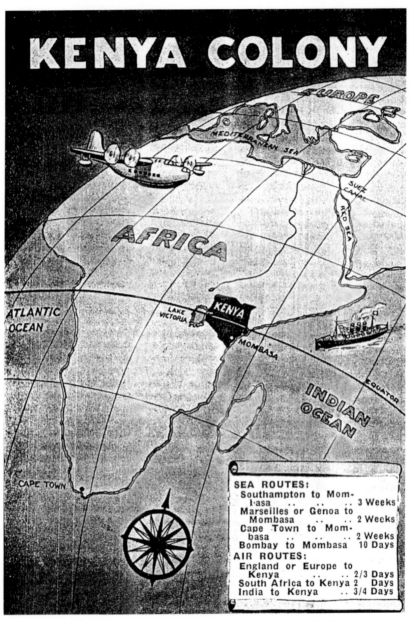

Kenya in 1945, from the Kenya Settlement Handbook,
promoting Kenya as a country for European colonization.

Introduction

Scram from Kenya! – from colony to republic is intended for readers in Britain, Kenya and elsewhere interested in the end of colonial power and the birth of a republic as experienced by people who were living in Kenya at the time or were involved in the dramatically unfolding story. It provides 'core-reading', a record of events rather than a scholar's analysis, and is the sequel to *Kenya – the colonial years*, which explores developments (outlined at the beginning of this book) from 1895, when Kenya became a British protectorate, until 1946, when the Second World War came to an end and Jomo Kenyatta, a potential leader of an independent nation, returned home from England.

The Kenyan experience can be viewed as a microcosm in a single colony of the end of the British empire. In a speech made at a Conference of All-African People in December 1958 Tom Mboya, one of the foremost Kenyan black African leaders, called for solidarity, urging delegates to 'tell these colonial nations – your time is past, Africa must be free, scram from Africa!' Five years later Britain did, indeed, 'scram' from the colony, and Kenya gained its independence.

A superficial perusal of the Sources section of the book indicates that there is no shortage of books about Kenya. This account draws on published material, but it also includes hitherto unpublished accounts of some 60 people, black, brown and white, who were involved in these momentous events. Audio-taped interviews, biographies, diaries, contemporary correspondence and documents are used to construct an account of significant happenings in forest, farm, Nairobi streets and political chamber.

Two aims have been uppermost in the mind while writing. First, that people, all too frequently in conflict, should be at the centre of the story. Secondly, that all sides should be presented in a balanced account. So it is, for example, that conflict in the forest draws on accounts by people such as Njama, Wachanga and Mwariama for Mau Mau and Campbell and Kitson for the British military. Nellie Grant, Joan Scott and others provide the white farmers' perspective. On the political front Odinga, Mboya, Kaggia, Blundell, Baring and Mitchell, to mention just a few names, provide views of political developments, while the Indian/Asian community and the Administration are also represented. Some contributors (most of those mentioned above and others) provide 'strands' which are unbroken for years on end and which are central to the plot, and the Index should help in tracing them. Others provide ephemeral local colour.

In the introduction to his autobiography, one of the Mau Mau leaders in the forest suggests that another leader wrote about events as he would have liked them to be rather than as they actually were. All writers have their own perspective and apply their own gloss; none is completely objective or impartial. Memories are notoriously unreliable, and some times people simply do not tell the truth. Most have a case to make, and interviewees tend to say what they think the researcher wishes to hear. Readers should continually note the source and draw their own conclusions.

Although *Scram from Kenya!* is concerned principally with the struggles to bring about change from colony to republic, the opening chapter paints the background against which that change may be understood. The epilogue, attempting to draw together the wealth of the material researched, presents questions, hypotheses and assessments. References and footnotes are given after this epilogue. The Sources and Acknowledgements sections indicate the breadth and scope of available information for research, by no means all of it used in this text.

1
Colonial Days

'For the furtherance of the British empire.' (Cecil Rhodes)

Kenya provides a microcosm of the British empire, which was for some centuries the largest and most powerful in the world. Roughly the size of France, three-quarters the size of Texas, the former colony sits on the east coast of Africa astride the equator. Late in the 19th century, during the 'scramble for Africa', European nations cut much of Africa into slices and divided them between themselves. Kenya and Uganda were Great Britain's slices in East Africa. Tanganyika joined them in 1919 when Britain acquired the former German colony as one of the spoils of the First World War.

Arab and Portuguese traders had long been familiar with both coast and hinterland, but it was during the 19th century that equatorial East Africa was brought to the attention of Europe, and not until the second half of it that a few European and American explorers ventured far inland. In 1871 the *New York Herald* sent Henry Morton Stanley, one of its reporters, to find a Scottish missionary/explorer who was not aware that he was lost. Their meeting gave rise to the legendary greeting 'Dr. Livingstone, I presume'.

British explorers were appalled by the extent of the slave traffic in East Africa. There are no reliable figures, but it is estimated that by 1875 12,000 black slaves were being exported by Arabian traders each year. By this time Britain, having been a successful slave trading nation until a decade or two earlier, had seen the wickedness of slavery and set out to abolish it with the zeal of the convert. Saving the natives seemed a justification for British protection, and further justification was contained in reports from Uganda, the land regarded as the prize for European occupation. These referred to the delightful climate and conditions ideal for settlement by Europeans. They referred, too – and luridly – to inhuman treatment of the native people by tyrannical rulers. It was suggested that the king and his people might undergo mass conversion to Islam. There was also the possibility of the natives being unduly influenced by Roman Catholic Portuguese missionaries. Given a choice between Islam or

Catholicism, Protestant missionaries found it difficult to decide which prospect offered the greater threat to the souls of the natives.

As if all that were not enough, protecting Uganda could also be regarded as protecting trade with India, an all-important consideration. The logic was that Uganda's Lake Victoria stood at the head of the Nile, providing access to Egypt and the Suez Canal, through which trade with India flowed. Protection of Uganda could therefore be justified on Christian, humanitarian, economic and imperialist grounds. No-one doubted the morality of imperialism. It had, it was argued, a long, respectable and well established history. It was a natural law and good for all concerned.

Uganda and Kenya became protectorates in 1895 and colonies in 1920. Many of the justifications for colonizing Uganda did not apply to Kenya, but it provided a route to Uganda from the Indian Ocean, and early in the 20th century a railway was built through Kenya. To pay for its construction and running costs, as well as for political reasons, the British government encouraged Europeans to emigrate, settle and farm in Kenya. True, its soil and climate were not as attractive for settlement as Uganda's, but it did have some advantages, and after the First World War the 'right kind' of ex-servicemen were offered financial inducement by the British government to settle there. To some extent, to say the least, the land they were offered was already occupied by black Africans, but when the white settlers first arrived at what were later to be known as the White Highlands (the seven million acres alienated for European settlement in the colony), the area had suffered a drought, causing a famine which had left the land virtually unoccupied. Such natural disasters had been part of Africa's history since man's earliest times, but not until the late 20th century, when television brought pictures of barren countryside, drought and mass starvation to European living rooms, was their full horror appreciated by the western world.

Although the White Highlands appeared unoccupied to the British colonists, part of the area had been occupied by the agriculturist Kikuyu. They had recently acquired land from the Ndorobo people, nomadic hunters who together with the small-statured, reclusive Gumba, a race of 'almost pygmies' who lived in burrows, had occupied the land until recent times. How the ownership of the land was transferred is uncertain. Neither Gumba nor Ndorobo was a match for the Kikuyu, with their political nous and well developed

4

tribal structure. Kikuyu expansion into Ndorobo territory was the movement, almost migration, of a well organized agricultural and socially developed people. The fate of the Gumba is uncertain: they may have emigrated west toward the Congo.

Both Gumba and Ndorobo faded away over the years, although the shy Ndorobo were seen by early European settlers from time to time. Some of them intermarried with the Kikuyu but others, who as nomads tended to be looked upon by the diligent Kikuyu as trespassers when seen on 'their' land, were killed on sight. Tribal boundaries were ill-defined, 'might was right' and genocide was the way of the world. The Masai and other nomadic people were sharing occupation of the land with the Kikuyu when the British arrived, and there is a strong oral history of inter-tribal warfare between Kikuyu and the pastoralists.

To early settlers the Kikuyu life seemed almost idyllic. They had so organized their lives that married men and elders had probably more leisure than any other people anywhere: a tree for shade, a gourd for beer, a horn for snuff, obedient wives, respectful sons, hard-working daughters, sun for warmth, milk, meat and millet for nourishment, fertile soil, a perfect climate. They sat under trees, drank beer and either talked of local matters or dispensed judgement, while their wives looked after crops and their sons herded cattle and fought wars. Every man was a councillor and a magistrate but attended to his duties more or less when he felt inclined, having to observe no hours or rotas. What more could one ask?

Although the White Highlands were largely unoccupied when Britain became protector of Kenya, it has to be said that dispatches between the British government's men on the spot and Whitehall suggest that the level of occupancy did not much influence local government attitudes and actions. In a dispatch to Whitehall about local people and conditions on 5th April 1897, HM Commissioner Sir Arthur Hardinge wrote that 'force, and the prestige which rests on a belief in force, are the only way you can do anything with these people, but once beaten and disarmed they will serve you.' He continued that the natives must learn submission by the bullet, followed by 'more modern and humane methods of education', concluding that 'in Africa to have peace you must first teach obedience, and the only tutor who impresses the lesson properly is the sword'.

A dispatch to the secretary of state from the then commissioner, Sir Charles Eliot, in 1904 provides a pragmatic view of British attitudes and actions regarding the acquisition of land at that time. 'No doubt on platforms and in reports we declare that we have no intention of depriving natives of their lands,' he wrote. 'But this has never prevented us from taking whatever land we want for Government purposes or from settling Europeans on land actually occupied by natives . . . Your Lordships had opened this protectorate to white immigration and colonization, and I think it is well that, in confidential correspondence at least, we should face the undoubted issue: viz that white man mates black in very few moves.'

Hardinge and Eliot were not irresponsible buccaneers. Eliot was the son of a clergyman, and a polymath, polyglot commissioner who would have appeared to be more at home occupying an academic appointment in Oxbridge than in the government of Kenya. He may not, however have fully reflected the views of the government, as he admitted to having a 'terrific row' with the foreign office over white settlement and the office's attitudes over grants of land in the Kikuyu country, which they regard as an infringement of native rights. Eliot hoped to attract thousands of Europeans to East Africa and appeared not to accept that natives had any rights. British attitudes were to change after the First World War.

The British Administration had military support to maintain the Pax Britannica but had less need to call on it as time went by.

More typical of later governors was Philip Mitchell, who first served as a colonial officer in East Africa in 1912. Before public school in England and Oxford University, he was brought up in Spain, where he learned to speak English, French and Spanish with equal facility. He added three Bantu languages to his collection. During the First World War he served in the King's African Rifles and fought in East Africa and was awarded the Military Cross. Between 1912 and 1925 he had covered, on foot or horse-back, the whole area between Zambese, the Kenyan border, the Indian Ocean and the Great Lakes. In his concluding years he was Governor of Kenya (1944–52), and after retirement he settled there.

A steady flow of white settlers continued during the 1920s and 1930s, and after the Second World War even greater encouragement and inducements were offered by British governments to prospective settlers, particularly ex-service people. Between the wars, however,

Elspeth Huxley (one of the people whose accounts provide a continual strand throughout this book) observed that 'Afrikaner transport riders, Scottish cattle traders, Italian mechanics, Irish garage owners, Jewish hoteliers and farmers drawn from the despised and mediocre middle classes' were all settling in the colony.

Settlers did not conform to a stereotype. In 1896 three couples made the six weeks' walk from the ship in Mombasa to Nairobi. They comprised a blacksmith, McQueen, and his wife; Dr. Boedeker, a Eurasian medical practitioner married to an English knight's daughter (he later combined medicine with experimental farming); and the Wallaces, she being seven months pregnant. They were among the earliest settlers and all made rewarding lives for themselves.

Typical of the settler-farmers who provided the backbone of the community were J.F. Lipscombe and Michael Blundell. Both arrived in the 1920s, started their working lives as assistants and managers, and worked their way up. Few of the settler-farmers can be described as having 'made their fortune', but most led full and interesting lives and raised families who provided the second and third generation European Africans.

Over the years a colonial administration had grown in order to preside over the activities of black, white and brown and endeavour to maintain harmony. It had its work cut out, as administrators and settlers were often at loggerheads. One incident must suffice by way of illustration. Early one morning two men were taking exercise – Girouard, the governor (1909–12), and a recently appointed assistant in the secretariat. They had not yet met formally. The assistant ignored the governor's first 'Good morning' greeting and he repeated it. The assistant looked coldly at the governor and said 'Oh, go to hell, you bloody settler'.

The main cause of the tension between settler and administrator was the settlers' conviction that they could and should govern themselves. Tribal resistance had been quelled and there was a sense of security. There was talk of an East African dominion to be created from a flow of white people from Europe, but nothing came of it. Little or no account was taken of the African population which already occupied the region. In 1919 the colonial legislative council (LEGCO) had 30 seats. Of these, eleven were for election from the 9,000 Europeans, two from the 25,000 Indians and one from the Arabs: the balance was occupied by members of the Administration.

These were heady days for European settlers, but the tide would turn to their disadvantage with the years. Policy was determined in Westminster, and the prime minister for much of the period we are concerned with here was Stanley Baldwin (1922–37), a religious and liberal man keen to improve the natives' conditions.

A policy more sympathetic to the interests of the natives appeared in 1923. A Conservative government White Paper, which was later confirmed by a Labour government in a further White Paper in 1930, set out policy which held good for the life of the colony. It stated that the interest of Africans 'should prevail' but that the interests of extant 'other communities' were not to be destroyed or impaired. It was a statement open to alternative interpretations, but at least until the end of the Second World War the European settlers were largely comfortable with the tenure provided by Westminster. Inevitably, administrator and settler had different perspectives and goals. The settler tended to regard officials as privileged, cosseted time-servers, while the official thought settlers were 'on the make'. It was a pre-scription for conflict.

Regardless of their aspirations, interests and motives for settling, the settler-farmers' lot was not easy. Insufficient capital, dependency on the good offices of the local bank-manager, lack of knowledge and lack of experience of farming in Africa (or, for many, of any sort of farming), plagues of locusts, unknown diseases of livestock and crops, drought and unreliable labour all played their part. The life was physically and mentally demanding, alternating between periods of hard, isolated toil and hectic socializing – with, always, the prospect of flood, drought, disease, crop or stock failure and financial disaster around the corner.

It might be said that at least some of these difficulties were common to most farmers, and that if they were not prepared to accept them they should have looked elsewhere for a living. What was more difficult to handle were the feelings of vulnerability. When it came to 'management' of their labour force, corporal punishment was not uncommon, particularly in earlier years: it was part of British culture until the 1980s. Most, if not all, Anglo-Saxon settlers had personal experience of being on the receiving end while at school. Flogging was a frequent, almost natural, method of regulating behaviour in British schools. The publication of a biography of a former headmaster of Eton in 1993 provoked a correspondence in the press which indicated that as late as the 1960s and 1970s flogging, occasionally sadistic, had been a regular occurrence in premier British schools of which many men in government and senior positions in the 1990s had had personal experience. There are, however, countless boring accounts of long and mutually happy relationships between European farmers and their workers which more than outweigh the sometimes harsh and occasionally brutal treatment referred to above.

One fact which speaks well for the relations which existed between African and European settlers was that in Kenya during the First World War no European estates were raided, no European women were harmed and there were no native 'outbreaks' while the men were away. The same could not be said of many other parts of Africa. Harmony makes less exciting and less interesting reading than strife, but for much of the time the white man was not set against the black. They worked together harmoniously, albeit with the European in the dominant role and, perhaps, over-conscious of the master-servant relationship.

A fundamental difference between African and European, however, was their attitude to change. As the Europeans became established it became increasingly apparent to them that the Kikuyu had not aspired to re-create or change or tame the country and to bring it under their control. They accepted what God, or nature, had given them without apparently wishing to improve upon it in any significant way. When they left a piece of land and abandoned their huts, the bush and vegetation grew up again and obliterated every trace of them. The Europeans on the other hand were dedicated to creating farms, importing new stock, planting crops which were hitherto unknown and building permanent (certainly by African standards) homes. Their ethos was directed at changing the country and the people to comply with their own standards and preferences.

How can one measure the standards of the time in order to assess the quality of black/white relationships in Kenya? In the USA, a democratic white nation with a significant black minority, the years leading to the Second World War saw unhappy relationships between black and white. Lynchings during the century had run at about a hundred per year. A bill introduced in 1900 to make lynching of negroes a federal crime was defeated, and lynching continued at much the same rate into the 1920s. There was ample evidence of whippings, hangings and other brutality. In 1919 white youths in Chicago invaded the Negro section of the town. Fifteen whites and 23 blacks were killed; 178 whites and 342 blacks were injured. The riots spread, and 76 Negroes were lynched nationwide. In 1920 it was estimated that the Ku Klux Klan had 4,000,000 members. A further 'lynching' bill was defeated in 1922. In 1923 the black village of Rosewood, Florida, including the church, was burned down by a drunken white posse. Negro men, women and children were dragged from their homes, tortured, shot and hanged. Little changed through the years: not until 1937 was a lynching bill approved by the federal government (not the individual states), and the bill was shelved. Only in 1937 was the first Negro federal judge appointed.

So much for black and white. How did the browns, the 'Indians', fit in? (Unless otherwise stated the term 'Indian' is used here to include people from the Indian sub-continent: partition of India did not take place until after the period covered in this chapter.) Churchill referred to the Indian as being versus both black and white. In many respects he was both against and between the European and the African communities.

Many Indians arrived in British East Africa at much the same time as the British, if not before, but it was the construction of the railway between Mombasa and Lake Victoria at the turn of the century which gave their immigration impetus. This project required considerable skilled and unskilled labour, which was not to be found among the native Africans. Some 32,000 Indians were imported, of whom about 7,000 chose to remain in East Africa after their contracts expired. The Indian presence was essential for the development of the protectorate at that time, and even when construction had been completed for some years there was talk of officially sponsored or indentured Indian immigration. However, in 1909 the Sanderson Committee stopped short of such moves in favour of voluntary immigration. By 1921 the Indian population had grown from the 7,000 who stayed on when the railway construction was complete earlier in the century to 23,000. Indians were to play a major part in the development of Kenya, but it was a part which was largely played separate from, but at the same time in close contact with, both the African and the European communities.

Over the years Indians grew in confidence and it might be said that there were now three classes, with Africans providing the unskilled labour, Indians clerical and craft work and Europeans supervising. Africans were paid very little, Europeans three times the wage of the Asians for doing the same job. Generally the Asians received, in their view, 'a cool reception' from both European and African.

By the 1930s the White Highlands (and particularly the area within it known as Happy Valley) had developed a reputation for being a resort of the aristocracy and upper class, an idle, drug taking, alcoholic group of rich people with a disproportionate number of old Etonians among them. Much was made of their alleged adulterous relationships, loose living and absence of principles. At all times they provided admirable copy for an eager press, and the impression of their irresponsibility was strengthened when, in the thick of the Second World War, Sir 'Jock' Delves Broughton was tried for the murder of Josslyn Hay, Earl of Erroll. Outside Happy Valley, geographically if not socially, was the Grant family, which in many respects typified the early farmer-settlers, except that few others stayed the course. Josceline and Nellie arrived in 1912. With breaks during the two world wars, when 'Jos' fought with his regiment in Europe, they lived and farmed in Kenya all their adult lives. By almost any method of English classification they would be regarded as upper class, even aristocracy, but as a result of English rules of primogeniture they were far from wealthy. They, too, provide a strand in this story.

A small minority of the White Highlands set undoubtedly deserved their discreditable reputation, but most white settlers, perhaps typified by the Grants, were conscientious, under-capitalized people who worked long and hard against every difficulty. Unless or until their bank foreclosed, they provided employment for local African workers and, it was maintained, made a significant contribution to the colony's economy, particularly during the war years. But it was a white master/black servant world.

There was no official colour-bar or racial discrimination in Kenya, but there was little or no social intercourse between races. That said, there were benefits other than financial for the African farm worker. Most European farmers were paternalistic in their approach to the welfare of their employees, many of whom lived on the farm together with their families and livestock. The farmer provided protection for their livestock, gave advice and assistance when sought, and sorted out feuds between families. It was, too, an exceptional woman farmer or farmer's wife who did not provide nursing cum medical care for workers, wives and children. The Europeans, albeit it for pragmatic reasons, were concerned for their 'extended families' and some provided schooling in the 3Rs for younger African children.

Colonial office advice on education was contained in an advisory committee report in 1925. It was that 'education should be adapted to the mentality, aptitudes, occupation and traditions of the various peoples . . . Its aims should be to render the individual more efficient in his or her condition of life . . . to promote the advancements of the community as a whole through the improvement of agriculture . . . the training of the people in the management of their own affairs and the inculcation of true ideals of citizenship and service'.

Lord Delamere's contribution to 'rendering individuals more efficient' was to start the national industrial training depot which 'turned out thousands of carpenters, masons, mechanics and other skilled men'. At much the same time the governor, Sir Edward Grigg (1925–30), referred to the natives as 'so primitive that for civilizing purposes they are almost a clean slate'.

In 1930 the Alliance High School was turning out teachers and clerks for government and railway offices. In 1939 a Masai graduate from the Alliance became a doctor, and during the second-half of the 1930s secondary classes were introduced at Nyanza. The schools were beginning to be victims of their own success. Archdeacon Owen called on the government to reduce higher education since it was giving rise to a new privileged class. Unfortunately the graduates were not as altruistic as their missionary teachers. Owen reported that educated Africans now formed a growing élite with bourgeois aspirations. This élite closed its ranks against the disadvantaged, who now found themselves squatters on African farms and had merely changed white masters for black.

Teachers were often more trusted than missionaries. Oginga Odinga, one of our strands, who freely admitted to benefitting from his missionary education, believed that in the villages the missionaries drove a wedge between Christians and pagans. He also accused the Catholic Union of supporting the government 'blindly on every possible issue, even the hated hut tax'. This came close to Tom Mboya's view of 'high-handed missionaries who stood against African traditions, customs and culture', while head teacher and devout Christian Carey Francis remarked that missionaries as a whole often let Africans down through fear, laziness or a desire to keep in with the government or Europeans. Other Africans suggested that the education they got was not out of love but to fit them to be 'obedient servants of the white government'.

Francis gave teaching and Christianity equal importance. Early in his career he had established a specification for Europeans intending to teach in Africans' schools. They should be keen Christians, but the particular brand of theology was not important. Their academic qualifications should be fully up to government standards and they should like boys, like teaching and not be touchy. The answer to the question 'Were the missions good for Africans?' depends on whom one asks.

African interests were first represented on LEGCO in 1923 – by one European missionary, Canon Leakey. It was not until 1935 that a second European was elected to represent Africans: still no Africans. Indians had taken up more seats in 1933, and in 1936 an Indian was unofficially appointed to the executive council. In 1944, Eliud Mathu was nominated to take the place of the two Europeans representing Africans. It would be interesting to know the thought processes which led to the conversion of two European seats to one African.

During the Second World War the tradition continued of Africans forming associations and/or unions which in due course became militant or anarchic and were banned by the Administration. Three were banned in 1940, their leaders being arrested. The Kenya/African Study Union was formed in that year. It was a body which would change its name, but not its membership, before too long.

For some African troops the Second World War started with a misunderstanding which led to trouble. Natives recruited for pioneer duties had mutinied and had been badly knocked about in the process of restoring discipline. The men's remittances to their families had gone astray, their clothing was in a shocking condition and their equipment almost non-existent. The men were bitter and felt that they had been cheated: they had volunteered to fight for their country, and the trouble arose because they were treated as a labour force with no military pretences at all.

It is impossible to know to what extent the mutiny was a reaction by the Africans to the massive loss of life among the carrier corps in the First World War. Their treatment by the Army in 1939 is difficult to square with assurances given after those appalling losses that the 'lesson in the First World War sank deep in the Army and nothing of the kind was ever allowed to happen again'. The 1939 mutiny was certainly not a mirage. However, when the troops' grievances had been resolved, good relationships were established between European officers and African men.

Unknown to the askaris (as the black African troops were known), similar questions were being asked by Negro troops in the American armed services, where discrimination was rife. Black troops were segregated from white and continued to be until it was forbidden in 1948. In 1943 there were race riots in New York, Los Angeles and Detroit, leaving forty dead and a thousand wounded.

In 1940, when German forces showed every sign of winning the war in Europe, Westminster demonstrated admirable confidence in the future of the British Empire by passing the Colonial Development and Welfare Act which provided for £5 million per year to be spent in the colony post-war.

The following year, with Hitler in the ascendancy, the settlement in Olenguruone of landless Kikuyu and some 50 families of Wanderobo did not attract much interest. As the government saw it, the Kikuyu 'settlers' had previously been living as trespassers in the Masai nature land unit. They had been settled at Olenguruone because they were landless, and not as a recommendation of the Carter Commission or as a promise for the future. However, Olenguruone was to become a place-name the Administration would later prefer not to hear. In the government's view, the Kikuyu and Mkamba incomers were at Olenguruone as tenants, not by right but as a favour. Olenguruone is a place name to remember: it becomes a focus for Kikuyu unrest in later years.

In 1942, with invasion of Britain imminent, the future of the British empire was the subject of debate in the House of Commons. In answer to a rhetorical question 'Why are the colonies poor?' Harold Macmillan suggested the reason was not capitalist exploitation, over or under-government or too many or too few white settlers. He maintained the reason was that they were 'four or five centuries behind us'. He concluded that it was the British government's job to move the colonies on. He admitted there would have to be long-term investment on capital development.

As the war came to an end, £120 million was set aside by the Colonial Development and Welfare Act for post-war development and welfare in the colonies. Even allowing for inflation over the intervening years, this was a significant increase on the £5 million proposed by the 1940 Act.

Times were changing. Africans were waiting in the wings and about to enter the central arena of politics.

Although few may have been aware of the constraints, Africans, Europeans and Indians were all reined in by political and economic forces over which they exercised little, if any, control. Politically, the great British empire, the largest in the world and before the war a matter for pride, was now increasingly seen as an embarrassment, something which needed constantly to be justified. Financially Britain had overseas debts of over £3,500 million and was dependent on the USA for massive aid. Britain never quite got over the shock of realising its dependence on the USA. This was the price of six years of war when, for a while, Britain had stood alone against Hitler. But perhaps even more important than the debt were Britain's changing attitudes. As the historian A.J.P Taylor put it, 'The British did not relinquish their empire by accident. They ceased to believe in it.'

That statement was certainly true for many, but by no means all, of the British people. The question was how to extricate oneself from empire without losing the investment one had made in it. The situation was aggravated by a new international climate created by the war, in which the leading colonial powers were put on the defensive and in which they felt obliged to introduce political as well as social and economic reforms. So much for the realities, the 'outside world' within which Kenya must live.

The tense relationship between white farmers and Administration continued, as in pre-war years, to be at best delicate and at worst turbulent. Living in a colony was, generally, precarious, whether in Algeria or South Africa, and the Kenyan settlers were not unique in this respect. Never mere farmers, traders or artisans, they were at once the strategic core and the most dangerous opponents of the colonial state which protected them.

With the benefit of hindsight and the passage of time it is difficult to understand how a small number of settlers could expect, in effect, to rule a colony with a population such as that numbered above. But one must remember the standards of the time and that these were relations of or, in some instances, members of the 'Few' that had recently and against all odds, kept the Wehrmacht at bay when the rest of Europe had fallen to Hitler.

So, in post-war Kenya, with black African discontent on the increase as the askaris returning from the war told what they had seen in the outside world, the African unions and associations, as ever, were making their presence felt. It would, however, be some time before they fully realized the changes the war had brought about and how much political muscle they now had.

The white community (and to a lesser extent the Indian) was still caught up in relative prosperity, and was perhaps reassured by the knowledge that Whitehall was looking for more 'suitable European people' to come to Kenya and farm. Surely, they could be excused for thinking, that must augur well for their future prospects in post-war Kenya.

2

Room for More White People

*The country is very young . . . There is still ample room for more
white people to speed the economic progress of all its people.'
(Kenya Settlement Handbook 1945)*

Hitler committed suicide ignominiously in a bunker in May 1945
and Germany surrendered unconditionally to the Allies. Then,
in August, the American Airforce dropped two atom bombs on Japan:
the Second World War was over and warfare would never be the same
again. It was not, however, until 1946 that British (including Kenyan)
servicemen and women were released from military service. Many,
in Britain, returned to houses wrecked by German bombing and to a
grey future. For some the prospect of starting afresh in a new
country with help promised by a grateful Government seemed very
attractive indeed, and they decided to have a go.

With the war won, imperialism (save in the expanding empire of
the USSR) was becoming unfashionable. For the Africans these years
were a time for them to step up pressure for more land to live in and
to re-kindle their resentment of racial discrimination. They were in
search of a leader, and he was to arrive in September 1946.

Nevertheless, the post-war years saw prosperity and development.
In Kenya many Europeans and Indians were enjoying considerable
prosperity, and there was an influx of soldier-settlers under the new
Kenya Settlement Scheme. There had been a ready market for farm
produce, and many farms which had been on the verge of bankruptcy in the 1930s had recovered. One side effect of this prosperity was
that in 1945 an Indian returning to Nairobi from study in India was
able to establish a building society catering for all races.

Although the prosperity of the Europeans and the Indians might
have improved, however, that of the urban African in Nairobi left
much to be desired. The vast majority of Nairobi Africans lived in
municipal housing estates or 'locations', where the drainage and
water-supply were extremely poor. They were the responsibility of
the municipal (later city) council which was run by and for European

and Asian business interests, with no great concern for Africans so long as disease and crime did not spill over into European and Asian areas. There were several inter-related issues in the post-war period:

- the future role of the European settler, more of whom continued to arrive
  - the relationship of settlers and the Administration
  - the Administration's role
  - improving the Africans' lot
  - racial discrimination
  - land ownership
  - the Africans' aspirations and their political awareness.

The role of the European settlers in any colonial society has been the subject of considerable debate. Some regarded the white farm in Africa, as distinct from the highly capitalised plantation, as a somewhat artificial construction. Some saw it as the highest as well as the most offensive form of colonialism, others as a colourful but unimportant feature of the drama of capitalist exploitation, which took other and more serious forms. Certainly the support given to white farms by finance capital was lukewarm at best.

Nevertheless, although Britain was still in shock from the war, she began recruiting more ex-servicemen settlers, a policy which in a few years' time would aggravate an already difficult situation. More European settlement was invited to a 'very young' country where, it was claimed, 'there is ample room for more white people who have the will to build up a strong and virile economy' – one which would, more than anything else, promote the welfare of Kenya and 'speed the economic prosperity of all its people'.

One of the settler's liberated daughters described the White Highlands as paradise. They had one of the most glorious regions in Africa reserved for their exclusive use, with government help to get cheap native labour and domestic servants, to provide facilities for research and to cater for their educational needs. They had the help of loans for distressed farmers, a land-bank, light taxation, the adventure of a new country, cheap sport and a sense of importance.

So, as the war came to an end, the British Agricultural Production and Settlement Board encouraged the 'right' people to settle in Kenya. It referred, in particular, to people who wished to settle as working farmers, as farm assistants or as residents who wished to enjoy, at low cost, their years of retirement. Suitable ex-servicemen were encouraged to farm in an area where the climate was described as unsurpassed and where there was 'an absence of the servant problem'.

The several references to the availability of servants may seem socially élitist with the passage of time, but the handbook was drafted at a time when, inevitably, the authors would have had in mind the pre-war years when employment of servants for cleaning, laundry and so on in all but the humblest British homes was the norm. The 'suitable ex-servicemen' were promised security of tenure. The handbook had several photographs of settlers' houses. The text explained that 'on account of the different cultural habits of the African, the servants quarters are always in a separate building'.

Pre-war settler-farmer Michael Blundell was involved at the Kenyan end of the agricultural aettlement scheme project in 1946, almost immediately after his demobilization. Selection criteria included ex-soldiers of pure European descent who were led to believe that Kenya would be administered as a British colony for the 44-year period of the schemes. That would have taken them to 1990. They were assured that the current way of life and standards of public administration would be maintained, and that their neighbours and the community around them would be men and women of like mind.

Nellie Grant, too, was a member of the settlement board and was closely involved with the newcomers' problems at Njoro and Nakuru. By this time she had lived in Kenya for more than 25 years. In a letter 'home' (10th June 1946), she recorded that she had interviewed 27 arrivals individually and that some were grand stuff, most were all right and, in her estimation, two were complete duds.

Who were these settlers selected under the scheme? Among the incomers were James and Elizabeth Stapleton who had seen an advertisement in a Sunday newspaper. He was the son of a Midlands women's hosiery manufacturer and was expected to enter the family business when he was demobbed from the Royal Air Force. The family, particularly the women of the family, were respectable Methodists. Ex-pilot Stapleton had considered and rejected the family business and work in civil aviation when he saw the Kenya advertisement and was attracted.

'All one needed,' he wrote, 'was £800 (later raised to £1,500) on which pound for pound could be borrowed on generous terms for working capital.' He and his wife attended a selection board comprising two Kenya farmers on holiday in England, an Australian working in the East Africa Office and another official in the Kenya government. The board enquired about the Stapletons' drinking habits and their dependence on amenities such as the cinema. They attended a farming course, sold their home in England and, in February 1947, man, wife and two young daughters were Kenya-bound on a troopship. Their land was between Timboroa and the Uasin Gishu Plateau, a fairly remote area. Contemporary settlers included two ex-RAF officers and an ex-naval man. One of the RAF men, had a distinguished war record and a wife and four children under five. The other was an ex-Stalag III escapee for whom 'after spending years in the "pen", Kenya with all its space seemed to be the answer'. They also had long-established Afrikaner neighbours who were welcoming but with whom they had little social contact.

Other arrivals were Erroll Whittall, his wife and three children, who landed in Kenya after the war with £3,500 and worked a cattle ranch for 18 months before their chance came to take up a farm. Whittall, who was in his late thirties, had attended an agricultural college in England in the 1920s and seen some of Africa before the war. The farm they took up was at Molo. From the settlement board he obtained money for various essential works on the property. They built a log house with thatched roof for £100 and lived simply on money borrowed from his wife which was subsequently repaid. They had a labour force of between 20 and 25 adults which cost him £500 per annum.

The incomers joined people like J.R. Lipscomb who had, by 1946, lived and farmed in Kenya for more than twenty years. He had every confidence in the future and considered that those who had made their homes in Kenya and whose children had been born there were natives of the country 'every bit as much as any African'. He regarded the black Africans as under-achievers and considered that it would be two or three generations before any but the most exceptional African headman would reach European standards of efficiency, direction and responsibility without having a European always at his shoulder.

Africans, some at least, were less than enthusiastic about some Europeans with whom they had come in contact. J.M. Kariuki (one of our strands), who had worked for them as farm labourer and had been a squatter's son, found that 'as a tribe the Europeans had certain characteristics which were, perhaps, not pleasant. Quick to anger, inhospitable, aloof, boorish and insensitive, they often behaved as if God had created Kenya and us for their use. They accepted the dignity of man as long as his skin was white'. He acknowledged, however, that there were many individual exceptions one of whom would, almost certainly, have been Nellie Grant.

She was widowed in 1947, but she stayed on in Kenya although her family was in Britain and she knew that her only grandchild would grow up a stranger if she returned to Kenya after a leave in England that year. But she was determinedly independent and she had 'no pension, annuity or anything of that nature'. Much of the farm had been sold off over the years, but she had commitments in Kenya, most of all to her Kikuyu families, which she did not feel that she could repudiate.

The relationship between white farmers and Administration continued, as in pre-war years, to be at best delicate and at worst turbulent. The Kenyan settlers were not unique in this respect. The dilemma of settler in a colony was, generally, precarious for settlers no matter where they settled, and the experiences of two visitors to the colony illustrate the character of the more extrovert settlers which contributed to the dilemma.

The first is provided by Colonel Campbell. As the independence movement developed, he came from Britain to take command of the Kenya Regiment, the principal role of which was to train European settlers for military service during what became known as 'the Emergency'. Campbell was told by a local that the true Kenyan was 'an extrovert who had never fully grown up, with a very simple out-look on life, who was quick to take offence and who would fight for a principle. There was no in-between: it was red or white, never pink'. Some, including settlers themselves, attributed this state of mind to the altitude of the Highlands. The air was, it was claimed, 'thin'.

The second account is by Laurens van der Post, the South African writer and frequent visitor to Kenya. He claimed to know many people in the country whom he liked and admired, but he added that 'they themselves are the first to admit they are eccentric. They take quite a conscious pride in their eccentricity. [They] have the knack of rousing passions and excitement far beyond their own frontier in a way unequalled in any other part of the continent. The people of Kenya appear to live in a permanent state of agitation, frenzy, rage, rebellion and resentment . . . [nevertheless] they are not the lazy, pleasure-loving decadent creatures that so many people in Britain think they are . . . Kenya is full of brave, hard-working Europeans . . . But they tend to behave at times like people walking in their sleep, and many of their excitements are dream excitements'.

The focus for the settlers' excitements was often the governor, and Governor Philip Mitchell readily realized that their aim was often 'the pursuit of an unobtainable objective . . . the attainment of a form of self-government based on legislature in which the European as such is to be entrenched in power by the terms of the constitution and has a majority over all other races combined'. It was an objective which both Conservative and Labour governments had long since ruled out.

Carey Francis, head of the (all African) Alliance School, a missionary at heart and a staunch supporter of the British empire, was highly respected within the settler community although he did not fit the mould. He wrote of the European settler that, to him, 'Africans are here to serve him and provide cheap labour'. Francis, could not identify with the many who clamoured for self-government by and for the 20,000 whites among the population of 3.5 million Africans and 60,000 Asians.

Michael Blundell, a representative of the white community and therefore at the centre of events, explains how the beliefs of the resident Europeans affected their actions when dealing with authority. There were those 'who believed in out-and-out opposition with mass public meetings, strongly worded resolutions and fiery debates in the legislature, and those who advocated government by agreement. This was a system by which the leader of the European settlers struck a compromise with the governor and his officials on any given issue, and both sides then supported the resultant policies.'

The latter approach had the advantage of associating the political views of the settlers with the decisions of government before they were formed, and facing their leading representatives with the fact that the government of Kenya was responsible for the advance of all races, a fact which the more vociferous were apt to ignore. The softer approach enabled the European political leaders to fall back upon outright opposition if their attempts at agreement failed, 'whereas the proponents of continuous and bitter opposition had discharged their major weapons in the first exchanges on any issue'.

Blundell illustrated the 'mass public meeting' approach with a description of a meeting in the Highlands in response to the Government's proposal to replace the 'kipandi' identity certificate, carried by male Africans who left their reserve, with a card that would incorporate the fingerprints of the bearer. The new card was to be carried by males of all races. 'All races' were the words which, with the addition of fingerprinting, aroused considerable opposition among some of the settlers. When he arrived he found that the room was packed, that they carried Union Jacks and tape recorders, and that one or two packed guns. Before they started they sang 'Land of Hope and Glory', and the meeting began in a tense and tempestuous atmosphere. Stirring speeches were made. An elderly gentleman from Blundell's constituency harangued the audience. One of his 'fiery opponents' strode up and down the gangway of the hall with two large pistols hanging from his belt during the voting, fixing with a threatening eye those casting against his views. At another settlers' meeting there was a resolution demanding 'immediate grant to Kenya of the same constitution as Southern Rhodesia'. All present were enthusiastic, but when asked what the grant was he replied, 'Well, madam, I don't know exactly the details, but I met a man in a bar in Salisbury and he told me that it was a jolly good thing'. The resolution was passed.

Van der Post had visited Nairobi when the Europeans were organizing their 'kipandi' protest, and he, too, was surprised at the strength of feeling aroused in an ex-army friend who had been in one of his guerilla groups during the war in the Far East. 'We just won't stand for it,' his normally rational and reasonable friend had said. 'We're organizing . . . we'll make these bloody officials retract . . . we'll go to London, to Downing Street, to the privy council, petition the king if necessary.'

Blundell considered the identity card controversy to have been of great political significance. It set alight the beginning of a reactionary and strongly racialist movement among the settlers, which drew great support from some of the newcomers to the colony who had left England because they could not adjust themselves to the changes and the social revolution of 1945, when Clement Attlee's Labour party took power with a significant majority. The newcomers were, on the whole, inflexible in their outlook and highly conservative, and they brought to the political scene an almost fascist concept of organization and massed emotion.

The administrator's role was at best onerous, and it became increasing difficult when he was faced by European settlers whose level of confidence was reinforced by incoming European settlers. The governor's oath of office bound him 'to do right by all manner of men without fear or favour, affection or ill-will'. The British government acted as 'trustee' for the colony, and Sir Philip Mitchell, a year or so in office as governor at the beginning of this period, believed that colonial government and legislature had to be constructed to ensure that it acted as the 'local agency of the trustee', creating in Kenya 'a Christian civilization, tolerant of other faiths, with equal rights for all civilised men as its major political principle'.

Mitchell saw the colonies as 'wards in trust', the major aim of the trustee being to create conditions in which his wards could advance in civilization, knowledge and capacity with all the help he could give to the furthest point they could reach. He regretted that the political organisation in Kenya was largely racial in structure and expression and that there were many Europeans who, in all good faith, believed that a policy which must lead to 'equal rights' was either wrong or at any rate impractical, and yet others who sincerely believed that Africans, and even most Indians, never could be civilized and for whom equality between people of white and of coloured skins was an impossible, even a wicked, idea. It was hardly a united 'ward'.

The administrative structure which Mitchell had in place in 1946–7, to help him realise the trustees' aim, had changed very little over the years, but he realized that some, perhaps many, British people outside the colony were rethinking their attitudes to their empire and had more regard for the lot of the local, 'native' populations. There were, he believed, opportunities to improve the African's lot in Kenya. He was in no doubt that colonies were going out of fashion.

For the Administration, the governor's tool, the post-war years saw great changes. Before the war the district officer (DO) had been the direct link between higher echelons of the Administration and the Africans, but the 1950s saw an end to the days when he went on safari around his territory with his wife and young children. One long-suffering wife later recalled her five-year-old son riding his pony on one of these expeditions, while his younger brothers sat in sawn-off oil-cans on either side of a donkey's back. Under canvas at night, with the lions roaring, she would wonder which child she would attempt to save should the animals attack.

The method of recruiting officers changed after the war, too. Previously, graduate recruits for the service entered as cadets more or less straight from university, most often Oxbridge, and worked their way up. Post-war recruits were men in their late twenties or early thirties, experienced officers who had travelled the world, had taken responsibilities and were now offering their well-developed talents for leadership in Africa. Some critics, perhaps in particular the men who had 'gone through the (pre-war) system', claimed that the post-war men rarely learned the tribal languages and rarely became quite as close to the tribesmen as the older generation had been. But many of the new men were university graduates, and all of them were sent on courses before serving an 'apprenticeship' under an experienced officer.

An essential difference between the pre- and post-war administration in the field was the increase in numbers and in specializations. No longer would the district commissioner (DC) be a man on his own in a distant outpost with one or two assistants, but the leader of a team of 10 to 20 specialists divided into different departments. Educated and articulate Africans were coming forward to represent their people, to communicate their problems and to be absorbed into government.

Typical of the post-war recruits were F.R. (Dick) Wilson and John Cumber. Wilson, who enjoyed a good rapport with settlers, was an ex-serviceman who had fought in India and Malaya. He was recruited for the colonial service, passed the examinations, married and spent his honeymoon aboard ship. He arrived in Kenya in 1947, was stationed 'in the blue' where the first thing was to learn the language. Cumber was another ex-serviceman, who had seen seven years service in India and elsewhere and who had undergone training in London before learning the tricks of the trade under Wally Coutts (DC Fort Hall), for whom he had great respect. He learned the local language to 'first standard' in three months and progressed to 'higher standard' – all of which is at variance with suggestions that the new men rarely learned the tribal language. In addition to learning the local language, the administrative officer was required, Cumber found, to pass the 'law exam' which would entitle him to sit as a magistrate with 'third power'.

Improving the African's lot was part of the governor's oath, and in 1946 Mitchell appointed seven Africans as administrative assistants to the provincial administration. In 1947 the Holmes Commission recommended that all posts should be open to all candidates regardless of race. There was really nothing novel about such an approach. Half a century earlier Queen Victoria, hearing about racial discrimination in India, declared, 'It is our further will that, so far as may be, our subjects, of whatever race or creed, be freely and impartially admitted to offices in our service, the duties of which they may be qualified, by their education, ability and integrity, duly to discharge'. But that was a royal command which had not always been honoured.

Education was the most obvious method for improvement. Carey Francis recalled that when Bishop Willis opened the Christian Missionary Society school in Luo country in 1905 people had said 'You might as well teach sheep as the Kavirondo'. Francis added that 'the sons of those sheep are achieving school certificate results which are well ahead of the Indian and at least as good as the Europeans'. But despite his confidence in the capabilities of the African, Carey Francis, at his first post-war speech day at the Alliance School, addressed his 'all African' school on a new and major difficulty which had arisen – politics. Sounding a warning note, he said 'It is natural and right that boys at school should take an intelligent interest in the government of their country and seek eagerly ways in which that country may go ahead . . . But in Kenya today it is coming to mean something far different – the process whereby immature minds are unsettled by racial propaganda of a purely destructive kind.'

Francis was proud of the British empire's achievements, and he believed that British education was of the best. He perpetuated the tradition of observing Empire Day, which before the Second World War and for some years afterwards was held on the 24th May. In some places, and in most British schools, it was a public holiday for pride in the Empire. Many schools celebrated with speeches, prize-givings and cricket matches, to which 'old boys' and distinguished guests were invited to attend. Francis followed the speech-day tradition, and in 1946 he developed his theme of pride, exhorting listeners to 'forget about what the politicians call imperialism. Take pride in belonging to a company of men of all races, who have achieved great things and are bound together by the high ideals of justice and freedom and service . . . Many men of today are living, not chiefly to get salaries or honour (some do, some don't) but to serve the people in their charge. You, as you take over their responsibilities, must serve in the same spirit.'

He was aware of criticisms which had, from time to time, been levelled at British imperialism, but he was no apologist: 'Of course there have been some pretty feeble specimens, but in my experience most missionaries and administrators and government educators have given devoted service, have really cared for their people, have not lined their own pockets, have gone out of their way to help, have lived upright, useful lives. I abhor the modern cult of apology in which we vie with one another in confessing our wickedness and explain away every African failure as being the result of our own.'

Francis ran a no-nonsense, highly successful school which, as it later transpired, was to produce the majority of Kenya's immediate post-independence leaders. In 1946 he was made a member of the Order of the British Empire.

European teachers found that the reluctance of tribal elders to release children to attend school was often a problem, but such was the demand from the Kikuyu for education that local district commissioners spent 90 per cent of their rates on it. The Kikuyu demand was met in part by the Kikuyu Independent Schools Association. Formed in 1929 by break-away teachers from the mission schools, this was closely linked with the Kikuyu Central Association to which reference is made below when tracing Jomo Kenyatta's early years. Some of these schools, for which funding was provided by a Kikuyu political party, KISA, were regarded by district officers as 'hotbeds of disaffection'.

Living conditions for Africans living in the towns, notably Nairobi, were somewhat squalid because of split responsibilities and administrative failures which it seemed impossible to overcome. In the reserves, administration was much simpler. District officers and commissioners had direct lines of communication with the African. Maintaining law and order, facilitating medical treatment and helping with food distribution in times of famine were important aspects of his work, but practical agricultural management by reduction of soil erosion and prevention of over-grazing by livestock and looking after labourers working on Europeans' farms all occupied his time.

When Mitchell became governor in 1944, he directed that soil conservation should be given top priority, as parts of some reserves were reverting to desert. He directed that steep slopes which were farmed should be terraced, although the Africans considered it unnecessary. The district officers relied on the chiefs and sub-headmen to provide communal (unpaid) labour. The work was far from popular, but it was regarded as essential and was done at an increasing rate through 1946 and the first half of 1947. The efficiency of a chief was judged by the 'terrace miles' completed on his location. This did not add to his popularity. Government-appointed chiefs were usually treated with suspicion by the Africans, and they were strongly criticized by those active in the movement for independence. It was generally agreed that many were underpaid, and some had feathered their own nests and put their families first.

There was no doubt that terracing created resentment against the administration and the chiefs. It was a gift to the propagandists of the Kenyan African Union (KAU), who argued that the beneficiaries of this labour would be the Europeans to whom the land would ultimately be given. Terracing was not as unpopular among the Luo as among the Kikuyu, because the Luo had a highly developed sense of 'community land', in contrast with the Kikuyu, who owned their land individually. Nevertheless, Luo Oginga Odinga was suspicious of the government's motive when it spoke of the need to discover and apply systems of land usage.

'It was,' wrote Odinga, 'obvious that the purpose of intensifying land use . . . was to block African demands for the return of their stolen lands.' He saw, too, an ulterior motive in a Royal Commission report which aimed at achieving 'economic mobility designed to ensure that the land finds its way into the hands of those best able to use it in the interests of the community as a whole'. The government's aim was, he believed, to create a stable middle class which would 'serve as a buffer between the government and the mass of people, and to absorb political resistance among the people as mission education and plums of minor office had done in a previous generation'.

Moreover, wrote Odinga, 'resistance to government soil conservation measures and land conservation gave mass backing to the political movement'. Terracing was an imposition by the government.

A dichotomy developed over the most appropriate way to advance agricultural holdings. Should the land in the reserves be developed collectively or as individual holdings? A conference of agricultural officers in 1947 passed a resolution that 'the policy [of terracing] shall in general be based on encouraging co-operative effort and organisation rather than individual holdings' and the government line was the same: 'collectives' were to be encouraged rather than 'kulaks'. The Administration, on the other hand, 'never wanted collective farming'. The Kikuyu were less committed than the Luo to communal working of land. It was not, therefore, surprising that the Kikuyu took to terracing less readily than the Luo. The Kikuyu were by nature individualists. Henry (Harry) Thuku and other individual Kikuyus had owned quite large farms which they had cultivated with hired labour since before the war. District officers' records show that providing water for the cattle and agricultural development in the reserves was a constant problem. Building dams, alleviating famine where crops had failed, seeking grazing for stock and carrying out health care were major activities. The reason for describing this controversy at some length will become apparent later.

Settlers, particularly post-war settlers, point out that there was no 'colour bar' in Kenya, but as the Kenya Settlement Handbook illustrates, the 'cultural habits of the African' separated them from the European in many ways, and there were few if any signs of equality between the races: Europeans were employers and Africans servants. The gap between employer and servant was well established and recognised in pre-war Britain, and would persist for some years to come, but differences in skin colour gave a special emphasis to the gap in Kenya.

In the 'nature or nurture' debate the daughter of a Scottish railway engineer/technician, who later married a Seychellois man, indicates that racial discrimination is nurtured rather than being part of an individual's nature. Growing up in post-war Nairobi she recalls 'getting it in the neck' for playing with the servants' children when she made friends with them behind her parents' back. 'It wasn't done to mix with the Kikuyu kids. It's only from their parents that children learn about segregation.' She could not fail to notice that her father, a modestly paid technician, employed African staff who lived in the 'boys' quarters', a small detached building which contained small rooms for each 'boy' (a kitchen, shower and toilet), who needed special permission for their wives to stay with them for even a short period. Anyone living in the colony at the time is able to provide examples of racial discrimination.

Two future African political leaders who suffered discrimination in their years before politics describe incidents which illustrate the causes of their humiliation and irritation. Tom Mboya, who served as a sanitary inspector for Nairobi city council, was testing samples in his laboratory when a European woman asked, in response to his 'Good morning, madam' greeting, 'Is there anybody here?'. On several occasions Mboya had been thrown out of premises that he had gone to inspect by Europeans who insisted they wanted a European not an African to do the job. He also resented the fact that African inspectors were paid only a fifth of the salary which a European inspector received for doing the same job, and that the Africans were required to wear khaki uniforms while Europeans wore lounge suits.

Oginga Odinga describes an incident which illustrates one European's attitude to educated Africans. In 1945-6 he taught mathematics at a veterinary school. His Scots veterinary officer headteacher, whom he regarded as 'a considerate liberal man', nevertheless told Odinga 'You are very intelligent, but you must understand that your brain is no better than the brain of my six year old son . . . it will take [Africans] three hundred years to reach the level of the Europeans'.

There was segregation on buses and in public toilets, and Africans were expected to stand if a European wanted a seat, although both had paid the same price for their ticket.

But unofficial initiatives were being taken to improve matters. Tom Askwith, DC Nairobi, a man with greater vision of harmony among the races than others, was in contact with urban Africans most of the working day and much of the night. He was aware of the feelings and of the bitterness felt by the better educated African against racial discrimination. It was, he observed, 'a flaw of the administration that it had little contact with educated, articulate, urban Africans' who were stigmatised as 'politicians', a word which was invariably used in pejorative sense. At the same time, white politicians 'were assumed to be anti-African and anti-Administration, black politicians to be anti-everything. One had as little as possible to do with both kinds'. Askwith's personal initiative to bridge the cultural gap was the formation of the United Kenya Club. He, with others, wanted 'to find a way in which "those of good will" in the white and Indian population could become aware of the point of view of better educated Africans and thus give support to easing tension'. The plan was to gather together once a week for lunch and once a week in the evening for informal discussion. They were to be represented by equal numbers from the three races, ten from each, and they met in a derelict building which, together, they worked on and restored. Initially, the majority of British members were government officers, most of the African members were politicians and the Asians were either professionals or businessmen. The group functioned as a social organisation and was not a vehicle for political protest. Derek Erskine a notably liberal man, one of the early candidates for membership, was rejected for having referred to Africans, using words from Kipling's poem 'The White Man's Burden', as 'the lesser breeds without the law'. Askwith suggested that Erskine should meet with the committee and apologise for his unintended offence, which he did and was accepted.

Indians were widening their horizons in post-war Kenya. Many, having qualified in Britain, became professionals: doctors, engineers, architects, lawyers. Previously they had been traders or working for the government, railways, local authorities and so forth. Now, they questioned, 'if we can be accepted in England, why can't we be accepted in Kenya?' India, now independent, began to champion the cause of the Asians and Africans.

As to the forms the discrimination took, it is often argued that its practice in Kenya was different from apartheid in South Africa. It could, however, be argued that for practical purposes it was apartheid without bearing that name. In residential areas substantial 'estates' were kept for housing Europeans, and in the title deeds and grants no person other than of pure European descent could own, lease, rent or mortgage a house – indeed, could even be a guest in a house, except as a pure domestic servant. In the restaurants the same thing applied: you had European restaurant licences, Asian eating houses and African eating houses. Nobody was allowed to eat in the restaurant of another race.

The prospect of eating near coloured people did appear to be objectionable to many European settlers. DO Leslie Whitehouse, who had by this time lived in Kenya as teacher and administrator for some 25 years, cited incidents by way of illustration. The first concerned the visit of Prince Ali Aga Khan and the Begum to his district. Whitehouse was ex-officio chairman of the golf club, and the royal couple were guests of the provincial commissioner (PC), who sought permission for the prince to play the course. The request was debated at length by the committee, at the end of which there was a nearly unanimous decision that the prince was welcome to use the course provided that he did not enter the club house.

Of the other incidents one involved very senior African officers, Ronald Ngala and Eliud Mathu, and the other a cabinet minister from Ceylon who was an anthropologist and an Oxford boxing blue. Whitehouse recalled that he was asked to entertain the African officers to lunch alone, while the rest of the committee members and the settler-farmers had their lunch in the club house. Later, the cabinet minister had lunch in the kitchen with the Ceylonese chef of a small wayside hotel because the European hotelier feared the other guests might leave if the minister were admitted to the dining room.

Discrimination (although 'exclusivity' might perhaps be a more appropriate word) was not restricted only to race, colour or religion. When Col Guy Campbell took command of the Kenya Regiment he discovered that the Muthaiga Country Club never admitted government officials and that the Nairobi catered for only officials and the business community. Both clubs opened their doors to members of the KAR and the Royal Navy. He makes no mention the RAF or army regiments other than the KAR. Asians, including the Aga Khan, and Africans were excluded from both the Muthaiga Country and Nairobi clubs and from the major hotels and restaurants.

The last word with regard to discrimination may be left to an elderly Kikuyu civil servant, talking of relationships between European farmers and the missionaries: 'We took every single European in this country to be a Christian . . . the missionaries would have done a wonderful job here if they had not given in so often to the settlers. They preached a gospel which did not recognise a colour bar, but there was a colour bar.' And the Africans resented it.

Land ownership was the other cause of resentment, perhaps the primary cause. No one disputed that the Kikuyu people, in particular, needed more land to accommodate their expanding population but, as mentioned earlier, Africans did not always make best use of the land they had. The arithmetic of the division of land proved conclusively that from the British Government's standpoint the Settlement Handbook was correct when it said there was still room for more white people. The Carter Commission inquiry in 1933, which had been amended and approved in two subsequent ordinances and two orders in council in 1938 and 1939, established the legality of the division.

The Kikuyu had, in the words of a commission to ascertain the causes of the growth of African unrest, been guilty of 'persistent misunderstanding and misrepresentation about the proportions of land in Kenya'. The facts were, the report continued, that the area in African occupation was 52,000 square miles, as compared with 16,000 square miles occupied by the Europeans in the Highlands. A quarter of this latter area was forest preserved for the benefit of the whole colony. The remaining 12,000 square miles comprised farms and ranches and, at the lowest estimate, not less than 9,000 square miles had been unoccupied until the coming of the Europeans, except for intermittent grazing by the Masai. The balance of 3,000 square miles was mainly uninhabited. The position was that 6,000 square miles were reserved for Kikuyu and kindred tribes and that many thousands of Kikuyu had settled in the land of other tribes, in Crown forests and on land leased to Europeans.

The Kikuyu's real grievance derived from the fact that the time had come when they could no longer provide themselves with land at will by the simple process of clearing forest and scrub. Governor Mitchell concluded that the Carter Commission settlement 'may have been wise and just or not; but . . . it was recent, authoritative and had been embodied in the law of the land; there could be no question of reopening the matter.'

From the British standpoint, that was that – but certainly not from the African standpoint. Indeed, much of what follows is concerned with the continuing controversy. How much more simple life would have been for the administration if either settlers or Africans had gone away or had grown to realize, as had other races in Europe, that the peasant culture of 'three acres and a cow' was not sustainable.

In 1946 the press began to develop as a medium for disseminating information to African readers (albeit only Kikuyu readers at first) and for providing them with a platform. The initiator was Henry Muoria, who started as a 'one man band'. His Kikuyu newspaper was conceived when he became angry at reading a letter in one of the major local newspapers suggesting that Europeans' rights should always prevail. His first letter by way of response was published, but when a subsequent letter was not, he decided to start his own newspaper 'in which African opinion would be expressed freely'.

The title was *Mumenyereria* – the caretaker. Using obsolescent plant, Muoria wrote and published the news sheet in Kikuyu twice weekly. He built up a circulation of 10,000 copies per issue. In addition he wrote and published several 30–40 page general pamphlets illustrated with photographs. *Mumenyereria* was concerned with how people could help themselves. The wages of black people and their living conditions were very low and the paper tried to express the feeling of the people and how they were put upon in many ways. The paper became very popular and was an alternative to militancy. The Kikuyu language is full of proverbs: its equivalent to 'the pen is mightier than the sword' is a saying to the effect that 'the one who is moved away by being convinced, will never come back, but he who is driven away by using weapons will come back when he is strong enough for revenge'.

By September 1947 *Mumenyereria* was embarrassing the administration. DC Kiambu wrote of the need to control 'journalistic activity in the vernacular press' and referred to the 'corruption of unbridled political agitation which has no regard for truth'. In October, following articles in *Mumenyereria* about evictions of Kikuyu in Olenguruone and the Uplands riot, Henry Muoria and the publisher were sentenced to fines or imprisonment in default of payment.

The askaris' aspirations were, without doubt, raised by their experiences during their war-time military service. They had not only seen another world, but had been given an opportunity to air their views during the Army Bureau of Current Affairs (ABCA) discussion groups – an established part of service life which encouraged 'other ranks' to think about life after the war. They observed, too, that while Europeans had received help of various sorts to establish themselves with farms, no credit system had been worked out to help African farmers.

So discontent was bubbling in post-war Kenya. The African unions and associations were in place, and lines of communication were being established. Only strong leadership was lacking.

3

Kenyatta Returns

'Gigantic meetings greeted Kenyatta.' (Oginga Odinga)

In 1946 Kenyan military service men and women, like the rest of the Allied service people, began to filter home to pick up their lives after six years of war. Jomo Kenyatta, too, returned in September of that year – not from the war, but after 15 years in Europe, most of which had been spent in England.

'The people were demanding a more dynamic leadership,' was Oginga Odinga's reading of the political scene in post-war Kenya. 'Never in the history of Kenya was there a more crucial period for the freedom struggle,' he wrote.

Much has been written about Kenyatta. He was born in 1897–8 at Ngenda, the son of Muigai and Wambui, ordinary Kikuyu shamba (small farming) folk. His tribal name was given as Kamau wa Ngendi when he enrolled at the Church of Scotland mission school in 1909. His early life was typical of that lived by any young boy in a polygamous society, and no doubt his book *Facing Mount Kenya* is based on his experiences at that time. He passed through the stages of initiation and eldership, became a member of the warrior class and witnessed many performances of magic rites, taking part in some.

At the age of eleven or twelve he joined the Scottish mission school at Thogoto some six miles from his village, wearing only three wire bracelets and a strip of cloth around his neck. Here, discipline was at the centre of his education, but the school's records suggest he displayed no marked intelligence or aptitude for education. When he left school his spoken and written English were below average. His teacher would not recommend him for employment, but in due course he worked as a 'kind of overseer' for a sisal company.

Never robust, in 1916 he had fallen seriously ill with a lung infection, but he recovered and escaped military or service as a porter by lying low in Masailand where the British press-gangs were less active. By the end of the war, he was living in Nairobi. Photographs taken at about that time show him dressed European style, 'the very image of one of the pioneers'. He signed his name, and was known to his friends, as K.N. Johnstone (alias Kamau wa Ngengi). In 1920 he made his first appearance as a representative of Kikuyu land ownership interests, but his presentation lacked credibility and they lost their case.

In 1920 he married a Kikuyu woman, Grace Wahu. The marriage was 'outside the church', which regarded him with consternation and made grave charges against his behaviour: Grace was pregnant and Kenyatta was 'a habitual drinker of intoxicating liquor'. He promised to try to mend his ways, but he had what in later years would be referred to as 'a drink problem'. Nevertheless, in 1922 he obtained one of the coveted, relatively well paid, jobs for Nairobi Council as a stores clerk and meter reader, and this set him up. He bought a bicycle and, later, land on which he built a family hut and simple shop called Kinyata Stores.

He had arrived as a modest entrepreneur, but this did not stand in the way of his political activities and 1925–6 saw his early involvement with the Kikuyu Central Association (KCA) as a translator and draftsman of letters. In 1927 he became a salaried employee, and at about this time he began to use the name Kenyatta. Johnstone Kenyatta was the name given as editor of the Kikuyu periodical *Muigwithani,* published in 1928, which bore the KCA slogan 'pray and work' on its title page. He was also shown as secretary of the KCA. He set up branches in Kikuyuland and wrote letters. One, to the governor, pleaded for the release of Harry Thuku, who was in exile and something of a *cause célèbre*. In February 1929 he achieved his ambition to represent the KCA in England, and he set sail in the face of discouragement from the Nairobi authorities.

In London Kenyatta was given succour by W. McGregor Ross, who had spent twenty-three years in Kenya (1900–23) and had written what might have been regarded by the British government as a mildly subversive book, *Kenya from Within*. Ross was a member of the British Labour party and provided Kenyatta with contacts such as Fenner Brockway MP who, later, was to be closely involved in Kenya's independence movement. Kenyatta was given the cold shoulder by the colonial office in Whitehall, and when he was given the opportunity to travel to mainland Europe at someone else's expense he took it, travelling to Germany, France, Holland and Russia. He returned to London in 1929, and inflammatory articles appeared under his name in the *Sunday Worker*, a communist newspaper, and the *Daily Worker*. The latter titled him 'Comrade Kenyatta' and showed a picture of him wearing military outfit.

Kenyatta continued to press the colonial office for an interview, and although the office, generally, was unresponsive, Drummond Shiels, the under secretary, took him up – albeit not very far. His advice was that Kenyatta should go back to Kenya, impress on his people the need for ordered constitutional advance and avoid at all costs talk of violence and extremism.

It was thanks to the Ross family that Kenyatta flourished and became accepted by the left-wing Hampstead set. He would have liked to return to Kenya but was uncertain of his reception by the government and had visions of being arrested and/or detained in some remote corner of the colony: there were precedents for such treatment. He had letters over his name, but assumed to be written by Ross, published in the *Manchester Guardian* and the *Times*. Both referred to the rights of Africans and issued a challenge to any fair-minded Briton to consider any of his aims as seditious.

A certain amount of mystery surrounds Kenyatta's activities during the summer months of 1930. He appears to have kept odd company and to have disappeared for days on end, but thanks again to Ross, who obtained money for his ticket, Kenyatta left London on 2nd September 1930 for his return to Kenya. During the next few months there he grew in stature. He helped to resolve the embarrassment which followed the clitoridectomy by Kikuyu 'surgeons' of the elderly American missionary, Hilda Stumf, which resulted in her death by suffocation when a pillow was held over her face to stifle her cries. He paid his respects to Harry Thuku, recently released from detention, and he mended bridges with the Thogoto Mission.

He left Mombasa for a second visit to Europe in May 1931 and re-established the contacts he had made the first time. He enjoyed a semester at the Quaker College of Woodbridge, Birmingham, and gave evidence to the Carter Land Commission, for which he had prepared a paper. Much was to be made of this in later years. Then he left for mainland Europe, visiting Berlin and Moscow. Whether he actually joined the communist party is in dispute: CID reports assumed he had, but there is no doubt that in Moscow he was being trained as a professional revolutionary. He reappeared in Hampstead in early September 1933, having been out of England for a year.

More publications appeared over Kenyatta's name which were, to say the least, critical of the British administration of Kenya. Speaking for 'the people', he said Africans were stooges, that missionaries were 'agents of the imperialists', that the Africans had been robbed of their lands and reduced to the status of serfs and that African girls were seduced by Europeans 'to satisfy their bestial lust'. He linked the Indians, the Irish and the South Africans as oppressed members of the British Slave Empire. The tone of these letters was quite different from those sent to the *Manchester Guardian* and the *Times* in 1930, which spoke of 'loyal subjects marching together': the more recent letters suggested a Moscow training.

But membership of the Communist Party in Britain in the 1930s did not mean too much. The rhyme 'Lives there a man with soul so dead who wasn't in the 30s red?' was often quoted in later years. Communism was fighting fascism in Spain, and many British people were were politically middle-of-the-road joined the International Brigade to fight the fascists. Whatever his political affiliation, if any, Kenyatta had to decide on his next move. From his pronouncements he appeared to be seeking African self-government, an aspiration which would not go down well in Kenya. With little formal education and no degree parchment, he lacked academic respectability. He opted to stay in England and improve his education. Had he returned to Kenya he might, like Harry Thuku, have found himself removed far from Nairobi to a place in the desert where he could cause no mischief.

Starting in 1935, he took various part-time courses, chiefly concerned with language, at University College London. In 1936 he obtained a grant to cover fees for a course at the London School of Economics, where he studied under Professor Malinowski, a celebrated anthropologist. In his introduction to *Facing Mount Kenya*, Kenyatta's magnum opus, Malinowski refers to the author's 'clarity of thought and expression' and to his being 'outspoken and honest to an extent rarely found in students of social science'. In his critique of the book he says it would 'rank as a pioneering achievement of outstanding merit'.

Elspeth Huxley was a fellow student at the LSE. She describes him as a student who was 'alert, intelligent, self-confident and concerned', with a mind 'subtle, keen but closely channeled'. Even then, his appearance had 'exotic touches such as a ring with a large semiprecious stone . . . a staff with a jewelled top, and flashy check trousers'. She found 'something a little intimidating about him despite his joviality'. Almost without exception, people who met him mention his eyes. Huxley refers to them as bright, quick and penetrating, putting her in mind of the Ancient Mariner. Later, Terence Gavaghan, an administrator who knew him well, referred to him as 'a potent figure . . . a perfect manifestation of maschismo'.

Kenyatta continued his political activities in England from the time he finished at the LSE until he returned to Kenya. He was attracted by women and was attractive to them in turn. He lived with several European women while in Europe and he enjoyed a drink. During the war he married an English woman, Edna Clarke, a children's governess. They lived in Sussex, where Kenyatta kept chickens, grew his own vegetables and worked as a farm-hand. Some of the older residents in the village of Storrington recall his visits to the local pub, where he was a popular 'regular'. He gave talks, and kept up with people, generally those left of centre, who might assist with his mission. He said he was happier with European than with African people, adding that the English were wonderful people to live with – in England. He returned to Kenya leaving his second wife and their two children behind in Sussex.

He was the first to leave the ship at Mombasa, and was greeted by his first wife, Grace Wahu, their two children and an excited deputation of people. When his train arrived at Nairobi, the density of the crowd prevented his stepping off it: he was carried shoulder high from the station. Odinga writes of his return that he 'had grown into a world-famous African figure'. Gigantic meetings greeted him, but when he suggested to the governor that he take an active part in political affairs he was told that he should start first in local government, on his area's native council.

Nevertheless, the 'dynamic' leader had arrived.

Kikuyu women were among the first to meet Kenyatta on his return from England. They considered he was on their side, and the enthusiastic welcome which had greeted him at Nairobi railway station continued, if not increased, as months went by. Henry Wachanga, a local leader who recalled Kenyatta's arrival for a meeting in January 1947 at the Kaloleni Hall in Shauri Moyo, a shanty town area of Nariobi, reported that 30,000 people of all tribes were there. Even some whites had come to tape his speech for the government. When he neared the stadium, the people lifted his car and carried it some thousand yards to the hall. There was much cheering and clapping as he entered, and they made much of him inside the hall. It was not long before he established that he was on the same side as all Africans – not just the Kikuyu – and he began a country-wide tour, visiting all the provinces in the district and securing the support of most tribal groups. By 1947–48, two years after his return to Kenya, one could say he had the support of them all.

A report dated 28th October 1946 from DC Fort Hall to the provincial commissioner stated that during the previous three months there had been a marked deterioration in the morale and discipline of the district. The main cause of this appeared to be the return of Jomo Kenyatta to the colony, which had been hailed by the African press. DC Nairobi reported with growing amazement the increase in anti-European sentiment among at least one section of the African population.

In his annual report for 1945, the commissioner for Central Province had referred to an unparalleled wave of financial prosperity, with increased prices of agricultural produce and higher wages. His report for 1946 told a different story. He wrote of outward signs of unrest among Africans, fostered by a pernicious African press, increased activities of known political agitators and opposition to many forms of government activity in the reserves, particularly if directed by Europeans or chiefs. In January 1947, only four months after Kenyatta's return, there was a general strike in Mombasa which paralysed the city and port for several days. Its chief organiser was Chege Kibachia, a Kikuyu far from his tribal lands, who reputedly made his point by arranging for African Workers' Federation 'police' to slice the ears off non-strikers. Soon Kenyatta was reported to be supervising oaths of secrecy binding on members of the KCA, which was now a proscribed organisation.

He sought an alliance with influential Koinange, a senior chief, and was given one of his daughters as a wife. He built a bungalow near to Gatundu and farmed the 32-acre estate, raised funds for a school with a large stone house in which he lived and made his headquarters.

On 1st June 1947 Kenyatta was elected president of KAU. Within a fortnight he made a speech at Nyeri which was greeted with enthusiasm by an exceptionally large crowd. Nyeri was followed by speeches at Kiambu and Fort Hall. In them he campaigned for inter-tribal unity, hard work and ordered progress. Nevertheless, he condemned thieving and thuggery which, he said, were getting Africans a bad name, and there is evidence , contained in confidential intelligence reports made in 1946–7, to suggest that Special Branch regarded Kenyatta as a purely pragmatic, even moderate, African nationalist who could be relied on to steer a straight course if he were free to return to politics.

Other African leaders began to emerge. Kenyatta was undoubtedly the best known but he was not the only leader to return in the immediate post-war years. Two, of several others, were Bildad Kaggia and Henry Kahinga Wachanga. Kaggia was later to be tried and to spend much of his time in detention with Kenyatta. Wachanga went into the forest until his capture in 1955, when he was detained with thousands of other suspected and convicted Mau Mau. Both names should be remembered, because they crop up later.

Kaggia was born in 1922 at Dagoretti of Kikuyu parents. His father was not a prudent farmer, and his land had been sold. His father, now a watchman, was poor but his mother was a good manager, and Kaggia attended the Santamor estate school before going to the Christian Missionary Society school at Kahuhia. Although he obtained a bursary to the Alliance School, his father would not, or could not, make up the difference to enable him to attend. He obtained work as a clerk in DC Fort Hall's office. In 1940 he joined the army as a clerk and quickly obtained promotion to staff sergeant, seeing service in Egypt before a posting to Britain. In Egypt he had seen how a concerted effort by African troops could be effectively employed against European authority, and in England and Wales he had mixed on equal terms with British working class people and been taken up by the Labour party. He was demobilized in 1946 feeling 'charged by God to liberate Kenya'.

So began the career of Kaggia the preacher. While on military service he had visited Jerusalem, which reinforced his already strong Christian belief. At first he preached as a guest in churches, but his continued denouncements of the church and the priests led to the churches being closed to him. So he preached in the open, attracting significant congregations until he was arrested for holding a public meeting without a licence. He was sentenced to two weeks of simple imprisonment – his first experience of jail. He fell out with the

Church, having formed a movement, Dini ya Kaggia, that was dedicated to creating a purely African movement outside the European church, free from European customs and with an independent doctrine to include African customs and tradition. Kaggia married without the involvement of a priest but, he maintained, within the Bible's teaching. Dini ya Kaggia 'spread like wildfire', to the extent that many mission churches had to be closed down. Arrests and imprisonment of adherents followed. Kaggia turned to trade unions as an outlet for his energy.

Wachanga was another activist contributing to the struggle for independence who saw the trade union movement as the way forward. Born in Karega village, Nyeri District, in 1923, he was educated to Form II and became 'a Protestant of the Presbyterian Church of East Africa'. He had several jobs before, in 1947, he became interested in politics – the way, he thought, to free his people 'of the white man's domination'. He became involved with the formation of the Forty Group, Aanake a 40, formed from the young men who had been circumcised in 1940 and which was, Wachanga suggests, a fore-runner of the Mau Mau movement. The Forty Group, of which Wachanga was both president and secretary, was opposed to several aspects of government agricultural development, the inoculation of children, government taxes, kipandis and church attendence, and it demanded the continuation of circumcision of girls.

The Forty Group was only the first step on Wachanga's political career. His biography provides a comprehensive picture of Kikuyu militant activity. The group organized ceremonial dances which ended in fights, but when its officers ceased to be paid it declined and fell in December 1948. Nevertheless, it was certainly a fore-runner of subversive activity, from the British point of view, which led directly to Mau Mau. Several future African leaders of subversion learnt their trade in Aanake a 40.

By no means all the African troops returning from the war were opposed to British rule, however. Some simply took up where they had left off, but with the benefit of technical skills they had been taught while in the services. John Carson, DC Samburu, accompanied a KAR recruiting officer among ochre-smeared tribesmen in post-war Kenya. The recruiting officer remarked to a moran (a young warrior) that the Bren-gun carrier would 'get him about nicely'. The herdsman grunted sceptically, felt the carrier's track and commented that it was much too loose: 'You'd never have got away with that in the 14th Army,' he said.

Without wishing to belittle the Forty Group's claim to be founding father of Mau Mau, it would be wrong to ignore the importance many Kikuyu placed on Olenguruone, the land near the Mau Forest where a large body of Kikuyu was resettled in 1941 and which was the subject of so much discontent. Olenguruone, referred to above, appears in later chapters as a place which kept alight the 'flame of hate'. The sequel to the 1941 resettlement occurred in 1947, following a surreptitious visit by Kenyatta in February. From the time of their arrival in 1941 the Kikuyu settlers had flouted the regulations and challenged the right of the government to exercise any control over them, but matters came to a head when the settlers informed the European settlement officer that he had no right to be there and asked him to leave. The PC's response to their demand was to inform them that any who were not prepared to accept the new and increased acreages which had been offered, or to abide by the settlement rules, would have to leave. They refused to listen and were given 14 days' notice to quit. This period was extended again and again, but in September 1949 eviction orders were issued, and in March 1950 action to evict was approved by LEGCO.

During the period 1947–50 matters went from bad to worse. Corfield, the government's official Mau Mau historian, came close to admitting governmental incompetence when he suggested in his report that while the action taken by the government to remove the Kikuyu from Olenguruone 'was strictly in accordance with the resident native labourers ordinance', sufficient thought had probably not been given to the effect of what the Kikuyu regarded as evictions. He reported that, as a protest, about 100 Kikuyu descended on Nairobi followed by a better organised group of 300 ex-squatters who invaded the grounds of Government House demanding an interview with the governor. They got it but there was a display of truculence and nine of the leaders were arrested and committed to prison.

The Kikuyu view expressed by Wachanga was that in 1941 about 10,000 Kikuyu were rounded up and taken to Olenguruone after the government had destroyed their crops and burned their huts. They stayed at Olenguruone for a period of ten years, during which they prospered in spite of hardships. Then 'the government became jealous [and] decided it had made a mistake in allocating such fertile soil to the Gikuyu . . . [and] . . . wanted to reclaim it for European settlement. Once again, the people's livestock and harvest were confiscated by the government'.

To summarize, the government regarded itself as owner of the land at Olenguruone and the Kikuyu as tenants or settlers. The Kikuyu believed they had the right to be there. The land provided a *cause célèbre* for the Kikuyu through which, in Wachanga's words, 'they rediscovered a unity which had almost been forgotten'. He recalled that the Kikuyu had not used their battle oaths since the British stopped inter-tribal warfare around the turn of the century, but so desperate were the people of Olenguruone that they returned to oath-taking. And, he suggests, the 'oath of unity' taken at Olenguruone between 1947 and 1950, not to sell land to white men or to co-operate in any way with them, was the beginning of the Mau Mau oaths. Few, if any, Kikuyu would have disagreed with him. Olenguruone turned out to be a disaster for the Administration and a tragedy for the Kikuyu, who later made great political capital from the sorry muddle.

But we are getting ahead of ourselves. There is, in 1947, no record of any colonial officer reporting that 'the natives are restless', but the combination of strikes in Mombasa and the support rallied far and wide for Jomo Kenyatta and others, must have made it a strenuous and worrying year for Governor Mitchell. With some 35 years experience of administration in East Africa, he gave the rotary club in Nairobi his opinion of British imperial achievement and the way ahead for the African. 'What we have already achieved here,' he said, 'is a living, growing, dynamic society pursuing as its objectives the creation of a polity in which all the human groups of which it is composed have a share and a vital interest according to their several needs and capacities.'

He made no apologies for British imperialism, although some saw the words 'as a term of abuse'. For him, and for others who had engaged themselves for life in the business, the achievement was 'an expression of faith and purpose'. And of the way ahead for the African, he suggested that 'the only way in which the multitude of East African tribes can hope to enjoy the benefit of civilized government, both central and local, now and for generations to come, before they have become themselves civilized . . . is under the forms of colonial Government'. He suggested that government should be 'administered by a strong and enlightened colonial power and directed, as British colonial policy has been for centuries, to the achievement . . . of a state of society in which the men and women of which it is composed – or at least a large part of them – have reached a stage of spiritual, moral, social, cultural and economic development capable of supporting and operating such democratic forms of government as may then appear desirable to them'.

He had seen significant change in the development of Kenya over 35 years. It was a long time since he had only his feet or horseback to cover his territory. Now, garden parties and similar gatherings at Government House were regarded as important occasions for social meetings between governor, administrators and 'the rest'. After the war black Africans were numbered among the rest and invited with increasing frequency. On one such occasion, in mid-1947, John Cumber, a war-time soldier and now a junior administrator, met Jomo Kenyatta. Cumber's short training for the service had included a course at the London School of Economics. He knew that Kenyatta had attended the LSE and he wore his LSE tie. Kenyatta, old enough to be Cumber's father, recognized the tie and entered into conversation. Cumber recalls that he told Kenyatta, 'We appreciate what you are up to, but if you wish to oppose the British government . . . for God's sake do not tackle us on the terracing [issue] because in the long run you are doing an unaccountable amount of harm . . . just see for yourself.'

Cumber added that 'he may have taken that to heart'. So he may, but soon after the meeting, on 20th July 1947, Kenyatta addressed a meeting of 10,000 people in Fort Hall denouncing, not the concept of terracing, but the employment of women on it. The following day, no women turned up for work. The issue was well-chosen: the idea of women being pressed to hard labour sent shudders of horror through the British Labour government, the United Nations and the International Labour Organisation. The irony was that, traditionally, the role of Kikuyu women in the tribal culture was to carry heavy loads and do the digging. Over the years Europeans had become accustomed to seeing long crocodiles of women bent double under enormous burdens, led by their husbands, unburdened, and swinging a stick. The complaint now, as in the past, was not about the fact that the women were undertaking heavy work but that they were working for someone other than their husbands. The reality was that Kikuyu women preferred to work for Europeans because they were paid for their work and did not get beaten, while at home they slaved for nothing and beatings were frequent. At least one British woman farmer did not employ men from the Kikuyu tribe on her farm because they would often get their women to do the heavy work.

Cumber's early impressions of Kenyatta were similar to those expressed by Elspeth Huxley. He found everything about him larger than life, that he was very upright, had a strong sense of humour and spoke very good English. It occurred to him that Kenyatta was a possible leader but he could not honestly say that he would have picked out Kenyatta as the leader among other distinguished looking Africans present at the garden party until he actually heard him speak. 'He knew exactly what he wanted out of life.'

Nellie Grant's letter to her daughter, now in England, dated 14th July 1947 included a simple report which was a sad indicator of things to come: 'The policeman called one day. He says there have been twenty-three homes broken into round Njoro.'

While Kenyatta was impressing Europeans at Government House garden parties, August and September 1947 saw two incidents which indicated unrest among the Kikuyu in the Highlands. The first, which occurred on Sunday 24th August, was a KAU meeting held in Fort Hall district in the location of Chief Ignatio Murai – regarded by the British administration as one of the best of the new type of chiefs and a very brave man. It was not legally possible to impose a general ban on KAU meetings, and the union's tactics were to drive a group of (in the Administration's view) 'rabble rousers' from Nairobi to chosen spots, hold a meeting and return to Nairobi before they could be banned. On this occasion speaker after speaker poured out hatred against the government, the chiefs and the Europeans, to the menacing shouts of the crowd.

'Clearly,' wrote Chenevix Trench, an articulate district officer, 'this was incitement to riot.' With only two tribal police constables, Murai pushed through the crowd and arrested the two most inflammatory orators, but while he was taking them to his headquarters they were stoned by the mob and Murai ordered the policemen each to fire one round. It was a classic response to a riot which led to one rioter being killed and another wounded.

The second incident occurred in September when there was a strike at the Uplands Bacon Factory staged by Makhan Singh, who had returned from India in August. Opinions of Singh varied. Trench saw 'an inflexible, card-carrying Sikh communist', but Ngugi wa Thiongo, an equally articulate and (having in mind his background) well educated African, regarded him as 'a remarkable Kenyan of Asian origins [whose name] is synonymous with the growth of a modern workers' movement and progressive trade unionism' – a view endorsed by other Indians sympathetic to the Africans' cause.

The strike cum riot was witnessed by recently appointed district officer Dick Wilson and reported during an interview soon after the event, which occurred on his first day in Kiambu district. Wilson and his colleague were informed of a riot and left immediately for the factory. They discovered that Singh had stopped at the factory to get members to join KAU. The clerk had refused to join and the whole of the factory was called out on strike. The two junior officers called for the district commissioner, who arrived with a small body of police and read the riot act. Some rioters were armed with pangas, but the police moved in with batons and were attacked, one having his arm virtually severed. The baton party was withdrawn and some shots were fired. When the rioters saw the bullets were not sham, they fled.

The wounded were taken for medical treatment to the station, but the Kikuyu surgeon refused to do anything for the Kamba or Luo policeman, whose arm was severed, on the grounds that he had been fighting with the Kikuyu. A European doctor was called up to sew his arm on. The official report on the incident records three rioters killed and six injured. Twenty-one Kikuyu were found guilty of rioting and sentenced to two years imprisonment.

Concern regarding the breakdown of law and order increased. In a report dated 19th September 1947, the acting provincial commissioner of Central Province sent a long secret letter to the chief secretary, expressing his concern at what he saw as 'a threat to good government'. He regretted having to inform the secretary that during the previous few weeks there had been a marked deterioration in the political situation.

The chiefs also expressed concern. In a letter to the acting provincial commissioner, Senior Chief Njiri Karanja reported, what was endorsed by 'chiefs one and all', that he considered it 'absolutely necessary that we should be given powers to prohibit all public meetings except with the written permission of the district commissioner . . . I foresee the greatest possible danger.'

The request fell on deaf ears. The only immediate response Karanja received was a note saying that his letter had been addressed to the wrong department. He was given instructions on 'getting the member system working properly' and on the need to send copies to other departments. That exchange between colonial officers did not go unnoticed by the Corfield Inquiry which, some years later and all too late, was to review what had gone wrong in the colony.

There were, inevitably, opposing views on the issue of proscribing public meetings. For the colonial, predominantly 'white', government banning them was tidy, simple and the only sensible course, but there was one, lone voice from Eliud Mathu that spoke out for 'freedom'. He was the first, almost token, African appointed to LEGCO. He made a speech in council which expressed resentment at the restrictions placed on the meetings of Africans. One of that bright group of African pupils educated by Carey Francis at Alliance High School in Nairobi, he later completed a course at Exeter College, Oxford. He was KAU's representative on LEGCO and was by no means a universally popular representative, although moderates (of whom there were few) regarded him as one of them.

Mathu's speech referred to resentment and eventual evasion of any law which pushed meetings underground. It contained a warning. 'Those,' he said, 'who still cherish their former freedom and common rights bitterly resent having to apply for permission to meet together for any purpose whatever. Naturally the law is evaded and they meet at night behind locked doors with a sentry outside; they meet in caves, in the depths of banana groves or in swampy valleys away from the habitations of their fellow men to avoid detection. They meet . . . like fellows . . . whispering and cursing the Europeans and their own headmen who administer an oppressive and unjustified law. One day their repressions are bound to burst out, with the usual unhappy consequences for all.'

It was a moving and impressive speech, and in the near future Europeans were to learn more of African meetings held behind locked doors and in remote places. It was the beginning of a five year period of secret organisation and oath-taking which was to end, or more correctly to become overt, in 1952.

Oath-taking did not originate in 1947, however : it was an integral part of African culture generally and of Kikuyu culture in particular. Kenyatta had written at some length on the subject, referring to to an oath or ordeal being the most important factor controlling court procedures. He described the three forms of oath 'which were so terribly feared, morally and religiously'. For minor disputes the appropriate procedure might be the muma oath, which involved eviscerating a lamb, mixing the contents of the stomach with herbs, blood and water and burying the compound in a hole dug by the medicine man. The disputants licked a brush dipped in it while kneeling, and asked that the 'symbol of truth' kill them should they lie, falsely accuse anyone or if the property they were claiming did not belong to them – many Kikuyu disputes involved land or property.

The second oath involved breaking all the limbs of a male goat, saying at the same time 'If the property I am now claiming is not mine, let my limbs be smashed to smithereens like the bones of this male goat.' The third oath was taken mostly in criminal cases, such as murder or stealing, and involved passing grass stalks through a red stone in which there were seven natural holes. No animals were sacrificed. Kikuyu society was dominated by the men and, Kenyatta wrote, women were excluded from taking any of the oaths, as they were not considered fit mentally and bodily to undertake the ordeal. Be that as it may, some Kikuyu women recalled women giving and taking oaths in 1930 when, angered by their exclusion from the activities of the Kikuyu Central Association (KCA), they formed the Women's Mumbi Central Association. The new oaths were concerned with undertaking to be a hero in the fight for land stolen by British settlers, for education for Africans and for loyalty to the cause.

Kikuyu land hunger is often suggested as a major reason for the unrest which was becoming apparent as 1947 drew to a close. In the 1930s Kenyatta had linked oath-taking and the soil when he wrote of an everlasting oath being sworn 'by the earth (koirugo)'. Now such an oath was applied to membership of the KCA, and oaths were administered *en masse*.

Kenyatta returned to Kenya in September 1946. By the end of 1947 mass meetings, strikes, riots and oath-taking hostile to the government were frequent occurrences. In a report to the director of intelligence at the close of 1947, DC Fort Hall wrote: 'There is a very strong rumour circulating that all the wrongs of the Kikuyu will be simultaneously righted by the murder of all the Europeans. This has come from two sources, but in neither case did the source say when the night of the long knives was going to be.'

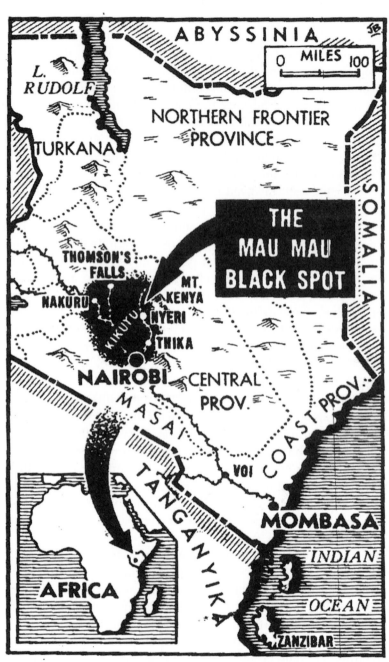

Map reproduced from Mau Mau in Kenya.

4

The Growth of Mau Mau

'There is bound to be . . . an armed clash between black and white in Kenya.' (Chief Wamboga)

Uhuru, translating as 'freedom' or 'independence', was a Swahili word first heard by Europeans in the late 1940s when the Mau Mau freedom fight began.

This was an unsettling time for the governor, whose relationship with the powerful settlers' lobby was as delicate as ever but who had, besides, to contend with an awakening black lobby. The settlers still had considerable muscle in Westminster, but there was generally more hate than love in their relationship with the legislative council. The governor therefore paid attention to the settlers, whose leader was also aware that their strength was not as great as it had been before the war, even if the decline had not been noticed by many of the settlers themselves.

This was the beginning of a period of strikes, which were largely the result of attempts by competing political parties to develop their power rather than because of trade union initiatives. These strikes cannot be described as more than moderately successful. They were more common in the towns, where the leaders had significant numbers of people to combine, than on the farms, where labourers usually worked closely with their employers and did not understand the principles of industrial action.

One incident, ironically, provided Kenyatta with an opportunity to demonstrate his influence and moderation to some influential Europeans. With wildebeest fly-whisk in one hand and ivory-topped, ebony walking stick in the other, he threatened railway workers in Nairobi that if anyone spoke of striking he would 'knock his block off'. Watching European colonial officers, including DC Askwith, were impressed by 'this remarkable and moderate man' who, it was suggested, might have been a force for good 'if the government had tried to work with him and meet him halfway.'

Talk of knocking blocks off was a generally understood opening gambit in industrial negotiations. Certainly it was understood by

Arthur Thompson, a farmer at Nanyuki, and his workforce. He enjoyed good relationships with his employees, but he was approached by his workers with talk of going on strike. Thompson had a large Scots foreman and was confident that they did not understand what striking involved. He simply but firmly told them to return to work without more ado and they did.

The hustings for forthcoming elections may have taken European minds off the strikes, particularly in rural communities. In 1948 there were elections for seats on LEGCO, and Michael Blundell stood against two respected opponents, one of whom was Lord Francis Scott. New to politics, he asked advice from a neighbour. 'All you need say,' he was told, 'is that you support the sanctity of the White Highlands, the communal roll and separate education for each race, and you will be elected.'

Nellie Grant wrote of her attendance at the hustings for the same constituency, 'where Grogan spoke for an hour and a half'. His thesis, Grant wrote to her daughter in England, 'was that calamity would overtake Kenya unless we all voted for Francis Scott next Wednesday'. Blundell, too, addressed meetings in the same constituency, which included part of the Rift Valley and parts of the highlands which rose all of 8,000ft (2,500m) above sea level. He noticed the difference in the outlook of those attending between those from the valley and those from the highlands, and the difference in the intensity of their politics. At the higher elevations 'the scene would often be electric, with undigested ideas jumping like sparks from the pole of one man's mind to another.'

Blundell won the seat. He had little or no idea that his electoral success would put him at the centre of Kenyan affairs during the colony's change to independence. Scott's daughter noted that he was initially disappointed by rejection (it was the first occasion on which he had had competition for the seat), but he realized that the people wanted a younger man. He liked Blundell, their policies were much the same and they became very friendly. Later, they would often discuss problems together.

With elections resolved, the White Highlands returned to normal. The earlier post-war settlers were establishing themselves, and more arrived in response to the British government's advertising. In addition, after Indian independence in 1947 there was an exodus of British officers from the sub-continent to settle in Kenya. In the

Timau area, at an altitude of 8,000ft, new settlers included senior army and RAF officers, many of whom were, in the view of some pre-war settlers, almost fascist: anti the Labour government in Britain, unable to cope with the restriction in post-war Britain and unable to settle down with each other, not to mention the long-established British farming community.

James Stapleton, a less exalted ex-RAF man, together with his wife and family, and John Carey, the Stalag Luft III escapee, had by now found their feet and were making their way. Sadly, however, there was another problem for some settlers, quite apart from those that normally beset farmers. Life on a farm where the altitude made a good log fire an almost essential comfort at night could be very lonely, especially for single men. One of their neighbours, a former medical student, was a batchelor. He took a Nandi woman shopping and to bed, paid the bride-price to her father and married her. She spoke no Swahili or English and he spoke no Nandi. It was a marriage doomed to disaster, and after a month he sent her back to her family. He was the first European in that community to go through a formal marriage ceremony with an African woman. His neighbours were both sympathetic and scornful.

At the political end of the black lobby was B.A. Ohanga, an African member of LEGCO, who concluded his speech at the 9th January 1948 meeting with a plea he had made before, that the council should 'treat the African as a man, nothing less, nothing more, and also as a fellow citizen of the British empire, with all the rights of citizenship'. His closing words were that, given such treatment, the African would respond well. And at that meeting Eliud Mathu, another African member of LEGCO, looked for specific steps that might advance the African cause and moved that the government should clearly state its policy with regards to public assembly and remove all restrictions not essential to good government. The right of public assembly was to be become a matter of major importance in the near future. The tenor of public meetings, too, was changing. A Scottish missionary recorded that until 1948 he was frequently invited to open African political meetings at Githunguri with prayers, but that 'things heated up a bit after that and contact stopped'.

The name Mau Mau, which had first appeared in 1947 and became established before the end of 1948, was thought by the British director of intelligence and security, to denote a branch of the Kikuyu

Central Association (KCA) responsible for dispensing oaths, the first of which ceremonies occurred in Naivasha. During 1948, however, Mau Mau groups were popping up everywhere: indeed, the intelligence director reported that the first Mau Mau oathing ceremony in Nairobi occurred in 1948, too. That was one of several reports, received and passed on by the Administration, of 'increasing unrest' – chiefly, they reported, the result of economic hardship and racial discrimination. The reports were largely if not completely ignored by the colonial government.

The 'increasing unrest' was not restricted to Nairobi. In September DC Fort Hall reported on his visits to independent schools. 'It may be fancy,' his report said, 'but in dealing with schoolboys of the impressionable age during the last two months it seems to me that they were imbued with a somewhat suspicious sullen attitude.' He felt that this had an anti-European flavour contrasting with their 'normally carefree and happy state'.

Similar reports were given by Sam Githu, a Kikuyu loyal to the British government, who also reported that the first Mau Mau oathing started in his district in 1948 and that it had spread without anyone noticing. In June an African missionary minister wrote to the chief native commissioner about oathing in the Rift Valley at dead of night. He reported hearing that the KCA were promising that only loyal oath-takers would share in the division of land between Gilgil and Kiambu which Jomo Kenyatta would have in his gift when the British left the country. The report referred to the KCA, not Mau Mau, but the impression was gaining ground that the KCA and Mau Mau were one and the same organization.

Much has been written about the origins of the name Mau Mau. At least three senior African leaders said that the word had no meaning in either Kikuyu or Swahili, and Kenyatta said time and time again that neither he nor his people knew the word. But the search for origins persisted, and extraordinary ingenuity was used to find or invent origins. The official British government historical survey of the origins and growth of Mau Mau, generally referred to as Corfield Report, was published in 1960. Commissioned to discover what went wrong in the colony of Kenya, it offers a theory that the words linked the society to the Mau Forest near Olenguruone, the site of an illegal settlement by Kikuyu peasant farmers from which they were subsequently removed by the colonial government. No plausible origin appears to have been suggested, but sources for research are given in the footnotes to this chapter. The leaders of the society which dispensed the secret oaths preferred to keep it as a society without a name or hinted at connections with the Kikuyu Central Association. KCA was a group formed in 1924 and banned in 1940, when many of its leaders were arrested. Whatever name the society administering oaths had, if any, it would be likely to appeal to the Kikuyu psyche, as oath-taking was at the centre of Kikuyu culture. All Kikuyu chroniclers of events at that time agree that the ceremonies ensured the secrecy of the society's activities and kept it united. As the celebrated Kikuyu pamphleteer Henry Muoria put it many years later: 'The oath helped to make the people fight whether they liked it or not. It made them angry.' He added that, bearing in mind the fact that many Kikuyu were reluctant participants, 'it was better to take the oath than be dead; to be chopped'.

Depending on one's perspective, Mau Mau was looking for either causes of dissent or opportunities to demonstrate the new nationalism. Well-intentioned government projects unintentionally presented Mau Mau leaders with suitable opportunities. The projects were an initiative set out in the Despatch on Community Development to British Colonial Territories dated 10th November 1948 from the British colonial secretary Arthur Creech Jones. The government's stated objective was to guide colonies to eventual self-government, and in tribal territories which wished to co-operate with the Administration it was implemented very successfully. In the Akamba, Kitui District, for example, development included public works such as dams, terracing, bush clearance and road improvements. Although work on these projects was compulsory for non-employed men, women and older children not in school, they were nevertheless, executed by the co-operative Akamba and by other tribes, too. They were, were they not, for the benefit of the community? Their agriculture and infrastructure were greatly improved.

But such schemes were a major issue on which Kikuyu new politicians mobilized their people against colonial authority. There was greater resistance from the Kikuyu than from other tribes. The entrepreneurial Kikuyu, with a tribal culture rooted in land owned by families, not by the tribe, were disinclined to take part in 'community development'.

This entrepreneurial streak was an important aspect of the nationalist movement, and Kenya saw the emergence of a significant number of African small traders and transporters whose antipathy to the Asians, traditionally the small shop-keepers and business people, rapidly increased. This was demonstrated late in 1948 when a secret meeting of the KCA at which Kenyatta was present, discussed boycotting Indian traders in the native reserves. Kenyatta reportedly declared that boycotts would have the effect of chasing them away to their own country. At a meeting on 7th November at Njoro Market a thenge oath was administered to 'boycott Indian traders in the reserves' as part of 'a general campaign against Indian traders'.

This was a marked change in African attitudes. Until this time the Indian had been everywhere. An Indian returning after the war observed that wherever one went, in railways, in post offices or at the airport, one would find nothing but Indians. People wondered whether it was an Indian colony or a British one. In Nairobi, the dependence of the African on the Asian did not disappear overnight. At first it was in the 'back parts' of Nairobi, where the African generally and Kikuyu in particular were strongest, but in the provinces African traders later began to push themselves in, learn how to finance themselves and, politically, put the Asian in his place.

An event detrimental to African/Asian relationships occurred in 1948 and received extensive publicity in the local press. It concerned the fatal beating of a number of African workmen employed by an Asian construction contractor. Two Asian directors and two African supervisors were found guilty of manslaughter. Their sentences ranged from three to 14 years' imprisonment.

DC Fort Hall's report for 1948 referred to a year which had been notable for its quietness and general apathy, but 'storms are brewing and gale warning should be sounded on an ever increasing scale'. Fort Hall was not alone. DC Kiambu reported a planned tour of all Kikuyu independent schools (always suspected breeding grounds of subversion) by Kenyatta and two Kikuyu leaders, and a leading missionary reported that 'an ideological war had been declared in Kenya' and that Kenyatta had been preaching that the Kikuyu 'must get back to their old religion'. The governor may have been confused rather than informed by Kiambu's comment that 'the continued quietness of the district was apt to make one suspicious', and that 'the subversive political temperature appears to be rising'.

So ended 1948, to be followed in the spring of 1949 by another warning. This was from Col Meinhertzhagen, whose connection with Kenya now exceeded 50 years, during which period he had distinguished himself in the First World War as a soldier and then, having retired from the army aged 46, became widely recognized as scientist, ornothologist and spy. He wrote to the governor about his recent visit to Nyeri for a meeting with the local chief, with whom he had, in 1902–3, 'been on very intimate terms'. Chief Wamboga had warned Meinertzhagen of an imminent outbreak of violence by the Kikuyu, caused by land hunger and theft of their lands by Europeans. The chief feared murder of Europeans 'on a large scale under the direction of a secret society now in existence called Maw Maw, whose influence in the tribe is rapidly growing and whose oaths, taken in the utmost secrecy, are binding on those who are compelled to take them'. The letter was not acknowledged by the governor and, when questioned later, he could not recall seeing it. Corfield sought, but was unable to trace, its existence at Government House or at Nyeri. He was, however, able to find reports from district commissioners referred to above.

Getting back to the old religion was, to all intents, the theme of another report from Meinertzhagen on what might be referred to as 'Wamboga's plea'. This plea, which included a measure of anti-Indian feeling, went: 'Give us back our old times, give us back our land. Remove the Indians with whom we cannot compete; remove our grievances; you have put yourself in the wrong by creating grievances. You have given us better health and security, which has increased the population, and we can no longer grow sufficient food in our restricted reserves.' Meinertzhagen had asked if Wamboga would prefer to return to paganism, Masai raids, epidemics and insecurity and was assured that he would. But he feared an armed clash between black and white in Kenya: 'I want to avoid that.'

Then followed rumours from the European farms in areas of the Rift Valley province of subversive activities by the KCA among farmers' squatter labour. In the hope of obtaining 'sufficient concrete evidence' against union managers in the Rift Valley 'to substantiate a charge of managing a proscribed society', the houses of four managers were searched in May by security forces, 'but nothing was discovered'. There were reports from DC Thika (another farming area) in both April and June that Kenyatta was encouraging Africans

57

to 'engage in petty theft and keep on annoying Europeans as much as they can, so that they will eventually be forced to leave the country'. There seemed to be no cogent response when an African chief asked why Kenyatta had been allowed to visit the reserves, but reports continued to arrive. The director of intelligence and security reported in June that frequent meetings of squatters were being held in the Limuru area, and that 'it was clear that these people have a grievance, and while a sense of grievance persists it will continue to be fostered by KCA . . . with the possibility of coming to a head at any time'. This was not a message to reassure either farmers or the Administration.

But many, probably the vast majority, of the European settler-farmers who did not live within the Mau Mau ambit were unaware of such reports and continued to develop their farms. Typical farmers were the Robathans who farmed with maximum economy near Mau Summit where, during 1949, house guests came and went, and cricket and polo provided a modest social life. New settlers arrived. In March 1949 the Seys took up Rhodora, 2,800 acres on the edge of Menengai, from Blundell. The Seys were followed by their pedigree livestock, antique furniture, pictures and jade. With little or no concern for cost (they were the envy of the Robothams), they undertook extensive building works for themselves and their farm workers and adopted the local life-style. Within days of their arrival Rosemary recorded in an early news-letter home: 'It is dark by seven and we have a bath and change into dressing-gown and housecoat for dinner – which is an old Kenya custom.' By September they had finally sited the 'new native village' which would have 'better water facilities and a better church'. The Seys had come to stay.

On African farms the good farming principles, established earlier, were beginning to make an impact. In Kitui, pressed labour of men only was used to provide terracing, gully plugging, scratch ploughing, and grass-planting works protecting 9,000 acres of land, and 34 dams were built. The Administration was quite pleased with itself.

On the debit side, the eviction of Kikuyu squatters from Olenguruone meant that many of those displaced returned perforce to reserves which were already over-crowded. Their grievances, real and imagined, were passed on to all and sundry. They were a rich source of unrest. In October DC Kiambu reported that the eviction acted as the breeding ground for subversive propaganda, and in

December DC Thika returned to his earlier theme of Europeans being forced by the African to leave the country. Matters had reached the stage where, he reported, 'natives are openly talking of the Kikuyus' assertion that they will one day take over Kenya and the Europeans will be driven away'.

At the fifth annual conference of KAU on 30th October, Jomo Kenyatta was elected president and Tom Mbotela vice-president. Mbotela was known to hold moderate views. He was one of the few activists who was not a Kikuyu (his father was from Nyasaland and his mother was Mkamba). The Kenya Intelligence Summary for 1949 recorded unrest among the Rift Valley squatters fostered by KCA, KPA and the Kikuyu Karinga Education Association. Summing up his 1949 report the provincial commissioner, Central Province (generally regarded as the leading province for unrest) was pleased to record how little headway KAU had made and that 'sounder and more moderate elements were in the ascendant'. He was so confident about 'this satisfactory state of affairs' that he paid tribute to his administrative officers, 'who handled their districts wisely, firmly and with discretion'.

The close of the 1940s saw little or no sign of racial equality or understanding. The bulletin of the East African Women's League, December 1949, contains a piece by J. R. P. Postlethwaite CBE, a self-confessed elderly male with 40 years' experience of living in East Africa. He invited his audience 'to remember that the African is a child and, like many children, is not given to concentrated effort and so [the reader] should make allowances'. He regretted that African ex-service men may have 'encountered [European] women whose manners and sometimes morals have upset the ideas of European superiority which they had formed in pre-war years'. An American, resident in Kenya, remarked that the United Kenya Club was the only place where Africans, Asians and Europeans were able to mix freely with each other and which provided members of all groups with a glimpse of the cultural patterns of the others. He suggested that the marriage of one member, Ismaili John Karmali, to an English woman was almost the first mixed marriage in Kenya, adding that husband and wife could not eat in the same restaurant and that the Karmali children were not allowed to enroll in white schools. In this last respect, conditions were not so different from southern states of the USA, where educational equality was more than a decade away.

The 'privatisation' of land in the Nandi Hills and Abadare highlands was observed by the authorities in 1950. Nandi ex-soldiers pegged out claims in the bush, cleared vegetation and grew crops without asking leave of anyone. There was plenty of bush and forest, and each man took as much as he could manage. In the Abadares, at Nyeri, two go-ahead chiefs, by purchase and the exchange of small plots within their own families, built up mixed farms of about 150 acres. These initiatives were mainly along the boundary with the settled area where people could see how Europeans did it. Most were between ten and 20 acres, well farmed, growing coffee and, in the higher altitudes, pyrethrum – profitable cash-crops. Outside Kikuyuland, more farmland had been created by the enclosure of common land, typically by the likes of Chief Willi arap Chirchir who started the whole enclosure movement in that area. They started a landslide, and by 1952 scarcely any land was left in communal ownership.

There was, then, evidence of shrewd and enterprising Africans making a success of farming, but there was also, as there always had been, a majority of less enterprising 'have nots' who were vulnerable for recruitment by the oath-dispensers. No doubt some were willing candidates, but there is ample evidence that many Africans were reluctant to become involved in subversive activities. They were caught up in 'the system'. Karari Njama, referred to earlier (and later at some length), was a 25-year-old Christian school teacher in February 1950 when he had his initial contact with the Kikuyu Central Association. His account of his first oathing, extracted in full but changed from first to third person, illustrates the vulnerability of the ordinary African and what lay behind the terse reports from numerous district commissioners of enforced oath-taking and similar activities.

'Njama's encounter started one evening when he went home to visit his girl friend who was staying in the house of a relative in their village. He arrived at the hut at about 7.30 pm to find that, although she was not there, a number of people from the village had gathered and were sitting about talking, laughing and telling tales. Curiosity made him stay to find out what sort of meeting this was and he joined in the conversation. At around 9pm a man entered the hut and said he was looking for a few strong young men like himself to assist with some work he was doing in a nearby hut. Three of them volunteered to help and followed the man out into the darkness. The hut was only a few yards away and inside Njama saw about 15 people. His father was there assisting some others slaughter a lamb. In the course of conversation he asked one of the men what sort of occasion it was and was told that they were awaiting the arrival of an important visitor. He knew all the people present and felt no cause for alarm even though he felt somewhat confused by the situation.

'In a matter of minutes he was once again called outside and led with six others to a hut located beneath the black wattle trees and separated from his home by a kei-apple fence. He felt a little scared at this point because he knew the third hut had been vacated long ago and he could see no point in going into a deserted house. Again, the people who were accompanying them acted as if they were guards – which in fact they were. Njama was upset because his clean clothes were getting wet and soiled by the high grass made wet by the early evening rain.

'As they approached the door, he saw a dim light inside and heard people whispering. But as they entered, the light went out and there was complete silence. They were all frightened at this point and entered with some reluctance, on the insistence of the guards. It was pitch dark inside but he could hear the whispered voices of many people who soon began asking them in turn who they were and other questions about themselves. He remembers suffering a few minutes of terror while being held around the neck and arms by three or four people. Moments later, however, someone ordered the lights turned on and soon three hurricane lamps illumined the inside of the hut. What struck him first was the sight of an arch made of banana leaves and the fact that three men stood guard armed with simis (the traditional double-edged Kikuyu swords). The door of the hut had been firmly bolted and, glancing around the room, he estimated that there were some 40 solemn-faced people inside. (Later he discovered that there were also people outside guarding the approaches to the hut.)

'One of the men in the room ordered the seven of them to form a queue by the arch, take off their shoes and remove any coins, watches or other metal objects they might have in their possession. It was at this point, as he relaxed a bit and saw that most of the people in the room were familiar to him, that he realised that this ceremony was probably the one he had earlier wished to undergo in order to become a member of the KCA. Though the people were stern-faced and would surely have harmed any who resisted, he was unafraid from this time onward.

'The man who had them remove their shoes and coins then instructed them to follows: "We want you young men to join us in the struggle for freedom and the return of our stolen land. That is why we have brought you here to swear an oath joining you with us in this struggle. Mind you, this is no joking matter. Any who refuse to take this oath will be killed and buried right here in this hut."

'At this point, one of the persons about to be initiated said that he had never heard of such an oath and was not willing to take it. Before he had completed his statement, however, he was hit very hard in the face. This convinced him and the rest of them that this was indeed no joking matter. The man pleaded to be allowed to take the oath and have his life spared. Njama explained how the oaths were arranged and the equipment used in the ceremony. He knew these things not only from having taken the oath, but from having attended dozens of such ceremonies in the months following his own initiation.

'He mentioned, above, that in the second house he entered a goat was being slaughtered. The meat was roasted to be eaten later and the skin was cut into thin ribbon-like strips which were twisted and joined to form rings. The eyes of the goat were removed together with the thorax and ngata, a bone which connects the head and the spinal column and contains seven holes. The eyes were stuck on either side of a 15-inch long piece of banana stalk which was hollowed out lengthwise so that it could be used as a container. Also attached were clusters of seven kei-apple thorns (from a particular tree known as Muthuthi or Mugaa) and sodom apples which were fixed to the three sides with the same thorns. This container was to hold a liquid formed by a mixture of goat's blood, soil and crushed grains, such as maize, sorghum and beans.

'The arch, which stood about five feet high, was constructed of long banana stalks dug into the ground and joined at the top by tying or intertwining their leaves. On this frame were put other plants and shrubs, such as sugar cane, maize stalks, etc. The ngata of the goat and the thorax, or large chest-piece of meat, were hung from the top of the arch near the centre.

'Throughout the ceremony, each initiate wore a ring of the twisted goatskin around his neck and held a damp ball of soil against his stomach with his right hand, a symbol of the person's willingness to do everything in his power to assist the association in regaining and protecting the land belonging to the Kikuyu people.

'Standing thus before the arch, he passed through it seven times while the oath administrator uttered and he repeated the following vows:

- If I am called upon at any time of the day or night to assist in the work of this association, I will respond without hesitation; and if I fail to do so, may this oath kill me.
- If I am required to raise subscriptions for this organisation, I will do so; and if I do not obey, may this oath kill me.
- I shall never decline to help a member of this organisation who is in need of assistance; and if I refuse such aid, may this oath kill me.
- I will never reveal the existence or secret of the association to government or to any person who is not himself a member; and if I violate this trust, may this oath kill me.

'Following this, and repeating these vows again on each occasion, he was instructed to take seven sips of liquid from the banana stalk container, seven small bites of the goat's thorax and – performing each act seven times – to prick the eyes of the dead goat and insert a piece of reed into the seven holes of the ngata. The administrator then had him take a bite of sugar cane, pour cold water over his feet and make a cross on his forehead with the blood and grain mixture. When this was completed, he was surrounded by a number of spectators who took hold of the skin ring around his neck and started counting. Reaching the number seven, they all pulled, breaking the ring and saying: "May you be destroyed like this ring if you violate any of these vows!" The rest of the people repeated this curse in unison.

'The oathing ceremony was thus completed and he was led into another hut with the others. A lamb, slaughtered earlier, was now roasting over the fire and they sat down to eat and talk till about midnight. Over 50 of them had taken the oath by this time and before departing they were all gathered together in a single hut to receive their final instructions. The administrator entered and told them they were now members of the KCA and linked by an oath of unity which would extend brotherhood to all members of the Kikuyu tribe. The white man, he said, was their enemy and they should have nothing to do with him. The land stolen from their people by the Europeans must be returned; and this could only be achieved through an unbreakable unity of all Kikuyu, who would act as a single man with a single purpose. They were then asked to pay an entrance fee of 2s 50 and told that an additional 62s 50 plus a ram were to be paid as soon as they were able. Njama's account refers to KCA administrators and makes no mention of Mau Mau.'

Njama's oathing was one of many. In his March report DC Kiambu wrote of two or three instances of Africans being intimidated and forced to take an oath of secrecy, people being taken from their huts at night and, usually, both man and wife being forced to take the oath under threats of violence. On the 4th April the city African affairs officer addressed a secret letter to the director of intelligence and security with copies to DC Kiambu and the chief native commissioner saying that a responsible and reliable Kikuyu had reported that political agitators in the Kikuyu area were going about the reserve administering an oath binding the oath-takers to complete silence concerning any political activities that the agitators might indulge in. The charge for the oath was said to be 80s.

One week later the police at Kiambu submitted a similar statement which gave the objects of the oath as to remove all Europeans and to obstruct the government. Jomo Kenyatta was reported to be a leading figure. Similar reports came in from the Rift Valley and elsewhere.

Then came the first of many trials concerned with oath-giving by what had been declared to be 'a society dangerous to good government and the colony'. Others were charged with being present They were tried at Kiambu and all were found guilty and sentenced to varying terms of imprisonment. A similar trial at Nakuru found the accused guilty. They were sentenced, but the case was successfully appealed. This result gave a great filip to Mau Mau supporters, and caused consternation and bitter resentment among the European farmers. Naivasha Settlers' Association recounted incidents of the increasingly subversive influence of Mau Mau on farm labour.

At about this time there appeared to be a remission of subversive activity. In May, DC Kiambu expressed his belief that there had been a virtual cessation of the administration of unlawful oaths during the previous month, and DC Fort Hall reported for April and May that an oath of allegiance to the Kikuyu Independent Schools Association had been given but had been taken voluntarily and was not therefore illegal.

However, the next few months produced further reports of KCA cum Mau Mau activity. An officer visiting a school at Kiagunya on the 7th June found a 'quiz' in progress:

Q. Who is our leader?
A. Jomo Kenyatta (*applause*).
Q. Which is the organisation which helps us?
A. KAU . . . (*etc.*)

That same day the director of intelligence and security reported on Mau Mau. He referred to the association first coming to his notice in the middle of 1948. It was undoubtedly the Kikuyu Central Association. He said there were reports of members joining it by taking an oath, and that details of the ritual were observed. The objects of Mau Mau appeared to be similar to those of the KCA and the two bodies shared some of their leading lights as officers. The report continued that little was heard of Mau Mau in 1949 and during the first four months of 1950, but that in May it reappeared in Naivasha. The driving force behind the increase in illegal oath-taking undoubtedly eminated from the Kiambu Reserve and followed closely on similar occurrences in the reserve.

On the 28th June 19 natives (17 Kikuyu, one Masai and one Kisii) were sentenced to imprisonment with hard labour for administering oaths at Naivasha. There followed two reports, one of which suggested an increased involvement of Kikuyu women in oath-taking, the other the existence of a central organisation which trained and directed Mau Mau activities. The district commissioner doubted the accuracy of the first report, as it would be utterly contrary to Kikuyu custom for a woman to administer a Muma oath, but he admitted that, until recently, it had been unknown for a woman to have a Muma oath administered to her. Corfield's report described several similar cases of oathing.

Central government appears to have taken no action on the report, which had been confirmed by Ian Henderson, the Kikuyu-speaking, Kikuyu-thinking special branch officer.

Kenyatta's involvement in corruption was also suggested in the reports. References to his return from England included mention of the natives' fund-raising meetings for the construction of a college at Githunguri. A report from DC Kiambu dated 25th July referred to there being 'absolutely nothing to show' for not less than £10,500 raised by the African public for the teachers' training college at Githunguri, and that there was 'good reason to believe that the college organisers were identified with the leaders of the proscribed KCA and were responsible for the administration of the secret unlawful oaths which were taking place in Kiambu and Rift Valley Province'.

In parallel with reports from the districts was a memorandum from the chief native commissioner to LEGCO on the 'Mau Mau Association'. It had regard to the probability that Mau Mau was really the proscribed KCA under another name, and it suggested that there were ample grounds for declaring it unlawful. Mau Mau was proscribed. Soon afterwards the police conducted a successful operation.

Covert meetings and oath-taking continued in several parts of Kikuyuland. One closely reported event occurred early in the morning of Sunday 27th August. Chief Nderi reported to DO Nyeri that a large meeting of the KCA was taking place, and that many people had been forced to take the muma oath. Nderi and two men who escaped with him were 'somewhat battered', having refused to take the oath. A group of 25 police surrounded the area and an informer who had escaped after being made to take the oath pointed out people participating in the ceremony. The meeting had taken place in the grounds of the Kyandu Roman Catholic school with the consent and co-operation of the African headmaster: the actual administration of the oath took place in one of the school buildings. Remains of goats, a flaying knife and other evidence associated with oath administration were collected by the police. Of the 37 Kikuyu arrested, 15 were charged, found guilty and sentenced.

As 1950 came to an end there were reports from various districts of 'sympathy' hymns being sung, chiefly by women in the Kikuyu reserve. The hymns contained 'words of prayer' for the families of convicted members of Mau Mau. They were sung at night and in secret and with every effort being made to avoid chiefs and headmen hearing them. On the 13th December a spear tied to a long pole was thrust at Chief Waruhiu through a window as he lay in bed in his house near Kiambu, but it missed its mark. It was rumoured that the attempt to assassinate him would not fail the second time. There was no doubt that unrest was growing in the countryside.

In Nairobi, too, there was unrest. The early part of 1950 was focused on raising its status to that of city. The Duke and Duchess of Gloucester presented the royal charter at the end of March. The East African Trades Union Congress (EATUC), led by Fred Kubai and Makham Singh, planned to boycott the civic celebrations. Rumours were abroad that the city was to be extended for 32 miles and that 12,000 families were to be removed from Kiambu to make way for European settlement. These rumours were without foundation but, as Corfield commented in his report, they were well calculated to cause intense local unrest. Mbotela, in KAU, gave full support to the granting of the charter and the civic celebrations. On the night when the charter was granted he was shot at by a Kikuyu-speaking assailant but the revolver misfired. KAU had held a large public meeting in Nairobi on 5th February, when Tom Mbotela stated that the aims of KAU were to unite and defend all Africans in Kenya and to fight for education, labour, housing, freedom of the press, equal rights with Europeans, freedom of speech and universal franchise. All were to be promoted through non-violence and full co-operation with the Government.

The Sansom family provide an almost detached, observer's view of the years to independence. In 1950 Dr Hugh Sansom took up a post as meteorologist in Nairobi. He found that all the top posts in the met office were occupied by Europeans, all the middle posts by Asians and all the junior posts by Africans: 'There was no easy way for them to get from one grade to the other.'

In May 1950 the authorities decided to take action against the EATUC in Nairobi and to obtain a decision in court as to the legality or otherwise of the congress. The congress's opposition to the royal visit may have prompted this decision. There was a strike in protest, and Makham Singh and Fred Kubai, both regarded as dangerous and unscrupulous agitators, were arrested. The strike was regarded as essentially political in origin and intent, claims for higher wages being added as an afterthought to the main demand. When mass meetings in Pumwani Park were resisted by the police, the strikers roamed the city, particularly in the Asian residential area, assaulting houseboys and others. Most of the victims were Nyanza Africans. When the police began to enrol special constables to deal with the gangs, they flocked to enlist, anxious to retaliate against their Kikuyu assailants. The strike, which began in Nairobi on 18th, petered out on 25th May.

Kenya began to attract the interest of Westminster, in particular Fenner Brockway, Labour MP for Eton and Slough. Previously the better connected white settlers had contacts with, and visits from, members of both houses of parliament, but Labour representatives were much less frequent visitors to the colony. Brockway was a dedicated socialist and humanitarian who was opposed to imperialism. Barbara Castle, another Labour MP, described him as totally devoid of racial prejudice. Brockway was not a communist: indeed, he resisted communist infiltration of the League Against Imperialism. It was suggested that his only sin was that he had a consistent record of anti-colonialism and tended to treat Africans with more respect than settlers did. This background is important, because Brockway would become a significant influence in Kenya in the next few years.

Brockway was one of the Labour party members who had given Kenyatta succour during his long stay in London. Now Kenyatta met him in Nairobi. Brockway affronted the Europeans by staying with the former senior chief Koinange. It was unprecedented for such a visitor not to stay at Government House or in a European hotel.

'I had not understood,' Brockway wrote, 'that racial separation was so rigid in this British colony.' His understanding was increased when he made a visit to a hospital which was equal to the highest standards in British hospitals but was racial – no Africans admitted.

Brockway was made comfortable by Koinange, but commented in his memoirs on the domestic arrangements under which the women and children lived in a kraal 50 yards from the bungalow. He also confided to Barbara Castle that he had experienced a moment of embarrassment when Koinange, having presented him to the tribe as a blood-brother, indicated that this meant he was entitled to share the chieftain's five wives. Brockway discovered, too, that he was now father to Koinange's children, who addressed him as such.

The governor was on leave, but Brockway had 'the friendliest time' with the acting governor and the chief secretary. He was told that Africans were prohibited from growing coffee because there was a danger that disease would spread from inexpertly cultivated African bushes to European farms, but he was not impressed by the argument. With the Koinanges, father and son, he planned a land petition to the

House of Commons supported by a 67,000 thumb-print petition. They decided, too, to press for elected African members of the legislation, with the aim of 'building up an African movement which would use political and not violent methods. Kenyatta was foremost in urging this'. Brockway was confident that Kenyatta was interested in political rather than subversive means of achieving independence. 'If,' he wrote, 'Jomo were at this time forming cells of Mau Mau, would he have encouraged Africans to look to Westminster? Would he have thrust into the public gaze the KCA, which the officials hold was the source of Mau Mau?'

He recorded his observations of Africans' living conditions during his visit. He witnessed Kikuyu being cleared from Masai land (probably at Olenguruone), and was sympathetic to the squatters' plight, likening them to serfs on European farms. He was not, however, uncritical of African customs. He discussed with them the 'servitude of women' and women's circumcision. He noted photographs of Lenin, Nehru and Paul Robeson on the walls, and books with 'a strong bias towards Marxism' on the shelves of the school library.

The climax of Brockway's visit was his speech at 'a racial goodwill garden party' arranged by ex-chief Koinange. The London *Times*, which reported the occasion with amazement, estimated the number of Africans present as 30,000: 'The gathering was attended by government officials, members of the Legislative, the United Nations representative in East Africa, the Commissioner for India, judges and lawyers, businessmen, doctors, religious leaders and settlers. Kenya had never before had such a representative inter-racial assembly.'

Brockway hit the right note and demonstrated that he was, as Barbara Castle wrote, totally devoid of racial prejudice with one sentence which 'set the women shrilling and the men clapping'. When, he said, a baby was born, 'it is not the pigment of the skin which makes it precious; it is the life, the spirit, within that little form, be it white, brown or black, which makes it sacred'.

At the conclusion of the meeting Koinange pronounced Brockway a chief of the Kikuyu tribe. He was proud of being one of only two whites to have been inducted as a Kikuyu chief, Louis Leakey being the other. Michael Blundell and A.B. Patel watched Brockway emerge from the KAU offices surrounded by excited Kikuyu and wearing a monkey-skin robe which had been presented to him. 'As I watched the scene,' Patel said to Blundell later, 'it occurred to me that we have already lost the mind of the African.'

Within a week or two of the Brockway visit Peter Mbui Koinange sponsored the inaugural meeting of the non-racial Kenya Citizens' Association at which it was decided that the association would be a forum for the fostering of human relationship and the free discussion of problems involved. Some 17 Europeans, eight Indians and 11 Africans attended, including Sir Charles Mortimer, Messrs Vasey, Askwith, Cooke, Sprott, La Fontaine, S.G. Amin, Ibrahim Nathoo, ex-chief Koinange, Peter Mbui Koinange, Jomo Kenyatta and Ambrosa Ofafa.

The association's aims had much in common with those of the United Kenya Club, which now had a membership of 325 and had outgrown its quarters. With five other Asian parents, Ismaili John Karmali, a club member whose children were not allowed to enroll in white schools, founded the Hospital Hill primary school, which opened in the Karmalis' home. The school was for children of all races, but it was to be several years before it received financial assistance from the colonial administration.

Ironically, as modest, almost covert, signs of racial harmony emerged, there were overt signs of rifts in KAU leadership. On 23rd September Tom Mbotela, the vice president, reported to DC Nyeri in a confidential letter that it had become obvious to him that some members and officers of KAU branches had been taking part in either administrating or taking illegal oaths in parts of Kenya. He emphasised that this was entirely contrary to the constitution of the KAU, and that some reputable Kikuyus as well as some chiefs agreed with him that they must co-operate in trying to get rid of the existing undesirable habit of administering 'these filthy oaths' among the people. He stressed that he, as vice-president, and Joseph Katithi, the general secretary, had been working very hard to drive it home to the people in Rift Valley province and Kiambu district that KAU's constitution was entirely different from that of the Kikuyu Central Association and the Mau Mau Association (if Mau Mau had a constitution), and that KAU members should not under any circumstances have anything to do with this terrible affair.

It is interesting that Mbotela wrote of KCA and Mau Mau as separate bodies. When passing the report up the line, DC Kiambu was guarded in his comments on Mbotela's letter, but he believed that the writer was genuine in his efforts to disassociate KAU from Mau Mau activities. He added that Mbotela hinted very strongly that Jomo Kenyatta had advised KAU branches to support Mau Mau, and commented on his difficulties as a non-Kikuyu in carrying weight if he made a comment on his own behalf. Announcements, he said, should come from Kenyatta as president of KAU. Mbotela failed to draw Kenyatta into such an announcement at a public meeting at Fort Hall.

Reporting on a meeting of KAU at Kiambu on 15th October, the DC said Mau Mau activities were stressed as not being connected with KAU, but they were not denounced. Kenyatta did support the government's terracing initiative but, the DC opined, it was chiefly with the object of avoiding KAU getting a bad name for slanging agricultural policy and thus being prevented from holding meetings in the reserve.

There were still few signs of Mau Mau activity on many European farms. Joan Scott, an early settler's daughter, returned to Kenya when she had completed her education in England working as a Land Army girl. Back in Kenya she worked on a farm producing principally pyrethrum, vegetables, flowers and milk, which she delivered locally. She took over management of the farm and found life remarkably similar to that of the pre-war settlers. They worked most of the time, and there was the club and gymkhana about three times a year, with weddings being the high-life which everybody went to.

Returning, she found the settlers very like people in English villages, introspective but kindly. She resented British people's ill-informed views of white Kenyans making a fortune and ill-treating the Africans, who enjoyed clinics, schooling and other benefits provided by the Europeans. She ran a mixed school on the farm for the children of the farm staff (*page 72*). They were keen to learn and, at their insistence, had only Christmas Day off school – and even then they resented the closure. This happy state was soon to be disrupted.

At Mau Summit the Robathan's farmhouse was extended in 1950. They had a brief leave in Britain, but returned to the trivial round of ensuring that mechanical plant and the water supply functioned efficiently. Their social life comprised local point-to-points and polo. The life of the Seys at Rhodora included holidays on the coast, a cruise on Lake Victoria, some travel around Kenya, a stay at Chiromo with the McMillans and tea with the Delameres, but on the farm the day started at 6.30am and finished at dinner time. Livestock management was taken seriously, and importance was placed on success at local shows as this enhanced the stock's value.

Nevertheless, news of unrest continued to flow through Government House. In August DC Nakuru noted that Mau Mau was known to the Kikuyu in Naivasha and was spreading. In October DC Nyeri said he was of the opinion that secret oaths were still being administered. In the same month DC Nanyuki reported a number of Africans taking the oath on Mr Bastard's farm in the school which he had built and staffed at his own expense for the benefit of his employees: the oath was administered by his cook to employees from his own and neighbouring farms. This was the first report of an oathing from the settled area of Central Province.

Although such reports rolled in with monotonous regularity, most appeared to be ignored. The provincial commissioner's frustration boiled over in DO John Cumber's presence. 'My God,' he asked, 'do they read these damned reports down there [at Government House]?'. Cumber reported that 'there were murders in the tribal reserves and

The school at Kangaita Farm, Nanyuki.

72

the odd headman, tribal police carrier, that sort of person was disappearing'.

The first reports of 'Njuku', a register supposedly kept by Jomo Kenyatta of the names of Africans who had taken the oath and paid the 60s fee, appeared in October. It was said that only those people whose names were recorded would be entitled to a free grant of land when the Africans achieved self-government, the others being expelled from the Kikuyu tribe. The register, if it existed, was never found but its possible existence had significant propaganda value.

Along similar lines was a report in November from the Nyeri divisional police that there was a common object in Kikuyu bodies or movements (KAU, KISA, KCA, Mau Mau and all) to teach the individual the importance of 'fighting for his land, complete freedom and the necessity of forcing the Britisher to abandon his interests in the colony'.

The African chiefs were closer to the natives than the administrators. Chief Nderi, whose name occurs in later pages, said Mau Mau had been founded some two or three years earlier in the house of a man called Kirori Mutuku in Aguthi – a meeting attended by Jomo Kenyatta and James Beuttah. This assertion gave weight to a memorandum from Eliud Mathu in July 1947 to the government reporting 'clandestine meetings of Kikuyu'.

Lest it be thought that all blame for the restlessness of the natives should be attributed to Mau Mau, DC Nakuru in his 1950 annual report said too many farmers were inclined to 'bully and subdue' rather than lead their African employees. The emergence of Mau Mau, he said, was due 'principally, to an entire lack of appreciation of the African and his mental processes by the majority of employers'.

The Corfield historical survey dealt with the events of 1950 at some length 'because it was during this year that the many and varied facets of the campaign of Mau Mau subversion came more definitely to notice'. Footnote 21 states that for the months of November and December the district intelligence reports of the Central Province alone cover some 28 pages. By the end of 1950, 142 people had been prosecuted in connection with administering Mau Mau oaths and 120 had been convicted.

There was, therefore, ample evidence of a well established secret society, and Mau Mau seemed as good a name to give it as any. The political temperature was rising.

ABOVE: *Jomo Kenyatta speaking at a mass rally at Kiambu in 1952.*

BELOW: *The house built by the Whittalls for £100. (See page 20)*

5

More Militant and Impatient

'A group of civil servants who were fumbling and indecisive.'
(The Earl of Portsmouth, Kenya resident)

The independence movement in 1951 was more a philosophy than an organization, and Oginga Odinga's assessment was that it was 'more militant and impatient'. KAU was central to much of the activity, but this body had members from LEGCO and other moderate individuals on its committees, making KAU less militant than some would have liked.

'KAU committees,' Odinga wrote, 'went on functioning, augmented by the few militants thrown up by trade union struggles and from the ranks of the returning ex-servicemen, but, most important, an inner core of the leadership began to prepare for a new type of struggle. The 1951 KAU elections threw out some of the moderates, the 'good boys'. The constitution was changed to include, for the first time, the demand for independence. Formal organizational structures were established and shadow parliaments and shadow groups were readied to take over the reins should the first rank of leaders be arrested.. Special groups were ordered to acquire arms: a counter intelligence organisation followed the moves of government security. In Nairobi taxi-drivers, black marketeers and gangs were enlisted, and a network of local committees was set up, later to be the vital supply and contact lines to fighters in the forests. These plans and preparations were not revealed to the official committees and leaders of KAU. Members of other tribes were involved and speakers at meetings warned that there could be no struggle without blood being shed – a fair summary of the events in 1951 covered by this chapter.

The friction between European farmers and administrators persisted, aggravated to some extent by African unrest. Not unusually, the farmers were divided among themselves, but more liberal elements were beginning to take control, while a series of right wing political parties emerged with different names but mainly composed of the same people. A continuing theme of all the parties, particularly those on the right wing, was a wish to escape the basic fact that Africa was largely populated by black Africans. A minority were vociferous and violently critical of the government almost all the time. They seemed incapable of understanding the realities of political life in Kenya, where a small white governing minority was accepted by a vast and still reasonably tranquil African population. But times were changing, and younger European settlers who had served with Africans in the military services were more aware of Africans' feelings than those who had not. But few Europeans seemed aware of the intensity of political feeling among many Africans. Such was Blundell's assessment of events at the time.

During 1951 there was a marked increase in meetings. Many were small gatherings of people with similar interests, but there were also mass meetings called by black African leaders to unite the public against the Administration. On 12th January, while the farmers were dividing, the Kenya Citizens' Association held its first meeting in the United Kenya Club. At the meeting Jomo Kenyatta complained that he had been attacked by *Kenya Weekly News* and had been requested by the editor to denounce Mau Mau publicly. He and his union, he said, had been working against it, and he had himself attempted to condemn Mau Mau publicly. He had said that KAU had nothing to do with Mau Mau. He agreed to hold a public meeting and denounce the movement, but he remarked that he feared talking about Mau Mau would probably strengthen its influence among Africans.

He was as good as his word, to some extent at least, but he spoke in riddles and parables which were capable of interpretation to suit the listener's taste. A meeting was held in Nairobi the following month, and Kenyatta denounced Mau Mau by saying that it was a bad thing but that he did not know of it – he did not even know what language it was. The police reported that this was greeted with mirth.

Another public meeting of KAU was arranged near Limuru on 25th February with the express purpose of denouncing Mau Mau, but Kenyatta did not attend. The chief speaker was the vice-president, Mbotela. He referred to the division of the tribe into oath-takers and non oath-takers as a highly undesirable matter because it would weaken the tribe. Joseph Katithi, the general secretary, was at one with Mbotela: both were 'good boys'.

A further meeting was held on the showground at Nyeri on 27th May. It was addressed by Anderson Wamuthenya, Samuel Gathogo and Victor Wokabi. Kikuyu-speaking Ian Henderson, the assistant superintendent of police, Nyeri, reported that they 'moved the meeting to a frenzy and called for the return of the White Highlands to the Kikuyu. By the time Anderson sat down,' he concluded, 'it would have been suicidal for anyone to pass a remark in favour of government.'

His analysis of the situation was that the most likely action would appear to be 'universal civil disobedience over road making, terracing etc, and a march by KAU members on Government House; the assassination of leading government supporters such as Chief Eliud and Senior Chief Nderi and/or an attack on chiefs' offices in the reserves. It was a bleak outlook.

KAU saw the need to be, and to be seen to be, more professional, and when Bildad Kaggia became general secretary the union acquired a single room in Kilburi House, Nairobi. It was, said Kaggia, as if KAU occupied the whole building, since it became 'the centre for dissemination of political and trade union propaganda among Africans, playing an important role in the struggle for independence.'

There was a lack of unanimity in reports coming in from the districts. Despite signs of increasing unrest and the spread of Mau Mau among Kikuyu labour in the settled areas of the Rift Valley, the member for law and order was informed by the director of intelligence and security on 22nd February that 'the general picture would appear that the Mau Mau is cracking up'. From the European farmer's point of view the reality in 1951 was the further from Nairobi and the fewer the Kikuyu employees, the better.

It was a routine matter for James Stapleton to give permission for an African dance or 'sheep event' to be held on his farm, but he was mildly surprised when, having sought permission, his Kikuyu workers cleared an area twice the size of a tennis court with a stand for elders and a space for a kitchen. The stand was decorated with green branches and a small area was roped off inside. On the night, four smartly dressed farm-workers acted as askaris (police/guards), his tractor driver acted as cook and his leading hand acted as cashier/accountant. Hundreds came, including some from Nairobi: all were Kikuyu. Some of the songs, he was told, were anti-European.

It was some time later that Stapleton realized the nature of the event he had hosted. A smaller but otherwise similar event was staged at Tom Aggett's farm in the Nanyuki area, which led to the arrest of the six Kikuyu leaders, all from farms in the vicinity. And 15 miles away, at much the same time, another oathing took place under cover of a traditional circumcision ceremony. Twelve were arrested.

Meanwhile, in Britain, people like Fenner Brockway were making much of the pleas from various colonies for independence. Britain had a Labour government and Brockway was by no means the only MP who was a member of the League Against Imperialism. One who became a member of the government recalled that most of the left became sponsors of the movement. James Griffiths, secretary of state for the colonies, had made a declaration of policy reaffirming that the central purpose of British policy was to guide people of the colonial territories to responsible self-government. The word 'people' included both immigrant communities and Africans. At a public meeting of KAU in Nairobi, with Jomo Kenyatta presiding, the meeting had welcomed the declaration. There was in fact little, if anything, new in the declaration: it was restatement of policy established by both Conservative and Labour governments before the war.

Later Griffiths visited Kenya and impressed Blundell as a man of 'warm determination' with great integrity. Blundell recalled that when European representatives in LEGCO asked him why he had given Ghana its independence Griffiths banged the table and cried 'in his lilting Welsh voice, And what was the alternative? Bloody revolution man, bloody revolution!'

Governor Philip Mitchell's diary records Griffiths' meeting a group from LEGCO which included Blundell and a cross-section of European, African, Arab and Indian members. Griffiths read a general proposition that; 'within twelve months of the election of the next council [May 1952], there would be set up an inter-racial consultative body under an independent chairman from outside Kenya', with Kenya government and colonial office representations. After a brief adjournment everyone accepted all the proposals. Mitchell was well pleased with the outcome, 'settled in an atmosphere of sober responsibility and goodwill . . . by the personal influence of this remarkable man, who has spread goodwill wherever he has been'.

Griffiths' visit had a major impact on political organizations of all shades in Kenya. Kenyatta had a meeting with the governor on constitutional changes and African representation on LEGCO, and Griffiths promised a constitutional conference in 1953 which all races would attend and at which political changes would be discussed. For reasons which will emerge, this conference was not held.

Visits from Britain were a feature of 1951. A master from an English public school taught for a term at the all-African Alliance School. At the conclusion of his stay he remarked that his school in England lacked 'the Christian atmosphere, and the good manners of the boys' which he had experienced at the Alliance School. When asked if he thought he could turn out African youngsters on a 19th century English public school pattern, Carey Francis replied: 'But I want my boys to be gentlemen, Christian gentlemen. Is there anything wrong with that?'

Subversion and lawlessness increased during the first half of the year. Bildad Kaggia was no doubt one of the Africans whom Oginga Odinga had in mind when referring to the independence movement becoming more militant and impatient. Kaggia was a man with 'new nationalist' aspirations, who knew that for many years African unions had had to tread a narrow path. If they lacked a measure of militancy they were unacceptable to some of their members, but if they overstepped the government's mark they would be proscribed. By 1951 KAU was regarded by the 'militant and revolutionary' Africans, with whom Kaggia wished to be identified, as an instrument of the governor through Mathu, his nominated member on LEGCO. Kaggia therefore looked to the unions rather than KAU as the way ahead for the ambitious would-be militant new nation leader, but he retained his place in KAU. The list of union officers elected in June 1951 included Kubai, Mungai, Kaggia, Kitabi and Ngei. All were names which would appear as militants in future years. The Nairobi branch of KAU was, too, wrote Kaggia, 'very unpopular' with militants. It was not the place for him, and as the unions grew in strength Kenyatta took a greater interest in them.

In June there were reports that Mau Mau meetings were being held in Kikuyu independent schools after Sunday church services in some districts, and during August and September there were three public meetings of KAU in Central Province. At the first, held at Thika with about 300 people present, Jomo Kenyatta reiterated that the land belonged to Africans and called for self-government and an end to European immigration. He urged KAU members not to be afraid to spill their blood to get the land: 'You must rule yourselves in your own lives if you want to rule the country,' he concluded.

The second meeting, held at Nyeri station, was attended by some 700 Africans, and Domenico Ndegwo attacked European immigration which, he said, was targeted to reach two million 'as rapidly as possible'. The third meeting, at Fort Hall, heard Andrew Nganga, a leading committee member, decry the Fort Hall African District Council as useless, and refer to the members as 'district commissioner's puppets'. He suggested killing the chiefs as a solution. Joseph Kanini then 'incited' the people (to use Corfield's word) to resist inoculations and to stop digging terraces for land conservation. The Administration recommended that the speakers be prosecuted, but no proceedings followed.

In addition to the mass meetings, Jomo Kenyatta and other leaders attended meetings of other bodies during September and October. At these they spoke against the government, chiefs, the police, the administration and terracing. News of these meetings filtered back to the Administration from various sources. With other leaders, Jomo Kenyatta campaigned against the Beecher Report on Education and was opposed to all government-sponsored education, urging its replacement by education 'locally controlled and on strong nationalistic lines'. There certainly appeared to be a 'meetings circuit', which may have been the cause of DC Nyeri's report that 'Mau Mau, KCA, KAU, Nyeri Education Society, KISA, the African Central Province Merchants and Growers Association etc are all the same old stiffs working under different guises in order to increase the number of public meetings they can hold and the amount of money they can extract from a gullible public'.

But in October words turned to deeds. There was a strike of coffee pickers on many farms in the Thika area and reports of picketing and intimidation of would-be pickers. These followed remarks Kenyatta made at a meeting of KAU in Katunda from which, the Administration alleged, the strike could be traced. It petered out in a few days, but there was, to say the least, tension at an 'inter-racial' meeting in Nairobi about the United Nations organization. The meeting was chaired by Eliud Mathu, with Chanan Singh and C.H. Adams as speakers: all three were members of LEGCO. It was not a subject one would expect to rouse strong passions, but the back of the hall was packed with 'extremist' Fred Kubai's followers, who shouted abusive remarks at the mentions of inter-racial co-operation and disrupted the meeting to a point where the speakers were forced to take refuge and escape by a side door. Tom Mbotela, ever the moderate, admitted that he was extremely frightened.

At the end of October a high level meeting, attended by the member for law and order and others, recognized that a policy involving repression was defeatist. Aims were agreed, which included pressing for longer sentences; investigating the possibility of providing an outlet for the expression of African feeling; continuing government community development; encouraging farm barazas (formal tribal meetings); appointing a district officer to Nakuru to assist in coordinating the work of the police, the administrator and the labour department; and discontinuing the practice of cancelling squatters' contracts as a repressive measure.

European farmers were generally oblivious to discussions at 'high level' and of the conclusions drawn at Government House, but people in the Nakuru area knew there was trouble coming at least a year before it was officially admitted. The local policeman had disturbed an oathing ceremony on the hill, and there were rumours of a night of the long knives. It was said that 'there seemed always to be trouble when Kenyatta made a speech', and he was making them all the time. Farmers noticed, too, changes in attitudes difficult to define – 'funny things going on and Africans acting in funny ways'. Thefts of stock and absenteeism increased in late 1951. Remarkably, more than 40 years later it was these months that farmers recalled perhaps more vividly than the violent times which were to follow.

It had to come, and in the second half of 1951 a power struggle developed among the leaders of KAU and the unions – a division Kaggia had foreseen and no doubt advanced. At the centre of the struggle were 'moderates' such as Tom Mbotela and Joseph Katithi, (KAU vice-president and secretary-general, respectively), and 'extremists' such as Fred Kubai and Bildad Kaggia on the other. However, with Kenyatta's encouragement Mbotela and Katithi were removed at a conference in November 1951, replacements being made from beyond Nairobi. By appointing people from outside, Kenyatta hoped to prevent KAU becoming a 'Kikuyu union'. Kaggia was appointed secretary-general of the Nairobi branch. He developed a role as a sort of liaison officer. 'Anybody who wanted to know anything had to see Kaggia,' he wrote.

On 27th November the government's internal security working committee submitted its first and last report. It ranged wide. It referred to Mau Mau as a Kikuyu secret society 'which is probably another manifestation of the suppressed Kikuyu Central Association'. It described the society as anti-European and its aim as dispossessing Europeans of the White Highlands. The Kikuyu were described as being, with the exception of the Somali, the most given to intrigue of any tribe, but, by nature and tradition, amongst the least war-like. The committee concluded that existing security arrangements were 'generally adequate' but considered that measures should include security checks against the setting up of connections with outside subversive bodies, the restriction of local agitators, appropriate control over publication, the strengthening of existing legislation relating to arms and explosives and the introduction of local immigration control which might involve undesirable contacts.

In his historical survey Corfield underscored the sentence in the report that read 'The potency of the organization depends on the extent to which it possesses the power, latent in all secret societies, of being more feared than the forces of law.' He found it difficult to appreciate on what grounds the committee 'reached the somewhat astonishing conclusion' that 'as soon as the sh.60 entrance fees [to Mau Mau] are not forthcoming, little more will be heard of the Mau Mau'. Cash continued 'pouring into the money-boxes', he wrote.

Perhaps an explanation of the apparently relaxed attitude of official reports may be explained by the form which communications between administrators and government were expected to take. At the end of 1951, an administrator wrote that a provincial commissioner's annual report was 'not supposed to include contentious arguments, clarion calls to action or dire warnings of troubles to come, all subjects for special secret letters and private talks'.

The facts were, Corfield concluded, that reports from all district commissioners and police formations showed intensification of oathing ceremonies during the latter part of 1951. Nevertheless, the Kenya Citizens' Association was satisfied that at a meeting of KAU in Nairobi on 24th February Jomo Kenyatta had denounced Mau Mau, although he had shown again 'that he was a master of circumlocution'. Also on the credit side were reports that 'a further advance in good African farming practice' had been achieved, with more than 12,000 miles of contour terrace having been completed that year compared with 10,327 the previous year. Tribute was paid to 'the cheerful and willing spirit of the majority of the people who have laboured so hard for so long'. 'In the interests of brevity,' wrote Corfield, 15 pages of the original annual report were omitted before publication. Deletions included references to:

• Gangs of criminals operating in and around Nairobi with the slogan 'More land'.
• embittered Kikuyu politicians.
• The worsening tone of public meetings, at most of which collections were taken.

The final report was, therefore, 'a bowdlerized version', on which Mitchell commented: 'It is a very good report of an excellent and encouraging year's work.'

Meanwhile, it had also been an encouraging year for the United Kenya Club's building fund, as contributions poured in from colonial government, a subvention, European and Asian companies and club members. Club officials took out a loan and Derek Erskine helped arrange the financing. George Vamos, architect and club member, designed the building.

By the end of 1951 Mitchell's term as governor was drawing to a close and he appeared pleased with the way that things were going. He recorded that they seemed to be following a set pattern: the governor made proposals which were rejected by one of the groups; there was much excitement for a while; and then the proposals, usually with some sensible modifications, were accepted with or without a visit from a minister. This was a rather wearing way of doing business, but it did get the business done. The governor made no reference to trouble ahead.

Certainly he had made an impression on some Europeans. Michael Blundell recalled that Sir Philip Mitchell had cautiously introduced the membership system into Kenya government which hitherto was 'an official, irremovable one, composed of colonial civil servants'.

January 1952 was 'musical chairs' time in the Administration. Henry Potter replaced J.D. Rankine as chief secretary in Government House. Potter was described by Chenevix Trench as a kindly, competent, somewhat colourless individual who had come from eight years in Uganda following 18 years in Kenya. He had no time for European politicians. Blundell echoed Trench's opinion, adding that Potter's years of loyal and sustained work 'had robbed him of the fire and energy required to deal with the mounting situation which now faced him'. Another change was the appointment of John Whyatt as member for law and order and attorney-general. A sincere man and a devout Catholic, he was a stranger to Africa. Faced with what was to prove a difficult year the senior government team therefore comprised a governor approaching the end of his term, three top officers with no recent experience of the Kikuyu and two who had none. Everyone acknowledged that the difficulties facing the colony involved the Kikuyu, but the Administration's greatest Kikuyu expert, Coutts, spent the years 1949 to 1957 administering St Vincent in the West Indies.

Michael Blundell sent two memoranda on Mau Mau to Whyatt in January, to which he received 'a rather condescending reply', Whyatt recording that he was encouraged by the interest which Blundell was showing. He suggested a meeting to discuss the problem. The committee that was set up as a result of the meeting had, wrote Blundell, no real teeth in it and was mainly designed to keep the unofficial members of the legislative council quiet if they proved to be too inquisitive or too restless in their enquiries on the security situation. Blundell and Chenevix Trench agree that the most the official side would concede to the European members was occasional discussion – not for mutual enlightenment but, in the words of the secretary for law and order, Cusack, 'to keep the buggers quiet'. Such were the relationships which greeted 1952 and the troubles ahead.

Intensification of oathing ceremonies continued into 1952. January saw arrests which converted into convictions. There was the first recorded case of a Mau Mau ceremony having taken place in Nairobi, and there were 11 cases of arson in Nyeri district. Arson continued into 6th February, the huts of 'loyal' Kikuyu providing targets. The attacks appeared to have been part of a pre-arranged and well organized plan, with several separate groups being responsible. A CID report stated that 'the object of the campaign appeared to be to intimidate loyal government supporters so that organiszed gangs of young Kikuyu, anti-government and anti-European fanatics' might operate with complete immunity. Loyal chiefs and headmen became less effective in the maintenance of law and order. To combat this subversion, six temporary police posts were established and manned, and one European and 15 other ranks were kept in reserve.

After considerable opposition from the member for law and order and with support from Eluid Mathu, the LEGCO representative, the governor signed the order imposing a fine of £2,500 on a sub-location under the collective punishment ordinance. This led to a question in the House of Commons.

On the 11th February 1952 500 women involved in burning farm equipment were convicted for causing malicious damage. The four male organisers were sentenced to two years hard labour. Frequently, however, Mau Mau leaders were not prosecuted because of the interpretation given by the courts to the law of sedition. Corfield reported that in the five years before the Emergency there were only five successful prosecutions for sedition. The sentences of fines usually awarded by the courts were quite useless and were paid without difficulty from the accumulated funds of Mau Mau.

There were outbreaks of arson in Timau, Naro Moru and Nanyuki areas and it was reported that Kikuyu women were very keen followers in these attacks. The outbreaks required Mitchell to make a difficult decision. Should he cancel the planned visit of Princess Elizabeth, heir to the throne, and the Duke of Edinburgh? To cancel it would hand a propaganda victory to the Mau Mau and end Mitchell's hopes of a peerage. To allow the royal couple to drive through the heart of Kikuyuland seemed an appalling risk.

The visit went ahead. For British settlers it was a major event, even for those not involved in high jinks at Government House. At Nanyuki they had been arranging flowers and were ready for the great day, and they all had their best clothes on. Sadly for them she passed through to the little Nanyuki air-strip in a car with the blinds down. While the royal couple were in Kenya King George VI died, making Kenya the first colony to be visited by Queen Elizabeth II.

In 1962 T.R. Johar, back in Nairobi from training in England, observed some softening of racial discrimination. During the war and soon after, Asians had never bothered to exercise their rights or demonstrate against the inequalities imposed by the colonial system. By 1952 things had started to move away from soft apartheid and more people accepted 'coloureds' in their societies, although they still had separate elections for Europeans, Africans and Asians. Restaurants gradually started taking down their barriers. Whites realized that they could not carry on as they had for the past 40 or 50 years. In April construction began on the two-storey United Kenya

Club building, comprising an office, library, dining hall, kitchen and store room.

Bildad Kaggia regarded himself as 'extremist' and 'revolutionary'. By 1952 he was KAU's member of the Nairobi African Advisory Council to Nairobi Municipal Council. One of his activities was to acquaint white municipal council members with African problems. The advisory council had a wide and varied membership, and as a member of it Kaggia managed to get recognition for societies led by members of Mau Mau. 'Having societies controlled by Mau Mau,' he said later, 'meant we could dominate the municipal halls.'

In parallel with the 'subversion' were public meetings. During February and March, meetings of KAU were held, supposedly to resist the spread of Mau Mau. The first was held at Tiekunu on 24th February. Some 200 people were addressed by the local branch president, Stephen Mwaura. Kiambu police attended the meeting and reported that the object of the meeting was to decry Mau Mau, but that proceedings were interrupted at intervals by shouts from individuals: 'Don't decry Mau Mau – I am one. It's the only policy that will save the African from being slaves of the European.'

DC Kiambu reported that everyone knew Kenyatta was president of KAU and was also believed to be one of the chief leaders of Mau Mau. The second meeting, held at Rukiaruambogo on 9th March, passed a resolution that Limuru KAU would not cooperate with the Mau Mau movement. This gave the government support in banning Mau Mau.

Jomo Kenyatta, Henry Muoria and Fred Kubai attended the meeting at Kamiirithu on 23rd March. Hinga Waiganjo, the acting chairman and two branch officers. DC Kiambu reported that Waiganjo and his officers 'courageously challenged' Jomo Kenyatta to declare whether he and KAU supported Mau Mau, but Kenyatta 'with his usual ability to evade the issue, and yet make his views quite plain, said he did not know Mau Mau'. He went on to berate the branch officers. In his newspaper *Mumenyereri* (26th March), Muoria gave a full report of the meeting. Kenyatta had invited people who said they knew about Mau Mau to explain it to him. They should, he said, 'take an axe and break its neck'. Forty years later the very metaphors used by Kenyatta in his heady speeches would be used by Muoria in an interview. DC Kiambu referred to the *Mumenyereri* report as one of Henry Muoria's usual clever articles.

Mau Mau adherents were delighted and their opponents dejected. That was the end of the KAU Limuru branch officers. They were summoned to Nairobi on 21st April and again on 22nd when they were taken to task. When they refused to accept as chairman Kungu Karumba, well known as the leader of Mau Mau in the Ndeiya district of Kiambu, the Limuru branch was closed down and replaced by a parallel organization under the chairmanship of Kungu Karumba.

In following months other meetings were held with similar outcomes. In April the DC Kiambu reported a rumour that Mau Mau members were being planted in twos and threes on European farms as labour and that they had been told, 'When the Europeans go, as they soon will, you will take over a farm'.

Opinions were divided regarding the extent to which Mau Mau was an established movement. The governor, Sir Philip Mitchell, speaking in London, was reported as saying that 'the general political feeling in Kenya was better than he had ever known it for many years', a statement which, as *Kenya Weekly News* (14th March) commented, 'must have surprised many who read it'.

In a speech at Londiani early in April, Hubert Buxton, a candidate for the constituency, said that he had been informed Mau Mau was universal amongst the Kikuyu, a statement which the commissioner of police on 9th April said was very far from being the case. He admitted that large numbers of Kikuyu had taken the oath, but he put their number at under 10 per cent. He described Mau Mau as a money making racket as well as being a racket to terrorise people. He was quite certain a considerable number of people earned their entire living by it – people of considerable prominence, too. He intimated that the police had certain information about those who were prominent in the movement, but that they needed more information before they could take action under the law.

Among European settlers there was 'extreme disquiet' when they read the commissioner's view that a 10 per cent membership of Mau Mau among the Kikuyu was 'an almost negligible figure'. A letter in *Kenya Weekly News* (14th April) from P.G.W. McMaster, from which the above quotations are taken, suggested that failure to punish the leaders of Mau Mau, who must be well known to the authorities, would be interpreted by the seditious as 'pure funk' and would encourage them to think they were immune from any punishment. And, concluded McMaster's letter, 'it looks as if they are right'.

Following the success of the arson attacks, district commissioners in both Kiambu and Nyeri reported that 'the increasing barbarity of the oaths and the forcible oathing of women and children had inflamed many of the Kikuyu who had so far managed to escape the clutches of Mau Mau'. On the initiative of chiefs in the Aguthi and Thegenge locations of Nyeri district (the locations in which the arson campaigns had been conducted) the district commissioner met them to discuss ways and means of combating the oath-taking. Following consultations with the athamaki (tribal elders), a thenge oath was invoked to cleanse their people and to expose the troublemakers. The ceremony was conducted by the people themselves and the thenge goat was ritually slaughtered by being beaten to death. About 4,000 people attended.

Subsequent reports indicated that the cleansing oath had rallied the reasonable members of the community to the side of law and order and upset the immediate programme of the Mau Mau organizers. The night before the athemaki supported the ceremony, Mau Mau organizers sacrificed two dogs, to which they attached notes warning the public of the dangers to themselves of taking the cleansing oath. Kikuyu custom was that the 'dog oath' was more important than the 'goat oath' but, despite the warning, the cleansing oath was regarded by the tribal elders as a success for 'law and order'.

These events led to a meeting in Kiambu on 23rd May attended by the district commissioner, Senior Chief Waruhiu, Dr Leakey, Chief Kabathi, Counsellor Mbira Githathu and Harry Thuku. The names of all those present occur later. On the Africans' recommendations a further 13 African-organized cleansing ceremonies were held in two districts with average attendances of 600 people. The DC reported that they gave an 'anti-Mau Mau focus of action and something definite to bolster up their morale', but the cleansing ceremonies led to threats on the lives of many headmen and chiefs, and on 15th May the mutilated bodies of two Kikuyu informers on the Mau Mau were found in the Kirichwa River near Nairobi. This was the first recorded instance of a Mau Mau execution. Many others followed. The police reported that the Mau Mau oath had been extended to killing Europeans and freeing Kenyatta, should he be arrested.

By April or May European farmers, particularly those with Kikuyu labour, were aware that all was not well. Elsa Pickering, farming near Nanyuki, attended a meeting at the club, arranged in order to discuss the greatly increased incidence of grass fires and measures to combat them. Members of the government who were present spoke of 'alarmist views, greatly exaggerated' and, while acknowledging that Mau Mau existed, claimed that the organisation was 'not by any means powerful enough to cause serious trouble'. Settlers, she wrote, 'were given the impression that government could stamp it out in five minutes and with no great effort. Most of us went home comforted and thought no more about it'.

Certainly LEGCO did not panic. During 1952 the council experimented with evening sessions, but not for long: 'No sooner did the sitting start but half the European elected members, and as many of the official side as dared, crept off to the bar of Torr's Hotel, returning an hour or two later in an unparliamentary condition.'

KAU prepared a memorandum on the land issue which Achieng Oneko and Peter Koinange (son of ex-Senior Chief Koinange with whom Fenner Brockway had stayed during his visit to Kenya in 1950), were deputed to present at Westminster. Some Africans, including Henry Muoria the reporter, editor, publisher and politician, believed the Kikuyu had significant support there. There were grounds for such belief. In 1950 Brockway and Jomo Kenyatta had prepared a land petition to the Commons with 67,000 thumb prints, and Brockway had arranged for a flow of information from Kenya to London so that a group of MPs could be constantly raising issues in the House.

Others were more cynical. Self-styled extremist Bildad Kaggia believed that there would be no favourable result from the deputation, but that it would strengthen their case when we went to argue in the country that deputations were useless and that other methods were necessary: 'We saw to it that the declarations left the door open for the adoption of other methods if the delegation failed.'.

In the event the British colonial secretary did not meet them, and Achieng described their treatment as insulting. As Kaggia had hoped, the British attitude towards Africans helped their committee to 'convince the people that deputations to London were useless, a waste of our money and time'. Indeed, Kaggia suggests that many Africans who had had high expectations of the deputation moved away from political to more militant means of obtaining recognition, and 'oath administration increased with great strides'. The collection of guns was accelerated, and their intelligence network strengthened.

The Mau Mau central committee authorised more and more aggressive methods and activities.

News of the appointment of the new governor, Sir Evelyn Baring, was made public in April. (He was actually appointed in March.) It was welcomed by the Kenyan press, which emphasized the breadth of his African experience, but greeted with concern by KAU, which referred to his 'disastrous handling of the Bechuanaland affairs'.

On 6th June Richard Gerrick was charged in Nairobi with assaulting an African by beating him on the head with a revolver. Gerrick was found guilty of the assaults and fined £5. He was also fined £20 for not having a licence for his firearm.

After the 1952 general election in Kenya, Michael Blundell was made leader of the European elected members. The choice, wrote Blundell, was not unanimous. Some would have preferred Lt Col Grogan: he personified attitudes and characteristics which appealed to many settlers, but he was an old man. Blundell's election as leader came at a time when the Administration was in a state of disarray. Seeking reasons for inaction over Mau Mau, Chenevix Trench notes that Mitchell, the governor, was in poor health and coasting downhill towards retirement, while the director of intelligence and security had knowledge only of subversive trade unions and was a little inclined to discount administrative warnings about Mau Mau, which was outside his own special interests and expertise. Potter was in much the same position. Whatever the reasons for inaction, the first half of 1952 had been hard going for Mitchell. Chenevix Trench suggests that he wanted to go down in history as one of the great colonial governors, retiring to a well-merited seat in the House of Lords: 'He resolutely closed his eyes and ears to the hideous possibility that his governorship might end not in glory, but in bloodshed.'

In the event his governorship ended somewhat abruptly. As the administrator A.D. Swann put it: 'Sir Philip Mitchell, having announced to the press that he "knew nothing of Mau Mau", collapsed with "exhaustion neurosis" and was invalided home in June.' Blundell wrote that, in a speech after laying down his office, Mitchell drew a happy picture of a fair country with a contented and prosperous population.

Mitchell had known East Africa for many years and he had proved himself to be an accomplished diplomat when serving as governor of

Fiji and high commissioner for the Western Pacific during the war. His governorship of Kenya should have been the summit of his career, but things had not gone well.

Negley Farson knew Mitchell professionally and socially. In 1949 he had written that 'Mitchell, like most other governors in Colonial Africa [found] it very hard to find men of the right calibre he [could] delegate responsibility to'.

It was four months before Baring took over his office. On his retirement Mitchell wrote a long letter to his successor. It referred to a genuine feeling of desire to co-operate and to be friendly at the present time, and discussed at length the ways in which Baring should behave towards divorced European people in the colony. The social niceties were, Mitchell wrote, a matter of 'somewhat unusual complexity'. There was no mention in the letter of increasing restlessness among the natives in either Mitchell's or the governor's private secretary's letters to Baring, but a letter dated 9th September from the latter closed: 'You are no doubt being kept informed of the difficult political situation through which we are going.'

There is no shortage of assessments of Mitchell the man and the governor, but the Earl of Portsmouth's is probably as fair as any. Portsmouth had himself been approached to be governor, but decided instead to farm at Kitale and Mount Elgon. In his autobiography he wrote of Mitchell that he was a brilliant man, but 'maybe for too long a Governor, he had surrounded himself with a group of senior civil servants who . . . were fumbling and indecisive'. Portsmouth's assessment of Mitchell's attitude at the end of his governorship confirmed the comments of others. He suggested that Mitchell 'by a sort of self induced myopia, in spite of warnings, had persuaded himself that everything in the garden was rosy. So, but for Mau Mau, it was'.

Mitchell's retirement left a gap. Baring, his successor, was not immediately ready to take up his appointment, so Sir Henry Potter, chief secretary since January, was appointed acting governor.

Much was happening in the field. Kenyatta spent considerable time travelling and meeting influential elders on their home-ground. He had visited Odinga in Kisumu and told him that economic independence would follow political power. In reply to Odinga's question 'How could the African take over government?' Kenyatta had replied 'By unity and sacrifice in struggle, preparing even to die for our cause'. He suggested that tribes should send elders into each other's country as 'the Kikuyu must know the Luo thoroughly . . . United we would be formidable'. Odinga admitted that Kenyatta's speeches in Kisumu had moved him deeply, and he wrote to him pledging his support.

Meanwhile Bildad Kaggia was building on the opportunities he had gained by his membership of the African Advisory Council which, as described above, meant that Mau Mau could dominate the municipal halls. By forming groups for specific purposes, 'we could,' wrote Kaggia, 'hold as many meetings as we liked without fear of being stopped'. One such group was the Study Circle. It was formed to research and draft resolutions and memoranda. In addition to four KAU members, there were Pio Gama Pinto, J. Murumbi, C.M.G. Argwings-Kodhek, Peter Wright and Commander John Miller. Through the Study Circle KAU formed connections with potentially sympathetic Europeans and Asians. Meetings were 'shifted from one house to another' and they were organized to introduce government officials to KAU leaders, 'giving us the opportunity to learn the feelings of government officials through ordinary social conversation'. Kaggia learned, for example, what sort of man Attorney General Whyatt was from a conversation with his wife when they met at Miller's house.

KAU embarked on a course of civil disobedience. People were to get themselves arrested on purpose, and 'we would raise hell about each arrest in the newspapers'. Kaggia was himself arrested, but soon afterwards the by-law was repealed. It was KAU policy to win over people potentially useful to its side, but the union was not above the use of shady methods, too: 'Bribes, force and prostitutes' were used by KAU to 'bring in people we wanted'. By this time Mau Mau had enlisted the help of all sorts of people, including thieves and robbers. 'Mau Mau had a hand in almost every theft, robbery, or other crime directed against Europeans. Most of these crimes were political.'

They also operated a protection racket in Nairobi which Commissioner of Police O'Rourke compared with the Chicago of Al Capone. O'Rourke discovered that the old Kikuyu who sold sweets and cigarettes outside police headquaters paid the 'society' 2s a week for the privilege. Similar levies were made on most Indian and African shopkeepers as well as on all African casual labour in search of a job.

Taxi drivers were the most active members of the movement. They made it easy to keep in touch with every corner of the town. Later they would 'transport oath administrators to the various districts outside Nairobi and return them to Nairobi before dawn . . . even during the actual fighting their importance in the city did not decrease'.

But Mau Mau was not the militant arm of KAU. Although many Mau Mau members were KAU members, others were not, and many KAU members were not members of Mau Mau. Furthermore, some leaders knew nothing about the militant movement within KAU. KAU took orders from its central committee: Mau Mau had a separate central committee. There was no organized link between the two. The only connections were Kubai and Kaggia, who were members of both committees

As time went by, Mau Mau central committee exercised closer control of oathing ceremonies, loyalty issues and security. Offenders incurred the death sentence. Part of Mau Mau's security involved its 'band of strong men', led by Stanley Mathenge, Kamurwa, Gachago and others used to spy on lonely policemen with guns. They snatched the gun and if necessary killed the policeman. Having killed a policeman, the 'strong men' would leave the policeman's booted and puttee'd leg behind as a trade mark.

In his report on the quarter ending 30th June, DC Rift Valley referred to an indication that Mau Mau was 'spreading very rapidly'. He also referred to criticisms of the Administration from Europeans, who asked why public meetings were allowed at which speakers accused Europeans of having stolen Kikuyu land and promoted the ideal of African self-government. One month later DC Nyeri reported that although the Kikuyu districts were 'outwardly more restful, inwardly tension was increasing steadily with Mau Mau ceremonies taking place in great secrecy in small numbers in numerous places', and that 'it was clear that one angle of the attack was switched to the Christian faith'. At Othaya, Victor Wokabi had demanded that a picture of Christ be removed 'as an enemy of the people'. And it was about this time that Carnally, another second generation settler, was told by his Kikuyu domestic staff, 'I'm afraid we have got to leave. If we stay we will have to kill you.'

Michael Blundell, now leader of the European elected members on LEGCO, became increasingly anxious about the whole attitude of the government. On 10th July he led a major debate in the legislative council on a motion moved as follows: 'This council notes the increasing disregard for law and order within the Colony and Protectorate and urges the Government to take the necessary measures to improve the situation.'

Corfield reported the debate in some detail, reflecting its importance. Blundell recognized the social evils and difficulties which beset the African, but he urged the government to take action. He advocated the introduction of a rigid pass system. Seconding Blundell, Humphrey Slade called for immediate and firm action so that 'subversive elements can no longer frolic with impunity'. He inquired how soon use could be made of the Emergency Powers Ordinance and submitted that early use should be made of these powers to arrest the suspected leaders. He called for the use of collective fines for political crimes and stricter control of political speeches.

In reply, Whyatt, the member for law and order, chided Blundell for not following the Westminster precedent of welcoming the governor's statement on 12th June, which viewed threats to law and order with concern and promised urgent and continuous attention to the task of maintaining it. He referred to the feeling of confidence that the police had created among these people, and in concluding he spoke of a movement among the Kikuyu to rid itself of Mau Mau.

Eliud Mathu suggested that had the government not proscribed the KCA after the war it would not have gone underground, with all the consequent troubles. He recounted the many African grievances and acknowledged steps being taken by the government, but he opposed the motion on the grounds that that action proposed would interfere with the lawful liberties of the African.

The member for African affairs made a long speech dealing with social and economic difficulties and the steps being taken to rectify them, but made only passing mention of subversive political activity. He added that most of the KAU branch office-bearers were people with known criminal records. Neither Mathu nor the last speaker mentioned Mau Mau.

It was, Corfield noted, a long debate. Winding up, Blundell said that he had hoped to see in the member for law and order 'a man of resolution', but he instead saw a man 'skilled in law, tilting and lancing over legal niceties, not a man of resolution'. Blundell was himself criticized by two settler members as being irresponsible and likely to give the colony a bad name by raising the issue. He was also criticized for his remarks on the need to improve the social and economic conditions of the Africans if law and order was not to be further undermined.

Corfield suggests that a schism divided the European elected members of LEGCO and the government at that time. He recognized that the European elected members acknowledged the existence of social and economic unbalance, that they had suggested methods for dealing with them and were genuinely convinced that public security was in serious jeopardy. They believed that it was essential to deal with the leaders of subversion. He added that the government did not consider that public security was in danger, and it believed that there was full confidence among the Africans in the action taken by government to maintain law and order.

There were, still, difficulties arising from clashes of personalities and entrenched attitudes which Churchill observed in his visit to Kenya in 1907, leading him him to refer to 'the official class against the unofficial'. The European elected members of LEGCO, to whom Whyatt and many other administrators would not listen, were, to quote administrator Chenevix Trench, 'well informed about Mau Mau. They had among their constituents farmers who had spoken Kikuyu since boyhood and were in close touch with their labour. All were reasonable, intelligent men, but endowed in Potter's and Whyatt's minds with horns, forked tails and cloven feet'.

In his history of Mau Mau Corfield noted that Whyatt's dislike of European politicians had a 'baleful effect on his judgment', and Chenevix Trench wrote of Whyatt that 'where the duties of his two portfolios [law and order/attorney-general] conflicted, he saw himself only as attorney-general'. He was a man whose 'real god was the English Common Law, and he fought to the last twist and turn against pressure to adapt this to the needs of the colony in a state of rebellion'. Clearly Whyatt was a man of high principles but, wrote Chenevix Trench, 'unfortunately he was rude and inconsiderate, making enemies wherever he went'.

When it came to crises of the sort which were developing in Kenya in 1952, 'Whyatt could be discounted as a man who knew nothing of Africa. Still less would he listen to settlers, whom he loathed; and they him'. Whyatt's deification of English common law may have been the reason for Lt Col Grogan's contribution to the 11th July LEGCO debate, in which he praised the type of young man passing into the Administration, 'a very large proportion of whom are today suffering from a serious sense of frustration . . . because of the law'.

The next month or two were filled with frenzied report writing and top level meetings at Government House – far more than the routine reports from district and provincial commissioners. The first, dated 14th July, on Kikuyu political activity, became known as the Momentous Memorandum. It was from the commissioner of police, O'Rourke, and was addressed 'top secret' to Whyatt as member for law and order. It was a detailed, lengthy report which referred to the Kikuyu people's strengths and weaknesses and the state of development of Mau Mau. He concluded that the situation called for 'immediate action, and action which must go far beyond that which lies in the hands of the police'.

In his report, Corfield stated: 'It is clear from perusal of the files then current in the secretariat that the central government had not yet appreciated the growing seriousness of the general situation . . . and the commissioner of police's letter had the effect of bringing the matter of unrest forcibly to the notice of the central government.'

Less than two weeks after the commissioner of police dispatched his letter, the first of two mass meetings was held at Nyeri.

6

Mass Meetings and Murder

'A political awareness was sweeping the land, which no one could ignore.' (Karari Njama)

July to October 1952 were the months when dissatisfaction and unrest became insurrection.

The public meetings held in 1951 had attracted crowds counted in hundreds, whereas those in the second half of 1952 attracted thousands. The first was held in Nyeri, some 50 miles from Nairobi, where there had been so much unrest in recent months. Memoirs of some of those attending illustrate the powerful influence of the public meetings on a people many of whom were illiterate but accustomed to following an articulate leader.

Nyeri showground was the place where the first meeting was held on 26th July. It may be regarded as a landmark in the development of African awareness of a prospect of change. Karari Njama, whose description of an oathing ceremony is given above, was one of those attending. The showground was his 'road to Damascus'. Opinions vary as to the number of people in attendance. Corfield suggests more than 20,000 men, women and children, Njama over 30,000. Corfield's number includes 'over forty bus loads of Nairobi thugs and prostitutes who were clearly under instructions to incite the crowd', and he recorded that the buses were decorated with Mau Mau paraphernalia and the KAU flag. Njama wrote that sitting in the packed showground where the Kenya African Union was holding a rally presided over by Jomo Kenyatta was a turning point in his political awareness and in his very life.

There were several speakers. Ochieng and Kaggia made attacking speeches. While Kenyatta 'soft-pedalled', thugs weaved through the crowd, many of whom heard nothing of the proceedings, announcing that 'the day of action had arrived'. The atmosphere was tense and 'the crowd was afraid of itself'. It took Jomo Kenyatta ten minutes to restore control after 'an excellent and balanced pro-government speech made by Senior Chief Nderi'. A spokesman, under official instructions, received a completely non-committal reply from

Kenyatta when he asked him what steps he would take to stamp out Mau Mau. The DC observed that Kenyatta was eager to get away. The DC made a mental note that in future he would have to restrict the size of his meetings.

Njama was very impressed by Kenyatta's words regarding land and freedom, and he was inspired by Kenyatta's explanation of the symbolism contained in the KAU flag, to which reference is made below. He summarized the five points covered by Jomo Kenyatta as land, freedom, education, wages and colour bar, all of which discriminated against the African on a racial basis and rested on nothing but the white man's selfishness. He made only passing reference to the contributions of other speakers, but he was excited by the new songs that were sung before the opening of the meeting, the chorus of one of which went:

> *Kenyatta leads,*
> *Koinange at the rear*
> *And Mbiyu on the flank,*
> *Each a good shepherd of the masses.*
> *We have been demanding the return of African lands*
> *And we will never give up.*

Songs and choruses played a major part in Kikuyu culture. 'Songs,' wrote the Kikuyu song-writer Kinuthia Mugai, 'win over speeches ever time. They are easily remembered and enter the head more quickly and more lastingly. Songs are a great prayer to God because he hears them quickly as a mother hears a loud cry from her baby.'

There is little doubt that Kenyatta's words had different meanings for different people. H.K. Wachanga, by this time well established as a Mau Mau leader, noted that many police spies attended. To confuse them, and yet to make his meaning clear to the people, 'Mzee Kenyatta' used proverbs. The donkey, for example, was used to represent the British. Kenyatta would ask the audience if they would 'hold the donkey's legs to keep it from kicking'. He told them that the tree of freedom had been planted, that it was the dry season and that the tree must be watered with human blood. 'Mzee asked them if they would give their blood and everyone shouted "Yes!"'

Long and (to others) obscure metaphors are an integral part of Kikuyu conversation, and Kenyatta inevitably used them when addressing an audience. ('He who is hit with a rungu returns, but he who is hit by justice never comes back.'). Some British settlers and others suspected that he used his walking stick to pass covert messages to an audience, and administrator John Cumber obtained persuasive evidence. Sitting next to Kenyatta at a meeting, he deliberately held on to the stick, hoping that Kenyatta might start the meeting without the dutch courage which it seemed to give him. When it came to speaking, Kenyatta indicated that he wanted his stick and put it on the table. Cumber noticed that when he put a rhetorical question to which he wanted a 'no' answer – such as 'We don't know a thing called Mau Mau, do we?' – his hand went over to the left and he put the stick at an angle of 45 degrees to twelve o'clock. If he wanted a 'yes', he would swing the stick over to ten o'clock as viewed by the audience.

The Nyeri meeting was one of the best platforms Kenyatta had to speak to so many Africans, and he made the most of it. What did he and the other speakers say during a meeting which lasted from 11am to 3pm? The government report indicates that perhaps an hour was lost while order was being restored, usually by Kenyatta himself. More time was lost to applause and jeers. But of a total of three hours spent on the speeches, Kenyatta spoke for 110 minutes, Achieng Oneko for 41, Kaggia for 14 and the two pro-government speakers for 12 minutes in all.

Kenyatta spoke six times. Traditionally he opened with a drawn-out 'eeeee', which was given enthusiastic applause. Shorn of the rhetoric, his principal themes were that this was a 'meeting of KAU', that he was 'the leader of Mumbi' (the Kikuyu people) and that he was telling them 'what God has hold me to say'. The purpose of KAU was to ask for freedom, and 'true democracy has no colour distinction'. The Africans must first achieve the right to elect their own representatives, and that was 'surely the first principle of democracy'. With regard to Mau Mau, he told his audience that 'he who calls us the Mau Mau is not truthful. We do not know this thing Mau Mau'. This statement was greeted with jeers and applause. Later, he added, 'I think Mau Mau is a new word. Elders do not know it.'. He stated that KAU was not a fighting union, and 'if any of you here think that force is good, I do not agree with you.'

A common theme of Kenyatta's speeches was to lay down the law. He despised bribery and corruption, as well as 'thieving, robbery and murder', which KAU also despised, and he 'would butcher the criminal'. When he told his audience that he would never ask them to be 'subversive', he used the English word which, the government report said, would not be understood by the audience.

He demanded equal pay for equal work 'right now', and a royal commission to enquire into the land problem. The last part of his speech was devoted to a description of the KAU flag, which had black at the top representing black people, red in the centre to show 'that the blood of an African is the same colour as the blood of a European' and green below the red 'to show that when we were given this country by God it was green, fertile and good'. But now, he continued, 'you see the green is below the red and is suppressed'. His closing words were greeted with tremendous applause.

Revd Wachira, the second speaker, told the audience that God had said one man cannot knock down a wall and continue to freedom, but if people unite and push together they could break the wall and pass over the ground towards independence. He blessed them 'in the name of Jesus Christ and the people of Mumbi'.

African District Officer Ebrahim asked what Kenyatta was going to do to stop Mau Mau. His question caused such a state of affairs that the rest of his speech could not be heard, and he left the platform a minute or two later.

Senior Chief Nderi urged the audience to 'stop doing bad things' and said that the police had helped them during their troubles. His talk about the land was greeted with jeers, and his remarks that 'night-time activity' was damning the Kikuyu people and that nobody but the government could help them produced barracking from the crowd and forced him to sit down. The crowd was evidently in a bad mood, and the reporter remarked, 'I personally feel that all that remains is for the cooking pot to be brought on.'

Achieng Oneko ranged wide, referring to Fenner Brockway as 'our friend', to the need to hit back if the African wanted freedom and to the Kikuyu's justifiable pride in their traditions. For the present, he concluded, he wanted no trouble and asked the audience to 'get together'. The reporter concluded that he was 'obviously fanatically anti-British, and speeches of this nature to primitive masses are extremely harmful'.

The closing speaker was Kaggia, who complained that Africans had been robbed of their land. Although Africans did not trust

LEGCO, he wanted Africans to dominate it 'for we are over 5,000,000 and this is our land . . . we will never stop.' Kenyatta spent all the time taken by Kaggia's speech trying to pacify the crowd. Oddly, Kaggia does not mention the meeting in his autobiography.

The final resolution at the meeting, put by Samual Kagotho following a lengthy hymn praising Jomo Kenyatta as the leader, was that the African be given freedom of assembly. It was passed unanimously, and the meeting ended.

Njama devoted seven pages of his autobiography to the Nyeri meeting. It was a time when 'a political awareness and excitement was sweeping the land, which no-one could ignore'. Kaggia made up his mind to join KAU, but he added that he was unable to make a clear cut between KAU and Mau Mau. An object of the meeting was to get Kenyatta to denounce Mau Mau, but Njama observed that 'though the speakers at the meeting were supposed to denounce the evil secret society which was spreading rapidly through Kikuyu land and had earned for itself the unheard-of name of Mau Mau, the latter organization was given considerable publicity because most of the organizers of the meeting were Mau Mau leaders and most of the crowd, Mau Mau members'. He noted that the meeting did not want to listen to anything about Mau Mau and that the African assistant district officer and Chief Nderi (both loyal to the government) were barracked and forced to sit down.

Commenting on the effects of the meeting, DC Nyeri was without doubt that it left the entire district in mental turmoil and that vigorous action was required to restore the morale of government supporters. Nothing that was said, however, was of a sufficiently criminal nature to justify the government taking action. Nevertheless, he continued, government supporters failed to see why it did not clamp down vigorously on the ring-leaders. He concluded that the people were in no doubt that the meeting was a dress rehearsal for the 'real thing' to start at the beginning of August, 'when they believed Peter Mbui would return with at least the gift of the White Highlands for the Kikuyu from Mr Fenner Brockway and his ilk'.

Henceforth there would be great activity at Government House. Three days after the meeting, on 29th July, the acting chief secretary chaired a meeting of top officers to discuss the letter from the commissioner of police and the action that needed to be taken. The chief secretary regarded the situation as 'extremely grave'. The minutes of the meeting record that all agreed, without 'concrete evidence to prove', although there was 'every reason to believe', that Kenyatta was behind the Mau Mau movement and that he was one of the leaders of the society. Their conviction was strengthened by the fact that Mau Mau activities had increased sharply in areas which he visited, and also by the display of Mau Mau emblems on the platform from which he addressed the crowd at Nyeri. The minutes record that all efforts to persuade him to denounce the society publicly had failed and that there could therefore be no doubt that he intended to pursue his '100 per cent programme', which was designed to secure the eviction of the European government and settlement from Kenya.

The meeting decided:

• That no more KAU meetings would be allowed.
• That early action should be taken against Kenyatta's 'lieutenants' under the Deportation (Immigrant British Subjects) Ordinance, but not against Kenyatta and his 'immediate lieutenants' unless they committed criminal offences.
• To consider special legislation for the award of corporal punishment to persons using bodily violence in connection with Mau Mau ceremonies.
• To enlist the aid of the churches, with the object of organising an anti-Mau Mau campaign
• To continue counter-oathing ceremonies.
• That important Mau Mau prisoners should serve their sentence in the Northern province.
• That KAU headquarters and the Kikuyu Club in Nairobi be raided, and that legislation should be introduced to ban the flying of the KAU flag.

Corfield commented that the commissioner of police, whose letter was the cause of the meeting, had not been invited to attend. He was given to understand that matters of higher policy would be discussed which were not the concern of the police. Subsequently the member for law and order decided that under certain circumstances KAU meetings might be allowed in Nairobi and that neither the KAU headquarters nor the Kikuyu Club should be searched. During discussions with Corfield, while the latter was compiling his report, the provincial commissioner said the memorandum from the commissioner of police had been intentionally drafted in strong terms in order to impress on the central government the urgency of taking more definite action than had been used in the past. He stated that administrative officers and police were well aware of the seriousness of the situation and were working at high pressure.

Four days after the Government House meeting KAU held an 'authorized' meeting in Kaloleni Hall, Nairobi. Jomo Kenyatta presided, and speakers included Jesse Kariuki and Paul Ngei. Kariuki was reported to have 'openly incited the police to disobey their orders'. He was arrested later in the month, and in September a restriction order under the deportation ordinance was signed. This was the first use of that ordinance for the leaders of Mau Mau, Kariuki having been 'a leading agitator of the worst type for some 27 years'.

On 5th August, two days after the meeting of KAU in Kaloleni Hall, Tom Mbotela, still a vice-president of KAU and one of very few moderate officers, wrote a personal letter to the member for law and order, asking why public meetings were allowed in the municipal social halls and reporting truculent Kikuyu thugs 'going round from house to house forcing the doors open and coercing the people to attend meetings and singing seditious songs'.

Soon after receipt of the above letter, 400 police were drafted into Nairobi and there was an extensive drive against the gangs, leading to a temporary improvement. The administrative officers in the field had seen, at first hand, an increasing number of incidents of violence during July and August, which included an old man at Ruathia who was chopped in two because he had given evidence in court. Further down the road the whole family of a chief's retainer was murdered for the same reason. And the strangled corpse of an African court process server who had given evidence in a Mau Mau case was found in the river below Gituga. The chiefs and head men were frightened, and the young men were beginning to wear Kenyatta beards and long hair. 'People laughed at us and spat,' reported the local administrator.

At last things began to move quickly, and there was a call for emergency powers. On 7th August the elected members prepared a case for presentation to the acting governor, asking that emergency powers should be brought into force immediately in some areas, that the leaders of KAU should be detained under the powers and that a special commissioner for security should be appointed, with power to co-ordinate and direct all government security operations.

103

On 8th August DC Rumuruti sent a 'special intelligence report' on Mau Mau to the PC Rift Valley. In it he wrote of his feelings that 'an emergency has arisen and strong measures should be taken before it has caused serious bloodshed involving countrywide attacks on European farms. He referred to exasperated and frustrated Kikuyu waiting for the government to take a strong line against Mau Mau, and of the collective punishment which should be taken.The PC told the member for law and order that this was an over-reaction. The difference of opinion was no doubt caused by the different perspectives of events and their relative proximity to the African. Michael Blundell noted that he always found officers up to district level most friendly and co-operative, but that a great change took place at provincial level. 'Most PCs were remote rather inaccessible, and I often felt suspicious of a political minister,' he wrote.

On 8th and 19th August two meetings were held with European elected members of LEGCO at which the member for law and order and the commissioner for police were present. During the former, the European elected members gave what amounted to a warning that 'there was a real danger that Europeans might take matters into their own hands if the forces of law and order did not deal immediately with the present lawlessness throughout the country'. Acting Governor Potter, in reply, commented that what the elected representatives really wanted was that the government should have the power to imprison dangerous agitators without trial. He concluded that the government could not stop nationalism, and that the situation, though grave, did not warrant the declaration of a state of emergency. It was decided to make further efforts to obtain sufficient evidence to support a prosecution for sedition and justify restriction orders against the KAU leaders.

Intelligence now arrived from various quarters, some covert, originating from a well educated Kikuyu known as 'Henry'. His letter, dated 9th August, was one of several which he referred to as 'dispatches'. He wrote that Mau Mau had almost completely shattered the average African's spiritual equilibrium, and he referred to 'a new extremism, a new barbarism . . . being created'. His dispatch contained the testimonies of three well-informed friends whose names were familiar to the recipient of the letter. His informants contributed to and confirmed intelligence which security forces received from other sources.

August was a month of high-level meetings (six in one week from the 11th) in Government House and out in the provinces. There were reports of chiefs' retainers being murdered, of the arrest of 550 people at oath taking ceremonies and of the administration's inability to deport Jesse Kariuki.

On the 12th August a few copies of a memorandum prepared by the director of intelligence and security (DIS), and originally issued on 30th April, was circulated to one or two departments. It expressed the view that 'until such time as the organiser of Mau Mau could be adequately dealt with, it was probable that the Mau Mau menace would continue to increase'. It was a first class document which had taken three and a half months to reach Government House.

On 13th August the Rift Valley PC attended a meeting of the executive committee of the Thomson's Falls Association. In spite of a résumé by the commissioner of proposed government measures to eradicate Mau Mau, referring to large scale raids by the police which had brought the situation under control, the meeting was adamant that a state of emergency already existed in the colony. The commissioner, however, opined that there was no reason why a state of emergency should be declared, and on 17th August the acting chief secretary and the member for law and order said they thought it was most unlikely that the secretary of state would agree to a state of emergency being declared.

There were meetings with the European elected representatives on the 19th August, when they put four proposals to the acting governor to improve security. They reiterated that they believed a state of emergency existed, but he categorically denied it and would not accede to their proposals. After further meetings and letters between all parties the elected members agreed to do all in their power to dissuade local district associations from taking any precipitate action, and agreed to give the local government authorities their full support.

On 17th August, however, the acting governor gave the first official warning to the colonial office of 'a progressive deterioration in the state of law and order in the areas of the colony where the Kikuyu tribe preponderate'. He referred to the proscribed secret society, Mau Mau, reporting that there should be little doubt, though there was no proof, that Kenyatta controlled the revolutionary organisation in so far as it was still susceptible to control. A press communiqué on 23rd August, drawing attention to repeated statements by certain African leaders claiming self-government and calling for the eviction of the other races from the colony, reiterated the declared government policy that the rights of all races would be respected. It warned that the government could not tolerate the continuance of the state of unrest and that it would use every means at its disposal to enforce respect for the law.

The PC Central Province, having consulted administrative officers and others, wrote to the chief secretary, noting that the communiqué had been translated into Kikuyu and distributed in pamphlet form. He complained that it had failed badly and was far too nebulous and emasculated to be effective. He regretted the fact that executive officers of government in the field had not been invited to give their opinions before the pamphlets had been distributed.

All that within a period of seven days!

In the locations, mayhem and murder increased. During the three weeks following DC Rumuruti's special intelligence report, three Kikuyu were murdered in that area alone. On the 27th August the Rift Valley PC signed a curfew order affecting two wards in the Aberdare district and two African locations. The increasing unrest among Mau Mau supporters provoked a response from the Kikuyu Christian community. On 22nd August 1952 Kikuyu elders and ministers from both Catholic and Protestant churches charged that Mau Mau 'thwarts God's wishes'. They adopted a six-point resolution to fight Mau Mau to the end.

Open rebellion did not start at the beginning of August, as DC Nyeri had feared at the time of the July meeting in his district, but further public meetings were arranged by Kikuyu elders and leaders, not by KAU. The organizers included senior chief Waruhiu, his son David and African church leaders. Later Eluid Mathu, Harry Thuku and other leading Kikuyu joined them. It was a last endeavour to persuade Jomo Kenyatta to denounce Mau Mau. The government planned a series of meetings to be held throughout Kikuyu country at which Kenyatta was asked to denounce Mau Mau. The Mau Mau central committee did not like this very much, but since only Kenyatta from among the KAU leaders was to speak they did not discuss it with him.

On 24th August, one month after the Nyeri meeting, KAU held a second mass meeting at Kiambu. Like the July meeting, it lasted four hours. Kenyatta made it clear at the beginning who had called and organized it, the aim being to 'see what the disease in Kikuyuland is and how this disease can be cured'. The government had bused in thousands of Africans to Kiambu, and cameras and sound recording equipment were in position. The estimated audience was 30,000. Chief Waruhiu MBE attended, smartly dressed and waving tufts of elephant grass to illustrate his comment that 'Kikuyuland is like this grass, blowing one way and another in the breeze of Mau Mau'. He announced, 'We have come to denounce this movement; it has spoiled our country and we do not want it.' He talked about the objects of KAU and disclaimed association between the union and Mau Mau activities. He concluded, 'Let us agree now not to engage in crime,' adding that a commission was coming to look into the land question: 'If you do not stop crime, those people who come out on the land commission will be told that we are thieves.'

'We must now work together,' Kenyatta said. 'Mau Mau has spoiled the country. Let Mau Mau perish forever . . . All people should search for Mau Mau and kill it.' Harry Thuku, Eliud Mathu and others continued this denunciation, and Chief Njiri said Mau Mau would 'put us back 50 years'. At that time 400 Kikuyu oath administrators were in jail and hundreds were awaiting trial.

The closing speaker was Chief Koinange (Fenner Brockway's former host), who singled out Europeans in the audience and said, 'I can remember when the first European came to Kenya. I worked alongside your father and you are my son. In the First World War you asked our young men to go to fight with the British against the Germans and many were killed.' He went on to say that Africans had fought with the British against the Germans and Italians during the Second World War but that now Germans and Italians lived in the White Highlands, from which Africans were banned. He concluded that he had lived, worked and known 'this country for eighty-four years . . . [and] I have never been able to find a piece of white land.'

The political intelligence summary was that the authorities could not consider the meeting to have been a success. It was dominated by Jomo Kenyatta, who was far from specific on the subject of Mau Mau. The unanimous opinion of the Administration and the Kikuyu was that Jomo Kenyatta had, as usual, evaded any personal or direct denunciation of Mau Mau. The front page of the *East African Standard* claimed that Kenyatta had cursed Mau Mau and that the meeting had been a resounding victory for African moderate opinion. The Administration was disappointed at what it considered to be Kenyatta's failure to denounce Mau Mau unequivocally, but the Mau Mau central committee thought he had gone too far. Bildad Kaggia, a member of it, recorded the committee's decision that meetings like the one at Kiambu could no longer be tolerated. 'We knew Kenyatta did not mean what he said. But his terms were too strong. There was always the possibility that some weaker members of Mau Mau might take him seriously and it could make the work more difficult.'

At this time there was great confusion about Kenyatta's relationship with Mau Mau among both Africans and European settlers. Although Mau Mau looked upon Kenyatta as the national leader, it was not under his direct control. Kaggia wrote that Kenyatta was aware of Mau Mau's existence but felt it 'politic' to keep some distance between himself and the organisation 'in order to throw more dust in the eyes of the authorities'. He deliberately knew little of what went on in the Mau Mau central committee meetings. Illustrating this independence, he told of being invited to meet the committee for the first time and his surprise on seeing that Kubai, Kaggia and other leaders whom he did not know were running Mau Mau. So successful was the impression of isolation of Kenyatta from Mau Mau that when on one occasion Kenyatta denounced Mau Mau the leaders of the movement called him to meet them. They warned him to temper his criticism. Some of the young leaders of Mau Mau were ready to kill him if he continued in this vein.

The threat of terrorism did not reach more remote farms. A letter to England from Rhodora, a hundred miles from Nairobi in the White Highlands, said that things were not as bad as reported and that the police were belatedly taking strong measures to combat them. It was nothing more than a passing reference in a letter which was generally devoted to farm matters and the garden, which was 'really quite lovely just now'.

In 1952 there was a growth in the number of vernacular newspapers, some of which were designed to report KAU meetings. A rush of small but intensely subversive news sheets catering principally for the Kikuyu also sprang into a brief existence during the months proceeding the emergency. Nine titles were listed between November 1951 and October 1952. Some editors and printers were charged with sedition.

Legislation requesting additional powers for the governor was sent to the secretary of state. In his confidential covering letter dated 2nd September, Whyatt, the member for law and order, wrote that things had been very much quieter during the past few weeks and that Jomo Kenyatta himself had publicly condemned Mau Mau at a meeting of 30000 Kikuyu, all of whom held up their hands at his request to signify that they approved of his denunciation. He wrote of succeeding in 'rolling back the Mau Mau movement before too long'.

But despite Whyatt's confidence, in Fort Hall alone, all of eight murders were reported with no prospect of arrest. On the Robinson farm more than 250 pedigree sheep and cattle had been found dead, disembowelled but still alive, or staggering about on two legs and two bloody stumps. Nonetheless, despite increasing fury from European farmers, Michael Blundell continued to advise members against forming vigilante committees and to support the government by enlisting in the Kenya Police Reserve.

On 12th September, in the wake of Whyatt's draft bill to the secretary of state, Eliud Mathu, a member of LEGCO, and Mbui Koinange, a delegate of KAU in Britain, issued their own paper titled 'The situation in Kenya', which played down the seriousness of the unrest. It referred to 'a propaganda campaign both in Kenya [and England] about a growing unrest and crime wave among the African people'. The paper denounced stories in the press of secret societies plotting to establish a 'reign of terror' and to 'massacre all whites'. It said no convincing evidence existed of a secret organization called Mau Mau and that the KAU and all African leaders publicly denied all knowledge of it and completely disassociated themselves from any subversive movements. The gist was that the word Mau Mau was not known in any of the African languages, but that if Mau Mau existed as an organization, which it didn't, there was no doubt that its significance could be only minimal and that 'its importance is being exaggerated, we fear, for political and economic reasons'.

The remainder of the paper referred to deteriorating economic conditions for the Africans, their peacefulness (there was only one policeman to 8,000 inhabitants in Kenya compared with 1:1,000 people 'in the most docile parts of England'), to political frustration caused by under-representation, to the need for a common roll, to African fears of new discriminatory legislation and to African demands for greater equality. Kenya was being brought to Whitehall's notice from all directions.

While confident reassurances were being sent to Whitehall regarding the relatively happy state of the colony, the senior superintendent of police CID had written a memorandum dated 12th September in preparation for the visit of the member for law and order and chief native commissioner to the colonial office. It provides a review of events and the problems facing law enforcement as seen by the police. They were that:

• The forceable administration of the Mau Mau oath was widespread in the predominantly Kikuyu populated area.
• The police, government, church and 'more responsible elements in the African population' were unable to diminish the strength of Mau Mau.
• The unwilling victim was helpless to prevent the oath being administered by the use of 'vicious methods'.
• The oath had a binding effect, not only on the 'superstitious and ignorant, but also on other Africans in a position to give information to the authorities'.

The memorandum described, by way of illustration, the case of a Kikuyu Catholic woman who was dragged from her house by night, stripped, beaten, threatened with death, beaten again and hoisted off the floor until she lost consciousness. As she regained her senses she was forced to drink blood and 'to perform other disgusting rites constituting the Mau Mau oath taking ceremony'. The report gave details of nine cases between May and September in which Africans who helped the authorities had been brutally murdered and mutilated. The cases involving assault and intimidation were 'too numerous to mention'. Eight of the nine murdered Africans were Kikuyu, the other being a Kipsigis policeman. Reference was made to:

• Charges brought against more than a hundred people for involvement in the administration of oaths, which subsequently had to be withdrawn because witnesses had turned hostile and had disappeared.
• The virtual powerlessness of the police and courts of justice in the absence of stronger legislation.

• The logicality of extending the penal code (which provided for the corporal punishment of people convicted of violence), to include those who compelled others to undergo 'a degrading and seditious oath'.

Clearly, the CID's view of the present state was, to say the least, at variance with those of the Administration and KAU.

On 19th September four eminent members of KAU (M. Gikonyo, J. M. Tameno, W.W.W. Awuori and F.W. Odede), were signatories to a paper titled 'Alleged unrest in Kenya – a statement of facts'. The paper was sent to the Colonial Office and circulated generally. In it, the authors accused the European elected members of misrepresenting and grossly exaggerating the extent of crime and subversive activities in Kenya with the intention of giving the new governor, Sir Evelyn Baring, 'a biased and prejudiced attitude to the legitimate demands and aspirations of the African people'. They also referred to attempts to destroy KAU, 'the only political organisation representative of all Africans in Kenya'.

The paper referred to Mau Mau as 'a localised organization of a few irresponsible gangs', if, indeed, such a subversive movement existed, and expressed surprise that Europeans connected Mau Mau with KAU, especially as the president of KAU had denounced Mau Mau at a public meeting on 24th August. It concluded by endorsing the recent suggestion to the secretary of state for the colonies made by E.W. Mathu, and for a royal commission to investigate the 'exaggerated unrest in Kenya'.

But several reports of events carried out within a few days of the KAU's paper tell a different story. On 23rd September, in the Timau area, some 60 African labourers were initiated. On 25th September around 50 Africans attacked stock and set fire to buildings on five farms. Approximately 120 valuable cattle were killed or had to be destroyed, and a further 26 were wounded. As many as 240 sheep were killed and 140 wounded. Damage by fire was extensive: the stock was wounded and left to die 'a slow and painful death'. Thirty-nine Kikuyu and three Meru were arrested. Nearly all were convicted and sentenced to imprisonment.

On 24th September the chief native commissioner prepared an appreciation statement for the incoming governor which built on a report submitted ten days earlier. During that period the number of known murders had increased from nine to 23, including two women and three children. There had been 12 attempted murders and four suicides. Many hundreds were awaiting trial, and 412 Mau Mau had been convicted and imprisoned. Most were 'small fry'. The appreciation concluded that:

• Mau Mau had succeeded in dominating three Kikuyu districts and areas of the Rift Valley province.
• Curfews, collective fines and additional police had no appreciable effect and the position was deteriorating.
• Mau Mau was emerging in Embu, Meru and Machakos districts, and expansion into Nyanza was feared
• Mau Mau was intensely anti-European.
• 'A number of factors' pointed to Kenyatta having 'a close association with the [Mau Mau] society'.

The interregnum was coming to an end. Sir Evelyn Baring, the new governor, was waiting in the wings. Why had he been kept waiting so long? And why, asks Douglas-Home, Baring's biographer, was the interregnum between governors in Kenya not brought to a speedy end? If it was not clear that Baring should have gone out to Kenya in the spring, why did he not at least go out in the summer when the change for worse in Kenya became more clear? In answering those questions he referred to 'a great deal of documentary evidence to show that it did not become clear in London, or even much clearer in governing circles in Nairobi, that there was any urgent need for the new governor to arrive before the end of September'.

Douglas-Home discusses the actions of the two principal British government representatives in Kenya during the months between Mitchell and Baring – Henry Potter, the acting governor, 'who was finding his feet in Nairobi', and John Whyatt, the attorney general, who 'by most accounts . . . clearly decided that the weight of his duty lay in the legal rather than administrative field'. With an acting governor expressing the kind of diffidence shown by Potter, Douglas-Home writes, and with his attorney general applying the strictly legalistic attitude to the unrest which Whyatt considered appropriate, 'it is not surprising that they did not perceive that a state of emergency had crept up on them until it became evident even to them that the courts had ceased to function properly because of intimidation of witnesses'.

Fenner Brockway, who met Potter when he visited Kenya in October, remarked, 'I was disturbed to think that he had been responsible for the administration of Kenya during the critical months between the governorships of Sir Philip Mitchell and Sir Evelyn Baring. It was during these months that the pattern of Mau Mau and its repression took place.' Brockway had previously encountered him two years earlier on a visit to Uganda: 'He was,' wrote Brockway, 'as dumb as he had been [there].'

Despite his strictly legalistic attitude to the unrest, which infuriated the European farmers, Whyatt told Fenner Brockway's fellow traveller Leslie Hale that he was appalled by Mau Mau atrocities and the savagery of the murders and the mutilation accompanying them. He said, too, that he was convinced of Kenyatta's guilt and that, in his view, 'Kenyatta spoke with his tongue in his cheek' when at mass public meetings he called on Africans to have nothing to do with Mau Mau. In this respect at least (and probably at most), European farmers would have agreed with Whyatt.

This was the inheritance of Sir Evelyn Baring' – the very model of a modern British governor – when he took up his office on 29th September. Blundell welcomed his arrival. 'I felt,' he wrote, 'as if a great load had been lifted from me, as I thought of the pressures which we had exerted earlier and the uncooperative way in which they had been met.'

Certainly Baring was not unknown to some of the 'well-connected' settlers such as the Scotts at Njoro, who had several family ties with the Barings. He had been born in London in 1903, the son of Lord Cromer. After prep school in Sussex he went to Winchester, and from there to New College, Oxford, where the authorities threatened to send him down when he got drunk for the fifth time. He was 'not thought very brilliant', but he got a first in history. He had 'no career and no money'. His mother told him he must always remember he was going to be poor. He qualified for the Indian civil service and in 1926 sailed for India, where he served for seven years until his resignation through ill-health. He married in London and joined Barings Bank.

Unfit for military service in the Second World War, he joined the foreign office, where he served with distinction, and was knighted in

1942. He was a young governor in South Africa, and at 41 was appointed high commissioner. He stood out against apartheid, observing that 'the British treat Africans like men and South Africans treat them like children'.

It is difficult to imagine a more challenging time for him to take up his appointment. In the reserves and on the European farms oathing, arson and mayhem flourished. But legislation was in the pipe-line which would make life easier for the Administration. On 22nd September, the same day as the Timau raids, LEGCO passed seven ordinances which were assented to by the governor on 3rd October. The ordinances:

• Allowed a confession made to a senior police officer to be accepted as evidence.
• Gave additional protection to witnesses.
• Gave the government the power to restrict the place of residence of persons associating with unlawful societies and to control traffic at night.
• Increased maximum penalties for certain offences.

The ordinances marked the end of one era and beginning of a new, but they came too late for Senior Chief Waruhiu. Four days after the passing of the ordinances he was murdered. For some months the 'loyal' government-appointed chiefs had 'stressed their great concern at the turn of events' and had warned DC Nyeri that unless the government took immediate action against Jomo Kenyatta their days were numbered. On 7th October Waruhiu, who had been party to arranging the public meeting on the 24th August at which it was hoped Kenyatta would denounce Mau Mau, was assassinated in broad daylight by a gunman in the accepted Chicago tradition, only seven miles from Nairobi. He was 62 years old, a Christian and opposed to Mau Mau. He had been warned that he was at risk, as Jomo Kenyatta did not like him and he must take great care of himself while in Nairobi.

His murder had a mixed reception. Karari Njama, soon to go into the forest as a full-time freedom-fighter or terrorist, noted that some people mourned the death but others rejoiced, celebrating with great applause and drinking parties. He remembered that 'when young I used to hear a song which wished Chief Waruhiu and Chief Koinange to be buried alive' – a reminder that chiefs appointed by the government were not always popular with their subjects. Sir Evelyn Baring and Jomo Kenyatta faced each other only once before the latter was detained – across Chief Waruhiu's open grave. On the next occasion Kenyatta would be Kenya's president.

For the district officer the ordinances were an important tool. Before, they had no special emergency powers and intimidation meant that murders, increasing every month, were impossible to deal with. Anyone giving evidence would be killed.

On the 6th October, five days after his arrival and the day before Waruhiu's murder, Baring made a tour which included Fort Hall (Kandara). Some years later he described his impressions. It was a tour he would never forget and which almost certainly set the seal on his future actions. He had never seen such scowling faces: the people looked unhappy and were intensely suspicious. 'It was an expression I saw a great deal during the early years of Mau Mau.' All the Kikuyu said that there had been a complete breakdown of law and order; there was a murder every night.

'If you don't get Kenyatta and all those round him and shut them up somewhere or other we are all in a terrible, hopeless position,' Baring was told. The next day, while he was at a meeting, he heard of the murder of Chief Waruhiu, one of the three leading men in the Kikuyu country. (The others were Njiri and Nderi.) He decided, 'Well, if we want to take extreme powers, this is the occasion.' Corfield opined that 'the murder of Chief Waruhiu set the seal on the conclusion of the governor that the most drastic action was required'.

Then, on the evening of 8th October at Kabete, a suburb of Nairobi, the elderly Colonel Tulloch and his wife were attacked as they prepared to take supper in their bedroom. Five men came into the house through the kitchen. The five Africans living in the house did not resist the attack. The colonel could not reach his revolver. The attackers ransacked the house and severed Mrs Tullock's nose with a panga. Next Mrs Margaret Wright was killed by stab-wounds outside her house in a Nairobi suburb, and Robert Hall was murdered by Kipsigis in his farmhouse at Ol Kalou. Hall's murder was typical of others to follow.

Nellie Grant's experience of Kenya was as long and balanced as that of most farmers who had worked with minimal capital, often with an overdraft. She was devoted to her African workers, albeit without illusions, and was certainly not given to panic. Her letters to her daughter Elspeth Huxley recommenced after a break of three years with one dated 9th October 1952. In addition to a mention of Waruhiu, she refers to a European woman stabbed to death (the second in a fortnight), the attack on the Bindloss family and an ineffective 'monster raid here last weekend [by] a company of KAR, police and police reserves'. She was alone on the farm. When, after two days away, she discovered that the house had been burgled she decided to take 'the firearms situation seriously' and go to the police 'to be told how to load my revolver'. She had decided that she would live at the far end of the house: 'How I hate firearms.' She closed with a mention of the headless bodies of eight loyal Africans found in a forest glade and lots of Christians [killed] near Nyeri . . . locked in their huts and the huts set on fire'.

On 9th October Baring sent a telegram and a personal letter to the secretary of state, Oliver Lyttelton. He described Mau Mau as a hydra that was planned and directed from Nairobi – a revolutionary movement which, if not stopped, would lead to administrative breakdown followed by bloodshed amounting to civil war. He predicted a planned assassination of the very reasonable European farmers, after which reprisals would be 'absolutely inevitable'. Baring, perceptively, was in no doubt that the instigators of Mau Mau were the leaders of KAU, although some of the leaders of the latter might not be implicated, and he saw that if they waited 'the trouble would become much worse and probably lead to the loss of so many lives that in the future bitter memories of bloodshed will bedevil all race relations'. His conclusion that KAU leaders, including Kenyatta, were the planners of the Mau Mau movement had been reached 'regretfully'. His detailed reasons for this conclusion included information he had been given by all his advisors, together with 'the pattern of events' such as speeches, oath taking and murder in areas which had previously been quiet; Kenyatta's actions and the incorporation of his name, blasphemously, in hymns and prayers; the murder of Chief Waruhiu; [and] two murderous attacks on Europeans which had 'produced a temper bound to lead to reprisals and then almost to civil war'.

In the closing paragraphs he suggested that the most likely way of avoiding bloodshed would be to declare an emergency and then immediately remove Kenyatta and his followers by executive action and the emergency regulations. 'If the operation was staged about October 23,' he added, 'we would have time to build up adequate police and military forces.'

Baring recognised that Mau Mau was not a 'colony-wide movement' but was restricted to the Kikuyu areas within an arc of about 100 miles' radius north and west of Nairobi. His calculation was that five per cent of the movement were fanatical African nationalists, 20 per cent thugs and the remaining 75 per cent people who had joined from fear. He hoped that Lyttelton would not think that he had 'been carried away by panic on the part of excitable Europeans', adding that he had reached his conclusions 'very unwillingly' and that he fully realised that the strong action he recommended would cause Lyttelton much political trouble, for which he was very sorry.

There was criticism by the European farming community of the way the growth of African unrest had been handled. Why had they not noticed it more quickly and, having noticed signs of unrest, taken appropriate action to deal with it? But, as DC Terence Gavaghan recalled, 'the growth of restiveness, of insurrection, of internal struggle among themselves spiritually and physically, was something which was very difficult to pin down, and any action could have been counter-productive. Any failure to act was probably predictive of worse things, but there was very little opportunity of seizing it by the neck and saying 'You are a rebellion, we will stop it'.

On the morning of 9th October the secretary for law and order held a meeting to estimate the security situation which might arise from the arrest of Jomo Kenyatta and other prominent agitators, and Operation Jock Scott was initiated on 10th October at a meeting presided over by the chief secretary. On 14th October the secretary of state in Whitehall approved the proposal to declare a state of emergency, to be followed by the immediate arrest of Jomo Kenyatta and leaders of Mau Mau. He also approved reinforcement by air and sea. On 16th October it was decided that the proclamation of the state of emergency would be signed on the evening of the 20th October and declared on the 21st. A British battalion would arrive the same day. Two Kikuyu were arrested and confessed to Waruhiu's murder. They stated they had been given a pistol and instructions to murder by John Mbiu Koinange, son of ex-Senior Chief Koinange.

On the 19th October military support in the form of 1st Lancashire Fusiliers arrived and Bildad Kaggia was warned that the government meant to arrest him. A letter sent by the Seys from Rhodora on the same day referred to doors being locked at night and a pistol being kept by the bed. They were taking 'special precautions . . . because of the present Mau Mau difficulties', which they thought were 'a passing phase' as the government 'is soon going to adopt very stern measures to put an end to the trouble'. But they took no measures 'which might indicate to the Africans that we are at all apprehensive, and we do not propose to do so'.

The military support was sent in response to a request from East Africa Command, regarded as the most drowsy out-station of GHQ Middle East, for a British battalion to be sent to reinforce the three battalions of KAR. It was intended to provide 'that reassuring sense of comfort so needed in the settled areas'. They spent Monday being seen in Nairobi and its suburbs, sitting upright in open trucks, engaged in that familiar ritual of imperial policing, 'a flag march'. The Africans merely gazed at them with that blank, inscrutable stare which was to become such a characteristic feature of the Emergency, but the Europeans felt a relaxing of the tension and did not conceal their joy at seeing the troops. Companies were posted in Naivasha, Nyeri and the Kikuyu reserve.

Kaggia was warned that the government planned to arrest all KAU leaders during the next 36 hours. The Mau Mau central committee's final resolution was of the need to push the struggle for independence to its bitter end. Kaggia was widely known to be a senior officer of KAU, and in recent months he had appeared with Jomo Kenyatta on platforms at mass meetings. On the eve of the emergency he must have surmised that British security knew he was a senior officer of Mau Mau, and that if there were to be arrests of leading African dissidents he was a strong candidate for detention. He and his colleagues made provision for their arrest and laid down a number of directives for subsequent use. Expecting to be picked up at any time, he left a message on his desk for his wife regarding laundry, debts to be paid and other matters.

The political leader Oginga Odinga was convinced that a crisis was imminent. He visited Achieng Oneko in Nairobi, where Achieng's wife told him that he had been collected that morning. There had been a swoop on political leaders. Odinga made to return by bus to Kisumu, but the bus was intercepted at Gilgil and the passengers were ordered to a detention centre. They spent the night squatting in the open before being released. An African policeman drove him to the railway station to catch the train to Kisumu.

At 5pm on 20th October the governor signed the proclamation declaring that a state of emergency existed in Kenya, and orders were assigned immediately authorising the detention of 183 Africans. Kaggia was arrested a few minutes after midnight. Locked up in Kilimani police station were Fred Kubai, Waira Kamau, Victor Wokabi, Mwai Koigi, Peter Gatabaki, Kiragu Kagotho and Achieng Oneko, who 'spent the rest of the night speculating on the future', wrote Kaggia. Ex-Senior Chief Koinange and some of his relatives were also arrested on a charge of having given false evidence in connection with the assassination of Senior Chief Waruhiu.

In the opening paragraph of Nellie Grant's letter dated 20th October she wrote, 'I do honestly think that it is utterly impossible to visualise doing a bolt . . . What happens to the animals, crops etc?' She expressed concern for the safety of her aged Tiriki (a non Kikuyu tribe) nightwatchman, and reported that Bishop Beecher had preached at Gilgil, likening the suffering of the 'wretched [Kikuyu] Christians' to that of the early martyrs. She reported her successes and failures at the Nakuru flower show on Friday, and referred to reports of 'dear little school children singing hymns, substituting Jomo's name for God,' concluding: 'They will get their little bottoms smacked here by me personally if I hear them.'

How did others receive news of the Emergency? For many European farmers the implications of Mau Mau were not appreciated until the approach or arrival of the state of emergency, when those nearer Nairobi noticed 'changes in attitude of labour'. The increasing 'unrest' had little affect on the Robathans, farming near Mau Summit. The only reference to it in Robathan's memoir was that 'a major crisis was brewing and came to a head with a state of emergency being declared on 21st October'. The response up in Timau, 120 miles north, when the Stapletons were told of the Emergency was that few could believe their ears: 'Very few of us had ever heard the word Mau Mau, and fewer still knew what it meant. We were far too busy on our farms and too far away from Nairobi.'

For Peter Jenkins, a young game warden out in the bush who had very little contact with 'civilization', the state of emergency was several days old before he learned of it by chance from a newspaper in an Asian trader's truck. Jenkins was coming back from Garissa to

119

Lamu in an old Ford truck when they broke down at 11 o'clock at night. The Asian truck driver stopped to offer assistance and gave them the news.

Meteorologist Hugh Sansom plays a minor part in events, but he is useful as a more or less independent observer. He had been living in Nairobi for two years when the state of emergency was declared. For many British people life in post-war Nairobi was not unlike living in a small cathedral city in England: indeed, the cathedral was at the centre of life for Hugh and his wife, Susan. From 1951, he kept a record of everyday life in 'five-year diary' form. The brief entries are concerned with the weather (as might be expected of a meteorologist), events in the office or laboratory, running the youth fellowship, his attendance in various connections at the cathedral, unreliable motor cars repaired at Devonshire Motors, sporting activities, social engagements and tea with the archdeacon. His courtship, marriage and daughters followed in due course. If it were not for occasional visits to the game-park and Treetops it could be a diary kept in Litchfield or Salisbury in England.

Basil Mitton, for many years a business man in Nairobi, noticed little change there. His immediate response was: 'If the natives are rising, let 'em rise as far as I am concerned. Let the army shoot them.'

7

State of Emergency:
Arrests, Trials, Murder and Massacre

'We are in the country to stay. Let there be no doubt about that.'
(Oliver Lyttelton, colonial secretary)

The six months from October 1952 to April 1953 saw a spate of frenetic activity. This included the arrest of many of the Mau Mau leaders and a number of their followers; the trial of Kenyatta and some of the more senior leaders, attracting world-wide interest; the murder of a respected European family, leading to a protest march on Government House by 1500 angry Europeans; and the massacre of the inhabitants of an African village, coinciding with the highly successful raid on a European police station. Mau Mau could no longer be ignored.

Hugh Sansom's diary for 21st October reads, 'State of Emergency declared – Jomo Kenyatta arrested. No disturbances but plenty of police and troops available. Eastleigh [airport] full of Valetta aircraft which brought battalions of troops.' Recent entries had mentioned the murder of Chief Waruhiu and a 'security meeting' in their area to prepare a roster to patrol the streets at night.

Operation Jock Scott, commonly known as 'the 'Jock Scott Pick Up', had been planned for 21st October 1952. The arrest of Mau Mau leaders, the first significant event of the Emergency, went very smoothly. Part of the preparation had been mobilization of the Kenya Regiment under Colonel Campbell, a British officer seconded to it in December 1951. He had found it to be a unique regiment, formed in 1936 as a territorial force and producing leaders for the King's African Rifles. It had been disbanded in 1945 and reformed in 1950. Only during the period of the Mau Mau Emergency, which Campbell dates as 1952–6, did it operate as a regiment. It recruited largely from European settler farmers, but included lawyers, architects and so on, together with some Asians. The wide range of recruitment produced anomalies. Campbell learnt, for example; that the owner of a 50,000-acre farm with a university degree was a private in the regiment, while another of limited means and often broke was his platoon commander. 'An officer in the regiment is only one favoured among equals,' he was told. There had been calls from some quarters to disband the Kenya Regiment, and criticism of its role and its intensive training, but Michael Blundell had been one who resisted the pressures.

When the call came for action, dozens of private cars loaded with sleeping bags, cases of beer, servants, dogs and drivers in various orders of dress arrived in HQ Square, with a 99 per cent turn-out by midnight. Most European settlers responded well in an emergency. Howard Williams, a settler with a coffee farm and pedigree herd to look after, who was also employed as information staff officer to the commissioner of police, described Jock Scott as 'the turning point in the story of mankind' and a brilliant operation during which 'not a shot was fired, not a drop of blood spilled'. Most of a battalion of the Lancashire Fusiliers arrived from Egypt by air that night, he wrote, and the Fusiliers, together with the Kenya Police Reserve, the Kenya Regiment and the King's African Rifles, 'took up their appointed places'. Williams was given to hyperbole, but about a hundred African leaders of Mau Mau were pulled in without much ado, including those mentioned by Bildad Kaggia in the previous chapter.

Kaggia recalls that the streets were deserted apart from some troops and police, but as dawn broke the police station was surrounded by armoured cars and armed soldiers. African house servants, the only Africans in the area, watched it all from behind windows. The leaders were handcuffed, taken by lorry to Wilson Airport and thence to their first place of detention – in Kaggia's case to Marsabit.

The Jock Scott Pick Up was successful as an action but, recalled Blundell, the government failed to maintain the initiative, and Mau Mau spread and rooted itself more deeply and widely wherever there were Kikuyu. The reason for its failure, he suggests, was the 'cellular form' adopted by the Mau Mau movement, which appealed to the secretiveness and individualism of the Kikuyu. Odinga agrees that from the British standpoint Jock Scott was, initially at least, successful. KAU was decapitated, and the arrest of its leaders 'created fright' among the people, even those who had taken the oath: it was some time before people found their nerve again, and before 'central secret organizations' could be revived. However, Karari Njama suggests, the arrest of political leaders strengthened ill-will against the government, and he was not alone in voicing that view.

As for the approximately 180 detainees; they were dispersed well away from Kikuyuland. Kenyatta was taken to Lokitaung in Turkana country, close to the border with Ethiopia – 400 miles from Nairobi as the crow flies. Twelve were taken to Marsabit in the Northern Frontier District and the rest to Kajiado, south of Nariobi in Masailand. For Bildad Kaggia 21st October was a significant day. 'Never did I think,' he wrote some 20 years later, 'that from that night onward I would be under some form of imprisonment until 17th November 1961, over nine years later.'

On Sunday 26th October, at morning service, the provost preached 'another very good sermon relevant to the situation', wrote Sansom. Tom Mboya recalled that most of the churches at first sided with the government and condemned the Africans outright. They concentrated on the atrocities which had been committed, and overlooked the background to these problems and the reason for the eruption. Several missionaries of all denominations condemned African leaders as 'agitators' who had misled their people and exploited the ignorance of the masses. At a Nairobi service it was suggested that any African who was suspected of Mau Mau activity should be excommunicated. Mboya was convinced the church had failed, as much as everybody else, to understand the sense of pride and nationalism among the African people.

As they went underground, new acronyms such as KEM became common currency, at least among the insurgents. The letters were the initial letters of the three tribes Kikuyu, Embu and Meru, and they indicated, wrote Wachanga, the 'common cause' of some members of those tribes. He calculated that by the time the Kenyan government awoke to the strength of Mau Mau about seven-eighths of KEM had taken the first oath. He gave no indication of KEM's numerical strength nor the form of its organization, but he claimed that the Kikuyu war council, formed early in 1952, had identifed KEM districts at Kiambu, Murang'a, Nyeri, Embu and Meru, each of which had a designated leader. He lists Charles Wambaa, Paul Njiri, Isaac Gathanju, Jesse Kariuki, James Beauttah and John Mungai as 'some of the leaders active in the Kikuyu war council'. He added that some of them, especially the older ones, did not want the Mau Mau revolt to be bloody, but that during a secret meeting they finally agreed that 'without bloodshed our revolt could not succeed'. Wachanga refers to Dedan Kimathi, Stanley Mathenge and himself as being among the freedom fighters already in the forest. Of those leaders, the name which became most famous (or infamous) was Dedan Kimathi. Several Kenyan towns in later years gave his name to a street.

Wachanga describes Kimathi as one of the powerful people in the Aberdares. He lived in Kahigaini village in North Tetu, Nyeri district, and was educated at Ihururu and the Church of Scotland mission at Tumutumu up to grade five. Stanley Mathenge, also from Nyeri district, was the forest leader who most closely rivaled Kimathi in the Mau Mau mythology. He was 6'3" tall, slender, very strong and with a very strong and loud voice, extremely fierce in battle and an excellent public speaker. Wachanga refers to Mbaria Kaniu as the third of the major leaders, another big man with Masai features. He was arrested in 1952 at Naivasha and repatriated to his home district of Murang'a.

In the second echelon of Mau Mau leaders were Waruhiu Itote (General China), Kago, Matenjagwo, Kerito ole Kisio, Nyoro Kiragu and Kahinga Wachanga. The first echelon leaders were, with one or two exceptions, given the rank of field marshal or assistant field marshal, while the second echelon were titled general. (More of most of these leaders anon.)

During the year the government's information department increased activities and brought in staff from Britain. 'Saucepan' radios were used four hours a day to make broadcasts in Swahili and Kikuyu throughout provinces where trouble was brewing, emphasizing what a retrograde step Mau Mau was taking. A few films were made and news sheets were distributed.

How did Jock Scott affect the European farms? By 26th October most of them, including the new Rhodora, had arranged for every European man to be enrolled in the KPR and to make two or three patrols per week. All the farms were visited at intervals day and night, wrote Tony Seys in a letter to England, 'so no one need feel lonely or neglected'. On another farm Jock Dawson, a second generation settler with a wife and five children, built a boma (a protective fence) around the house for the cattle, and he gave his African workers a display of his expertise with a pistol. He left them in no doubt of his willingness to use it should Mau Mau terrorists, or his own staff, attack any of his family.

Within a few days of the declaration of the state of emergency, Nellie Grant wrote home that 'the Kenya Police Reserve are marvellous' and gave as an example a neighbouring settler John Adams who, in addition to all his farm work, was 'patrolling every single night around the farms'. She added that all the telephones had been taken over by Europeans, with all messages screened and only English ones allowed.

The secretary of state, Oliver Lyttelton, and his parliamentary secretary, Hugh Fraser, made their first visit to Kenya in the early days of the Emergency, and Lyttelton put many noses out of joint. They arrived a week after the murder, by a mob, of Chief Nderi and his two police escorts at a gathering for Mau Mau oath administration. Michael Blundell did not enjoy the visit. It was 'not a success', he wrote later. Elected members informed Lyttelton that they regarded government and police action as 'fumbling and ineffective', and they asked that the European community should be part of the government, with a view to influencing the decisions which had to be taken. 'Lyttelton,' wrote Blundell, 'turned down our request bluntly.'

Lyttelton admitted that he spoke to the settlers 'with brutal candour', explaining that 60,000 Europeans could not expect to hold all the political power, and he warned that the exclusion of the Africans would 'build up pressures which will burst into rebellion and bloodshed'. He referred to settlers' suspicions and criticisms of colonial office rule, but reminded them that they were 'not slow' to ask for troops, aeroplanes and money to suppress a rebellion. He told them they must turn their minds to political reform and measures which would gradually 'engage the consent and help of the governed'.

This was probably the first occasion on which many of the white community learned direct from Westminster that 'minority rule' was not an option for the future. Lyttelton's plain speaking was not welcomed by the Europeans, but he appears to have done nothing to endear himself to the African leaders, either. Odede, Awuori and Murumbi, stand-in leaders of KAU, told Fenner Brockway that an 'interview' with Lyttelton had consisted of his entering the room, taking a seat 'without even shaking hands', nodding to the governor to go ahead and leaving 'without saying a word' to the African leaders. He won no friends anywhere. Nevertheless, Lyttelton demonstrated to those in the know that he was an astute politician who saw anomalies in the present system of representation, and he observed Blundell to be 'a man of liberal inclinations who carried the banner unflinchingly in the face of much abuse and hostility from a large section of his fellow countrymen'.

The early 1950s were the time of the McCarthy witch-hunts in the USA, and the search for 'reds under the bed' was not restricted to North America. Lyttelton opined that on the evidence available it could not be established that Mau Mau 'had been the creation of Soviet policy', although he acknowledged that large sums of money and other help came from the Congress Party in India and that the activities of the Indian high commission went 'far beyond the bounds of diplomatic propriety'. He recalled that the Catholic church ascribed most of the evils and distempers in the world to communism, and he asked Bishop McCarthy in Nairobi why he thought everything bad in Kenya was inspired by communism when there was no evidence whatever to support it. 'Well,' replied the Bishop, 'if you have a back like a duck and you have webbed feet like a duck and you quack like a duck, it's just as well to call it a duck.'

When discussing terrorist trials the Europeans' pressure for 'summary justice' was a recurrent issue facing Lyttelton. It was claimed that 'too many safeguards watched over the accused'. He succeeded in speeding up the machinery of justice by cancelling or curtailing the proceedings of courts of the first instance, although it seemed likely that such a proposal might create a parliamentary storm in Westminster. Lyttelton pointed out that it was normal practice in Scotland to bring people charged with a serious offence straight to a high court. Administration of justice was speeded up by practical means 'without in any way eroding the indefeasible rights of the accused'.

Lyttelton was clearly impressed by Baring, whom he regarded as a governor endowed with balance and wisdom. 'He didn't always act very quickly,' he wrote, 'but his slowness sprang from the mature nature of his mind; he wished to be sure before being forceful; his eyes were on the future, never diverted from the great objectives by expediency in the face of some unexpected but transitory danger. Once he had decided, he acted with a bland and unshakable determination.' His assessment concurred largely with Blundell's, which found him 'deeply conscious of his position', but 'once he found it necessary to exercise his prerogative as the governor, the chief executive of the colony, no amount of argument would prevail'.

That said, however, his poor health and his apparent hesitancy to take decisive action to contain Mau Mau activities were too much for the European elected members of LEGCO in the early weeks after the Emergency was declared. Blundell recalls that they were driven to desperation by the lack of decision and co-operation against Mau Mau in the field. They considered that they must ask for his recall and replacement, and Blundell was deputed to go and see him and tell him of their strongly held opinions and worries. He conveyed his colleagues' ultimatum as best he could. 'Instead,' Blundell wrote, 'of being faced with the delegated authority of the British government in all its irremovable force, a tired and almost humble man said to me, "I see. I had only wanted to serve this country as best I could, but I would not wish to continue if the people lost confidence in me." '

Blundell wrote: 'I felt strangely drawn to him. We discussed the situation, and I tried to tell him what was going wrong and how matters could, in our judgement, be improved. I returned and reported fully to the elected members, and that was the last of this particular incident.' Blundell endorsed Lyttelton's assessment of Baring as a man of 'unshakable determination', adding, 'he had the confidence of the British government, he understood the intricacies of the Tory political scene and he would refuse to be brushed aside.'

The European settler-farmers may have considered that Baring did less than he might to advance their interests, but in Britain, where an increasing number of people who mattered had little sympathy for the settlers' cause, there was a view that Baring did too much. His biographer suggests three reasons for Baring's attention to settlers' opinion: they were too often within the danger area as farmers and employers for him to ignore them and their potential; they were, because of their agricultural output, a vital element in maintaining the Kenyan economy which would, ultimately, help to pay for the Emergency; and they had influence in parliament and the world press.

It was, furthermore, always a nightmare of Baring's that, unless the war against Mau Mau was seen to be prosecuted with firmness by the official security forces, both settlers and some elements of the administration would start to take the law into their own hands. There appears to have been mutual respect between Baring, Blundell and Lyttelton despite, or perhaps because of, the latter's unpalatable response to the settlers' 'demands'.

Fenner Brockway and Leslie Hale also visited Kenya in October. Blundell considered their arrival ill-considered and ill-timed. He had spoken against the visit in LEGCO, at that time recording that Brockway had a history of affiliation and sympathy to the communist movement and that his arrival could only give encouragement to the terrorists. Blundell had, he said, obtained his information as to his communist sympathies 'from an unimpeachable source in the United Kingdom'.

Brockway and Hale were startled by the barrage of cameras which met the aircraft's arrival in Nairobi. It had been hot in the plane and Hale had removed his tie and socks. 'Arrived like a poor white,' whispered a shocked official. The press informed them of the European settlers' resentment and outrage at their visit, and asked them to confirm that Kenyatta had signed the cheque for their flights. Told of Blundell's allegations, Brockway denied that he was a communist and that he had attended a communist conference. He confirmed that they had come at the invitation of KAU and that KAU had paid their fares. (Many settlers might well have regarded KAU and Kenyatta as much the same thing.) They were met by Odede and Awori of LEGCO and Joseph Murumbi the new secretary of KAU. 'For a mile Africans stood on the pavement clapping us,' Brockway later commented to the press. 'Splendid KAU organization.'

After some hesitation Brockway and Hale decided to accept the invitation to stay with ex-Senior Chief Koinange, whose son Mbiu was in custody charged with the murder of Chief Waruhiu. The father had been charged with complicity in the murder. At Charles Koinange's suggestion it was agreed that they would make Mrs Desai's house in Nairobi their headquarters. For most Europeans, visits from Labour members of parliament were unwelcome at any time, but they were particularly unwelcome when the visitor appeared to favour the Africans. Tony Seys, a recent settler, wrote that 'a great deal of damage has been done to race relations in this country by people from outside it'. He referred to Fenner Brockway and other socialist MPs 'who came out for a very short visit, their minds entirely set on taking the part of the black man . . . they cannot realize what terrible damage they do in a short time'. In a letter dated 26th October he quoted from a leading article in a local paper which referred to 'responsibility for this tragic state of emergency [resting] with the remote doctrinaires of the demagogues who have so recklessly and so unrealistically intervened in the communists' affairs and policies'. His letter on 2nd November concluded, 'we think it quite deplorable that Hale and Fenner Brockway (both socialist MPs) should have been allowed to come here at this time. (The former wearing no hat, tie or socks). These two men are at this moment in the Kikuyu reserve, staying at the house of Chief Koinange, who is one of the chiefs at present in prison, accused of the murder of Senior Chief Waruhiu. In other words they are staying in the house of one of the Mau Mau leaders. Our Africans knew they had arrived before we did. "The Bwana Mau Mau has come," they said'.

Hale's socks became a memorable feature of the visit. DO John Cumber recounts an incident during a garden party given by African leaders, at which a number of local African leaders, Fenner Brockway, another 'left-wing member of parliament' and others, including himself, were present. The MPs were dressed 'like a couple of Greek traders who had been dragged through a prickly hedge backwards' and were wearing sandals on their bare feet. This was in contrast with the rest of the African leaders who were 'in their smart Sunday best because that is how the Kikuyu like to throw these parties'. A Kenya police aeroplane dropped a brick wrapped in two pairs of socks in the middle of the lawn, the label on the parcel reading 'To Mr Fenner Brockway and friend with the courtesy of the Kenya Police Airwing.' The African leaders, who had previously expressed surprise to John Cumber at the informality of the MPs' dress, were highly amused at the message, 'rolling on the ground holding their stomachs in near mortality of laughter,' Cumber remarked, 'much to the discomfort of the two messiahs from the left-wing side of the House of Commons'.

The Hale's socks incidents at the airport and the Government House garden party entered into Kenyan 1950s folklore. All colours and cultures enjoyed a common joke in these trivial matters during otherwise tense times. They were a subject for the press at the time, mentioned in several biographies of leaders from both sides in the struggle, and 40 years on were remembered with a wistful smile when recalling the turbulent 1950s.

Brockway and Hale met members of the government, administrators and a cross-section of the people from the African, Asian and European communities. They urged the governor to allow the African leaders to speak freely with him and to give the new leaders, like Odede, Awari and Murumbi, the opportunity to go among the people – as they were willing to do – and 'urge them not to touch Mau Mau'. In silencing leaders opposed to Mau Mau, said Brockway, 'Mr Lyttelton and the governor encouraged many Africans to come to the conclusion that there was no alternative to Mau Mau. This was a disastrous mistake – had they been permitted to conduct a campaign against Mau Mau, they might have saved the situation. Instead they were cold-shouldered.'

After their visit to the governor, Brockway and Hale met their 'African sponsors'. They discussed the failure of the new KAU leaders to obtain permission from the governor for Odede and Awari to broadcast a warning to Africans against Mau Mau. Odede suggested that Brockway and Hale might approach him to seek permission to make an appeal. Hale prepared a draft which identified them, on the one hand, with African demands for land, wages, education, elected representation to LEGCO and elimination of the colour bar and, on the other, with an appeal to Africans 'not to associate with Mau Mau'. The draft was endorsed by Odede, Awari and Murumbi and was distributed in translation by KAU.

'We asked . . . to be allowed to broadcast ourselves,' wrote Brockway. 'Our association with KAU would guarantee African confidence,' but among Europeans we were Public Enemy Number One.' The governor refused.

During their stay Brockway and Hale were provided with an armed guard, 'to defend us,' wrote Brockway, 'not from Mau Mau terrorists, but from fanatical Europeans'. They travelled in the colony under heavy escort, attending meetings with both Europeans and Africans. The latter were often inhibited by the presence of their escort, but when they met them in the Desai's household they found that Indian grievances were the same as those of the Kikuyu – land, hunger, and prohibition of coffee and sisal growing. They were very critical of the chief, 'a stooge of the British', they said.

Brockway and Hale had lunch with Col Grogan at an exclusive hotel, but although Brockway had expected a serious discussion about Kenya, that was 'the last thing' in their host's mind. He was content to tell them stories. Kenya's 'leading woman farmer', who was 'well tailored, clear-cut in features and gave the impression of competence and strength of will', told the politicians: 'You ask us to regard Africans as equals? You insult us. Every African is dishonest, a liar, lazy. Their language has no words for love, gratitude, loyalty.' Later Brockway asked the Kikuyu sergeant for translations of the words, which he wrote down as 'wendo', 'ngatho' and 'wathikeri'.

Towards the end of their visit, Brockway and Hale noticed that the Nairobi press had reversed its tone towards them: 'Even the Tory papers in London said we had behaved correctly, and the Europeans acknowledged our reasonableness.'

At Hale's suggestion a round-table conference was held, attended by Blundell, Havelock and Asian, African and Arab members of the legislative council. Many of the items on Hale's list of 'immediate reforms' were agreed in principle, but a meeting arranged for the following day was cancelled because, returning to his farmhouse the evening after the initial meeting, Blundell found a threat from Mau Mau. 'The proposed declaration would appear to be appeasement in the face of threat,' Brockway records. 'For the first time on our visit Leslie and I felt beaten and tired. We left the next day.' He wrote that 'Mau Mau with its murders, atrocities and its killings of fellow Africans was a great shock. I knew so many of the Kikuyu. I attacked Mau Mau'.

Brockway's impression of Sir Evelyn Baring was that he looked a governor, distinguished in appearance, charming in manner, open-minded and liberal in his approach. His summary of the governor's capability, on the other hand, was that 'with all his charms and breadth of outlook, he left me worried'. Brockway doubted whether he was dominant enough for his immensely difficult task – strong enough to control Mau Mau, on the one hand, and to resist the pressures of the European minority on the other. 'I hope,' he concluded, 'I am wrong.'

Blundell made good with Brockway. He accepted his assurance that he had no connections with communism. He concluded that Brockway was 'a sincere, emotional, rather muddled thinker, who felt in some way that he could resolve the conflict, which was gathering force and speed, by some great social and humanitarian gesture. He did not realise until much later that he appeared as a sympathiser and supporter to a bestial anti-Christian, inhuman and evil movement'.

Nairobi's social life was not entirely neglected during these times of strife. Kenya's National Theatre was opened on 31st October. Despite his undeniable problems, Nellie Grant wrote in a letter to

131

England, Baring sounded 'in rattling form and made a cheerful, carefree, funny speech'. He had had 'a jolly good dinner at GH'.

Nor was Karari Njama's social life neglected. During the mass meeting, a few months earlier, he had been 'drawn to the Mau Mau cause', and now his third oath was administered near the school at which he taught. His assistant teacher stood with him, naked, facing Mount Kenya. Once again the ceremony involved the sacrifice of a goat. Then, holding high a ball of soil dampened with milk, fat and blood from the goat in his right hand and another ball against his navel with his left hand, he took a series of steps over lengths of intestine which had been arranged on the floor of the hut and completed a set of seven vows. The vows required him:

- To become a soldier of Gikuyu and Mumbi, and to fight for the land and freedom.
- To come when called to accompany a raid or bring in the head of any enemy.
- To refuse to spy or inform on his people.
- To steal firearms whenever possible.
- To obey the orders of his leaders.
- Never to leave a member in difficulty.
- Never to sell land to any white man.

He was then ordered to hold a skinned goat against him and put his penis in a hole in the carcass while repeating the vows for a second time. The ceremony continued, using bones with seven holes, sticks, goat's eyes, kei-apple thorns, sodom apples, a sword, a knife and a needle. Walking back to school, he and his fellow candidate and assistant David Wahome decided that it was 'a horrible oath, though typically Kikuyu'. They spoke of 'Utuku wa Hiu Ndaihu' (which they translated as The Night of the Long Swords), rumoured to be 3rd November, when all Europeans would be killed at a given time. They noted that all the vows they made were of 'fighting plans'.

In the event, settler/staff officer Williams, working with the police, recorded that November 3rd passed as quietly as he imagined it would, 'although several people took precautions'. However, a second generation settler, Tony Coulson, surmised that 'if the Africans had had their night of the long knives it would have been very successful. We wouldn't have had a dog's chance in hell'.

One night, shortly after the declaration of the state of emergency, police patrolmen flagged down Michael Blundell on the road from Nairobi to Nakuru to tell him that he had been put on the death list during a Mau Mau meeting in the forest. It had been decreed that he should be hanged. For a brief period Blundell was the number one target of the terrorists, and for three years he was accompanied by a police bodyguard wherever he went.

On 25th November Sir Percy Sillitoe, head of MI5 in Britain, visited Kenya as security adviser. This led to the appointment of a British security service official and other staff, while the police special branch was greatly expanded and a senior intelligence staff officer for military operations was established at GHQ. This recognition of the need for finer security was generally welcomed, but there is ample evidence that the main problem facing the Administration was not lack of intelligence but failure of the Kenya government to believe it or act on it. Baring and his advisers, including Sillitoe, were of the opinion that the Emergency would be short-lived, and Dr Louis Leakey, a Kikuyu elder and recognised authority on the Kikuyu, endorsed that view. 'Mau Mau', he opined, 'was like a fire made of kindling wood and not coal, which burnt with intense violence and was unstoppable, but would presently abate with equal speed.' Estimates were that the Emergency was unlikely to last more than a few weeks. Sillitoe also thought the insurrection would end once they had removed the Kikuyu leadership. Then, he believed, witnesses would come forward and cases could be tried.

The security and administration experts were proved wrong. The insurrection did not end when the known leaders were behind bars, for other leaders emerged to take their place. In some respects it was a return to the early days of the colony when the Pax Britannica was being established. Then, the local administrator managed his patch by his wits, and if his people needed 'discipline', the police were there to assist. Should the problem be too much for the police the KAR was in the background and could be called on for help. Thereafter, when Africans were established in the lands reserved for their occupation, white settlers occupied their farms and the rest of the land was open, Kenya had in effect two police forces. 'The Kenya police extended colony-wide in all the settled and main areas, but it did not cover the tribal reserves.' Those were patrolled by the able tribal police service, which came under the district commissioner.

They were good 'village constables and NCOs' but they did not run CID, Special Branch or traffic. The administrative structure of the colony was not conducive to overcoming the Mau Mau movement. Traditionally each district officer was master of his area, with the district commissioner and the provincial commission one above the other. The Emergency undermined that hierarchy, with security forces operating across provincial boundaries.

Military support came through Lt Col George Coles, a regular officer in the Uganda Battalion of the KAR who had served with the KAR during the war. He became involved in what became a cat-and-mouse game between government forces and Mau Mau terrorists who had gone underground and were denied food supplies.

Mau Mau's immediate source of food was the European and African farms, and Coles's strategy was to deny access to these cultivated areas to Mau Mau now living in camps in the forests. As and when necessity dictated they would sally forth and attack a village area and retreat into the forest. The KAR would then try to round them up, in the course of which they might kill one or two. They would try, too, to locate the camps and destroy them so that the occupants would have to move somewhere else. The idea was to keep them away from the villages, where they had been successfully intimidating the local Kikuyu people, many of whom were supporting Mau Mau and would not give information to the military. 'You would go to surround a village in a round up and hear the women calling out right across the hills, letting everybody know'.

A curfew, enforced by the military, was imposed to restrict the movement of terrorists by night. They would go out, and if they saw anyone out in the village or on forest tracks at night they could arrest them. If they ran away 'you could shout at and then shoot them. You were very unlikely to hit anybody, but it would frighten them and discourage them from going out again. If you met a group you could be pretty sure they were up to no good. And, again, you could challenge them. On occasions we managed to shoot the odd one. There were always armed groups with pangas or occasionally with rifles. They had quite a few with shot guns and so on'. Law abiding villagers did not suffer as a result of the curfew, 'but it was a hardship for the Mau Mau because they were not able to move from A to B and carry out their next oath-takings or other nefarious tricks that they were up to'.

A deterrent to Mau Mau supporters which received little publicity among the European population but which did not go unnoticed was the erection of gallows where they were visible to passers by. Kahinga Wachanga, now one of the new underground leaders, observed them during November and December throughout Central Province. Others were built in Nyeri town, Embu, Meru and Murang'a town. In his paper on counter-insurgency, Anthony Clayton records that a public gallows was put up on Nyeri golf course 'which may have been in response to settler demands'. The intention, he suggests, was that it should be erected in a sentenced man's home area as a warning the day before the execution at dawn.

November saw the beginning of what might be regarded as a siege of the European settlers. Wherever they went, night or day, a pistol had to be to hand. When darkness fell, they would be alone with windows and doors barricaded and barbed wire embracing the buildings. Sofas and chairs would be pulled across the room to act as obstacles between the inmates and the doors. The farmer and his wife would sit reading or quietly talking, each with their pistol ready, half listening all the time for noises outside the house.

Nellie Grant's letter dated 17th November referred to her trying to recruit two armed Dorobo to supplement her 'very indifferent' nightwatchman. She discovered that Dorobo watchmen had become 'extremely fashionable and very hard to get'. By 25th November she was trying to remember to carry her revolver on her person and to hide her ammunition. She had an electric fence as part of her so-called 'farm plan', and her two Dorobo had arrived, 'complete with bows and arrows'.

Loyal people of whatever colour (in this context meaning loyal to the government), were at risk day and night in town or country. On 26th November Tom Mbolela was murdered in Nairobi while walking home. He had spoken against terrorism and, as vice-president of KAU, had urged a moderate course for that union. Bildad Kaggia had claimed some credit for removing Mbolela from his office, but it was Kenyatta who dismissed him. Now he was dead.

An Indian shopkeeper near Thika was killed in his home at 3am on 9th December. His wife and children were injured. As the attackers left they said to the family, 'We don't want you here. Don't come back; return to India'. And the week before Christmas 11 African loyalists were killed while attending church.

European settlers' leaders were emerging and becoming recognized. The Seys letter on the 30th November praised Michael Blundell's 'excellent speech at Kabazi for the annual general meeting of the Solai [local farmers'] Association'. Michael and Gerry Blundell were described as 'superb examples of how to behave in danger', and Michael was described as becoming a first class leader. Seys recognized that the composition of their labour force and their distance from Nairobi made their farm less at risk from Mau Mau attack. At Rhodora they had 20 Kikuyu, 90 Jaluo and 38 Kipsigis, and they were not near the forest or the reserve. Seys compared their lot with that of Michael Blundell, whose farm was on the edge of the forest and surrounded by Kikuyu. Furthermore, the Blundells had been informed that their farm had been selected for attack by Mau Mau. By the 7th December the Seys had formed the Rhodora Defence Force, consisting of eight of their most trusted Kipsigis braves. They carried out night exercises.

Nellie Grant was not really a candidate for a 'settler under siege' role. Early in December she mislaid her revolver. She searched behind the radio and down the side of the sofa, where she usually secreted it while listening to the radio, but without success. Europeans were required to notify the police of lost firearms so, reluctantly, she contacted them. The next morning Karanja, one of her staff, 'discovered' it in the armchair where the police and Nellie had looked. The facts behind the reappearance of the revolver were not known. (She wrote home that, soon after her mishap, an emergency law was published 'saying that anyone leaving a firearm in any place not absolutely safe would get six months in gaol and a £100 fine.) In the same letter she reported that livestock had been slashed or killed on various farms, and that an Indian storekeeper had been murdered 'by an armed gang of forty'.

Mau Mau was becoming more brazen. Leader Kahinga Wachanga described the murder of Chiefs Waruhiu and Nderi Wang'ombe as part of a plan to assassinate all senior chiefs, priests and other government servants between October and December 1952. He recorded his own part in an action when 'five men and I burned homes of non-oath-takers. We burnt more than twenty houses, many of them containing goats and sheep'.

At Westminster on the 25th November the colonial secretary announced the government's 'distasteful but necessary' decision to impose communal punishment (including the removal of livestock) on certain areas. The decision followed an attack by 2,000 members of the Kikuyu tribe on 20 policemen at Kirawara on 23rd November. Communal (collective) punishment had been a recognized aspect of Black African 'law' which had been adopted by the British administration over the years but which the Administration had been most reluctant to use.

Then came an unhappy Christmas. For both Nellie Grant and Mau Mau's recent recruit Karari Njama, Christmas 1952 was gloomy. For Nellie, because all KPR and home guard were working overtime to keep things quiet. In her letter of 28th December she wrote of the burning of Osborne's saw mills, of 11 Christian Kikuyu murdered in one night at Nyeri and of a chief attacked and his retainers hacked to pieces. And she was 'out of knitting, which is so boring'. She hoped her grandson could be persuaded to stand still for long enough to be measured for a cricket sweater.

For Njama, who was still teaching at Nyeri, 'instead of the good Christmas songs, bullets echoed everywhere', and 'there were cries for the deceased, for blazing houses, for the robbing and raping; the cry of beatings and tortures in the chiefs' centres, in police and prison cells'. A curfew was in force from 6pm to 6am, and he could not travel to Mahinga, his location.

Alliance School headmaster Carey Francis spent Christmas with a missionary friend in the heart of the Mau Mau area. He wrote that '95 percent of the people belong.' He met an Alliance old boy, July Jerome, a former pupil of Makerere school, who was now an assistant DC and had been condemned to death by the local Mau Mau.

The closing months of 1952 were depressing for Kenya. There were interminable delays in initiating new legislation to deal with Mau Mau during which time, wrote Blundell, 'our people, both black and white, were shot with pistols, slashed with pangas, tried by illegal Mau Mau courts and garroted. Hundreds of the Kikuyu . . . were murdered . . . their bodies found months later'. He gave an example from his own experience. His wife telephoned him from their farm to tell him that a Mau Mau ceremony had taken place on the slopes of a hill near their house. She had been awakened late at night by her brother-in-law, who managed the farm in Blundell's absence. A Kikuyu who was working on the farm was taken at night to a secret meeting place where he was told to take the Mau Mau oaths. He refused, whereupon the administrator and his gang stripped him of his clothing and threatened him with a panga pressed into his stomach. He still resisted until a knotted rope was tied round his neck, and he was strung up until he was nearly throttled when, in desperation, he accepted the oath.

After the ceremony was over, he was told to return to his home without contacting anyone on the farm. He was badly bruised and damaged, but he had no intention of giving in. He told the whole story. The police were telephoned and arrived in time to arrest the gang, including the oath administrator, who proved to be 'an extremely well paid young carpenter of attractive personality and outlook, who had recently worked temporarily in their own house'. At the trial, the farm worker had the courage to go into the witness box and openly identify each of the men who had taken part in the ceremony. This was a particularly brave thing to do, because intimidation and murder made it almost impossible to get witnesses to come forward.

The December issue of the East African Women's League newsletter devoted two pages to the Emergency. The theme was, 'Something is happening at last!' It described the role of the women as providing succour, warned against spreading rumours and gave advice on security.

Karari Njama was not enjoying life. At Christmas he had prayed that the New Year would come quickly 'and change our horror and sorrow into happiness, in which we would be victorious'. Instead, the new year produced 'a mass compulsory cleansing ceremony sponsored by Government'. The cleansing was performed by 'witch doctors' (often called Her Majesty's witch doctors), who were 'mainly Mau Mau members or sympathisers'. Njama adds that 'in reality they were only deceiving the Government that they were cleansing people'. As a Christian, Njama did not have to undergo cleansing but instead (having already taken the third Mau Mau oath) 'I swore on a bible at the DC's office that I was not a member of Mau Mau'. After the holidays he returned to teaching, and on 21st January his wife delivered a daughter at the Consolata Catholic maternity hospital, Nyeri.

The Indians, Kenya's middle-class, were in an invidious position. There are few reports of them 'in the forest' on the government side. In January 1953 Diwan Chamanlal, who had close ties with the Indian government, advocated civil disobedience at a large meeting in Nakuru, and the Indian commissioner, Shri Apa Pant, took an interest in Mau Mau developments. Indian nationalists, still aflame with the spirit of their own independence in 1947, saw in the Kenyan scene a kindred spectacle to their own struggle. Indians in Kenya at that time were not unanimous regarding their allegiances, but most businessmen have little doubt that Indians did not fight for independence in Kenya. 'What we want is stability in the country. We look after our own business. As long as the government keeps law and prosperity'.

The *Times* newspaper of 28th July 1953 reported that during the Emergency thousands of Indians volunteered for military service, and that at least one all-Indian unit saw action in the forests. However, 'the unit performed so badly it was not used again'. Edgerton, a reasonably dispassionate historian, concludes, having weighed the evidence, that most of the Indians openly sided with the government during the Emergency but that some, such as Makhan Singh and Pio Gama Pinto, played important roles in launching Mau Mau. But later, when Koigi wa Wamwere argued that with only two exceptions the Indians had remained passive in 'Kenya's fight for independence', Mansukh Shah named between 20 and 30 who were Mau Mau supporters and 'prominent in the fight'. The list was by no means exhaustive, he said. Nevertheless, Mansukh Shah admits that in the 1950s 'most Indians were regarded as allies of the colonial regime'. A notable exception was K.P. Shah, a Nairobi businessman who supported independence before many Indians.

So much for attitudes, actions and allegiances. Having, courtesy of Jock Scott, arrested more than a hundred leaders, not to mention the more humble members of Mau Mau, the authorities had to make decisions regarding their future. For a variety of reasons the government found it difficult to bring Jomo Kenyatta and five leaders to trial, but evidence was eventually obtained which the Crown felt enabled it to charge Kenyatta with being the manager of Mau Mau. The evidence was, however, pretty thin. Kenyatta was no doubt guilty by association with the spirit of Mau Mau but almost certainly not guilty of technical management of its operations before the Emergency. Many Europeans had not even heard of Jomo Kenyatta before he was arrested.

Nevertheless, the trial of Jomo Kenyatta, Fred Kubai, Achieng Oneko, Bildad Kaggia, Paul Ngei and Kungu Kurumba opened on 24th

November at Kapenguria some 250 miles north of Nairobi, not far from the Ugandan border – a peaceful, beautiful setting on the edge of the Rift Valley, which could hardly have been more inconvenient for a major trial. Communications with Nairobi, let alone the outside world, were appalling, and the trial was held in a cramped old red-roofed structure normally used as the schoolroom of an agricultural training college. Few people had heard of Kapenguria or knew where it was. It lacked telephone, railway and hotel, and participants in the trial had to stay in and travel from Kitale, some 20 miles to the south.

The charges against the prisoners listed by Bildad Kaggia were:

- Management of an unlawful society known as Mau Mau between 12th August 1950 and 21st October 1952.
- Conspiring to commit a felony by act of physical force or by threat or intimidation, to compel persons to take an oath.
- Conspiring to promote feelings of ill-will and hostility between different classes of the population.
- Inciting disaffection against the government.

Against Kaggia there was a further charge of being a member of Mau Mau.

District Officer Dick Wilson, who was responsible for the arrangements, described the court accommodation as a large hall cum classroom with a dais (on which the magistrate sat) and a few little offices at the back. The premises were taken over entirely. Sitting in school desks behind the public, the world press was heavily represented. Kaggia, who had ample time to observe the arrangements, referred to a small high table which served as the bench. The dock was a bare wooden bench, and there was a portable witness box. During the proceedings only police, army officers and civilian settlers from Kitale were present. No Africans except policemen were allowed in court. Outside there were armoured cars, police on horseback and armed soldiers.

Counsel for the defence were drawn from the four corners of the earth. D.N. Pritt QC from London led Chaman Lall (India), H.O. Davies (Nigeria), Davis (Scotland), Dudley Thomson (a Jamaican from Tanga), A.R. Kapila, Fitz de Souza and Jaswant Singh from Kenya. The Crown was more modestly represented by DPP Somerhough. Dr Louis Leakey acted as interpreter.

The case was heard by Ransley Samuel Thacker QC, who had officially retired from the service on 5th August. For five years he had been a senior puisne judge in Kenya. He was now appointed as a first class magistrate rather than judge, which avoided the need for a preliminary enquiry by a magistrate. He was paid by the day for a case which it was assumed would soon be over. Thacker required a 'realistic' rate in view of the danger he would be in for the rest of his life. In the event, the trial ran until 8th April 1953, when he delivered judgement.

The course of the trial was far from smooth. The defence objected to Leakey as interpreter, and he was replaced. Witnesses proved unreliable or were threatened and, wrote Kaggia, Pritt said 'No case to answer' over and over again.

Fitz de Souza, one of the defence counsel, referred to written evidence that the charges were 'trumped up' – and, indeed, the most senior witness who gave evidence against Kenyatta eventually confessed and said that he had been bribed by the authorities and offered a scholarship and so much money to give evidence against him. The alleged paying of witnesses at the Kapenguria trial later became an established fact. Detailed accounts of money paid over were prepared and signed. 'The director of prosecutions told us during the trial that he himself believed that Kenyatta was not the leader of Mau Mau,' said Milner, one of the participants.

Wilson, himself a first class magistrate, believed the defence counsel's aim 'was 'to collapse the case on grounds that it was a mistrial'. There was a tremendous amount of political speech-making. 'The main tub that Pritt thumped,' Wilson recalled, was that it was a political, not a criminal, trial. 'Virtually every day he had a go at the government and me'. Every day tempers became frayed between him and the magistrate, whom he taunted the whole time. He would turn his back on the magistrate and address the press and public. The magistrate would say, "That's enough for today," and adjourn. I would then take him off into his room at the back and calm him down. And so it went on.' Wilson believed Kenyatta *et al* had a very powerful QC in Pritt. Later, the defence counsel all joked very happily with Wilson that he ran quite a good hotel and looked after them. 'There was certainly no hard feeling.'

The transcript of the trial fills some 2,000 pages. Montague Slater, in *The Trial of Jomo Kenyatta*, provides what he is convinced is a fair and true account of it in 252 pages. All six prisoners were sentenced to seven years' imprisonment with hard labour. The magistrate recommended that restriction orders be made. He was careful to explain his rejection of the defence evidence by saying that he had done so from his long experience of the African as a witness. By implication he was protecting himself from any subsequent appeal, since there was no point of law on which Pritt could criticise the sentence, only the allegation that the judge's assessment of the prosecution and defence evidence was very biased.

Kaggia records that after the trial there was an appeal to Justice Rudd and Justice Meyers. Pritt submitted that the magistrate who convicted had no jurisdiction because he had been especially appointed to the Northern Province, whereas Kapenguria was in the Rift Valley Province. 'On these grounds,' wrote Kaggia, 'the court acquitted us.' But as they stepped out of the building they were re-arrested under the emergency regulations.

There were further appeals to the Supreme Court of Kenya, the East African Court of Appeal and the Privy Council. Pritt's appeal to the latter was that the magistrate had accepted practically every application, motion or submission made by the prosecution and rejected those made by the defence; that every witness called by the prosecution was accepted as truthful, no matter what their character or history etc, while every defence witness was rejected; that the magistrate adjourned the hearing for more than a fortnight while the leading defence counsel was tried for contempt of court; and that the magistrate admitted such a large body of inadmissable evidence as to make his findings of the fact untenable.

Baring's biographer wrote that he 'seems to have been a party to improper discussions during the trial', and that Thacker asked for an honour after it was over. Thacker told the governor that, should he reach a conclusion that Kenyatta was guilty, his own life in Kenya would not be worth a penny; he would have to leave the country. What arrangements would be made for him? Not surprisingly there is no record of such a conversation in the files, but Thacker received an *ex gratia* payment of £20,000 from the Kenya government, drawn against some special emergency fund on Baring's own instructions. Thacker had an eye for the importance of his judgement and sought to capitalise on the situation, and Baring, 'acting with unusual cynicism and ruthlessness', saw that he could not afford to take any risk.

Was Kenyatta justly convicted? Was he managing Mau Mau? Delf, one of Kenyatta's biographers, sounded many people about Kenyatta's leadership of Mau Mau, including a Scottish missionary who offered, 'It is quite clear that he accepted a certain amount of bloodshed as necessary, but I am sure he made some attempt to stop it. I don't believe for a moment that Kenyatta organised Mau Mau. My impression was that by 1952 he had largely lost control, and that to some extent things had ceased to matter for him'. Fitz de Souza, one of his counsel, said many years after the event, 'Kenyatta himself was a full nationalist, he wanted independence, he wanted everything but he didn't want violence'.

There is evidence from Kaggia later that Kenyatta's refusal to moderate his condemnation of Mau Mau at public meetings made him extremely unpopular with the more militant Mau Mau leaders. Kaggia states that Kenyatta was never a member of the Mau Mau central committee, and although Mau Mau looked upon Kenyatta as the national leader, it was not under his direct control. Indeed, as we have seen, when Kenyatta was asked to meet them for the first time he did not know who comprised the committee. Mau Mau leader Jesse Kariuki records, 'As it was, even Kenyatta himself became an object of suspicion to the thugs [Mau Mau], and there is strong evidence of plots to assasinate him both at a meeting in Kaloleni Hall, Nairobi, and also at the burial of Senior Chief Waruhiu.'

The politician/journalist Henry Muoria, who was close to Kenyatta, maintained that he was 'a very peaceful man who didn't like violence', and he endorsed the story that the people who were leading Mau Mau threatened to kill him if he didn't withdraw his statement that the Kikuyu rejected Mau Mau. But Muoria added, with a grin and twinkle, that 'Kenyatta was a very clever man; he was a politician of the highest order. He had to see which side was likely to gain politically, so that if Mau Mau was the side that won he would have completely sided with Mau Mau'.

The barrister T.R. Johar, who represented several Mau Mau terrorists and met Kenyatta on friendly terms on several occasions, thought the alleged plot that Mau Mau wanted to kill Kenyatta was probably propaganda: 'The fact is that people who were Mau Mau regarded him as their leader.' Fitz de Souza maintained that the director of prosecutions 'told us during the trial that he himself believed that Kenyatta was not the leader of Mau Mau'.

There are two comments in this connection attributed to Jomo Kenyatta himself. When Malcolm MacDonald, Kenya's last governor, was asked if he believed in Kenyatta's guilt, he replied, 'I can best answer that by repeating what Kenyatta said to me when he was prime minister. I told him that the chief justice was leaving, and asked who we should appoint in his place. He replied, "I think we should appoint the judge who convicted me at Kapenguria. I thought he was a very good judge. Certainly he did listen to lying evidence about me, but he wasn't to know they were". '

When Baring visited Kenya after independence, he met Kenyatta in the president's office. Baring said, 'I was sitting at that table when I signed your detention order twenty years ago.' Kenyatta replied, 'I know in your shoes, at that time, I'd have done exactly the same. And I've signed a good few detention orders on it myself.' Like so many stories concerned with Kenyatta, one may read into those incidents what one wishes.

While the leaders were in court at Kapenguria, Mau Mau activities continued – indeed, increased. Nellie Grant's letter of 1st January 1953 provides an insight into the basic nature of many Europeans' living conditions. The dilemma European farmers faced, she reported, was how to protect themselves and their farm staff from Mau Mau attack. Should house staff be locked in the house with them or locked out before dark at 6.00 to 6.30 pm? Early in the Emergency it became apparent that one's most loyal servants might have taken a Mau Mau oath which included murdering all Europeans.

No doubt many European settlers felt isolated and insecure. 'It wasn't very pleasant to switch on the radio and hear that some settler on a lonely farm had been slashed to an atrocious death with pangas,' commented Stapleton. 'After all, the bedroom of an isolated farm is a very vulnerable place.' On Joan Scott's farm they were very strict. Every night they locked up at six and had a cold supper or something off a little stove inside. They had no servants come in. They were aware that most of the Europeans were murdered by a gang coming at night, seizing the cook or houseboy and being let into the house. They locked up for the servants' sake as much as for their own.

On post-war farmer Arthur Thompson's farm at Nanyuki the family accommodation was joined to the kitchen and staff quarters, with a passage behind. At night the staff and house quarters were locked with the staff indoors. The passage door between farmer and servants was locked, too. Guns were to hand at all times, as Mau Mau 'had a habit of coming in with the soup'. Outside, after a raid on the labour camp, Thompson constructed a 20ft-high tower. They formed their own home guard and 'never had a raid'. At Timau, second generation settler Tim Llewelyn locked up everything, and meals were cooked in the sitting room, with the verandah enclosed in barbed wire and wire mesh. All the cattle were in small bomas, with a watch-tower, searchlights and armed guards.

Only a few miles away the Murrays, second generation settlers, did not allow Africans in the house at night, securing the farm in a similar manner to the Llewelyns. They experienced very little trouble from Mau Mau, but they were conscious that their small children could not be let out of sight at any time. They believed they had faithful people but knew that they were under enormous pressure from Mau Mau. The Campbell-Clauses were very worried when, temporarily, they lost their young son, who had wandered off. They, too, had a watch tower, barricaded farm house and cattle secured within bomas. They had no trouble with terrorists, and life seemed to be fairly normal, but 'one walked about carrying a revolver at one's belt. At the time it didn't seem very unusual'. They practised with their weapons, but these were never used in anger. All 20 of their Kikuyu men and women squatters were oathed by Mau Mau.

The Pickerings were post-war European farmers whose farm was attacked and livestock mutilated. After the attack they put a high barbed wired fence all round, with pointed stakes pushed into the earth outside the wire. Every night when work was finished they locked the men in their camp so that nobody could get at them. Only then did they feel safe.

Distance from Kikuyuland, the number of Kikuyu employees, size of farm and other factors affected the precautions taken by European farmers. At well established, relatively large and rich Deloraine, at Njoro (not a high risk area), the Scotts did not take such extreme security measures as some other European farmers. Kikuyu workers were a minority. Farms dependent largely or wholly on Kikuyu labour were at high risk, not only from Mau Mau terrorists but from 'attack' by security forces. The Scotts observed that farms with almost 100 per cent Kikuyu labour force had great difficulty, because at times the security forces would sweep down on them and arrest their entire labour force.

The high level of security being adopted was most apparent to people who knew the country but had been out away for some time. Early in January Canon T.F.C. Bewes, the Africa secretary of the Church Missionary Society, returned 'home' to Kenya. Previously he had been a missionary among the Kikuyu for 20 years. He was amazed to see the town of Fort Hall (Murang'a) looking like a fort, with barbed wire stockades, police on one side of the road, military in tanks on the other, lorries and armoured cars coming and going and a general air of preparedness.

Despite careful security, however, at 9pm on 2nd January, while listening to the 9 o'clock news, Mrs Rayne Simpson and Mrs Kitty Hesselburger were attacked by a Mau Mau gang armed with spears at a farm eight miles north-west of Mweiga. The women shot four of their attackers, killing two of them. In the commotion they also had the misfortune to shoot their cook, whose hands had been tied, and their boxer dog.

With relationships between black and white generally as poor as they had become, Nellie Grant saw the need to bring the races together socially. Arieta, the wife of her house servant Karanja (who discovered the pistol under the cushion), returned from a Jeanes School homecraft course with a good report, and Grant decided to urge the East African Women's League (EAWL) branch at Njoro to start women's clubs which would include African women such as Arieta. 'It seems to me,' she wrote, 'absolutely vital to make contact with the women and bring them along friendly-like.'

Perhaps 1953 saw some movement towards a greater concern for racial integration. Canon Bewes, on returning to Nairobi, wrote that there was no colour bar in Kenya, 'yet the African finds himself shut out from most of the social activities of the European; the two races scarcely ever eat and drink in each other's company, play games or meet at the same parties. At the moment most of the best hotels and restaurants are closed to Africans'. But he reported that 'there are rumours that the hotel keepers in Nairobi are beginning to throw open their doors to Africans'. This he considered to be a courageous move, of which he approved..

At much the same time Blundell and Wilfrid Havelock tackled the Hotel Keepers' Association on the elimination of the colour bar in hotels throughout Kenya, and pressed on with ideas for the association of all races in the government of the country. On this occasion 'the little group of fiery men were intent on going out and shooting every Kikuyu whom they met on the streets of Nairobi' as reprisals for the tragedy at Thika: 'For two hours in the evening, Wilfrid Havelock and I argued with them, and gradually forced them to give up their mad and dangerous intention.'

Governor Sir Evelyn Baring opened the new multi-racial United Kenya Club building in Nairobi.

Also in Nairobi, meteorologist Hugh Sansom and his wife Susan noticed that within about six months of Mau Mau erupting the Mothers Union (MU) had become multi-racial. It had been English, but she realized that African women were now facing 'a much bigger challenge than us because they were being asked to take the Mau Mau oath or have their children killed'. Many of the Christian Kikuyu women refused the oath. The MU, she said, took the view that 'we English Christians must do something to be able to get alongside people like this, and it sort of broke out of its English ghetto'. However, Susan Sansom recalls that when their eldest daughter was baptized in the cathedral early in 1953, they 'cut the ground under everybody's feet' by inviting all those who worked with her husband in the Nairobi meteorological office – 'from the boss to the office boy, and it really shattered people when they found themselves having tea with Africans after the baptism'.

The Sansoms did not carry firearms other than when Hugh was on night security patrol. They let this be known to friends and servants, because it was general knowledge that some break-ins were aimed at stealing firearms. Sansom's diary during these months is spattered with entries such as this, made on his return from bible school: '5th November. Find I'm on patrol in night when I get home; 1am to 4.'

It took KAU some time to pick itself up following the arrest of so many of its leaders during the Jock Scott operation. Lawrence Karugo Kihuria became chairman of the Nairobi branch. Then all key secret organizers were summoned to a meeting at which a war council was formed. Headquarters was at Mathari in Nairobi, where recruits were trained until the building was destroyed by security forces in April. Preference was given to recruits from the army, police and prison services. 'As many as 500 recruits went from Nairobi to the forest.'

Opinions in England were not as supportive of their British settlers in Kenya as the latter would have wished. Seys was not alone in believing that these attitudes influenced the Kenyan government which, he wrote, 'is afraid to take sufficiently strong measures' against the Kikuyu. 'It is,' he continued, 'a pity that many newspapers and politicians (and presumably, members of the public, too) in Britain are so anti-British and pro-African.' In his 4th January letter he included an extract from an editorial in the *Daily Mirror* which took the form of an open letter to Sir Evelyn Baring. It was widely publicized in Kenya and caused deep resentment. Baring was in London at that time. The letter read, 'You have to contend with a revolting pagan organization trying to undermine you on one side and a trigger-happy white minority on the other, already howling for Kikuyu blood. Let the settlers howl: we shall be for you, and there are more of us than there are of them.'

Seys wrote that British Kenyans felt British policy in Africa was vacillating and weak, and that a large section of the British people were less concerned for the safety of their own people and for respect for the law than for the opportunity to use African problems 'as a football in the political arena'. He pointed to Southern Rhodesia's break from the colonial office as a course which Kenya might follow. 'Is it not high time that, in the face of inept interference in African affairs by powers outside the African continent, there should be some closer association of all peoples of European descent living in the countries of Africa?' he suggested. A footnote in the Seys book observes, however, that 'life went on nonetheless. Alain and Mary de Rothschild visited Rhodora from Europe, and we set off for the Nakuru Horse Show'.

In January Government House acquired a military presence in the form of Maj Gen W.R.M. Hinde, who was appointed as personal staff officer to the governor. He soon became director of operations. Hinde had relations among the Kenyan settlers and, it was said, shared some of their prejudices. His instruction from C-I-C Middle East was 'to jolly them all along'. He had a good war record, and his appointment was popular among many settlers, who took credit for having 'pressured' for him and 'were prepared to tell him exactly what to do'. The *Times* described him as a man 'with an unusual gift for getting on with people', but he may have lacked discretion when he told a private meeting that '100,000 Kikuyu should be put to work in a vast swill-tub'. That remark led to a parliamentary question.

Then came an incident which hardened hearts against Mau Mau terrorism in the world beyond Kenya, and roused the European settlers to march. The murder of Roger and Esme Ruck and their young son at Molo, some 100 miles north of Nairobi, on 24th January 'woke the colony', wrote Howard Williams, 'as had nothing else'. Their former farm manager, Joan Scott, described Ruck as 'a rough, tough diamond'. He was slashed to death when called out of his house by one of his staff. His pregnant wife was slashed when she ran from the house with a shotgun in response to her husband's screams. The gang then killed their six-and-a-half year old son in his bed and a Kikuyu farm boy. The Kikuyu farm-workers were in tears. Like Mrs Meikeljohn, seriously wounded in an attack two months earlier, Esme Ruck was a doctor who had treated many native families on various farms. She 'did an awful lot for the Africans', Scott said.

Two days after the Ruck murders European settlers marched on Government House. It was an event reported by the international media. A photograph of 'some of the 1,500 angry white settlers who marched against terrorism' was one of only four illustrating the events in Kenya between 1952 and 1956 included in *The Chronicle of the Twentieth Century:* they sought, it said, 'to put their case for a bigger say in running the colony and for tougher action against the anti-white Mau Mau terrorist society'. The same report referred to a settler meeting at Nakuru, when a speaker demanded the shooting of 50,000 Kikuyu, and an attack in a local paper written by Elspeth Huxley in which she compared Jomo Kenyatta with Hitler.

Feelings were running high. The march was a significant incident, which Michael Blundell recorded in detail. He suggests that, among other things, it demonstrates how unmoved Baring could be at times of tension.

Elected Members of LEGCO, including Blundell, gathered in the afternoon of Sunday 25th January in Nairobi, prior to a meeting with Baring planned for 9am the following day. These meetings were concerned with requests to Baring for greater co-ordination of government efforts through the creation of a defence council, the appointment of an overall commander for all operations against Mau Mau, both civil and military, and the direction of labour on a compulsory basis. Blundell was at his club that Sunday evening when he heard that a mass march was to be initiated by the more extreme elements in the city the following day. He telephoned two members whom he thought might be implicated in the demonstration and urged them to use their influence against any such idea.

Early on Monday morning he rang Baring to warn him of the intended march. Blundell and the elected members would be responsible for handling matters, he said, should the crowd get out of control. He urged Baring not to have any African police on duty around Government House, as this might enrage the crowd who, although armed, were only intending a demonstration. Blundell's advice was not followed.

While the elected members were meeting the governor the demonstrators arrived and their noise grew. Baring left the members to discuss among themselves the measures which the government proposed taking, by which time the noise outside was ominous. Those at the meeting could hear the national anthem being sung and shouts of 'We want the governor!' Blundell observed that when the settlers of Kenya were about to indulge in some desperate action to demonstrate their contempt for colonial office rule, they invariably prefaced it by singing the anthem in order to show their loyalty. The governor asked Blundell to come to his room, and explained that he had no intention of going outside to meet them since one day other crowds might likewise be demanding the governor's presence. The writer John Gunther who was, soon after the event, a guest of the governor, records that 'women jabbed cigarette ends into the bare arms and legs of black policemen'.

Blundell urged the crowd to return to the grass below the terrace, but he recalls that they were worked up and refused to do so. He next ordered a senior policeman to march off the police askaris, but he refused to do so until ordered by the commissioner. By now tempers, not least Blundell's, were becoming frayed, but the commissioner gave the order and the crowd, with a great cheer, fell back on the grass. A dull thumping sound now indicated that the entrance doors were being assaulted. Two African and two European members of staff wedged two heavy tables against the doors and pushed with all their might to hold the doors in place.

Standing on a chair in the window of the Cipher Room, accompanied by a number of elected members, Blundell addressed the crowd. He had had no time to prepare a speech, but before he had begun there was a crescendo of shouts and curses rising to an intense pitch. The cause of the uproar was the appearance on the balcony of the Sultana of Zanzibar, a guest at Government House, together with Lady Baring. They had come to see the cause of the commotion.

'They're there!' yelled a furious, normally respected, proprietress of a Nairobi shop. 'They've given the house over to the fucking niggers, the bloody bastards!'

When Blundell failed to make progress with his address, he passed the chair to the lawyer Humphrey Slade, another elected member. 'Slade started well,' wrote Blundell, 'but when he remonstrated with the crowd he antagonized them and they began to seethe around us once more.' Two other elected members took the chair, and Blundell made the final address. The crowd seeped away. He was congratulated by L.E. Vigar, one of his bitterest political opponents.

The fracas had lasted about an hour. Blundell returned to Baring's room, where he found him reading Thucidydes. He thanked Blundell and said 'Well done'. Sitting in a chair, Blundell began to shake all over as if with the ague. He was resuscitated with a strong whisky. Gunther, probably quoting Blundell, with whom he spent a weekend during his visit to Kenya, writes that the governor, 'with perfect composure and detachment, expressed no pronounced curiosity as to what had been going on'.

Howard Williams recalled that the government and municipal servants outnumbered the settlers in the crowd: 'Most were good humoured, if a little concerned. A few were excitable. No damage was done. At midday they left quietly, amid much good natured banter.' He concludes, 'Notwithstanding, the event had its effect.' Blundell told Baring that he had committed him to 'the direction of manpower, and an offical statement must be made at once'. Gunther observed that 'forty years of evolution in Kenya could have been destroyed that day if the African police had been obliged to fire on a white mob, or if the white mob had fired on their own kind and marched into the house'. In the event, 'Blundell single-handed kept this from happening'.

Any Government House tended to take on the character of the governor. Gunther wrote of Baring as 'one of the most aristocratic aristocrats I have ever met, and the atmosphere of Government House as almost that of eighteenth-century England, caking a little at the edges. The principal private secretary is a Howard and one of the ADCs is a Ridley. People emerged down corridors as if they had just stepped out of antique frames. They were fastidious, generous, with beautiful manners and refinement. but they made Government House resemble a stately island lost in time, drowned in forces nobody could comprehend.'

151

The 'stately island lost in time' must indeed have seemed incomprehensible and far removed from everyday life on the settlers' farms. 'The situation in the country continued to deteriorate,' wrote Blundell. The terrorist gangs had the initiative and could strike when and where they liked. The European farmers, police and administrators lacked co-ordination and he saw great danger ahead. On 3rd February he wrote to Baring very frankly about the political situation, assuring him of the Europeans' 'great confidence' in him personally but of 'a great lack of confidence in Government generally' and with 'demands for self government' from and for the European community. He cautioned that lack of leadership was tending to encourage people to turn to any movement or suggestion that would 'fill the void', which was Blundell's code for the settlers taking matters into their own hands. He had in mind irresponsible counter-terrorist police forces; vigilantes. He urged Baring 'to put a proper commandant in command' and he repeated his idea for a defence committee, concluding by recording his certainty that the political structure would not survive the strain of the Emergency unless it was made 'more flexible and more representative of unofficial opinion, and especially European opinion'. Blundell was not worried by the prospect of moderate home guard patrols such as those at Rhodora but those being formed by Europeans, whose opinion was 'that until some of the Mau Mau leaders were hanged or shot' the problem would not be solved.

During earlier years in the colony, Masai levees had been used to supplement the KAR when natives were restless. Now there was nostalgic talk of recalling them. 'Given the opportunity and if left alone I guarantee to have settled it in three months,' were the views. 'You could have raised a levy force of 10,000 men in a week, I promise you. That would have finished it', and, 'It would have been a bit cruel but it could have been done'. Post-war settler J.W. Stapleton recorded other proposals for resolution of the Mau Mau problem which were put forward by 'old-school' European settlers. Old Mrs Van Malander's personal solution was 'to line ten of them up where other Kikuyu could see them and I'd shoot them. And I'd do it every day until the crazy devils came to their senses'.

The other 'solution' was, perhaps, suggested with tongue in cheek or in the club bar. It was to 'put 'em on the game licence'. For their annual licence fee, farmers were entitled to shoot a given number of game of various species. The settler's proposition was that 'we ought to be allowed two Africans on our game licenses'. He was a reasonable man and was prepared to make concessions, so he added, 'even if it means reducing on something else – a buck or a buffalo'. The object of extending the scope of the game licence in this way was to restore the balance of nature, which the British had upset by stopping the de-population of the Africans through disease and epidemics and putting an end to tribal wars. The result of the British interference, it was suggested, was that the Africans had bred like rabbits and would, unless stopped, 'overrun the earth'.

It was widely rumoured that Mau Mau terrorist attacks were directed against settlers who treated their workers with the greatest concern and consideration. Farm manager Joan Scott's experience supported this hypothesis. She referred to the Rucks, among others, who provided excellent conditions and medical care but were among the early victims.

On a different tack, there appears to have been a strong causal link between good security on the part of the Europeans and minimal attacks by Mau Mau terrorists. European settlers who took thorough security precautions had not been attacked. A simple correlation suggested by a second generation settler (a Sandhurst-trained, former regular KAR officer) is that Mau Mau made the military appraisal of the situation 'common to soldier, terrorist, bandit, whatever: always go for a soft target'. The terrorists knew a soft target when they saw one and went for it rather than risk tackling 'the cynical old bastard living further down the road'. Mau Mau were certainly selective with their targetting. On several occasions one of the settler's relatives, (whom he equated with the cynics) had been stopped by terrorists while driving home drunk and sent on his way with a 'Sorry effendi'.

In the meantime, 'official' security forces were active. Africans generally, but political leaders such as Oginga Odinga in particular, were vulnerable to the knock on the door by the security forces. Odinga was taken from his bed and driven into the bush in the hills round Kisumu, where four armed men questioned him about what he had discussed with Nehru in India. It was said that he was hiding arms, and they demanded to be shown the hiding places. 'It was sheer intimidation.' After some hours he was taken back to his house. 'If I reported them, they said, I would be found dead.'

While urging Baring to take more positive steps to counter Mau Mau, Michael Blundell was aware that wages for the African in Nairobi were extremely low, and in February he moved, on behalf of the elected members, a motion asking for a minimum wage structure for all workers in the larger towns. Not all of the members supported the motion, but the Carpenter Committee was set up to investigate.

Then, on the 11th February, only eight days after his previous demands for the Administration to take action to counter Mau Mau, Blundell sent a minute to Baring, setting out his views at that time. The principal points were that:

- The administration had the capacity to contain but not to eliminate the Mau Mau movement.
- The root of the trouble lay in the reserves.
- Action should be taken on three locations, 'to give us experience and to test out the ideas'.
- Plans must be considered for the long term and could be costly.
- The morale of loyal Kikuyu people should be built up by promises of government support and co-operation between the government and the Kikuyu people.
- 'The best of the Kenya Regiment boys' be used as district officers 'constantly in touch with the people'.
- Mobile police patrols should be built up in each location.
- Steps should be taken to feed the influx of Kikuyu returning to the reserves from the European farms where they had been squatters.
- Finance should be made available to develop services such as education, water supplies, roads, hospitals etc.
- The 'right people' were 'amongst us', and only imagination, enthusiasm and a sense of mission were necessary to overcome the Mau Mau movement.

Nellie Grant, at almost grass roots level, wrote to her daughter on 1st March while in the throes of installing a siren on her croquet lawn along with 'a huge G-R-A-N-T in whitewashed bricks . . . to help the air-wing of KPR know where they are when fire-hunting'. Blundell, too, had his name 'spelled out in big white stones' when writer John Gunther spent time with him in 1953 'during the blistering height of the Mau Mau crisis'. Gunther wrote, 'Seldom have I met anybody with a more acute intelligence or a livelier, pithier sense of phrase.' He commented on his Yorkshireman's sense of humour, but suggested that the chief thing to say about him was that he was 'of the earth earthy . . . a born leader, packed with magnetism, bounce and defiance'. He prophesied that Blundell would 'almost certainly be Kenya's first Prime Minister – I am sure about this'.

Gunther placed 'Kenya whites' in one of three schools:

- The 'knock-em-on-the-head' school of extremist settler.
- The 'drink-a-cup-of-tea-with-them' school of a small minority of social workers and intellectuals.
- The moderate, 'lead-them-by-the-hand – but slowly' school, in which he placed Blundell.

Isolated as she was, Nellie Grant had time to read, and she was disconcerted to discover that 'in 1920, in Ireland, we had sixty thousand regular troops and fifteen thousand regular police, and they failed to cope with three thousand guerillas'. She mused that in Kenya 'we have six hundred Lancashire fusiliers, possibly two thousand KAR, police and police reserve, and about a million and a half potential guerillas'. She drew comfort from the fact that Mau Mau were not as well armed as 'the Shinners' (Sinn Fein).

The early months of 1953 saw extensive movements of Kikuyu for various, often unknown, reasons. Nellie Grant noted (12th February), a thousand lifted from Elburgon and a most odd migration of women and children going on, on their own, no one knows why. Thousands from Ol Kalou, 'and now it seems to have begun here'. In her 8th March letter she reported that Njoro station was a sad, refugee-like sight, with streams of forestry Kikuyu taking themselves off to the reserve, 'no one knows why'. It appears, however, that one reason was that the government advised some Europeans to sack Kikuyu workers. This advice probably made a bad situation worse because many farmers took the advice. Their workers who were squatting on European farms were sent back with their families to the Kikuyu reserves. These soon became overcrowded and formed a perfect recruiting ground for the illegal oath administrators.

European farmers adapted quickly to their changed living conditions. Nellie Grant was shadowed by her Dorobo bodyguard. 'They attend me to the aunt,' she reported, 'and thence to bath and bed (they do stay outside)'. She continued: 'One most important security measure is never to do anything at the same time every day, i.e. one day you have your bath before dinner, next day in the morning, next day no bath at all'.

By March Mau Mau terrorists were generally in the ascendancy. Blundell recorded that in the upper locations of the Fort Hall district the administrative machinery of government had virtually ceased to exist. The power of the gangs and the organizations of the passive wing were so complete that the area was to all intents and purposes a Mau Mau republic. Chiefs and headmen were eliminated or cowed into acceptance of the situation and, through the breakdown of the whole system of evidence upon which British law is built, justice had ceased to operate. Most people were either in hiding or had taken to the forest, and 'the whole atmosphere was sullen and resentful'.

The 'oathed and faithful' were moving to the forest, but Karari Njama was still teaching in school when, in March, he started to take a more active part in Mau Mau affairs. His home was only 300 yards from the Aberdare forest, and by this time thousands of young men passed his way *en route* to join the terrorists. He was invited by the North Tetu sub-location committee of Mau Mau to help with passing on orders, enrolling members and assisting at oathing ceremonies, intelligence gathering, fund-raising and equipping recruits. In the beginning his contribution was not great.

Then came what became known as the Lari Massacre. With the benefit of 40 years' hindsight, Blundell wrote that 'up to that time, world opinion on the whole was sympathetic to Gikuyu [sic] activities and the Mau Mau movement, which were perceived as oppressed colonial subjects fighting against imperial rule'. Furthermore, he wrote, 'the massacre not only alienated international support for Mau Mau, which began to be seen as a savage atavistic tribal affair rather than a genuine and widely supported nationalist movement, but also set in motion a resistance movement by Christian Gikuyu to the methods of Mau Mau which later grew into the Home Guard or Loyalist organisations'.

He emphasized that the Christian Gikuyu had the same ideas as the terrorist Mau Mau leaders, namely the independence of the Kikuyu people, and hence Kenya, from colonial rule, but felt that this could best be achieved by evolutionary and constitutional means rather than by revolution or terrorism.

Nor, when looking for causes of the massacre, should one ignore the economic changes which had come about in post-war Kenya, which had by no means bypassed the Africans. 'If,' wrote Crowder, 'capital had engineered growth, growth had engineered change, so that it was not surprising that in Kenya the process of economic development had produced not only an African élite but also an African property owning class, primarily among the Kikuyu.' The Kikuyu were, he concludes, 'divided into landed and landless, with a land-owning gentry dominant within the society'.

In the 'have and have not' society of Lari, the 'loyal' Chief Luka Kahangaria and his followers were the 'haves', and the massacre was directed against him. He had prospered under the British rule to the extent that he owned a thousand acres of land and had ten wives. Mau Mau leader Kahinga Wachanga refers to Luka as a government 'stooge' who was given land at Lari 'as a reward for his treachery', which involved selling his people to the government when many of them were removed to Olenguruone. (That place name crops up again.) Wachanga was not alone in his opinion of the 'haves' treatment of the 'have nots'. There appears to be,' wrote Furedi, 'no doubt that, the loyalist camp at Lari in Kiambu had an odious reputation for treating the refugees from the Rift Valley with cruelty and disdain. Furthermore, Luka and his kin had sold land for office. Increasingly most people living around Lari 'had come to look upon Luka and his family as the root and symbol of all their troubles'.

The Lari operation was carefully planned and executed. Having set out to destroy Luka, the militant leaders of the area met for four days preparing plans. It was decided to kill all the chiefs, headmen and home guards in the area on the night of 26th March. Moreover, anyone who might be able to give evidence in court afterwards would also have to be killed. The operation was planned to synchronize with the attack on the Naivasha police station, planned independently by the Naivasha secret committee. Luka had been summoned to appear before the local terrorist committee to answer charges of collaboration with Europeans, but he refused to attend.

After the massacre, Luka's fourth and sixth wives, Rachel Wanjiru and Muthoni, gave interviews to the *East African Standard*, from which the following account of events leading to the massacre is drawn. They revealed that during the afternoon of 26th March, 3,000 'freedom fighters' [Wanjiru's words] met in the forest and recited the oath of unity. Facing Mount Kenya, they swore to destroy those people who conducted the case of Jomo Kenyatta, who assisted the white man to hunt the freedom fighters and who sold their lands. All were to be destroyed 'messily', but the last mentioned group were to be castrated and have their eyes gouged out, and they were to be kept alive for seven days and nights, when their hands and legs were to be cut off and their blood drunk before they were beheaded.

At 3pm the terrorists took up their positions in the bush around Githithirioni. Most were neighbours of Luka, his family and his servants. For no known reason the loyalists felt tired and went to sleep earlier than usual, recalled Rachel Wanjiru. At approximately 10.30pm an area of approximately four by seven kilometres was surrounded, and the attackers were armed with pangas, swords, clubs and one home-made gun. The huts known to be occupied by men were bound with cable and barbed wire and the doors secured to prevent the occupants escaping. Firewood and dry grass were piled on and around the buildings. At 11.00pm petrol or paraffin was poured on and ignited. Terrorists took up positions to hack any who escaped from the buildings.

Luka was with his youngest wife when he was 'arrested' by the terrorists at approximately 11.45pm. They were half-dressed when four of Luka's other wives (two of them later the subjects of the *Standard* interviews), were taken to witness his murder. Rachel Wanjiru recorded that a number of men with frightening shaggy beards and dreadlocks slowly cut his private parts and gouged out his eyes with swords. When Muthoni, Luka's sixth wife, attempted to intervene the terrorists held her down and cut off her hand at the wrist. They continued to slowly behead Luka and when complete, the head was crushed with a hammer on a stone, before his body was dismembered. They then turned on the youngest wife and cut her breasts and 'reduced her to nothingness' too. Some 200 huts were fired and more than 100 villagers killed. The Luka wives escaped and ran off into the night. One was shot and a small child carried by another was beheaded with a sword. 'He was the last of my six children to die that night,' said his mother.

John Cumber witnessed the aftermath. Through the intelligence network he had warnings that his area, Kiambu, had been singled out by Mau Mau for punishment as the villagers had been 'too loyal to the Brits', and he first heard about a possible Mau Mau attack on the 18th

March. He called a meeting immediately and warned chiefs, headmen, groups of home guard, influential farmers, both European and African, that it might happen. A KAR unit had recently been withdrawn from his area, so he thought an attack might be made the following night. He saw flames spreading, and later it was estimated that some 800 to 1,000 terrorists took part. They had put a rope around some of the doors to prevent them being opened, and set light to the thatched roofs of the rondavel huts. When the poor occupants were half suffocated and tried to beat their way out of the little windows and door, they were hacked down or shot. They sent for the KAR, but they couldn't arrive in time. The Mau Mau disappeared but they met the Kenya police with two Bren guns guarding the road and went back into the forest. The police and the home guard caused a lot of casualties.

Oliver Lyttelton, the secretary of state, was visiting Kenya at the time, and he arrived on the scene in the early hours of the 27th to witness the mayhem of the night – hut after hut burned to the ground, corpses lying within those huts burnt to death.

Sid Moscoff, an NCO in the Kenya Regiment, arrived in the morning and was confronted with lorry loads of chopped-up women and children. He would 'never forget . . . the look of horror on the faces of our Wakamba askari who suddenly realised what Mau Mau was all about . . . when they saw the mutilated bodies of kids'. They met some loyalists who had captured a dozen or so Mau Mau suspects who were piled into a lorry to take back to Uplands police station. On the way they were confronted by more loyalists demanding the prisoners. 'Suddenly out of nowhere a car appeared, driven by a Catholic missionary who pleaded in the name of the Almighty that justice be done.' Moscoff pointed his Patchett (machine gun) at the loyalists over the cab of the truck and ordered the driver to drive through them while his prisoners lay flat on the floor of the truck, shivering with fear. 'I shall never forget the look of disgust on the faces of the loyalists and later the loss of respect by my Wakamba askaris.'

Mau Mau leader Karari Njama refers to the massacre as 'successful', and writes that he learned from friends who witnessed it that 'in the morning the government killed ten times as many persons as the ones who had been killed and set more houses on fire. It was then claimed that the whole action had been committed by

Mau Mau'. And Kahinga Wachanga claims that only white soldiers were sent to Lari, where they killed many of the people and animals and gathered the bodies and 'claimed that the atrocities had been committed by Mau Mau'.

There appears to be no evidence from either African or European writers sympathetic to the Africans' cause which supports Njama's and Wachanga's allegations of government forces killing Africans in order to discredit Mau Mau. In general, students of all colours agree with Berman and Lonsdale (and Blundell) that Lari was the outcome of a 'specific land dispute, a tragedy not separate from Mau Mau, which hardened the Kikuyu Guard to fight', and after which Mau Mau 'seems to have been determined that such an atrocity should not recur'.

Whatever European opinion may have been on the Lari Massacre, there was a feeling of respect amounting to admiration for the Mau Mau attack on the police station at Naivasha, which synchronized with the Lari attack. No European officers were on duty, and there were gaps in the barbed wire. Only five or six African police were awake, and their weapons were locked in the armoury 300 yards away. The terrorists shot the sentry in the tower, killed another and others were taken prisoner.

In his 29th March letter Seys referred to the Mau Mau attack on the 'police armoury at Naivasha [which] had the dash and precision of a commando raid in the last war, and achieved spectacular success. It begins to look as though the bandits are becoming better armed and better trained in the acts of hit-and-run warfare'. Williams shared Seys respect for 'a first-class raid, in the very jaws of the enemy. Had we but done it'.

Mau Mau forest leader Kahinga Wachanga describes the Naivasha raid as perhaps the most important of 1953 because it provided weapons which were used in later raids. His account provides a useful starting point. Mbaria Kaniu and Kihara Kagumu led 75 fighters armed with .303 rifles, one shot gun, one pistol, swords and pangas. They reached Naivasha at 10pm, went to the entrance of the station and shot the guard. Each of the other soldiers fired a single bullet into the station, following 'the Mau Mau regulations of using only one bullet unless ordered to use more'. They were, he wrote, under orders not to kill civilians unless it was necessary for their own safety. They released more than 500 men, women and children who were in detention, and raided the armoury. One Mau Mau fighter was killed by a bullet. The raiding party, together with some of the released Kikuyu and a cache of stolen weapons, marched some 30 miles to the Aberdares. They stole 30 head of cattle from a European farm on the way.

Karari Njama's account of the attack agrees with Wachanga's, although on other matters they often differ profoundly. He records that the government's report of the number of weapons stolen was 47 precision weapons and 3,780 rounds of ammunition. The Mau Mau claim to have stolen 100 precision weapons, while another account of the raid refers to 18 sub-machine guns, 29 rifles and a 'truck-load of ammunition' being taken. Njama recounts the story of a mute named Mungai who had recently started speaking. 'His name was used, spreading propaganda that he was God's prophet and had led the raid with supernatural powers – that his little Kikuyu knife turned all the bullets into water. After the raid he disappeared but became a legend.'

The raids on Lari and on Naivasha police station appear to have been independent of each other and organized by different Mau Mau groups. Kahinga Wachanga wrote of a meeting he had with Mbaria Kaniu, who was involved in the Naivasha raid 'first hand', and Wachanga's editor wrote that as far as Kahinga knew 'there was no connection between these two raids. That they both happened on the same night was a coincidence'. Much criticism fell on the commissioner of police, M.S. O'Rorke, who, as Blundell wrote, 'was coping as best he could with an almost impossible situation'.

All was by no means well with the police. Even the European farming community considered them heavy-handed with the Africans. Joan Scott suggests where the government went wrong: 'They recruited temporary policemen from England. They were out-of-work people, rough, tough people who came out and they were quite capable of behaving badly. They didn't mind if they shot people or didn't. They were unpleasant, some of them. They didn't understand. You've got to have lived in Africa to understand Africans at all.'

Friction was also caused between the security forces and European settlers when the latter's staff were detained under suspicion of assisting terrorists. On more than one occasion the Pickering farm's female workers were arrested under suspicion of feeding Mau Mau. The Pickerings considered the arrests as 'patently absurd', and fought for their release, but it took the police a month in which to satisfy themselves that the two girls were innocent.

Blundell and others were aware of the problems and concerned over the increasing signs of indiscipline among the police and the police reservists. These sometimes led to illegal actions against Kikuyu who had been arrested for suspected complicity in Mau Mau. As a result of their representations Maj Gen C.C. Fowkes was appointed as inspector general of the Kenya police reserve, with a view to restoring discipline and co-ordinating its activities more closely with the regular police force. An immediate improvement did come about, but the situation in the country continued to deteriorate. The terrorist gangs had the initiative and could strike when and where they liked. The farmers in the country districts organized patrols and the general defence of individual homesteads within the framework of the Kenya police reserve, but co-ordination with the regular police was poor. The police themselves were far too few in numbers, and a firm general direction of all the forces of government had not been evolved. The farmers were under constant strain, and this was increased by their night patrols and efforts to protect their families and homes during the hours of darkness.

Rhodora, situated on the edge of Menengai, was now scheduled, wrote Seys in March, as a 'dangerous area' but not as 'very dangerous'. Seys, who in October 1952 had praised the Kenyan government's firm action to stamp out the Mau Mau fire before it became a conflagration, now wrote of the 'imcompetent and lily-livered administration'. In Nairobi that April there were notices on view: 'What, no Governor?'

Europeans were, by now, generally suspicious of their Kikuyu workers. In a letter to England (29th March) Seys wrote of a young and very nice boy . . . born and bred on the farm who had no stake in the Reserve, but all the same we watch him closely and so do the other houseboys of the other tribes. So far I think he is loyal but . . .'

By the end of March the massacre at Lari and the successful attack on Naivasha police station had demonstrated that, despite the detention of Jomo Kenyatta and other African leaders who would shortly be sentenced to long periods of imprisonment, Mau Mau was both ruthless and well organized. The morale of European settlers in the most affected area was low, as they awaited attacks and grew increasingly dissatisfied with the management of affairs by government at Westminster and in Kenya.

8

Civil War

'It is, of course, a civil war.' (Nellie Grant)

The highly successful raid on Naivasha police station and the massacre at Lari had established that Mau Mau was both an efficient and a ruthless a body to be reckoned with. Until then the government and military forces had been largely reacting to Mau Mau pressures. Now British troops were put in forest and reserve. The Europeans' frustration with the government led to some to acts of violence as they saw their former way of life and the fruits of their labours in jeopardy. But this was a civil war and involved everyone, not only armies.

The 'best' or 'worst' is largely a matter of perspective. As far as the women were concerned, the Mau Mau civil war demonstrated that the capacity to organize resistance and to fight was not the sole prerogative of Europeans such as Joan Scott. Kikuyu women showed a remarkable capacity to demonstrate their respective strengths as both Christians and tribal loyalists. Civil wars are notoriously divisive, and this was no exception.

Canon Bewes, by now well re-established in Kenya, spoke of 'the wonderful potential of Kikuyu girls', who had been among the bravest to make a stand for their Christian faith. Carey Francis was impressed by their bravery: he referred to poor men and women, and boys and girls, for whom Christ came first and who provided 'the core of resistance to the new faith' – by which he meant Mau Mau. Before these days of being put to the test, he said, he had 'never believed that there were African Christians of their quality'.

On the other hand, when is a terrorist a freedom fighter? The 'wonderful potential' of Kikuyu women was demonstrated in the ranks of Mau Mau women who participated in the full spectrum of the organization's violent activities, serving as recruiters, organizers, spies, soldiers and prisoners of war. To the surprise of the British administrators, women not only took Mau Mau oaths but administered them, too. This was a break with Kikuyu custom, but women leaders undoubtedly gave the oath to mixed groups of men, women and children, and some districts had a women's central committee responsible for arranging safe places and smuggling supplies. One woman was chosen to be responsible for the co-ordination of women's activities to that end. They combined these clandestine activities with their day-to-day work, so that a nurse working in a hospital would pass on medicine to Mau Mau. Other women took provisions to them in the forest, or would cook and/or carry, usually at night: during the daytime they would probably be working on terracing or similar activities, supervised by the Kikuyu home guard.

The successful provision of succour to the terrorists was an activity the government sought to control. It was decided that the forest sheltering the terrorists had to be separated from the land which provided the resources they needed for their survival. Loyal Africans (often difficult to identify with certainty) must be protected from terrorists, and the forest needed to be provided with a cordon sanitaire. This was difficult to provide, as Kikuyu families traditionally lived in defensible, largely self-sufficient homesteads apart from each other. During the early days of the Emergency, district officers would make practically daily visits to areas where there had been murders in the night, food had been given to Mau Mau gangs or oaths had been taken, but people were too frightened to speak out for fear of vengeance.

The counter-measure adopted was 'villagization', the creation of defensible stockades with barbed wire fences, ditches, drawbridges and watch-towers in which the villagers would be safe from Mau Mau attack and infiltration. Both the Administration and the Kikuyu were initially opposed to the principle of fortified villages, but Baring nevertheless issued a directive for their creation. Once they were established the villagers often formed a local home guard. 'In a few weeks,' wrote Blundell, 'the Nyeri landscape was marked out with straight regimented rows of little houses, and I would not have believed that such a change could have taken place in so short a time.'

The redundant homesteads were burned when the villages were complete. Karari Njama, school teacher cum Mau Mau leader, saw puffs of smoke all along the forest boundary, and these quickly spread. All the houses between one and three miles from the forest boundary had been burned. Their owners were told they would be shot on sight if they entered the sanitized strip. A battlefield had been created. The Kikuyu hated going into villages, because it was contrary to their custom, but it was a great relief, once inside, to know that there wasn't someone hammering on the door every night demanding food or money – or else! From the government's standpoint, villagization was a success. An immediate improvement followed, and this was increased still further when guarded stores with paddocks enabled the Administration to control food supplies and animals.

The 'one-mile strip' was conceived at much the same time as villagization because the Mau Mau gangs up in the forest looked on the Embu and Meru, their immediate neighbours, as easy pickings for their foraging activities. 'One-mile' was an exaggeration, because the strip varied in width depending on the rocky outcrops, but now any Mau Mau gang intent on raiding standing crops or cattle had to cross an open no-man's land before he could get there. This made it much easier for the security forces to defend. In one district where soil conditions made it practical a wide trench was dug, and anyone seen in the strip could be shot.

In the front line, as it were, the first close contact Nellie Grant had with Mau Mau occurred in April, not long after the Lari massacre. A local reserve policeman 'flushed ten armed chaps, ordered them to halt; they didn't, so he shot one dead; the others went off.' Police patrols were out the next day hunting them, and they killed one. Mau Mau activity continued through April. Grant heard (18th April) that a gang of 35 had been liquidated nearby, but her workers got 'terrifically jittery' when the Mau Mau murdered four of their number. In May they had another 'do' during which seven terrorists were killed and 'five captured out of fourteen'. But some Kikuyu guards were killed too, and 'Pip Beverley, KPR, was shot in the mouth and lung'. It was by no means a one-sided battle: sometimes more loyal Kikuyu than terrorists were killed.

During April, troops from several British 'county' regiments arrived in the colony, and by the end of the month there were eight-and-a-half regular battalions of infantry, the first African Independent Armoured Car Squadron, the 156th Heavy Anti-Aircraft Battery and the Kenya Regiment. Their initial tasks were acclimatization and training, 'bolstering the morale and fortifications of the police and . . . visiting farms for the sake of reassurance'. Much of the 'forest' fighting was to be in the Aberdare Mountains, also called Nyandarua. Karari Njama, as a Mau Mau leader, knew the area intimately and describes the terrain vividly. From its southern reaches in the Kiambu District to Nderagwa near Thomson's Falls it is some 120 miles long and 50 miles wide. It rises about 1,000ft. 'Extremely thick,' it is 'the real home of the wild game'. One could hardly see beyond ten yards, 'and in parts the sun never shines'. The coniferous 'black' forest gave way as one climbed to the bamboo forest, which in turn levelled out to the moorlands, where clouds were often close to the ground which, combined with strong winds, made it damp and cold. During the nights, all the dew froze to ice.

For British troops, acclimatization was extremely difficult. The area was, to say the least, inhospitable. Certainly, there was no shortage of water. Njama writes that the mountain rivers and streams were extremely cold, and freezing to death or drowning was a danger, particularly when one of the larger rivers had to be crossed during the flooding season. To this must be added the constant risk of being charged by rhinos, elephants and buffaloes. Contrary to popular European belief, many Africans had little or no experience of living in the forest, and for British troops it was an entirely new experience which they found frightening. Those troops who had served in Malaysia were less intimidated, as the terrains had much in common.

Nevertheless, military patrolling began when the troops were as acclimatized as possible in the time available. African trackers led them, and officers and NCOs of the Kenya Regiment provided general guidance and handled interrogation of the natives. Air support was provided by a special unit of the Kenya police reserve. The forested parts of the Aberdares and Mount Kenya were declared prohibited areas 'where troops had the right to open fire on sight'. Nearly all the Highlands was declared a special area, where troops had the right to halt and question, to open fire if a challenge were defied and to open fire on sight during the hours of curfew'. The altitude made men breathless, and wild animals gave cause for fear.

With many of the men serving in the Kenya Regiment or the Kenya police reserve, European women played a major part in running farms and defending them if needs must. On the one Joan Scott managed they attempted to isolate their workforce from infiltration by Mau Mau oath commissioners and terrorists. They had their own brand of villagization on the farm. Before the Mau Mau, the Kikuyu workers had lived all over the farm in little huts, but Scott moved them all into one camp. They built a watchtower in which the loyal home guard lived. Everybody was provided with a four-gallon paraffin can and a stick: they were told to beat it if they got attacked and that the Europeans would come to the rescue.

Scott's experiences caught the imagination of the British and Kenyan press in April. More than one report referred to her as the 'tally-ho' woman because, the *Daily Express* reported, she 'blew a horn as a clarion call and rallied a party of Africans armed with pangas to beat off thirty terrorists' during the second attack on the farm she managed. An abbreviated account of the attack, which she wrote in 1969 at the request of her former employer's son, provides a useful description of a Mau Mau attack from the perspective of Scott and Mrs Oulton, the wife of her employer, who was away at the time. They were woken at approximately 3am to hear the most deafening noise going on. Shots were ringing out, a bugle was playing military calls and all the boys were beating the petrol debbis (cans). She and Mrs Oulton were the only Europeans in the house. Scott discovered that the phone wires to Nanyuki had been cut, but the farm wires were intact and one of her African workers phoned to say that the camp was full of Mau Mau and that they were shooting everybody. The two women had their own pistols and her employer's 'brute' of a Mauser. They let off rockets in an attempt to alert a nearby military camp, and had a frightening moment leaving the house because they didn't know whether the gang was waiting outside. Together with the house staff they left by truck for the workers' camp, which had been shot at, to discover that two had been kidnapped. One rose to be a Mau Mau brigadier and the other made his way back to the farm after about a month. The army arrived quickly, having seen their rockets.

On 20th April, the day the *Daily Express* published its account of Joan Scott's battle with Mau Mau terrorists, Maj Gen Hinde formally issued a directive establishing the home guard as the Kikuyu Guard and defining its tasks in the fight against Mau Mau as: 'In co-operation with the other forces of law and order, so to deny to Mau Mau the Kikuyu reserves that they become in due course a secure base from which our regular forces be withdrawn to hunt down Mau Mau in the forests and mountains and to provide information of Mau Mau activities and plans.'

Following the murders of settlers in the early months of 1953 a series of meetings was called in various locations at which Blundell was invited to speak. He found European settlers concerned by the authorities' apparent inability to govern, and by the influence of the international press. The murders of their friends and neighbours had left them with a deep sense of insecurity and shock, and in some cases with brutal memories of hideously mutilated bodies. It was difficult to convince the crowds that the European members of LEGCO were trying to persuade the government to act. Already there were signs of splinter movements spreading, dissipating their energies. Extreme and fierce speeches were made, and there was always the danger of the crowd being incited to unconstitutional and independent action of its own. This was inevitably covered by the press overseas, presenting an unfavourable image of the European farmer on the international stage. At Nakuru, there was a demand for the immediate shooting of 50,000 Kikuyu until they were literally killed into submission. This demand hit the international press. Throughout these days there was extraordinary situation in which a crowd would demand the most drastic action against the Kikuyu as an impersonal whole, followed by individual members of the crowd going to great lengths to protect from violence and abuse those Kikuyu whom they knew personally. On one occasion when Blundell pointed out the contradiction of the settler's demands 'the anger and tension dissolved in gales of laughter'.

At the same time the editorial in the East African Women's League's bulletin for May noted how much darker it must seem to the loyal Africans 'for whom all is now obscured by fear; how greatly must they now need our compassion and our help'.

The conduct of the fighting and the actions of the British forces were reported in the local and European press, and led to considerable controversy. Military historian Blaxland records that the 'first blood' was drawn by the Devons. 'On May 11th,' he wrote, 'two of their patrols simultaneously claimed the £5 offered by the commanding officer for the first kill.' He admitted that none of the previous experiences of the British battalions could rival it 'for the sheer exhilaration it afforded'. The men lived rough and they lived hard but, in Brigadier Tweedie's words, 'the keenness was tremendous. In spite of the very isolated conditions and lack of things that everyone believed young soldiers must have, they were entirely happy'.

Keenness was sustained by encouraging competition between battalions and companies in the number of Mau Mau killed. As

Blaxland puts it, 'Since they had come there to kill Mau Mau, this seemed a reasonable enough thing to do.' Colonel Campbell states that the Kenya Regiment did not keep a tally of Mau Mau 'kills', but this does not accord with the recollections of some members of the KR who served for the whole period of the Emergency and beyond. We have not heard the last of scoring 'kills' and bounty payments.

Some of the European settlers appear to have been less than convinced that the British troops were sufficiently militant in their approach to Mau Mau. The Seys letter home (29th March), refers to 'the rank and file, and some of the officers, too, being generally left-wing and pro-native in their attitude'. But, it adds, without being specific as to the nature of the attitude, 'we have heard tales of serious misconduct on the part of the troops towards the Africans'.

In spite of the colony being at war with itself, a royal celebration was recognised in Nairobi. The coronation of Queen Elizabeth II produced a parade which was reported in the *East African Standard* on 3rd June. It was difficult to regard it as anything other than a joyous occasion. The report included the scene in the African reserve at Kiambu, where thousands of Kikuyu crowded the boma from early morning with Kikuyu police, special police, guards and military, as askaris mingled freely with the happy flag-waving throng. There was dancing in front of the district commissioner's office and a parade of floats, many designed by Africans. At least 3,000 Africans took part in processions led by the Limuru Catholic Mission, followed by Kikuyu warriors and dancers with spears, sticks or musical instruments, and with Union Jacks everywhere. It went on until late afternoon, while at Fort Hall and other reserves there were smaller celebrations.

The newspaper reports accord with Nellie Grant's experiences of the day. She refers to the Nairobi parade outside the cathedral. There were representatives from the navy, county regiments and KAR, and New Zealand Air Force planes screamed past. 'About ten very dirty and weary Kenya Regiment lads quite rightly got all the cheering there was,' wrote Grant. She gave away prizes at the Egerton College African sports 'with a KPR sten-gun in the small of [my] back'. She observed that 'European manners were shocking'. She 'saw someone snatch a chair away from under an African . . . and the racial segregation was terrific'.

This was a time of bluff and double bluff, when no one was sure who was on whose side. Karari Njama estimated that only five of approximately 50 members of the local Kikuyu home guard had not taken the Mau Mau oath in the first half of 1953. He had played a cat-and-mouse game with the home guard, during which he hid terrorists in the school building. On at least one occasion they came close to detection by the headman, Chief Muhoya. Skirmishes increased in intensity and frequency, with Njama's school never far away. There was a raid on the Gatumbiro home guard post, during which three members were killed and 17 others were burnt to death inside the post. There were, says Njama, no casualties on the side of Mau Mau. In contrast, the Mau Mau raid on the Kariaini headquarters resulted in Mau Mau losses.

Njama's double life was coming to an end. He had been observed by a Mau Mau collaborator tending the wounds of the supervisor of the Church of Scotland mission school, and he received a written warning from Mau Mau AB court no. 7 that he could not serve two masters. The letter concluded, 'We advise you to leave [his job as a Government teacher] and join us, or else you will find yourself in trouble.' Shortly after that warning he took all the pupils and teachers to a funeral of a member of the home guard who had been killed by Mau Mau, and he received a second strong warning that if he did not resign from teaching they would take it for granted that he wholly supported the government and they would regard him as an enemy and not hesitate to kill him. The letter was signed by Dedan Kimathi.

Njama collected the remainder of the school fees (300s.) and took them to the education officer on 30th May. He had calculated that Mau Mau was winning and that 'Kenya was ripe for independence'. Early in June he left for the forest, where his intention was to record the Kenyan revolution. He wrote of his transition from Mau Mau collaborator to terrorist in the forest without enthusiasm for the change: 'I had no alternative but to go.' He asked that his wife be shown a piece of land which she could cultivate and get food during his absence, and without any preparation he tied up his blankets and some clothing, bid his wife and five-month-old daughter goodbye and set off, 'leaving my bicycle to Johnson Ndungu'.

By May, Mau Mau units recognized the advantage of liaison with others, while at the same time exercising their own initiative regarding the targets they selected within their designated area. Kahinga Wachanga held a meeting with three other leaders at Mathioya on 25th May when Stanley Mathenge told of a raid he was planning to make on home guard posts requiring about 600 soldiers. He sought assistance, particularly, with reliable men and weapons. He was given rifles, a machine gun, pistols, grenades, swords and bugles – they usually went into battle with a bugle call.

The askaris were in their element. The murder of Europeans in their homes and on their farms, the massacre at Lari and numerous killings of 'loyal' Africans on farms and in the reserves all created a fighting climate for both European and askari, but the troops varied in their dedication to the cause. By June the professional European soldiers and the few national servicemen were finding their feet, but British military units varied significantly and their origins determined their competence and motivation. The most committed were undoubtedly the Kenya Regiment. Njama contrasted the KR's performance with that of the British county regiments. The former, as the sons of settlers, showed no mercy and wanted to kill, while the Devons wanted to capture.

The intensive training which members of the Kenya Regiment had undergone paid off. The regiment provided a tough operational company of young men who had complete conviction in the rightness of their cause. Masai elders and warriors considered that it was the only military unit which could equal their own powers of marching long distances and living rough.

They were an odd bunch. Sid Moscoff, a young white farmer and Kenya Regiment volunteer to whom reference was made in connection with the aftermath of the Lari massacre, suggests that enlisting in the regiment was akin to joining a club of which they were members by birth and education. He refers to the light-hearted description of the white farmers as chaps 'Kenya born, Kenya bred, strong in the arm, weak in the head', but Brigadier Cornah, 70th East Africa Brigade, likened their spirit to that of RAF pilots in Britain during the Second World War. The regiment's commandant, Colonel Campbell, was, as a regular British army officer, in no doubt as to its role: 'Our sole aim was to locate and kill terrorists. British battalions did not have the same dedication to killing the enemy as the Kenya boys.'

Next to the Kenya Regiment in commitment and experience of Africa were the King's Africa Rifles, whose battalions were widespread. Most KAR officers held regular commissions in British guards or county regiments. The majority developed an affection for the

African non-commissioned officers and other ranks. Ian Ferguson, from the Scots Guards, had high regard for his askaris, who were loyal and very good in their own terrain, although they varied from tribe to tribe. By the time his battalion was involved in Kenya the Kikuyu were regarded as no longer trustworthy, because the Mau Mau were all Kikuyu and their families might come under pressure and make loyal service impossible. In action Ferguson thought of his askaris as a pack of foxhounds. They hated the Kikuyu, which was 'a very disliked tribe', so the majority were delighted to have a go at them. 'They treated the chase as if they were chasing an animal.'

George Coles, who had served in the Second World War with African troops, arrived in Kenya with the Uganda Battalion of the KAR. He was told their job was to round up Mau Mau terrorists and 'Mau Mau and Kikuyu were synonymous really'. Cole's askaris had absolutely no sympathy for the Kikuyu. His appraisal echoes Ferugson's: they liked hunting, and they went to hunt Kikuyu as they went out to hunt an animal.

Ugandan askaris were kept apart from the Kikuyu civilians, and had their own, quite separate, encampments. The battalion included in its ranks Sgt Idi Amin, who later became president of Uganda. It was over-promotion, Coles felt, that led to his downfall. 'He would tear ahead and catch them rather than kill them. He was an amazing patrol commander. I don't know how he killed them.' Amin was not well educated. He was sent off to see if he could pass the exams to become a warrant officer, 'but he was so thick he couldn't get it into him, and he didn't do very well'. He would, suggests Coles, have made a fine sergeant major, but 'that was his limit'.

In addition to experienced officers such as Ferguson and Cole, the KAR was recruiting newly commissioned officers, including a few national servicemen. Some were there from county regiments, while some came 'looking for a bit of adventure' and one preferred it to a posting with his regiment to Germany. They expressed surprise at the primitive nature of most Kenyan towns (Nanyuki had hitching rails in the main streets) and the high level of responsibility they were given when carrying out their duties.

DO John Cumber, with the benefit of his Second World War military experience, was involved in Operation Schemozzle. This was primarily a military operation, but it was also 'a test of the willingness of the Meru people, of the men and women (some with children in arms), to go into the forest on a carefully organized basis, self-contained, with food and bedding for the night and various coloured arm-bands to distinguish them in companies. They would march by the compass in strength, and when they met the smaller enemy numbers the latter would run away from them, only to run into the arms of a company coming the other way. The first of these Schemozzle operations accounted for something like thirty dead Mau Mau in various areas, more wounded. Others followed. It virtually put paid to the use of the forest in Meru by Mau Mau gangs for fodder-raiding and terrorist activities and turning the heat on the Meru people.'

Nellie Grant described an operation as 'just like a buffalo hunt, or even more a grouse drive, with beaters advancing in line and whacking the bushes . . . It's an extraordinary sort of war – vast quantities of troops with their red-tabbed generals and armoured cars, lorries and jeeps, huge camps, engineers, aircraft, modern guns and heaven knows what, ranged against gangs of thugs armed with pangas or home-made rifles . . . It makes fools of us really . . . Later we heard the result of "our" battle. The gang was 13 strong and of those 11 were killed and two captured.'

Incidents which endorse the relative popularity of the British regiments in Africans' eyes are mentioned in Oliver Lyttelton's memoirs. As colonial secretary he witnessed a sweep by two battalions from county regiments, who later drove back to their Kikuyu owners cattle that had strayed. 'They helped to mend the fences, they played with the children, milked the cows and swore genially at everyone.' Driving through a village with the commander-in-chief 'in full fig . . . and flying the Union Jack from the forepeak', they were greeted by the 'whole population . . . chattering and smiling and waving their hands . . . the children greeted us with delighted cries of 'Fuck off!', a term of obviously military origin which they clearly thought to be one of endearment or a variant of cheerio.'

Would that all relationships between military and African were as sweet as Lyttelton described. On the 11th June, a few days after Coronation Day, an incident during one sweep led to the court martial of Acting Major G.S.L. Griffiths KAR. A summary of the evidence records that the sweep was across a patch of forest onto a narrow road where askaris were posted at 'stops'. At the court martial Co Sgt-Maj Llewellyn stated that Griffiths had told them, 'You can shoot who you like if they are black. We are out to raise our score of kills to fifty.'

Two askaris held up three African civilians on the road. Griffiths arrived in a jeep in which a Bren gun was mounted. He was angry and swore. He said to the askaris, 'Why have you not killed them?' He called for and examined the three civilians passes, and dismissed an old man who ran away. Then he handed back the passes to the other two Africans and said, 'Go forward, stop'. They did – they were going to work in the forest. Griffiths shot them at ten paces range with his Bren gun and they lay screaming.

Capt R.E. Joy, who was driving the jeep, gave evidence that he saw Griffiths shoot the men. CSM Llewellyn arrived and heard Griffiths say, 'Let them scream – they killed my horse and it screamed more than that.' (It was general knowledge that his horse had been killed by Mau Mau terrorists, who forced a stick up its rectum and through its gut.) Llewellyn stopped the traffic and Griffiths came back. One African was dead and Griffiths ordered the CSM to kill the other. He refused. Griffiths then shot the man in the head with a revolver and he died. CSM Llewellyn stopped a civilian lorry, and the bodies were put in it. The CSM said, 'Take them to the police station,' and Griffiths added, 'Tell them to take them to the police station with the compliments of Major Griffiths.'

Relatives identified the bodies at the police station. There was no post-mortem. Llewellyn did not, himself, see Griffiths shoot the wounded man, but the evidence was that he saw him get out of the jeep, pull out his pistol and walk to the back of the jeep where the African was lying, 'groaning and screaming'. Llewellyn heard two shots, after which 'there was complete silence'. KAR Pte Kiptarius Mpyal and other soldiers saw the shooting and gave evidence which supported Llewellyn's, as did that given by Capt Joy. He stated that Griffiths had told the Africans to go and shoot them in the back with bursts from the Bren gun. They were 'walking at normal pace' when shot. Griffiths, who later asked Joy not to mention the incident to anyone, gave evidence that the Africans 'went off at a shambling trot towards the right where there was a corner', that he called to them to stop and when they did not do so he opened fire'. He admitted shooting the wounded man, 'who was obviously in very great pain', with his pistol. It was to be some months before more was heard of this incident.

In March, Rhodora had been listed by the Administration as being in a 'dangerous' but not 'very dangerous' area. At 7am one morning in June one of the Rhodora night guards reported to the Seys that three of their Kikuyu house staff had, the previous night, left their huts at 11pm and returned at 2.30am. Seys' letter (28th June) read: 'I had no option but to take all three to the police for questioning. It is unfortunate that there was only the evidence of the one guard against them, but we cannot afford to take risks, and I therefore said that even if the police can get nothing out of them, I do not want them back and they must be repatriated to their reserves'. This must be typical of many such incidents which led to massive overcrowding in the reserves.

By now teacher Njama had new and very different responsibilities as 'Mau Mau Staff Officer Karari Njama'. He reports June as the month when the Kenya Regiment arrived in the reserves and the brutality of shooting civilians in cold blood increased. He wrote that in his location four suspects, whom he names, 'were called out of their homes, taken to Kamoko home guard centre where they were badly beaten [it being] alleged that they had helped Mau Mau with food. Each was then taken out of the camp in turn and shot'.

There was another game of musical chairs in Government House. Gen Sir George Erskine arrived in Nairobi on 7th June to take up the appointment of commander-in-chief of the upgraded East African Command. He had full control over all security forces and was to be accorded such help as he needed by the governor, who remained in administrative control of the colony. Erskine's arrival led to a series of staff changes. Gen Cameron became Erskine's deputy with special responsibility for territories outside the emergency area. Gen Hinde was moved from police to army headquarters, carrying out the same duties as before but as deputy director of operations. He was field commander, thus freeing Erskine for political problems. Sir Frederick Crawford's appointment as deputy governor coincided with that of Gen Erskine and took a great deal of the day-to-day load off Governor Baring's shoulders.

Erskine's appointment provided a delicate compromise. He had sought overall command of military and civil machines, but the British government did not wish to alter the position of the governor, to whom the armed forces were ultimately responsible. The compromise was that Erskine had a letter allowing him, with the full authority of the government, to take over the civil as well as the military administration of Kenya if at any time he deemed that the civil power was incapable of carrying out its tasks. Should Baring and Erskine reach an impasse, each had to appeal to his respective secretary of state. Erskine kept his letter of appointment in his spectacles case, and Blundell recalls that 'on one occasion when the war council had a 'severe disagreement' Erskine sat opening and shutting the lid of the case with a loud popping sound'. Blundell wondered if the gesture was a natural and unconscious one or a method of adding due weight to the military view he was presenting.

Erskine stepped up the tempo of offensive operations, making the forces for which he was responsible clear as to his expectations and expressing his confidence that the army and police would 'uphold their honour and integrity' while dealing with the present situation. 'I will not,' he stated, 'tolerate breaches of discipline leading to unfair treatment of anybody . . . I most strongly disapprove of "beating up" the inhabitants of this country just because they are inhabitants.' He ordered that every officer in the police and army should stamp at once on any conduct which he would be ashamed to see used against his own people.

News that troops kept a score of kills was the subject of debate at Westminster and was frowned on by some members of parliament. Erskine issued orders prohibiting all forms of competition regarding 'kills' or encouragement to soldiers by way of bounty payments.

It did not take him long to assess British weaknesses in the field and in Government House, and his letters home provide a frank, critical account of events as he saw them. An early observation was that 'half the trouble is that all these civil servants and police sit in their offices behind barbed wire fences and so do not know what goes on in their districts'. At the end of June he concluded: 'Baring is a very sick man and I do not believe he will last.'

There were, indeed, feelings circulating in June and July of the governor's unfitness to continue. There was talk of introducing a military governor similar to Templar in Malaya. It is understood that there was discussion in Westminster of Erskine taking over as governor, but there is no known record of it.

By mid-1953 the British forces comprised 10,000 British and King's African Rifles troops, 21,000 police and more than 20,000 Kikuyu home guard, 3,000 of whom were equipped with firearms. Erskine had under his command a squadron of RAF Lincoln heavy bombers and several flights of Harvard light bombers.

Nevertheless, although they had against them some 54,000 assorted troops and 'irregulars', not to mention aircraft, it was the undoubted success of the Mau Mau attack on Naivasha Police Station in March which caught the imagination. Even if that raid was not a guarantee of future victories, it increased the confidence of their leaders. By June the liaison between Mau Mau leaders regarding targets for raids appears to have become more professional. During the previous month Stanley Mathenge had met leaders to plan raids on home guard posts. On 11th June, the day Maj Griffiths shot dead the two Africans at the road block, a dozen or more leaders from several areas attended a meeting convened by Mathenge to make plans for 'raids that would shake the government'.

The meeting opened with the usual prayers, all standing and facing Mount Kenya. Mathenge explained a strategy, planned with Dedan Kimathi and involving all the areas. The aim was that the raids should be carried out over all the country on the same day and at exactly the same time.

Njama, as clerk, read aloud a letter signed by Kimathi which set out seven objectives. These included seizing all livestock; destroying roads, railways, bridges and lines of communication; killing as many enemies as possible; raiding trading centres for clothing and goods and dispensaries for medical supplies; firing Europeans' houses; and stealing water pipes to make guns. (Professionally manufactured weapons were always in short supply.) The leaders were given four days for preparations and told that any leader who failed to carry out the raid would be demoted to a regular warrior. Njama records that Nyeri district had 5,800 warriors in the Aberdare Forest, 1,800 of whom had joined that week. The 'raids that would shake the Government' were planned for 7.30pm on 25th June. Njama wrote on Stanley Mathenge's behalf to each leader under his command, notifying him of the 'all-out attack'. He also wrote the governor a 'propaganda' letter about the attack, which was 'an example of our planned series of attacks'. The letter was confident that 'the next all-out attack will make you flee our country or commit suicide'. It concluded, 'Yours Victoriously, General Stanley Mathenge'.

Final arrangements were made for 1,600 warriors to attack in 32 groups of 50 men. However, on the morning of the planned attack a warrior was injured by a grenade, and later in the day 800 troops of the Devonshire Regiment, together with members of the home guard, were seen near the attack paths. The warriors feared they might not be able to retire after the raids. Furthermore, on two occasions a group of warriors had seen a deer and a gazelle cross their path – a certain omen of bad luck. Then 'many warriors . . . said that they disobeyed the same rule when they were going to raid Othaya and the result was very bad'. It was decided to put off the raids. The government remained unshaken.

The Kenya Regiment was less susceptible to omens. At 3am on 11th July, some two weeks after Mau Mau abandoned its planned series of attacks, the regiment entered the Mau Mau headquarters at Kariaini without being noticed. Njama records that the Mau Mau warriors fled when they heard shots. They had received a message from a seer saying that they should not sleep in the camp, as the government would raid it during the night. Many had heeded the warning and slept on the mountain. Mathenge, their leader, chided those who had 'disobeyed' the seer. A considerable number of them had been killed and some wounded. The corpses had one hand removed by their attackers. Huts had been burned, but the hospital had not been observed and was undamaged. Njama, who doubled as a medical dresser, treated the wounded. The female warriors acted as luggage carriers for the men.

Njama records that four days earlier Mau Mau leaders knew that KR troops were in the forest in groups of about a dozen, but the attack nevertheless appears to have taken them by surprise. The Devons and Buffs also made successful night attacks on Mau Mau camps, inflicting significant casualties. British troops were in 'constant amazement' at how a Mau Mau could be hit without being felled. News of these government successes was reported to the European community.

July Jerome, the assistant district commissioner, an ex-Makerere School pupil and a former pupil of Carey Francis at Alliance School, was killed in an ambush. Francis had met him at Christmas, shortly after he had been condemned to death by the local Mau Mau group.

Despite Erskine's orders that 'kills' should not be rewarded with bounty payments, the rewards and 'league tables' continued, and a reference to them in the Devons' magazine led to a question in the Commons from a Labour MP. A court of enquiry exonerated all

British battalions from charges of indiscriminate firing. The KAR and the police were not so blameless in their treatment of Mau Mau suspects, as the forthcoming court martial of Capt Griffiths would bear witness.

Although attacks on European farms continued, Europeans were not the only victims. In her letter dated 8th July Nellie Grant reported an awful raid on one of the Bastard farms while the family was away at the coast. A Seychelles fundi (craftsman), his wife and three young children were burned alive; all the farm guards and the dogs were shot; and the house was looted and burned. The battle-ground was everywhere, but particularly near the European farmers' yards. Elsa Pickering's husband joined with the army in a battle in the long paddock beyond the front lawn. 'It started with a sudden burst of firing, and at the end the bodies of eight dead terrorists were laid out on our farm road.' In a letter dated 25th July Grant refers to the murder of Irene MacDougall's ex-husband, who was slashed to death four miles outside Nyeri township. A gang of 40 Mau Mau had been seen behind the Fishels' farm, while a smaller force, at Egerton, gouged out the eyes of a cow at Chauvain's.

As if contending with Mau Mau attacks were not enough in itself, the weather in July continued to be, in Grant's words, 'catastrophic'. Some farmers expected a 95 percent failure of crops. Her letter of 25th July reported that the drought was raging and that the Fishels' entire crop of maize, over an area of 90 acres, was lying flat on the ground and brown as paper. Four months later, however, Elspeth Huxley, visiting her mother on the farm, wrote home to her husband that the post-war settlers seemed to have done exceedingly well almost to a man, and were mostly hard-working and desirable types.

These settlers were quickly assimilated into the European farming community. James Stapleton was one of those to whom Elspeth Huxley referred. He recorded a conversation with one of his old settler neighbours, who concluded that the only way to put a stop to 'all this nonsense' would be to introduce summary justice. Public hangings and floggings, even the use of the stocks, should be the remedy for all hard-core terrorists that were caught. How could you expect the African to understand laws that gave him medical attention, a long drawn-out trial full of technicalities and the right to appeal if he was found guilty – when, for countless generations, he had suffered a law of torture that gave him no right to speak? Africa simply wasn't ready for British-type justice, he argued. And, noted Stapleton, 'most of us had to agree'.

Stapleton had more than 50 Kikuyu families living and working on the farm at the time of Mau Mau. Most of them had been there for years, and they seemed settled and contented. His wife Elizabeth gave advice when sought, doctored families and helped at time of sickness. The workforce consulted Stapleton with their matrimonial and financial problems. Most of his Kikuyu had little recollection of the Kikuyu reserve. They or their parents had come with the early settlers to work and raise their families in safety as far away as possible from 'the dreaded Masai'. But the influence of the dark forests they had so recently left was still with them. Fear and witchcraft, such an inherent part of their forefathers' lives, broke out 'like a festering sore'. Stapleton observed the same culture-gap that had separated earlier settlers from the African. He listened to their troubles and sometimes become their confidant, but the gap made by generations of civilization prevented any intimacy.

'We have nothing in common from the way we dress to the way we eat,' he found, 'from our ambitions and pastimes to our morals and ethics. There is no social ground on which we could meet after the sun had gone down.' He seems not to have been surprised or unduly concerned when he learned that all his Kikuyu, 'men, women, Christian and all, had taken the oath, some as far back as 1950'.

On Deloraine farm the Scott family found that the Emergency had little effect on everyday life. They had plenty of non-Kikuyu labour, and their only incident, which was never explained, concerned an old man who was found hanging from a tree. When some of the Deloraine Kikuyu announced that they wished to go 'back' to the Kikuyu reserve, even though some of them had never been there in their lives, Pamela Scott arranged transport for them but told them that if they went they must never come back. Most of them stayed. Their head Masai had a simple solution to the Mau Mau problem. If he were the government he would collect all the Kikuyu together, put them in an enclosure, pour petrol over them, then send an aeroplane with a bomb and drop it on them and 'do in' the lot. The Kikuyu on the farm were to some extent marginalized. All the Europeans and some of the non-Kikuyu Africans were enlisted into the Kenya Police Reserve. They were often called out at night. On one occasion they 'shot one person who was trying to run away'.

On the farm that Joan Scott managed, not to be confused with Deloraine, they tried to keep their work-force away from Mau Mau by diverting them into other activities. They formed a football league and had sports days. Their football team played the local army teams, and they were taught sewing and to wash every day. Because it was a pyrethrum farm the women all had work, and they were better off than on some other farms. But as time went on Joan Scott, like James Stapleton, had no illusions about the relationship of her workforce with Mau Mau. She believed that most of their workers were Mau Mau; they had no option but to be. They had a very loyal Meru night-guard, but only one or two loyalists out of more than a hundred. 'We only had one worker killed and he was working right out with the herd a long way from anywhere where he was shot by the British security forces. They accused him of running away.' Scott has little doubt that the man had co-operated with Mau Mau. 'Attending herds in remote areas he would not have survived long had he not done so,' she observed.

There were lighter moments. Apart from the successful Mau Mau raid on the Naivasha police station (which Europeans tried to forget), perhaps the most memorable military engagement in Naivasha was the British bombardment of a papyrus bed near the lake. Unidentified Africans had been seen in the papyrus, and the army was called up. Mervyn Carnally, who had spent the war years, 1939-45, in the KAR watched with interest as a 'creeping barrage' of mortar fire, 'which must have cost the British tax payer £200,000 to £250,000', spread through the papyrus – a constant threat, as it provided good cover. In the event, the terrorists had almost certainly disappeared by the time the army arrived and the only casualty was the papyrus. Blaxland makes no mention of the encounter.

On another occasion one of the Carnally's Masai guards was shot in the arm while on patrol. The wound required whisky as an anaesthetic and the cook with his knife. 'He returned on patrol with his bow and arrow in a matter of minutes.'

By August Europeans began to realise the strength of Mau Mau. There was an alternative perspective, of which Njama provides the most comprehensive account – that of the 'fight in the forest' from the standpoint of the Mau Mau fighters. His accounts of the Mau Mau leaders' endeavours to manage their affairs in a constitutional manner are the most detailed of those used in this text. The reports by Kahinga Wachanga and others support Njama's in broad terms, but Wachanga is sceptical of Njama's description of the tidy, democratic, parliamentary nature of the forest meetings. According to Wachanga; 'Our meetings were not very organised. Decisions were made by our big leaders and set before the itungati [warriors]. The itungati did not question decisions made by the accepted leaders, even though they were not consulted. They followed our orders.'

Inevitably there are differences in the accounts of the Mau Mau recorders on the relative importance of the various leaders, indicating that African autobiographies are as subjective as those from other cultures. Njama tends to enhance the importance of Dedan Kimathi to the detriment of Wachanga and Mathenge. Wachanga writes that he knew Njama in the forest, where he served as Kimathi's personal secretary during most of his time there. Although he was thus in a position to know a great deal of what happened, 'he was not the big leader he says he was'. He suggests that Njama relates events as he thinks they should have happened rather than as they actually took place. As he relates them, wrote Wachanga, 'things are just too tidy to have occurred in the chaotic forest setting'.

Njama and Wachanga (the latter is usually know in Njama's texts as Kahinga, his 'given' name), had both attended Christian missionary schools and were better educated than the majority of the Mau Mau warriors. They were both engaged as secretaries – Njama to Kimathi and Wachanga to Mathenge – but Njama was Mathenge's secretary for some weeks, so he knew two of the 'big leaders' from close personal experience. Njama was both schoolmaster and scoutmaster before he entered the forest, and he had a good command of the English language. He also had a more than adequate knowledge of first aid, but he was frequently asked to operate on injuries which were far beyond his skills. Reference was made earlier to his Christianity, and in the forest camps he was invited to 'speak to the people'. On several occasions he read to the officers and warriors from the books of Lamentations and Ecclesiastes. The subjects he chose were orphans, widows, persecutions and iniquities, which Njama considered to be particularly apposite.

The following extracts from his biography are abridged, but attempt to provide representative samples of the many skirmishes which occurred. Mau Mau warriors avoided contact with larger groups of government forces if at all possible. In one skirmish, Njama says, 'I set out with 20 men and armed with 12 rifles and six home-made guns. It was about 5am that we ran into a government ambush. By the time we realised it we were completely surrounded by security forces. I directed my group to aim all of our guns at one point in the circle around us. When I gave the signal we all opened fire and ran through the hole which our bullets prepared'. They lost three of their 20 men.

The following day his group was escorted by 50 'fighters'. He noticed a government reconnaissance plane overhead, but felt quite confident they hadn't been spotted. After a day's tiring journey, as they were sitting on the ground eating, one of their guards ran up excitedly and told him that they were being surrounded by a large force of tribal police, home guards and military units. A fight began, which lasted until dark. One fighter was killed, but they managed to capture 12 enemy rifles. He sent back to Narok for reinforcements and by the following morning he had 300 additional men. Government forces, too, had increased in numbers. 'A day-long battle began,' Njama continues, 'ending at night-fall with a loss of 11 of our fighters. We had captured no enemy guns and it was decided that we should move out of the area.' It is difficult to verify details, but Njama's account suggests that significant numbers of combatants were involved in these skirmishes.

In 1953, Mau Mau groups occasionally ambushed each other. The absence of military uniforms no doubt added to their difficulties in identifying friend or foe. Njama recalls that 'In many cases the guards posted around the camp of a group of forest fighters wore stolen home guard uniforms and when seeing strangers approach would signal them in a manner requiring a special response. As sometimes happened, new recruits first entering the forest did not know these signals and hence could easily be taken for enemies and ambushed. On the other hand, if they spotted the guard before he saw them, they might in ignorance open fire on what appeared to them a home guard, and so initiate a battle'.

While many attacks on Europeans' farms came as a surprise to the farmers, in August 1953 Njama used a small typewriter, the (stolen) property of General Kimbo, to type eviction notices. On the 22nd August he issued 'first notices' which gave each settler seven days to quit. The long notices recited the complaints of the African and were signed 'Your New Kenyan, Karari Njama, Chief Secretary, Kenya

Defence Council'. The notices were planted by labourers employed by the farmers in bamboo tubes placed just outside the front doors of their houses. Up in Timau the Murrays discovered such notes from Mau Mau, thanking them for sheep which had been stolen and inviting them to come to 'Box Mau Mau, Mount Kenya' if they wanted payment.

Most women joined the Mau Mau groups in the forest to escape from the reserves where the Kikuyu home guards might harass them, particularly if their husband was known as a Mau Mau member or supporter. Some were abducted. Njama's estimate was that seven per cent of the women in the forest were either lured or abducted by Mau Mau warriors. The Mau Mau section in which he worked in September 1953 had 288 warriors, of whom a dozen were girls. And another camp of 40 had 13 women warriors. One of Njama's co-leaders told him that his section had 184 itungati, of whom four were girls. Two of them were very brave and had trapped a KAR man, killed him and brought his gun to the forest. He also confirmed that all the girls in his and Kimbo's section had been taught how to use any weapon.

The presence of women in Mau Mau groups could cause problems, particularly if they included a witchdoctor's abducted wife. One fighter lamented to Njama, 'We believe that women have brought all this calamity to our mbutu [group]. Last week Kiruthi Gikuri abducted a woman named Wariu who was only recently married to Kamotho, the great witchdoctor in Mahinga Location. We suspect that we might be bewitched by Kamotho or else that [trouble] would be the punishment for our intercourse with women inside our camp against the taboos.' Kikuyu customary law did not give women equality with men. The penalty for the murder of a man was a hundred goats, but for a woman it was 30.

Mau Mau officers did their best to maintain good order and military discipline in the field and forest. Njama lists 17 camp rules covering such matters as the time to rise, communal prayers, sentry duties, prohibition of sexual intercourse in camp, control of firearms, restrictions on fire-lighting, hygiene and observing the privacy of the leaders. He acted as secretary to Stanley Mathenge, who admitted to being uneducated but is described by Njama as being one of three 'big leaders', the others being Dedan Kimathi and Mbaria Kaniu. Njama was involved in making and recording seven 'rules and regulations' for their warriors, which covered rape, theft of various kinds, including theft from the enemy, and distribution of captured items. Failure to maintain discipline might lead to punishment, but the accused was entitled to a trial, and Mau Mau courts martial were held from time to time.

Karari Njama acted as clerk to three trials convened by Stanley Mathenge which were concerned with the rape and continuous beating of a girl, robbery and murder. Under Kikuyu law the punishment for rape was the payment of seven rams to the elders, a ewe for cleansing the girl and the brewing of some beer. In the forest money, livestock and beer were not available for a fine, and 'strokes on the buttocks' appeared to be the only available remedy. There was argument regarding how many there should be, but in the event the sentence was 25 strokes dispensed 'on the spot'.

The robbery was from the house of a Mau Mau supporter but there was some confusion and the accused was cautioned. The third case concerned Gicuhi Mugo, who 'shot dead his comrade and took his gun'. The accused admitted the shooting, and the incident was regarded as an accident by the court. Mugo was warned to take more care.

One of Njama's tasks was to investigate incidents in which their men were involved. Offenders were punished, often harshly: beatings were frequently given, typically for the mistreatment of, or theft from, Kikuyu villagers.

In mid-1953 what appears to have been a relatively trivial incident caused, or perhaps aggravated, a rift between Kimathi and Mathenge, who were already rivals. The 'fire-bullet' incident, as it came to be known, occupies more than one of the Kikuyu chronicles of Mau Mau activities. A bullet exploded in the camp fire around which several leaders were sitting. Mathenge suspected Kimathi of making an attempt on his life in order to eliminate a rival, and decided against continuing their planned journey together. The incident grew in significance with the passage of time.

As time went by, Mau Mau leaders experienced increasing difficulty in keeping control of their warriors, and British government forces began to regain control of the forest. Njama referred to the dispersal of Mau Mau warriors into many small sections, out of which grew many 'incapable self-styled leaders' whose main objective was getting food and hiding. The breakaway groups, which the dedicated Mau Mau leaders called komerera, 'took the law into their own hands and fulfilled their pleasures', which included robbery, abduction, rape and administering 'absurd and illegal types of oath'. They embarrassed the dedicated Mau Mau leaders, who went to great trouble hunting them down and disciplining them. Eventually, most returned to the fold.

Njama refers to an increase in 'repressive measures of government, with sweeps of the villages becoming more frequent and with beatings, arrests, theft of property and the rape of our women becoming the order of the day', adding that 'many of our fighters were leaving to join their comrades in the forests'. He continued assisting the committee in its work of investigating government atrocities. Most of the repressive measures were from home guard and tribal police, but he alleges that European Special Branch agents would place a bullet or two in the pocket of a man they were searching during a sweep – they would then 'discover' the bullets in the presence of witnesses, and charge the man of being in possession of ammunition. Attempts were being made to bring these facts before the eyes of the world through the press and a few sympathetic Europeans.

Standards of living in the reserves slipped for several reasons. Many Kikuyu squatters had returned from European farms in the Rift Valley and elsewhere. Njama suggests that 250,000 people were 'homeless, landless, jobless and helpless' by June 1953. He refers to thousands of children and the elderly dying from starvation, a suffering accelerated by 'killings, beatings and torture'. The cold rain-sodden months of June to August in the Highlands contributed to their misery. Denying Mau Mau fighters access to food led them to take it from African farms and gardens. The position continued to deteriorate during 1953 and, indeed, would do so henceforth. Nevertheless, some Kikuyus managed to keep their feet in several camps at once. At Gweiga, Patrick Wachira kept his small hotel running. He had taken three Mau Mau oaths ('You couldn't go into the forest with Mau Mau unless you had taken three oaths'), but he worked in detention centres as a spy for the British Special Branch while at the same time passing on intelligence to Mau Mau.

The Mwatha meeting of August 1953 in the Aberdare forests was a landmark gathering of all Mau Mau leaders and warriors which endeavoured to provide a structure for Mau Mau operations. Njama's account of the meeting occupies some 30 pages of his text and records the Mau Mau leaders' aspirations. Some of the more significant aspects are given below. Oginga Odinga, whose activities were political rather than military, refers to the meeting as the 'Kenya Parliament'. It set out to plan an overall strategy that reflected, not a narrow tribalism but the aim of a united independent African Kenya. It is not recorded to what extent tribes other than Kikuyu (taken for this purpose to include the Embu and Meru people) were represented, but their influence is generally believed to have been negligible. The leaders' suspicions and jealousies were not conducive to a happy meeting – the 'fire-bullet' incident was still fresh in some minds. Stanley Mathenge resented receiving the letter from Dedan Kimathi convening the meeting, as he considered himself to be of equal status to Kimathi.

The agenda included the election of a Kenya-wide council, making rules and regulations, instructing leaders, making plans for raids and issuing 'ranks'. Mathenge declined the invitation, on the grounds that he was retrieving warriors scattered by the Kenya Regiment during the previous months' operations. Some of his officers remained with him, but many travelled for several days to the venue high in the Aberdares where blankets froze at night. Njama was one of that number.

The assembled warriors queued in hundreds to be ritually cleansed by witchdoctors, General Macharia Kimemia and others. When cleansed, officers were separated from the warriors: they camped and ate separately. Kimathi selected a meeting place which was central to Mau Mau operations and obscured from observation by aeroplane by mists. More than 4,600 attended. The meetings were chaired by Kimathi, who opened with prayers.

The first business was military formation. Eight armies and their leaders were named, together with the districts in which they would operate. Warriors or their heirs were to be rewarded with land and be remembered. Memorial halls would be built.

'Rank' was an item on the agenda which was discussed at some length. It was resolved that, 'from the lowest to the highest', these should relate to individual activities, and Kimathi invited leaders to propose a list of 12 people in each camp who would be issued with ranks from lance corporal to general. It was resolved to allocate money to the ranks in the order of '2s, 5s, 10s, up to 100s by 10s'. The cash was to come from oathing fees. A proposal which was greeted with applause by leaders was that Europeans' farms should be taken over by Mau Mau officers as their pensions.

The keeping of records occupied the closing session. It was stressed that leaders needed to keep very detailed records of damage caused by the government; Mau Mau personnel injured or killed; the names of enemies; cash receipts and expenditure; and daily events, in the form of a history book. As 'the most educated and capable man', Njama was appointed chief secretary. Before the meeting was closed, he instructed 63 clerks in record keeping. Four secretaries, including Njama, were given letters of appointment.

The closing prayers were led by Kimathi with considerable ceremony. The other leaders, including Njama, were then invited to speak to the warriors for two minutes. Their contributions included the need for obedience, exhortations 'never to surrender' and promises that they would 'share the Kenya Highlands'. Njama promised them immortality. He read them a few verses from the Holy Bible, which were the 'words of the great wise prophets of ancient days', and he took his final message from Revelations 22, 12–14: 'My reward is with me to give to every man according as his work shall be.'

The meeting was not without its dark side. Discussions revealed that many teachers had been killed and many schools destroyed by Mau Mau, the people who were seeking freedom. Kimathi admitted ordering the destruction of some schools.

At 10am the following day, after morning prayers, eight planes bombed and machine-gunned the camp and the adjoining forest causing 'strong winds, earth tremors and much fear', but there were no casualties.

Njama's diary makes frequent references to group prayers. Whatever the conditions, the day started and ended with prayers. Many entries illustrate this devotion. Prayers conducted by Njama included readings from the Bible.

In the forests military order and discipline prevailed, and in Kimathi's camp there were distinctions between officers and warriors. He had issued ranks to many warriors who were respected and showed real character. Each fireplace had a girl attendant, who collected firewood and kept the fire burning. In Mathenge's camp, however, distinctions of rank were not so marked. Njama found him mixing with the men, and he criticized him, pointing out that he should have a private fire even though he was the only leader in the camp and enjoyed the company of others in the kitchen.

In 1953 Henry Wachanga formed a battalion known as the Kenya African Military Soldiers Investigation no.1 (KAMSI No.1), which operated throughout Mukur-weini Division and numbered about 5,000. Under his command were one major-general and nine brigadiers. A number of home guard posts or government buildings were attacked by KAMSI No.1 in 1953, but they did not take many captives, 'and if we did they were usually sentenced to a quick death, generally by strangulation. The executioner had to return with the captive's penis and testicles as a sign he had done his duty'. Bodies were hacked to pieces so that they could not be discovered and given a proper burial.

For Mau Mau officers and men the closing months of 1953 were more of the same. Much time was spent on organizing the army; foraging continued; the smiths made more guns; more Africans were oathed; and more Europeans cattle and sheep were slaughtered or maimed. On the 31st December they held an annual ceremony attended by about 800 fighters. Sheep were sacrificed, prayers were offered up, speeches were made and anthems were sung. The concept of the Kenya Young Stars Association was announced and greeted with applause. It was a time of hope.

British troops continued to arrive during the second half of the year. The Lancashire Fusiliers were relieved by the 1st Black Watch early in August and they moved up next to the Devons. Near the end of September the 1st Royal Inniskillin Fusiliers and the 1st Royal Northumberland Fusiliers moved to Kenya. By mid-August the Royal Engineers had cut deep tracks into the forest, which enabled the infantry to penetrate and engage the terrorists.

Even so, there was at high level a lack of confidence in the governor's ability to govern. Baring was away for three weeks in October, and it was expected that he would come back rested and fit, but the reverse happened. Erskine wrote, 'I like Baring very much and the whole family are charming, but he can make no decision, and that is fatal. I don't feel in any way optimistic on the long term policy.' Erskine was, however, confident of victory over Mau Mau, and wrote, 'I am sure I can put down the gangs in a reasonable time, but I can't do much to alter the outlook of the Kikuyu tribe as C-in-C except to knock them on the head when they are troublesome, and that is no answer to the real problem, though it is an essential preliminary.'

In addition to the stresses of everyday life, many white women felt insecure and rejected by public opinion in Britain. The September issue of the East African Women's League bulletin provides a perspective on the European woman's role. An emergency committee had been appointed in January 'to deal with matters immediately affecting or arising out of the Emergency'. Their tasks were, mainly, offering security advice, arranging accommodation for women and children from troubled areas and providing notes for women speaking overseas. The League appreciated that European settlers were not necessarily being regarded as the victims of war.

'Sidelights on the Emergency' were gathered from the League's branches. In Naro Moru they were providing baths, meals and beds at all hours for One Force, police and KAR. In Molo they found waiting the most difficult thing. There was a fear of 'game paths easily ambushed and the diabolical cunning of the Mau Mau'. Adjoining the Aberdares, a woman whose husband was away was warned one night by an African who had been shot at, that Mau Mau were nearby. She locked up the farm, collected her spearmen and Maragoli guard and went to assist a neighbour. One of the terrorists was killed on the lawn and three arrested. A member wrote of the difficulty of explaining to children the need for vigilance, without 'destroying that inherent trust that has been nurtured in their minds since birth'. As children could no longer ride over the farms, a skating rink had been opened. Soldiers from the Devons patrolled the area. The need to carry side arms was understood but, the article concluded, 'All the women are heartily sick of our dresses hanging badly with a belt and revolver'. And 'the men's pockets always need mending'.

In Nairobi, meteorologist Hugh Sansom's home guard patrols continued once or twice each week throughout 1953. On 28th August he had to go to Guthenguri to give weather evidence at the Lari massacre trial. He was 'impressed by the friendly spirit in the Kikuyu reserve'. On 14th and 15th September he visited a Mau Mau screening camp to help Africans who were working for the meteorological department and who had been detained. He recalls that the detainees were treated heavy handedly. 'I don't remember any of our staff being beaten up, but they were treated pretty roughly'. His wife Susan recalls that 'facilities in the detention areas were not good, and the detainees came back dirty and tired, and were resentful'. She did not, however, feel threatened. She drove from Nairobi to Kikuyuland and Limuru in an open-top car with a new baby in the back, attending multi-racial Mothers Union meetings, and it never occurred to her to be 'fussed'. 'We were more concerned for our African friends than we were for our European friends.'

Joan Baralon, then a teenager in Nairobi, noticed no animosity between the whites and natives during the troubles, but there was a curfew and the servants had to be in at night. Their servants were Luo, and therefore not as proscribed as Kikuyu servants. She remembers 'mum and dad' walking about with guns, but says the children would go with them to the railway company club and that there was Saturday morning cinema for them.

But for Ruth, later wife of Henry Muoria, life in Nairobi was stressful. There would be a knock on the door, and people would be taken out for screening: when they went back they discovered that everything left inside, including money and clothes, had been taken by the police. There were false accusations by paid informers, and 'if you had an enemy they'd just pick you up'.

There was a sharp contrast between life in Nairobi and life on the farms or in the reserves. The reserves developed defensible areas manned by the loyal Kikuyu home guards. As the home guard movement spread, a chain of forts, protected with deep, spiked ditches and rounded projecting corners, was ranged across the steep ridges of the Kikuyu country from Ndeiya in the south to Nyeri in the north. Each was complete with central grass-covered sleeping quarters and a tall, commanding watch-tower complete with a piece of metal to sound a tocsin across the countryside. 'We were,' wrote Blundell, 'transported back to the days of Caesar and the fortified camps of the Gallic wars.' He constantly visited these forts and the men in them. They appeared to have a curiously dedicated air, with a remarkably tranquil and steadfast look in their eyes, as if they were buoyed up by some inner conviction. Always the guard on the watch-tower would be on the alert against sudden attack and overrunning of the post by the enemy. The young European boys and the Kikuyu home guards would be together for weeks on end, each vitally dependent on the other. During a visit to Fort Hall, Nellie Grant saw Kikuyu guard posts – stockades – all over the place, manned by unpaid guards. But, she observed, both Mau Mau and home guards had killed, and continued to do so. 'It is, of course, a civil war,' she wrote and, with accurate foresight, 'there will be a terrible legacy of feuds and hatreds when it's over'.

Europeans held a wide range of views over the way ahead. In the late summer Blundell detected the first clear indication of the concept of a Kenya nation which would gradually dismantle the old racial barriers and compartments, and which would be supported by men of all races with the same civilized ideals. Such thoughts were the product of a sub-committee of the European elected member organization of which Blundell was a member. The paper generated by the sub-committee was followed at the end of November by a policy statement, in which the principle of all races together in the government figured largely. This statement had not been produced without a considerable amount of indigestion within the organization, wrote Blundell, and such thinking was not unanimous. But the devil was driving, in the form of 'the revolt in our midst', and some of Blundell's colleagues 'who would never have looked at multi-racialism in normal times . . . were prepared to accept it in order to get greater effectiveness in the actions of government'. Others were in favour of multi-racialism but would accept nothing which did not give Europeans outright control of the government. Failing that, they felt that continuing sustained opposition was the answer.

The possibility of European racist 'extremists' gaining control in government was a matter of great concern for the Africans and Asians,who became frightened at the prospect of such a concentration of power. The result, observed Blundell, was that 'a wedge was thus driven between the races at the very moment when unity was most required'.

The weakness of the government, apparent to all, was a major cause of the European settlers' feeling of insecurity. Many became increasingly irritated by the time it took the Administration to bring Mau Mau to trial and by the legal procedures which appeared to favour the terrorists. Six months after the Lari massacre not a single terrorist involved in the outburst had been brought to trial. Even when they eventually did, incompetence on the part of the Administration all too often prevented justice being done. During one trial 19 oath-administrators had been found guilty of oath-giving in the lower court and were awarded suitable punishments, but all the sentences were quashed by the court of appeal – not over the judgement of the magistrate, with which the court of appeal agreed, but because of a small clerical error in the charge sheet of one of the accused. 'The terrorists learnt from this and other instances to exploit to the full the cumbersome British legal system, which was never evolved to deal with full scale revolt in the dark continent of Africa,' Blundell wrote.

The 'cumbersome British legal system' could be exploited by a competent defence lawyer. Barrister T.R. Johar recalls an occasion when 80 trials were stopped because the submission was flawed. He discovered, too, flaws in the method of screening suspects in detention camps, and the court accepted his argument. He discovered that 90 per cent of cases arose from confessions which had been extracted by inducement which, when it came to light, led to the accused being acquitted.

Understandably, settlers became frustrated with the state of affairs. The battle against Mau Mau was being fought in the law courts – troops and guns were being withheld because it wasn't recognised as war. Stapleton, along with many others, felt the apparent failure of the government to control Mau Mau was a factor which led to a lowering of some Europeans' ethical standards. Some, having come face to face with the utter brutality of massacres such as those at Lari, took the law into their own hands.

There were, as Oginga Odinga wrote, 'brutalities and massacres on both sides'. Inevitably it is difficult to discover the truth. Both sides coloured their accounts, and on occasions, one suspects, they even elaborate the brutalities they inflicted on the enemy. Mau Mau Field Marshal Musa Mwariama, for example, describes in detail the 'execution' of Manley, a British soldier, a boy of about 20 whom they captured. 'We slaughtered him like a cow.' Then, his account ran, they skinned, sliced and roasted him, having severed his head and put it on top of a pole as if he were watching his own flesh roast. On the other side, Lt Simon MacLaughlan believed 'it was a sort of "macho" act on the part of the whites to pretend they acted badly to the natives'.

Nevertheless, Johar knew, as friends, a number of Europeans who served in the Kenya Regiment and who openly admitted that they arrested suspected Mau Mau men, put them in their lorries, stopped the lorry, told them to run away and, 'for the fun of it', shot them. Johar recalled too, a case where his African client's case was that he had been shot when coming to surrender, but the 20-year-old member of the Kenya Regiment maintained that the African had been shot while running away. Medical evidence proved that the bullet/s entered his body from the front. In the face of this evidence the soldier suggested that the African had been running backwards.

Some Europeans openly boasted of atrocities they had committed, and there is ample evidence from both sides. In his closely referenced account of Mau Mau, Edgerton, a writer considered by many to be sympathetic to the Mau Mau cause, provides several examples. These include a white prisoner being bound, put in an empty beehive at the top of a hill and rolled down to the river to drown. Others were doused in kerosene and burned alive and used as target practice. Three prisoners were placed in a row so that they could be shot together with one bullet, and British soldiers, taken prisoner, were made to kneel while their captors tried to shoot them so that the bullet entered the anus and exited through the mouth. When genitals were hacked off and bodies were dismembered by Mau Mau (sometimes into as many as 50 pieces), they were taken to the reserves and displayed. Edgerton's list of Mau Mau atrocities is by no means exhaustive.

On the credit side, he notes that no European or Indian women were raped in the earlier attacks, and that there were no accusations of white women being raped during the whole period of the rebellion. The list of Mau Mau atrocities in the field is, at least, matched by those committed by the Europeans. Edgerton's research provides well-documented and undisputed examples of European brutalities during the year, often as part of an interrogation. Electric shock and fire were widely used. Women were choked and held under water, and gun barrels, beer bottles and knives were thrust into vaginas. Men had bottles thrust up their rectums, fingers chopped off and testicles crushed with pliers. Beating and whipping were routine, as was shooting for failure to answer questions.

Europeans who opposed it might, too, be subject to brutality from those they confronted. Late in the year Sir Henry Dalrymple, who was serving as a home guard district officer, took a suspected Mau Mau prisoner to the local police station where he was kicked in the face by a European police officer. Another said he would have the man shot. Sir Henry reported the incident to his superior. When the police officers heard of his report they broke into his room and beat him so badly with a bottle that he was hospitalized for eight days. In court, the officers admitted their guilt and apologized. One was fined £50 and the other £30. Civil war is notoriously messy and brutal.

Which brings us to the court martial of Captain Griffiths of the Durham Light Infantry for the murder recorded on pages 173–4. It ran for three days from 25th November and provides evidence of individual, regimental and official military attitudes. Griffiths, a major at the time of the murder, pleaded not guilty to what was a civil offence committed while on active service. Sixteen witnesses were called, and the record of the proceedings runs to 105 pages. Eighty percent of the record is given to evidence (much through interpreters), four pages to closing speeches and the remaining 24 pages of closely typed text to the summing-up by the president, Maj-Gen T. Brodie CBE, DSO. The closing speeches are almost entirely occupied with questioning the credibility of the opposition's witnesses.

The opening paragraph of the president's summing-up reads: 'Gentlemen, there is one thing which I would like to say now which I think may commend itself to you all and it is this, that in a case of this importance and seriousness we must all be thankful that the accused has had the advantage of being so ably defended, and we must all be grateful to his learned counsel for his assistance.' The competence, or otherwise, of the prosecution is not mentioned.

Having spent four pages explaining to the court its duties and defining murder and malice, the president states that 'for the purpose of this case, killing with malice aforethought is killing by an act which is done unlawfully and on purpose and with the intention to kill or to do grievous bodily harm. That is the kernel of the matter.' The president then describes the actions of the accused, with which the court is concerned, as 'firstly, firing into the backs of two men purposely with a Bren gun at a length of a few yards; and, secondly, firing at the head of one man with a revolver at a length of about a foot – and you may think that these acts were, each of them, quite obviously likely to cause death. And as the accused *admitted he did them on purpose* [the author's italic here and below] he can be presumed, whatever he may say, to have intended, or at least to have been prepared, to bring about their obviously probable consequences. The real issue here is not on this point at all; it is on whether the man whom the accused killed, if he killed anyone, was Ndegwa and *whether there was any lawful excuse for what was done.'*

The summing-up continues for 17 pages. The president's closing paragraph reminds the court that it is 'for the prosecution to prove its case. But if you are able to find yourselves satisfied that the murder of Ndegwa has been brought home to the accused either because on the evidence you can discern a reliable indication that it was Ndegwa who was shot at on the head by the accused, or that you are satisfied on the evidence that both these men were killed by the accused, and by no one but the accused, and killed unlawfully and without any shadow of justification . . . your verdict should be one of guilty of murder'.

The court adjourned at 2.15pm and re-opened at 3.30pm and the accused was brought before it. The court found him not guilty and closed at 3.32pm. Just two minutes.

A side issue which was aired during the trial was the 'tremendous rivalry' between army units as to which could kill the most Mau Mau and that every encouragement was given officially to the achievement of high scores.

It transpired that 23rd KAR had a barometer on which Mau Mau kills were marked, with official kills on the front and unofficial kills on the back. Sgt Maj Llewellyn stated that 23rd KAR were very proud of having killed over a hundred Mau Mau, and that other units were encouraged to beat that record. He had heard of it being the usual practice for commanders to offer five or ten shillings per head. Griffiths gave evidence to the court of making 5s payments for kills and to keeping a score board with columns for prisoners, kills, hide-outs and CSOs. The last mentioned, it was explained, stood for 'cock shot off'. The following questions and answers illustrate the tenor of Griffiths' responses to examination:

Q. Why do you allow that sort of thing (keeping the score board) to happen?
Griffiths. Because it was laughed at.
Q. Because the only thing you were interested in was killing black men?
Griffiths. No, I put it up because it was a joke.
Q. Do you have any specific orders from Colonel Evans as to how to shoot?
Griffiths. No.
Q. Did Colonel Evans ever see the score board, did he laugh?

Griffiths. Yes.
Q. What number appeared under the heading CSO?
Griffiths. One.

Griffiths was described as 'an embittered, passed-over officer in a KAR unit, who owned a farm in Kenya', and his acquittal on the technical point of the prosecution's 'inability to prove the identity of the murdered man' was made 'to the surprise and fury of Erskine'. Griffiths was, however, put on trial again for torturing prisoners, 'in particular one prisoner's ear had been removed and another had a large hole bored into an ear'. On this charge Griffiths was convicted, cashiered and sentenced to five years in prison.

KAR officers heard of the Griffiths case with mixed feelings. His first company commander when he was being court martialled was Lt MacLaughlan, whose comments in an interview afterwards may cast some light on the defendant's state of mind and motivation. All the junior officers had been told of 'the things Mau Mau did to his horses', MacLaughlan recalled, and it had been explained to them 'in subtle and not so subtle propaganda so that we pointed the rifle the right way . . . I think in retrospect I felt relieved that [Griffiths' action] was clearly righting a wrong. It was as simple as that.' Company gossip suggested that 'more senior officers should have spotted what he was doing and sooner. The colonel and second-in-command were relieved of their commands . . . partly because they hadn't got the vision of leadership to lead a battalion in the field'. When Griffiths was relieved of his command it was received as 'good news'. MacLaughlan is not sure that the askaris understood what it was about, but 'I think they understood that they were fighting, and when you are fighting and sent out to shoot people, the way you shoot them is, to someone less sophisticated, a grey one'.

Indicators emerged of regimental practice, customs and attitudes with regard to the Kikuyu. There is no doubt that it was quite common for troops to cut off the hands of Mau Mau slain in the field as evidence of a 'kill'. MacLaughlan also refers to askaris who 'used to cut off people's hands while they were still alive' to verify an encounter with the enemy. 'If you were ten hours march away, bringing back a body was quite difficult.' Later, troops were required to bring back fingerprints, rather than a hand. The award of bounty payments may have encouraged such dismemberment.

MacLaughlan believed Kikuyu civilians were frightened of both Mau Mau and government troops. 'They felt they might get kicked around a bit.' It was well known that askaris from other tribes had contempt for the Kikuyu, and 'one did have to stop one's troops from time to time knocking somebody about who really hadn't done anything except not immediately hand over his pass'. They were, however, impressed by the Kikuyu who 'opposed the Mau Mau and their terror tactics', but understood the pressures which led them to provide food and shelter for the terrorists.

The Mau Mau warriors' attempts to kill the Ukambani Chief Kasina did nothing to improve inter-tribal relationships or the standing of Mau Mau. They caught him in one of his huts and hacked him, they thought, to death. They severed both his arms and 'practically decapitated him'. It was done as a warning to the Wakamba. But Kasina survived, and toured his tribal area decrying Mau Mau and all its works. He raised troops and medical orderlies from his tribe, and retired Wakamba KAR NCOs gave them basic training using rifles made out of wood. Kasina handed them over to the KAR as semi-trained troops.

Mau Mau, and by association the Kikuyu tribe, became increasingly isolated. During the civil war most other tribes wanted no truck with Mau Mau. A strongly held European farmers' impression, long after the events, was that the strife was not a rebellion for independence, it was 'Kikuyu against Kikuyu, anti-Christian, anti-order and pro-chaos'. Mau Mau required its followers to abandon good farming techniques, terracing etc, because they were a colonial imposition. Mau Mau did not constitute an independence movement.

Most Europeans and Africans saw the conflict in terms of good versus evil. The government troops and what they stood for were good, while Mau Mau were evil. Jomo Kenyatta, Dedan Kimathi and other leaders and witchdoctors were evil, too. One had been told again and again about the horrible things they had done to people and to animals. Throughout 1953 countless Christian Kikuyu were murdered by Mau Mau terrorists. A dilemma of the Christian Kikuyu was that they broke the tradition of the tribe. Somewhere between was Karari Njama, the reluctant oath-taker, Mau Mau brigadier and historian, who led prayers in Mau Mau camps facing Mount Kenya and used the Bible as the source of his texts.

Within a few days of the Griffiths court martial, Richard Crossman MP, one of Labour's leaders and intellectuals, visited Kenya and listened for five hours to 'horrifying stories of atrocities by the police and the home guard from the African point of view'. He concluded that there seemed to be little difference between Mau Mau terror and police counter-action. Furthermore, no-one denied 'that before the British troops arrived, lynch law was widely prevalent, and many policemen are now in prison for excesses committed last spring'. He was however impressed by the benign and likeable commissioner of police, Col O'Rourke, who made no attempt to pretend that all was well. At the time of Crossman's visit the force numbered 10,000 full-time policemen and 11,000 armed reservists. Many had been recruited to meet the crisis and Crossman observed that, inevitably, they were inadequately trained at all levels. Far too often they took justice into their own hands, torturing or killing prisoners who were trying to escape.

There was no shortage of evidence of torture and murder. Canon Bewes saw 'a hospital ward of inoffensive, yet badly injured men [who] had been questioned by the police'. The workers of the second generation settler George Murray, suspected of Mau Mau activities, had a 'rough time' while prisoners, and African workers from Deloraine, the Scotts' farm, were 'screened' – which involved interrogation as to whether they had taken oaths. 'Sometimes they would come back with bumps and bruises and even cigarette burns on them.' Nevertheless barrister T.R. Johar, who spent much of his time defending Africans accused of Mau Mau activities, maintained that 'beating was more a matter of people than policy'. During his short stay in Kenya Crossman learned that the Africans regarded the British troops as their 'protectors', whom they liked in the reserves because they were the first white men they had ever seen work with their hands.

The Africans who were the subject of these atrocities were, perhaps, more sanguine than many Europeans about their treatment. Those from Deloraine Farm who suffered cigarette burns, for example, described their treatment as 'quite right . . . If they don't do this to us, how can they find out if we have taken the oath?' George Murray observed that his workers 'never seemed to hold a grudge', and when released they returned to the farm, where some were still working in 1994. And Michael Kemp, a lawyer who served in the Intelligence

Corps and interrogated many Mau Mau prisoners, including a number of the leaders, was pleased that 'some of the Mau Mau prisoners whom I helped to interrogate later became my clients. Muraya Muchera and other ex-prisoners evidently trusted me personally and our firm (which included several former members of the Kenya Regiment) both to understand them and to represent them effectively and honestly'.

As 1953 came to its end, there was a faint glimmer of reconciliation. Elspeth Huxley and Canon Bewes were both returning, separately, to Kenya from England after lengthy periods of absence, and they knew Kenya as it had been before Mau Mau. Huxley stayed with her mother from October until mid-December. She observed 'an early Christmas atmosphere', at Weithaga Church of Scotland Mission. 'Christians are favourite targets for Mau Mau and many have been killed and still are being.' Bewes' observations, quite independent of Huxley's, were remarkably similar. He records numerous cases of such shootings and slashings. He also recounts that 'something very significant is happening up in the Kikuyu hills; it is a new experiment in Christian living, all the more wonderful because it was never deliberately planned. It has simply grown out of the present situation'. He describes some of the larger mission stations which became 'cities of refuge . . . [where] . . . Africans and Europeans live in one community together, sharing everything on terms of equality and brotherhood'.

By the end of the year the Buffs had killed well over a hundred Mau Mau terrorists 'in the most productive period of Mau Mau-hunting enjoyed by any British battalion,' wrote military historian Blaxland. It was estimated that Mau Mau had lost 3,064 confirmed killed and that a thousand had been captured. No-one knew the number of the enemy wounded but 100,000 Mau Mau supporters had been arrested and 64,000 of them brought to trial. The British casualties were relatively light, but they included Maj Archibald Wavell, son of Field Marshall Wavell, who was killed on Christmas Eve near Thika.

The end of 1953 also provides a time for review of changing attitudes. Post-war settler James Stapleton had, understandably, regarded Mau Mau as sole perpetrators of evil and atrocities but, he wrote, 'news came that trusted home guards had been arrested for murders and atrocities committed on the prisoners they had taken.

Private feuds and old scores were, it seemed, being conveniently settled. So the home guard, who thought they had the law behind them, were finding themselves in the dock, and what is more they were being found guilty and sentenced'.

No one was better qualified to pass judgment on this sad year than our strand Carey Francis, headmaster of the Alliance School for Africans. He had always expressed confidence in the British Empire as a power for good in the world. He told pupils earlier in 1953, when Mau Mau was at its peak, that the school was 'an oasis in a grim desert, hardly affected by what [was] going on outside'. He referred to the school as 'as happy a family as ever, boys, masters, black, white, Kikuyu, non-Kikuyu'. Out of school in the holidays, however, many of the boys had a hard time, and some took the Mau Mau oath. Francis had addressed the school: 'You . . . are living in comparative peace because the security forces are fighting Mau Mau on your behalf . . . You should see what the Mau Mau do. You do not fight guerrilla warfare by the methods of the YMCA . . . We have to make them afraid of us as they are of Mau Mau.' It was his belief that 'we cannot destroy Mau Mau by killing gangsters or by imprisoning oath-takers, but only by destroying the foundation on which the whole monument rests, by showing that we are not enemy invaders'.

As time went by, his confidence in the ways in which the fight against Mau Mau was being conducted began to waver. At the end of the year he wrote, 'I am no defender of Mau Mau; it is wholly wicked. But it is not the ultimate enemy'. All round he heard tales of injustice and abuse of power. He was reluctant to believe them, but gradually the evidence had convinced him. He wrote a memo to 'a very senior Government official' whom he trusted, to express 'what I believe to be the feelings of a considerable body of men of goodwill, Europeans and Africans, the men in whom I see hope for the future, ordinary folk from many walks of life, usually Christian, who believe in truth and who fear that the present tendencies are turning the present conflict into one of White v Black instead of Good v Evil'. He continued, 'I have no doubt whatever that the security forces, and particularly the police, have been involved in many acts of brutality to prisoners (sometimes amounting to deliberate and despicable torture) and of callous ill-treatment of innocent Africans, and of looting and destruction of private property. These acts have not been 'occasional errors of judgement', they have been so widespread as to be regarded as the normal policy of the security forces. European officers have often taken part and still more often connived at them. The police are feared and loathed and never trusted by the great bulk of Africans. The police force as a whole seems banded together to resist any criticism, particularly of the European personnel. No unknown African has much chance of getting redress; indeed, he believes that if he makes a complaint he is in personal danger from the forces which should be protecting him.

'The essential trouble is one of attitude. So many of the members of the Security Forces seem to understand nothing about Africans, do not even regard them as fellow human beings. They shout at them, demand that they take off their hats at their approach, speak contemptuously of them in their presence, have no respect for their feelings or their convenience. Some even speak as though they enjoyed killing Africans, and I fear that it is true. Why do so many Africans attempt to escape? Why are they almost invariably shot dead? I know the other side. Security forces have a most difficult, dangerous, unenviable task. Africans are hard to understand and can be desperately aggravating. Full allowance must be made for these things. And yet that does not account for what is happening. The unjust attitudes and unjust actions which are commonplace today are building up a legacy of hatred which will be far harder to overcome than one of the bands of terrorists.'

He continued that he could not prove anything in court, 'but I believe that if they say what they honestly think, most responsible officers of the Administration in Central Province, most missionaries and most loyal Africans in the same area will agree with me'. He gave instances of European policemen on trains – one who drew his revolver and waved it about and slapped and banged boys, and the other who slapped boys for answering him in English, which 'behaviour does not enhance the reputation of the police'.

Francis had personal experience of 'heavy-handedness' which endorsed reports he had received. On one occasion the war had come into the 'oasis in a grim desert' and Francis found the school cook 'disgracefully beaten up' by members of the Kikuyu home guard. He found a European in the Kenya Regiment who appeared to sanction the beating but who refused to give his name. Francis ordered him out. It was an action which caused 'some unpopularity but resulted in a great improvement'.

It was no doubt the reports he had received, coupled with his own experience, which led Francis to propose the government make a statement guaranteeing better treatment, which 'would do more to restore confidence and to end the emergency than the killing of thousands of terrorists'. He campaigned with Scottish missionaries George Calderwood, Robert Macpherson and Walter Scott-Dickson, and investigated incidents of torture and deliberate killing by the security forces. He interviewed 'the highest authorities, military and civil'. He threatened writing to the *Times,* but did not post his draft.

Francis was, however, party to a letter from the Christian Council of Kenya to the *East African Standard* dated 4th December 1953, which recorded 'the abhorrence with which we read the published records of evidence given before a civil court and a recent court martial'. It urged the security forces not to indulge in cruel abuse of power: 'You are Christians and such action is unchristian.' Such action 'establishes a legacy of hate that will last for generations, thereby endangering the whole future of this country'.

The Prince of Wales and the Duke of York schools went along with him, and he spoke at both schools using Matthew 7:12 as his text: 'Always treat others as you would like them to treat you.'

ABOVE: *Mau Mau detention camp.*

BELOW: *Settlers march on Government House, Nairobi. (See page 149)*

9

The Decline and Fall of Mau Mau

'Secure [Kikuyu] co-operation amd cease the slaughter.'
(Winston Churchill to Blundell, December 1954)

The concern of post-war settler James Stapleton and headmaster
Carey Frances regarding the conduct of the war against Mau Mau
by some, perhaps too many, members of the military and the police
did not end when the 1953 calendar was replaced by the one for 1954.
The change of calendars did, however, mark a transition from civil to
internecine war.

This chapter and the next are concerned with the period from
January 1954 to December 1956, during which Mau Mau ceased to
function as a cohesive entity. There were numerous attacks on
Europeans and some Indians as well as on property in the early
months of 1954, but these were reduced in scale, particularly in
Nairobi, by the government's Operation Anvil in April. Running
parallel to these events were Westminster's attempts to find a form of
government that would be acceptable to all subjects in the future and
that would bring order to the prevailing chaos. The Administration
also pushed on with agrarian reform for the Africans.

If there was a Mau Mau decline in the early months of 1954 it was
not apparent in January, when the Kenya government read a bleak
assessment of the Mau Mau situation in the report of a colonial office
parliamentary delegation to the colony. 'It is our view,' the report
said, 'based upon all the evidence available to us, both from official
and responsible unofficial sources, that the influence of Mau Mau in
the Kikuyu area, except in certain localities, has not declined; it has,
on the contrary, increased; in this respect the situation has
deteriorated and the danger of infection outside the Kikuyu area is
now greater, not less, than it was at the beginning of the state of
emergency. In Nairobi, the situation is both grave and acute. Mau
Mau orders are carried out in the heart of the city, Mau Mau "courts"
sit in judgement and their sentences are carried out by gangsters.'

It must have made worrying reading for the governor, Sir Evelyn
Baring, who had to deal with a number of thorny issues all at once.

Not only was he receiving open opposition from the newly appointed commissioner of police, Arthur Young, but his attorney general was demanding enquiries into prosecutions of the Administration. He also had to weigh the consequences of the government's amnesty with Mau Mau against strong opposition from the settler lobby while initiating an agrarian revolution which would change the nature of Africans' land ownership. Had he but known it, he might have drawn some comfort from the position in which Mau Mau now found itself.

At much the same time Mau Mau leaders of the Kenya Parliament, which existed more in name than practice, were less than sanguine regarding their military organization. On the 5th February, some 750 warriors and 40 leaders representing most Mau Mau interests met 'in a grassy open area under some big trees' to discuss the way ahead. Five aims were identified which may be summarized as:

• To establish its authority and legitimacy among Aberdares guerrilla groups.
• To initiate a new military offensive, aimed at enemy property.
• To separate itself from the military hierarchy and dissociate its members from particular sections or territorial groupings.
• To demonstrate its national character and gain added military support by extending the revolt to other tribes and regions.
• To reorganize and assume authority over the civilian population in the reserves.

More immediately, the leaders sought a more centralized organization. One must keep in mind the nature of the 'grassy open area' venue, the condition of the participants (mostly warrior leaders fighting a war against what would be overwhelming odds) and that tendency of Njama to see things as he would like them to be rather than as they were. But his report suggests that some, at least, of the leaders were thinking ahead and were not the disorganized rabble they were regarded as being in the outside world.

Njama criticised the Ituma Nderi Trinity Council for failing to hold meetings and Mau Mau for its lack of organization and failure to manage the affairs of Africans in the reserves. They 'lacked central organization,' he concluded. At that time the 'armies' were generally district-based and largely autonomous. Mau Mau's Kenya Defence Council had met only once, in September, a month after its formation.

Plans were made for the first meeting of the Kenya Parliament. How many members should there be? After a heated exchange of opinions it was agreed that, since Jesus Christ had only 12 disciples whose preaching had reached all over the world, they should elect 12 members, excluding Kimathi, the president of the parliament, to represent the whole of Kenya rather than regions, class or tribes. A form of secret ballot was devised for selection. The outcome was that Dedan Kimathi was elected president 'by unspoken consensus'. The elected members all bore high military rank, and when the election was over they stood facing Mount Kenya and prayed to God, asking him to bless, guard and guide their Kenya Parliament members and grant them power and wisdom.

They returned to camp from their meeting place in the glade and enjoyed an evening of singing, dancing and military drill. After writing letters of appointment they decided that every man should contribute 10s and every woman, including girls, 5s. The newly elected members of parliament concentrated their talks on 'attacking plans' concerned with destroying any enemy property; using fire to burn all the grass, cornfields, wheat and barley, stores and houses; stealing and spraying the grass with cattle dip so that cattle and sheep would die; and using pangas and swords to cut down coffee, tea and any enemy property they came across. They agreed that members of parliament should not participate in raids but stay in the forest.

While the leaders of the principal parties were considering reports and making plans, conditions in town and country were no better, probably worse, than they had been at the close of 1953. To illustrate the 'present condition' early in 1954 Louis Leakey extracted some 50 lengthy quotations from the *East African Standard* for a random period of six days from Friday 29th January to Thursday 4th February. This period 'was not an unusual week, in any way', wrote Leakey. 'It has been going on each and every day for the past twenty months.' His extracts included descriptions of:

• Discoveries of Mau Mau gun factories in the Meru forest and at Thika.
• European encounters with Mau Mau involving home-made weapons in the Eastern Aberdares, near Kiambu, South Nyeri, south of Nairobi, in Gatundu Location, Magutu Location (2), north east of Kijabi and near Rumuruti.

• Other encounters, skirmishes etc. near Nyeri, on the Kijabe road, near Embu, in Nairobi (2), North Kinangop, in the Masai reserve, in Muthaiga area, north-west of Thika, east of Embu and Meru area.

• Europeans' carelessness with gun security, which in the six days which Leakey monitored led to two European women and three European and one Seychellois man being prosecuted and fined. The thefts were all from motor cars and occurred in Nairobi (2), Nanyuki, Nakuru, Kisumu and Thika.

• A Luo pleading guilty to being 'a member of the Mau Mau and being sentenced to 12 months' hard labour'.

• Five attacks on Kikuyu farms and reserves by Mau Mau gangs, during which several Kikuyu were wounded and killed and property destroyed in Thika, Rumuruti, South Nyeri and Fort Hall.

• Three trials of 14 Africans. The charges were of being in possession of fire-arms, oath giving and taking and murder.

• An unsuccessful attempt to rob Khalsa School during which two men were detained.

• A Kikuyu found shot in the back in Eastleigh.

• Searches for terrorists in the Rumuruti swamps.

• Two attacks by Mau Mau on farms at North Minangop.

• Two sweeps in Kilimani (Nairobi) and in Bihati Location during which 3,000 Africans were rounded up. They were screened and the majority released.

• Two pistols recovered from Africans arrested at Thika and Kiambu.

• Two armed gangs in Nairobi carrying out robberies of Indians.

• A Forestry Department Land Rover ambushed in the Mount Kenya Forest. A Sten gun and £1,00 in cash were stolen.

• An African sentenced to death for possessing a home-made gun and ammunition in Mgutu location.

• Eight Kikuyu and two Embu tribesmen hanged at Nairobi Prison, six for illegal possession of fire-arms and four for murder.

The list was by no means exhaustive, and had Leakey's survey been made a month or so later it would have included a report of an incident which was picked up by the British press. Farm manager Joan Scott experienced her third attack by Mau Mau. Front page in the *Sunday Graphic*, this was described as similar to those the previous year but there were only eight terrorists, led by 'Brigadier Mahommed Mwai', formerly Scott's house-boy, who joined Mau Mau when they attacked the farm in April 1953. 'The raiders fled.'

From Leakey's extracts and the Scott report, above, it is apparent that the early weeks of 1954 witnessed a country in chaos. Murder and mayhem ruled across the whole length and breadth of Kikuyuland and, occasionally, beyond.

There was, however, one success for the Administration – the wounding and capture of Mau Mau's General China, Waruhiu Itote, in January. It was an event which shocked Njama, who was in the forest, and no doubt other Mau Mau fighters, too. China was, perhaps, second in prestige only to Dedan Kimathi. The government made much of his capture, and thousands of leaflets were dropped from aircraft which also carried loudspeakers. Mau Mau fighters were invited to surrender, taking green branches with them. 'You will be welcomed by the Devons,' said the speakers.

China was sentenced to death. Ten days later Kimathi received a typed copy of a letter signed by China, asking that he send two men to represent the Mau Mau fighters in negotiations with the government about surrender terms. Njama's recollections of the letter was that it expressed concern about the lives of the Mau Mau fighters saying, 'We had better stop this bloodshed.' The China letter, as it became known, went on to list seven questions which, it said, the government had asked Kimathi to put to other Mau Mau leaders. Similar letters had been sent to other leaders in the forest. The questions were concerned with:

- The reasons for the fighting.
- Steps which must be taken to get Mau Mau to come out of the forest with their arms.
- What Mau Mau would do if they failed to get land and freedom.
- What retaliation Mau Mau would take on the home guards, traitors and loyal (to the government) Africans in the event of their achieving their freedom.
- Whether Mau Mau would agree to suspend the fighting while talks took place.
- Whether Mau Mau saw these government overtures as a trap?
- Who would get land and freedom if the Mau Mau fought 'to the last man's drop of blood'.

Mau Mau General Ndiritu Thuita and Njama were elected by their parliament to negotiate with the Kenyan government. They prepared answers to the questions in the China letter and gave conditions which had to be fulfilled by the government in order to demonstrate its willingness to negotiate. They sought the return of the White Highlands, full independence under African leadership, the hand-over to Kenya African government of all the alienated lands (which they would redistribute), the demolition of the 'villages' and military bases, the release of all revolutionary prisoners and detainees, and the opening of schools closed by the government. Kapila, Ralph Bunch and D.N. Pritt (the counsel who had defended Jomo Kenyatta) should negotiate and advise Mau Mau. Jomo Kenyatta or his representative from the Lokitaung should also take part in the negotiations – of which more later.

Only a week or two after General China's capture, General Omera was captured by government forces and was known to be co-operating with Kenya police reserve. His capture was linked in Mau Mau mythology with an incident referred to as the Kayahwe Massacre. Mau Mau fighters had successfully attacked Kandara government base, killing many while they were fleeing and burning all the houses. One of the leaders, General Mboko, then split his group into small units, one of which was ambushed by the Kayahwe River. Finding that they were surrounded, the inexperienced troops surrendered and 'ninety-two men were shot in cold blood'. Two, left for dead, survived to tell the tale. The incident became the subject of a Kikuyu song.

British commanders confirm that their orders in the KAR were to destroy Mau Mau wherever they could find them. Very few were caught alive, and those who survived were probably badly wounded. They were very frightened, on the run and looking very much like animals, with their long hair all matted, wearing some sort of animal skin and using their arms as feet in the very close jungle. Their ages varied from, probably, 40 down to 16. Coles' askaris came from Uganda and 'didn't have a history of capturing their enemy. They were trained to find the enemy and kill him. And they did'. But Liddle maintained that he had no experience of his KAR company taking part in 'what you might call aggressive action with captured people'. Many years on, former General Ndirangu recalled that 'if an African soldier got hold of you he would kill you, [but] a white soldier would arrest you and take you to be tried. There was more justice under the Europeans'.

Blundell saw the events of early 1954 as follows:

- That the government was 'disunited and lacking in unity of thought and direction'.
- That by June at the latest they would have lost the whole country (this from a secret intelligence summary).
- That private European armies were being formed, and it would not be easy to control them because 'the public' saw only the appalling delays and lack of urgency in the general situation.

Blundell expressed his concerns to Baring and urged that there should be an effective war cabinet. That was the consensus of European opinion. They looked for a war cabinet that was for political purposes independent of the Administration.

The perennial rift between Administration and European settlers persisted and was augmented by differences between the Administration and the military. There had been long discussions between General Harding and Oliver Lyttelton in February about the wisdom of replacing Baring with a military governor. In a letter dated 28th February 1954 General Erskine wrote, 'I gather everybody wants to do something but nobody knows what to do. Baring is a sick man and I do not think he can possibly carry on. The settlers hate me just as much as I hate them and I do not reckon I'm a starter.' The European settlers compared Erskine unfavourably with General Hinde, and he was never popular with the Administration. In a letter home in June, Erskine wrote, 'I frankly loathe this place and the job . . . Kenya is the Mecca of the middle class, so I have been told. I have coined a new phrase, "a sunny place for shady people". I never want to see another Kenya man or woman, and I dislike them all with few exceptions'.

In March Governor Baring had taken six weeks sick leave, and there was a spate of rumours that he would not return. These were denied by the colonial office but firmly believed in the junior ranks of the army and the Administration. He returned, however, at the end of June.

Rifts were not restricted to the higher echelons. Former governor Mitchell described the divisions in the views of the Europeans in a letter on 'the current organization'. There are, he wrote, 'many who in all good faith, believe that a policy which must lead to equal rights for all civilized men is either wrong or at any rate impracticable; there are others who sincerely believe that Africans and most Indians never can be civilized; there are a great many for whom equality between people of white and of coloured skin is an impossible, even a wicked idea'. Mitchell thought, however, that many European settlers of whom he was now one, still held to the policy 'steadfastly pursued by the Trustee (the British government) that any hope for the future depended on the belief that all human beings are inherently capable of civilization'. This, from an administrator who had spent almost all his working life in East Africa, should have carried weight.

There was pressure for partition ('dividing the country between black and white') from the European right-wing Kenya Empire Party, and this found favour with some. However, as Mitchell wrote in a letter to Blundell, 'With a population mix of 45,000 Europeans, 100,000 Asians and 5,000,000 Africans, a European community insistent on separation, special rights and refusal to cooperate with other races would isolate itself and not be able to maintain even its present privileges, including representation in the Legislature'. But those Europeans who favoured 'continued sustained opposition' to multi-racialism did not, as Blundell put it, 'have the tempering effect of responsibility [of government] upon them'. He was aware that the Africans and Asians had become frightened of European influence and of what might happen to them if extreme European opinion achieved control.

Blundell's approach appears to have been a balance of liberalism and pragmatism. In a letter he wrote to Baring the previous November he had warned that the general opinion of the European community was that there was at that time no African really qualified to accept ministerial responsibility, and that he could accept no com- mitment to an African at ministerial level. He attempted to reconcile the consensus of European preferences, insofar as they could be determined, with what he believed might be achievable.

The prospect of changes in the balance of representation on the legislative council concentrated European minds on the future representation of the Asian community. In his November 1953 letter to Baring, Blundell had acknowledged that at that time the European representatives had looked on the 'Asian group' on LEGCO as representing both Hindu and Muslim sections of that community. Now, with the people in the Indian sub-continent independent and the continent partitioned, it was becoming increasingly apparent that their demands 'would need to be considered independently'.

The Indian community was, in the words of barrister Johar, prone to get metaphorically 'bashed' from both sides – not only were they second class citizens by virtue of the fact that Kenya was a colony, but the Africans regarded them as having taken over things that rightly belonged to them. They were, during the years 1954–6, between the devil and the deep blue sea.

In the early months of 1954 LEGCO member A.B. Patel, faced with the prospect of possible rule by the European settlers, declared that there was no alternative to the government at present or, indeed, until the three major communities could reach agreement to form a government acceptable to all. Patel therefore pushed Lyttelton for greater African, Asian and Arab representation, but the response of Asian leaders to the Lyttelton Plan, referred to in the previous chapter, was generally favourable. Blundell developed a strong liking for Patel, who in 1956 urged him to secure as many seats as possible for the Europeans in the legislative council as a bulwark behind which the Asian people might shelter.

Blundell's appreciation was not shared with all Africans. The Labour MP Barbara Castle observed the friction which existed between African and Asian when, during her visit to Kenya in 1955, Tom Mboya's deputy, Gaya, chanted almost monotonously, 'Oh, how I hate the Asians' as he saw 'not a single African shop, only Asian ones', in an African location which he and the MP were visiting.

Castle also met Mr Mangat QC of the East African Indian National Congress (EAINC), who felt caught between the Africans, whose cause the EAINC supported, and the whites, who were prepared to give the Asians preferential treatment which they refused to Africans. She herself stayed in the home of Mr Desai, 'a friendly if frightened little Asian businessman' with whom Brockway had stayed. Desai, she wrote, welcomed any Asian, African or European who cared to come.

The Asians continued to take a middle-of-the-road stance, and in August 1956 the EAINC affirmed Patel's stand while pressing for Indian representation on LEGCO and local government bodies.

Whatever the views of various groups within the European community, the arrival of the secretary of state, Oliver Lyttelton, in March 1954 was the decisive factor in determining the way ahead for Kenya. 'Straight out' he required a future government which would represent 'the national scene'. This applied, particularly, to the Europeans' proposals for a war cabinet, of which more anon. There followed a period of intense negotiation, near the end of which Lyttelton likened his position to that of a juggler 'trying to keep all three coloured balls in the air at once'. Blundell saw these negotiations as 'a decisive moment in the political history of Kenya'. The new generation of African political thinkers and leaders were, he wrote, even then standing in the wings awaiting their cue. They noted 'what appeared to be a lack of generosity in dealing with African claims. As a result, they began to move away from the idea of partnership and association between the races towards a policy of straightforward majority rule'.

The term 'multi-racialism' became common parlance during the Lyttelton negotiations. All races were to be represented on LEGCO. The European members gave the notion grudging support, and the report won the support of the great majority of African opinion until attacks on it from a section of the Europeans made them think there must be something wrong with the whole arrangement. Kamba leaders pointed out that 650,000 Kamba were now represented by a man they had called a 'Kikuyu rebel'. Strong feelings were emerging among the Africans that they wanted their system of voting and representation to be the same as that of the Europeans, namely 'one man, one vote'.

The African members were well aware of Lyttelton's insistence on representation of 'the national scene', but they appeared to go along with the proposal until the last minute. The European elected members were disturbed at this change of mind and were in no mood to make what they regarded as further concessions. Certainly the majority of European settlers did not favour universal suffrage. As post-war settler Errol Whittall put it, 'It is useless to give a vote to a man and a woman with a hoe and half a dozen goats'. He recognized that at the time he was writing, 1955–6, such an idea was not even suggested, but he saw from the way the wind was blowing that 'through force of [African] numbers' the Europeans would be liquidated – a daunting prospect.

Tom Mboya, the Luo trade union leader and one of the few 'political' Africans not in gaol and still active in Nairobi, observed that with almost all the KAU leaders (mostly Kikuyu) in prison, it fell to the Kenya Federation of Labour to express the African reaction to the Lyttelton Plan. They rejected it because there was no direct representation of Africans on LEGCO and because, Mboya wrote, 'the African minister was clearly going to be used to make the world believe Africans were participating in government, although in fact he was a tiny minority with no policy making responsibility'. Furthermore, as Mboya added, it was the first time Africans had the chance to decide whether or not to take part in the colonial government, and they took the opportunity of making their presence known. The compromise they adopted rejected the constitution but did not stop members of the group from taking part individually.

The middle of 1954 saw the publication of a 43-page book entitled *The Mau Mau in Kenya*. It contained a map of 'the Mau Mau black spot' (*page 50*) and 33 photographs showing mutilated cattle, a hanged cat, burning huts and European and African leaders talking to loyal troops or viewing the aftermath of Mau Mau attacks. Two showed RAF military aircraft. No author was acknowledged, but the foreword was by Granville Roberts, the Kenya public relations officer. The stated intention of the book was 'to throw light upon the Mau Mau secret society and the foul atrocities it [had] committed'. 'The horror of Mau Mau' should, said the book, 'be viewed against the background of nation-building under peaceful and progressive conditions. The African peasant agriculture was being nourished by constant instruction and encouragement, and rural life and rural economy were being modernized as quickly as the resources of the colony would permit'.

The massacre at Lari, and Mau Mau oath-taking provided the main thrusts of the book. It stated that the Kikuyu Christians had suffered martyrdom for their faith, and that by no means all the Kikuyu tribe were members of Mau Mau. It concluded that the Kikuyu tribe constituted roughly a fifth of a population of 5,250,000 and that, save for isolated incidents, all Kenya's tribes remained peaceful, contented and progressive, despite the Mau Mau troubles.

During the middle months of 1954 'multi-racialism' was the theme of the day, wrote Oginga Odinga, and, under a 'deceptive formula', one ministry was allocated to an African, two to Asians and three to whites – three non-Europeans balanced by three Europeans, in a country where Africans outnumbered whites by a hundred to one.

Nevertheless, the government had a commitment to multi-racialism. The Europeans were still divided in their views of the way ahead, but the multi-racialism policy statement was regarded by the overseas press as a remarkably liberal document from people under the pressures of a rebellion, and by this time the European community in Kenya recognized the importance of favourable publicity. Blundell considered himself to be among the more moderate and progressive elements of the European community, whom the more conservative labelled as 'multi-racialists', attacking and denigrating them wherever possible. Barbara Castle endorsed Blundell's self-assessment and referred to him as both intelligent and progressive.

Blundell believed that more than the old rigid racial outlook was required if the effort necessary to contain the Mau Mau revolt were to be mobilized. He admitted that some of his colleagues would never have looked at multi-racialism in normal times (and even now some would accept nothing which did not give the Europeans 'outright control of the government'), but he knew that many were prepared to accept it in order to get more effective government action.

European farmers must have been somewhat reassured when Baring, opening a conference in Nairobi on the 1st November 1954, told his audience that 'the prospective [European] immigrant' who hoped to work on a farm in the highlands had several reasons for looking hopefully to the future. He referred to a recent statement by the secretary of state for the colonies that 'the British settler is really here to stay' and that he had 'an essential part to play'. He added: 'Her Majesty's Government are not likely to lend themselves to encouraging people to come if they intend to betray them. They will be entitled to full confidence in the possession of the homes they have built for themselves and for their children.'

There was more than altruism in Blundell's willingness to accept the concept of multi-racialism. In a letter to a colleague early in 1954 he had said that it had been made quite clear to him that there could be no real advance for the European community unless Oliver Lyttelton could present to the parliament 'some measure of participation by other groups and some measure of agreement between them'. The effect of the Mau Mau rebellion was, he continued, that it was becoming more and more a test case for black versus white in Africa, 'and the world, much encouraged from Delhi, was lining up on those lines'. Furthermore, the autumn of 1956 would see an election which was important for Kenya's future, because the electorate would be asked to endorse the general principles of the Lyttelton Plan. In the event of its rejection, the secretary of state had made it clear that he would initially return to the existing 'pure colonial form of government'.

Come the day, Blundell stood opposite the right-wing Maj B.P. Roberts – Blundell for multi-racialism and Roberts for partition. Roberts, wrote Seys in his letter home, wanted 'Kenya split up into provinces, with the white settlers entirely responsible for their own province, the Africans controlled by the colonial office in their provinces and the Asians excluded from all executive participation in the government'. Blundell was returned by a majority of nearly two to one. 'We placed the principle of multi-racialism first and planned to move steadily to the other changes,' he wrote.

An important item in the Lyttelton talks, the most important in the eyes of many Europeans, was the formation of a war council which could fight Mau Mau effectively. It consisted of Baring, Erskine, the deputy governor and one unofficial member of the legislature. Blundell became the minister without portfolio. Constitutionally the war council was part of the general colonial framework whereby everyone was advisory to the governor. Erskine was directly responsible to the secretary of state for war. Blundell had the right of direct approach to the secretary of state for the colonies, and attended as an independent minister with his own relationship with London. Whyatt, the attorney general, accused the war council (he was not a member), of being an illegal body. Baring privately admitted that 'according to strict constitution' that was the case.

There had been great pressure from settlers for the removal of Whyatt. He had been known to lose his temper at executive council meetings, and his normal reaction to an enquiry by Baring was to say 'out of the question; against the law', almost snapping it out and showing no inclination to see a way round. In a private conversation, Baring said that Whyatt was right from the very beginning and had not deviated from his principles. Right or not, Whyatt's principles resulted in many headaches for Baring and for many members of the Administration. Few can have been sorry to learn that he was appointed chief justice of Singapore.

Blundell became, in his own words, 'a sort of political shock absorber between the public and the war council'. The council may not have been perfect, but some of the personalities in the old government had gone, and responsibility for law and order had been divorced from the appointment of attorney general. One effect of the war council was to reduce the influence of senior members of the Administration, less able to adapt to the changing circumstances than the young district officers in the front line against Mau Mau. The war council was, wrote Chenevix Trench, small enough and high-powered enough to reach decisions quickly, and it arranged the final defeat of the Mau Mau very efficiently. But that defeat remained some way off.

What motivated Mau Mau? In April 1954, in an attempt to understand its psychology, the government of Kenya commissioned an expert report by a distinguished psychologist with extensive experience in Africa, Dr J.C. Carothers. His report was published in Nairobi in 1955. It comprised 29 pages of analysis, summarized in a five-page synopsis which included a number of recommendations. A lay précis of his report might include the following conclusions:

• Minds are the product of culture, and the stability of a primitive (pre-literate) culture such as that of the Kikuyu was based on the absence of internal strife.

• Unlike European children, who are taught to exercise their curiosity and think logically, the children of primitive people lack curiosity or have their curiosity stifled.

• Primitive peoples tend to oscillate between good and evil, and as they are highly dependent on their tribal group they consider that 'aliens' have no rights.

• European social misfits tend to be contained; this is less likely to apply in primitive societies.

• Primitive people see their environment as a dangerous place in which the individual is vulnerable. He may, however, obtain support from more powerful sources, such as witchdoctors.

• The Kikuyu people regard European farmers as an alien power living in close proximity and having a great impact on their culture.

• In the 1950s the Kikuyu culture was at essentially the same stage of development as that reached in Europe in the 16th century, when witchcraft, ritual murder and cannibalism, necrophilia and sexual orgies were not uncommon.

Carothers' recommendations included:

• Villagization (to which reference is made elsewhere) as 'a step in the right direction' of providing psychological as well as physical security.
• Education
　　– to enable students to think things out for themselves.
　　– to enable them to see themselves as part of a vast human organisation with tentacles which stretch a long way.
• The instillation of general principles of social conduct, and ideals of truthfulness and honesty.
• That the European population should practise Christian principles in their dealings with their fellow men, both black and white, or 'the missionaries might just as well pack up their bags and go'.
• That prospective immigrants to Kenya should be interviewed by a selection board to assess their qualifications for living in a land where their every act will have much wider repercussions than is the case in the land they aim to leave.
• The need for strong leadership at every administrative level by men chosen for their jobs on the basis of their sophistication, their personalities and their prestige, all of which needs to be paid for in accordance with their responsibilities, and they should be left on their own, as far as possible, to exercise those responsibilities.

The cover of the report states that it was published for information, but it had not yet (at the time of the 8th impression in 1955) been considered by government.

British troops and the RAF arrived in Kenya in 1953, but policing and security were still far from perfect. The police, Special Branch and military were under separate commands, but they worked closely for most of the time. Obtaining any personnel in sufficient numbers to provide even scant coverage was difficult. Britain provided almost full employment in the 1950s, and this created a situation in which there was not the incentive which developed in later years to look for work overseas.

The Kenya police force had to be expanded from a contingent of 7,000 for the whole colony to one which could cope with a tribal revolution. The benign and likable commissioner, M.S. O'Rourke, had

had an extremely onerous burden, his force hopelessly inadequate for the task which confronted it and with no proper intelligence section. By 1954 the recommendations of the British director general were in place, and Kenya had a good police intelligence and special branch section which became a model for other colonies.

O'Rourke, however, was by this time worn out, and he resigned. He was aware that Crossman had, during his visit, heard what he described as 'horrifying stories of atrocities by the police and home guard'. Policing problems did not disappear with O'Rourke's departure: in some respects they increased. He was succeeded by Col Arthur Young, commissioner of police for the City of London, who had earned a great reputation in Malaya and was on secondment to Kenya for a year.

Baring had been on rest leave in England and he was not consulted about the appointment. Young's offer to see Baring before taking it up was declined by Lyttelton, who told him that Baring was likely to retire through ill health without returning to Kenya, but in the event Baring was back in Kenya before Young arrived. Young had, however, paid a lightning visit to Kenya, after which he returned to Westminster and lobbied the cabinet for a change of governor and commander-in-chief. He also told correspondents of the *Times* that Kenya lacked both a leader and a plan. Such lobbying and announcements to the press were not conducive to a happy professional relationship between Baring and Young.

Young sought, too, policing changes based on a published white paper on the Kenya police, which recommended its independence from the Administration. Baring and Young clashed. An independent constabulary was considered appropriate for Britain's parliamentary democracy but was, the Kenyan administration maintained, 'totally out of context in the enlightened dictatorship of a Crown colony', particularly with a state of emergency at its peak. Young failed to have his proposals adopted by the executive council of ministers, and he resigned.His letter of resignation in December 1954 ran to 30 paragraphs. It was not published. 'If my report had been published,' Young contended, 'the governor and colonial secretary would have been in a very hazardous position'.

During his short term in office he had pressed for some tribal chiefs and some Europeans to be prosecuted, and eight cases (seven black and one white) were eventually assembled by the police for prosecution. Government House was well aware of occasional incidents of brutality on the part of the police, and had introduced special police inspectors whose duty it was to report on misconduct by the regular police, by those recently recruited from Britain (referred to by the settlers as '£80 jobs') and by the Kenya Police Reserve, in which almost all European and many Asian civilians served on a part-time basis. The 'snoopers' were resented by many on whom they snooped. Baring thought he might lose the enthusiasm of loyal Africans if he allowed the cases to proceed and the prosecution won. He used the prospect of an amnesty with Mau Mau to justify delaying taking action against the 'loyals'.

This was the time of visits by members of parliament most of whom, like Crossman, were opposed to the continuation of the British empire and were looking for present failings in order to bring about future changes. Barbara Castle was such an MP. She stayed for some time on Michael Blundell's farm, where she took a particular interest in cases in which she thought the security forces had exceeded their legal powers or had abused their position. The cases were there for her to see or, at least, to hear about. Everyone, she wrote, seemed to have some story about the brutality of the police. She focused on the killing of Kamau Kichini, who had been brutality handled and flogged to death over a period of days at a police station manned by two European police officers, Fuller and Waters, who were charged with murder. Resident magistrate Harrison reduced the charge to causing grievous bodily harm, and they were sentenced to three-and-a-half years' imprisonment. Chief Inspector Coppen and DO Bosch, who had been privy to what was going on, were fined £25 and £10 respectively. Richmond, a regular, fully trained member of the colonial service, who had overall responsibility for Kichini's treatment, was not initially punished, but he was later dismissed from the service. Soon after his dismissal he was given a top job as African affairs officer with Aberdare county council.

Castle saw this action as illustrative of Britain's brutal colonial policy, and she was never afraid to give her opinion. She prided herself on not letting go. She expressed a preference for Blundell's 'bluff, blunt manner to the soapy smoothness of Evelyn Baring'. Blundell she considered 'intelligent enough to realise that white privilege could not continue indefinitely'. She regarded Alan Lennox-Boyd, the colonial secretary, as her main target of attack, describing him as 'a Guardsman type of man . . . with the conviction that the British ruling classes at home and overseas, could do no wrong'. Her view of him was confirmed when, 'at his most truculent', Lennox-Boyd told her at Westminster that he was glad Richmond had been given another chance in life as African affairs officer.

At much the same time as Castle was visiting Kenya there was a recruiting drive for police, in Britain and elsewhere. Douglas Walker and William Furner volunteered. Two or three volunteers in their respective cohorts had been constables in Britain and some were ex-servicemen, but the majority had been 'plumbers, bus drivers, anything'. The advertisements sought an 'A' Level in English and two other subjects, but at the training school Walker discovered that 'one chap was illiterate and most of the others didn't have half the advertised qualifications'. Walker had, on arrival in Kenya, been given a revolver but no uniform. Next day he was out on the streets as a policeman, implementing the laws of Kenya 'which none of us knew anything about'. Only after some three months was a place found for them in the training school. The course, which lasted three months and was mainly concerned with learning chunks of appropriate law, was very boring. Weapon training predominated at Furner's school, but as he had recently served in a Guards regiment he had no difficulty with this aspect of his training. Walker, too, found no difficulty.

Formation of the Kikuyu Guard commenced as Mau Mau grew in strength, by which time many Kikuyu had taken the oath. Before they were accepted they were required to confess and were encouraged to name members of Mau Mau. They were provided with uniforms and weapons as available.

Intelligence work required people with different skills. F.R. (Dick) Wilson was personal assistant to Sir Percy Sillitoe, the advisor from London responsible for organising an intelligence network in Kenya. With another officer and a secretary, Wilson set up the Kenyan Intelligence Committee. This was responsible for co-ordinating reports from the district intelligence committees and other sources, and drafting composite reports for the governor and for London. The unit grew from such small beginnings to become a big organization with numerous staff.

Recruitment for intelligence gathering was even more difficult than for policing; recruits were not necessarily volunteers. Frank

Kitson, a junior officer in the Rifle Brigade, was told by his adjutant that he had been posted to Kenya to do a job connected with intelligence – 'at once'. He had no idea of how to get information, and no training on the subject even though his family had an unbroken tradition of military service over a period of more than 200 years. He undertook background reading on Kenya while waiting for his posting, and when he arrived in Nairobi he was given Elspeth Huxley's book on the Kikuyu, *The Red Strangers*, to read. Two days later he was briefed and appointed district military intelligence officer (DMIO) for the Kiambu district. He defined his aim in Kenya as being 'to provide the security forces with the information they needed to destroy Mau Mau'. He soon learned that alternative ways of achieving his aims were either killing all members of Mau Mau or 'assembling a dossier giving a full list of all that was known against a person to the governor, who could then sign an order for detention during the Emergency provided he was satisfied'. Kitson regarded the second way as kinder. That was the extent of his training. Beyond that, it was learning as he went along.

Recruitment and training was a continuing process, but in April 1954 came the sequel to Operation Jock Scott, namely Operation Anvil. One concern of the war council was the possibility of Mau Mau influence spreading to other tribes, and there were signs of the spread of the oaths and the cult of the movement amongst the Kamba of the Machakos district, together with reports of 'a deteriorating scene' among the Masai.

There were reports, too, of Kamba people in Nairobi being oathed, but such infiltration as there had been was annihilated by the Kamba themselves, and one district commissioner asked for fewer Kenya police in the district because there was nothing for them to do.

In Nairobi, however, there were Mau Mau murders almost every night, and men were shot in broad daylight. The Mau Mau central committee continued to recruit in the towns, and Kahinga Wachanga estimated that over 6,000 warriors were sent to the forest in the first half of 1954. In the Aberdares around Mount Kenya they were trained for two days, being shown how to kill enemies, how to escape from danger and how to raid settlers' farms and steal property. The last large group left Nairobi in early April.

Operation Anvil was launched on 24th April 1954 and involved the removal of 30,000 Kikuyu from Nairobi to the reception camps.

Here they were 'screened', and those heavily involved in Mau Mau were moved to detention camps. The 'innocent' returned to their ordinary way of life and work. Similar operations had followed at Kiambu, Fort Hall and Nyeri. The operations were aggressive action against the gangs, coupled with the strengthening of the administration and the build up of the home guard in each location.

The Kenya Regiment played an important part in the operation, as they had extensive local knowledge. At dawn a ring encircled the area in Nairobi where wanted men were thought to be located. There were four British battalions, one KAR battalion and the equivalent of two and a half companies of the Kenya Regiment, supplemented by clerks, artisans and HQ staff. Police were out in full strength, including 24 combat teams of Europeans, Asians and Africans. Barricaded doors were broken down and suspects were hauled out from under beds or inside cupboards. Others broke through windows, only to be caught by the searchers outside. Suspected Mau Mau sympathizers were collected into groups, searched, questioned and documented by special screening teams. The police decided that suspects should be graded into 'hardcore', 'softcore' and 'followers'.

Two incidents illustrate the Kenya Regiment's approach. A 'very thorough search' of the Nairobi Glassworks was, to say the least, heavy-handed. Campbell admits that there were demonstrations of 'over-enthusiasm' by his men.

The raid on the glassworks took off many of the staff to the detainees' pen with their hands on their heads. The detention of these men was later the cause of major concern, because what had been overlooked was that the machinery continued to function until, becoming choked, it ground to a halt.

Yet more serious was the search at the Indian High Commission. Four 'badly wanted' men were apprehended, but over-enthusiasm was an understatement of the approach used. Campbell records that doors were shot off hinges, contents of drawers and filing cabinets were strewn around rooms and pictures were left hanging askew on walls. Such an invasion was an act of war. Campbell's report to the commander-in-chief included reference to the above incidents, and the next day the regiment made its apologies to Mr Pandon, the high commissioner, who luckily was very understanding.

After Anvil the Kenya Regiment came under examination. Blundell strongly resisted proposals for its abolition, but it was reduced to one operational company and a headquarters. Nevertheless, the operation was regarded as an operational success by the Administration. Anvil was brutal, but it broke the back of Mau Mau activities. Henceforth Africans were required to carry pass-books, and camps were built rapidly at Langata, near Nairobi, and at two other sites. Within 48 hours 8,300 of the 11,600 detained were sent to Langata, and within one month 24,000 Africans were in detention camps.

Tom Mboya was one of those rounded up in what he referred to as 'the biggest sweep of the whole Emergency'. He was not Kikuyu, but as a leading trade unionist he was questioned, released and warned not to come back into the cordoned area. And Oginga Odinga, a fellow Luo, refers to 'the entire African population of Nairobi . . . just over 100,000' being effectively screened. The last resistance groups in Nairobi were disrupted, and their supply of arms, ammunition, money, clothing and medical supplies to the freedom-fighters was severed. Karari Njama, who was liaising between Mau Mau camps, found the warriors without medicine and wearing animal skins due to lack of clothes. Europeans had feared the operation would paralyse Nairobi but the fears were unfounded, and although it was not by any means the end of Mau Mau, the hardcore gangsters were driven to mountain and forest.

Anvil marked the intensification of activities in the forest. Erskine produced an overall military plan which, area by area, was destined to restore control and law and order to each district. He deserves credit for the eventual clearing up of the gangs in the forest. Erskine's military appreciation was that the Mau Mau leaders were fighting to unite the Kikuyu people to destroy British influence and secure Kikuyu domination throughout the country in its place. He considered that the priority was to re-establish firm control in the heart of the Kikuyu country, where the maximum help could be given to the resistance movement.

It remained for the soldier, mainly in the forest, to expedite the plan. Coles, Ferguson, Liddle and MacLachlan, all of whose names appear elsewhere, provide detailed accounts of the contribution of government soldiers, and Njama and Wachanga provide the same service on behalf of the Mau Mau. Their accounts are remarkably similar – preparing ambushes and being ambushed, patrolling day and night, skirmishes and, occasionally, battles.

Some units used tracker-dogs but MacLachlan found African trackers better than dogs, because the latter 'made a dreadful noise all the time'. The arrest of General Kaleba illustrates a typical 'combined operation'. Late at night 'a very senior member of the Kenya Police Special Branch' sought military help to apprehend Kaleba, one of the two most wanted terrorists, who was believed to be lying up. Liddle took a small group and after two hours march arrived, in the half light before dawn, at the entrance to a cave. They rushed it and, without a shot being fired, captured General Kaleba, a woman and three or four of his henchmen, who were all armed and fast asleep.

During his perambulations among Mau Mau camps, Njama found many instances of poor sentry-posting at night, and Coles describes an operation in the Aberdare (Nyandarua) Forest when a KAR night patrol quietly infiltrated a group of Mau Mau camps at dawn, opened fire and captured or killed the enemy as they tried to escape. Njama admitted Mau Mau leaders never expected the military to move at night and were unprepared. On one occasion he was, himself, almost captured when a camp in the forest which he was visiting was attacked at 8.30 one morning while they were still asleep.

By mid-1954 the Mau Mau fighters in the forest were often cut off from food supplies. This led to relaxation of traditional taboos, including not eating meat from animals with 'one hoof (toe)' or from 'clawed animals'. In General Gikonyo's camp, for example, most of the people ate elephant, and there is no reason to believe that that camp was exceptional. The air attacks may not have killed many people in the forest, but Njama records the fear the warriors experienced as they were machine-gunned and bombed. '[We] lay down on our stomachs with our noses almost touching the ground and held soil in our hands amidst the horrible thunder of exploding bombs which echoed as death hoots to me, and the frightening earth tremors.' Warriors swore that they would prefer to die 'exchanging gunfire with the enemy rather than endure the unassailable Lincoln bombers'.

The role of women in support of Mau Mau has been the subject of some discussion. Ferguson's experience was that they were mainly camp followers, but Njama writes of a group of warriors at Ruthaithi where more than half were women, or 'girls' as he calls them. The annual prison reports provide an indication of the part played by the

226

women. They record that that during the years 1954–6 31,774 African women were admitted to prisons and 27,867 were sentenced. The majority, 24,444, were first offenders.

The following table shows that the percentage of African women admitted into detention camps increased significantly between 1954 and 1956 when the Mau Mau fighting in forest and field was at its most intense. Of the 30,247 African detainees in 1954, 44 per cent were women.

Year	Total (men & women)	Women	% women
1952	23,201	347	1
1953	32,862	4,415	13
1954	25,979	9,609	37
1955	30,247	13,265	44
1956	41,441	8,900	21
1957	53,080	8,854	17

AFRICANS ADMITTED TO DETENTION CAMPS 1952–7

(Source: Government Reports ex. Presley 1992: 137–9)

In the course of her research Cora Presley interviewed a number of Kikuyu women, who explained that the main work of women supporters of Mau Mau was in the supply lines. Each district had a central committee responsible for arranging safe places and smuggling supplies. The women lived generally in the villages or towns. Nurses' aids would steal medicines and pass them to the fighters, who came out at night. Other women went into the forest with their husbands, leaving their children with grandparents. The women built huts out of junk, and obtained food from their former villages. They participated in military operations with male warriors and were 'doing just like men'. The women 'could shoot and so forth'. They went on raids, and when they had taken the oath they were 'men and women together . . . girls are very tough'. Elizabeth Wanjiko, one of Presley's interviewees, was shot and captured. She made her way to Kamiti Camp, to which reference is made elsewhere. Better known as a woman fighter was Muthoni Kirima, who took her first oath in the reserve having grown up on a 'colonist's farm'. She took part in raids on Europeans' farms and experienced 'the most severe bombings' while in the forest. She attended at least two Mau Mau parliaments, sharing Njama's disappointment at the way Mau Mau became increasingly rejected by the Kikuyu people in the reserves.

In October Njama, who was probably one of the best educated Africans in the forest, saw evidence of a split developing between educated and uneducated Mau Mau. Much to Njama's surprise he found the vice-president, Brigadier Kahiu-Itina, very disgruntled by a feeling that he and other leaders who lacked education had not been given 'chances of rising'. He had a list of grievances which it took much of Njama's diplomacy to address and satisfy. He noticed that Kahiu-Itina was living almost at the same level with his warriors so as to enable him to preach equality. In order to gain popularity by criticizing other leaders, he had dropped most of his own privileges.

The second and third meetings of the Mau Mau parliament, (Njama's records of all of the meetings provide a good indication of the progress of the war in the forest), were held in May and November 1954 with what had become appropriate reverence and ceremony. The May meeting lasted three days, and minutes record:

- The failure of the China negotiations, with suspicions of treason on the part of General China.
- Their channels of communication with Fenner Brockway MP and, through him, to the United Nations (copies had been sent to Russia, India and Egypt).
- Their pride in influencing Lyttelton's proposals for a multi-racial government which were the 'result of Mau Mau's militancy'.
- Parliament expressed confidence in their victory.
- Njama was promoted to brigadier general and made knight commander of East Africa by Dedan Kimathi.

Conditions for Mau Mau warriors in the forest deteriorated between the May and November meetings. Travelling around, Njama observed that tents and huts were few, and that warriors slept under trees in the open. Most 'were dressed in oily, dirty, stinky rags'. They carried, too, a distinctive smell, to which reference is made later, and they were unshaven, with their hair long and unkempt. Many had lost weight, and 'their bright faces had turned to be thin and black'. There was an increase in the number who deserted from Mau Mau fighting units and set up camps as komereras (bandits) inside settlers' farms. The suggested reasons for these desertions were a wish to escape from their leaders' rules, avoidance of British bombing, a lust for leadership among some of the warriors and a wish to be near food that could be foraged from European and African farms. Their numbers increased as time passed. The komereras were an embarrassment to Mau Mau. They were, to say the least, unscrupulous in their foraging, giving the Mau Mau fighting units a bad name with both Europeans (which was not, perhaps, important) and the Africans upon whom the future depended – which was.

During the 24th–25th November meeting, held in a 'big memorial hall in Nairobi', members observed the usual formalities but no significant resolutions were recorded. The previous day Muthenge and Kimathi had called upon God to witness that they would never hurt each other. Kimathi had suggested they take an oath binding them as brothers, but they did not do so. Njama found that Mau Mau was losing the support of many in the reserves, and that even their own members were going over to the enemy. News from the reserves was not pleasing because the government, having greatly increased its numbers and its arms, had 'forced all people in the Central Province into villages which were as strongly supervised as prison camps'. Mau Mau had been cut off from Nairobi supplies and communication and, worse still, from their supporters in the reserves.

For the last two months Njama had notified their Nairobi base that the little ammunition they had could only be used for defending or fighting for food, and they could no longer make offensive attacks. In addition, 'our itungati who had either surrendered or were captured had given the enemy sufficient information about the forest fighters and, worst of all [some] had joined the enemy's pseudo-platoons and had become their guides to our mbuci [camps]. In fact the wind had changed, this time against us'. As if all that were not enough, the Mau Mau were divided among themselves, and Mathenge and Kimathi were not fully reconciled. Njama saw the main division as between those who saw a future Kenya as a progressive nation and those who wished for a return to the tribal past.

Nevertheless, it was decided to increase the membership of the Mau Mau Kenya Parliament from five to twelve, and the seven generals were elected as members. Njama said the qualifications for nomination were 'cleverness, national feelings as opposed to tribal, leadership ability and regional representation in Nyandarua'. The progressive nationalists rather than the reactionists appear to have been in the ascendancy.

On the 5th March 1955 some members of the parliament attempted to assess their strengths and weaknesses. Njama calculated that 22,000 fighters throughout Kenya had been killed and 800 captured while in action, and that there had been 700 'surrenderees'. Taking an average death rate of 200 people daily, they calculated that up to the end of 1954 the total killed by both government and Mau Mau forces amounted to at least 150,000. A recent issue of the *East African Standard* had reported Mau Mau losses as 8,000 killed, 700 hanged, 880 captured injured, 300 captured unhurt and 888 surrenderees, against 68 Europeans, 21 Asians and 1,800 Africans killed by Mau Mau forces. It made depressing reading. The AGM planned for 30th December was postponed

Early in 1955 Njama noticed a change in government tactics. Their forces 'did not enter the forest and instead of fighting against us they instructed our parents, wives, friends and the home guards to do all they could to convince us that the government had really given us an amnesty and they wished us to stop fighting in order to save our lives and release them from government's punishments and enable them to return to a peaceful life'. Government forces stopped guarding the villages and the forest boundary and, instead, sent their wives and mothers into the forest with food for them. The relatives were given time to discuss their surrender. Njama was told that the women showed 'great love and sorrow' and always shed tears when Mau Mau 'fighters' rejected the surrender offer. A few did surrender and were set free in their villages without any supervision in order to induce others to follow suit.

This was part of Gen Erskine's strategy, which was that if an army was to intervene in a rebellion or civil war, 'it should try to do so in such a way that it does not prejudice the natural progressive development of the territory. Measures must be designed to support and protect the loyal members of the community and to round up the real trouble-makers who have resorted to force and lawlessness'.

Njama discovered that 'more than half the people in the reserves had become tired and longed for peace'. At the beginning of the

Emergency there had been rumours that the communists would help them but now, in the third year of their fight, there was no help, nor had they received any supply of arms. Many European settlers, and some members of the Administration too, had suspected that the communists were Mau Mau supporters, but as time went by it became increasingly evident that such support had not been forthcoming. Baring noted that many attempts had been made during 1953 and 1954 to link communism with Mau Mau, but at no time did the Administration find evidence which would support those accusations. There was the odd communist in Kenya, and one or two from outside attempted to fish in the troubled waters of Mau Mau, but their efforts were nullified.

Many Mau Mau were aware that the war was not a simple white versus black struggle. Njama's estimate of the forces against Mau Mau was that over 75 per cent of the '100,000-man' government force was African, comprising over 30,000 home guards (KEM) 10,000 regular police, 8,000 Kenya police reserves and 4,000 tribal police. The rest were regular soldiers in the KAR and the Kenya Regiment plus the four battalions of British troops. The government had drawn its African forces from many tribes. In his opinion most of these soldiers, who had either been badly trained or had not been trained at all, insulted, scorned and despised the whole Kikuyu tribe. Comments made by some of the government military leaders during interviews, and which are quoted elsewhere in this text, confirm that Njama was correct in believing that many of the African troops had little or no respect for his tribe.

Perhaps what most hurt the Mau Mau in the forest was the lack of respect shown to them by members of their tribe in positions of authority. Njama's frustration can be sensed when he says, 'In addition to the bad treatment, shame and guilt senses created by the goverment's propaganda, the chiefs, the headmen, the churches, the traders, the educated Africans, the African representatives in the Legislative Council, the Kenya African Union leaders, free or detained, were continuously denouncing and disassociating themselves from the revolution.'

So with seemingly everyone opposed to Mau Mau, and with Jomo Kenyatta, 'the symbol of the revolution' (Njama's words) in prison and referred to by government leaders as 'the leader of darkness and death', the Mau Mau leaders could be forgiven their despair.

But worse was to come. Victims were unearthed of earlier Mau Mau murders of those who did not support them. 'It was,' says Njama, 'at this crucial period that I first heard of willing confessions in the villages, which were reported to have unearthed skeletons of informers and traitors who were assassinated two and a half years ago. All this news really shocked me. It made me think that our people had lost the way and were moving in the darkness to the government's surrender-offer trap.' As a cohesive force, Mau Mau's day was coming to its end.

During this period Blundell made visits to London, and on 10th December 1954 he had a private conversation with Winston Churchill at 10 Downing Street which must have endorsed the firm, yet moderate, approach Blundell had been adopting. He made a record of the 45-minute meeting immediately afterwards. Blundell noted that Churchill referred to the 'terrible situation' in Kenya, which was 'getting Great Britain into very bad odour in the world that we, the home of culture, magnanimity of thought, with all the traditions of our country and democracy, should be in a situation of using power against these people'. He returned time and time again to the necessity of negotiations, his arguments being that the tenacity of the hold of Mau Mau on the Kikuyu showed that 'they were not the primitive, unintelligent, gutless people we had imagined. That they were persons of considerable fibre and ability and steel, who could be brought to our side by just and wise treatment'. Churchill returned again and again to 'devices to secure their co-operation and cease the slaughter'. He emphasized 'the bad odour that the shootings, the brutalities and the detention camps gave to Britain in the world'.

The great man, near the end of his political life, saw a broader picture of affairs than Blundell and most of the Europeans in Kenya, who were engrossed in their own survival. He was well aware that all the former European imperial powers were experiencing difficulties with their disappearing empires, and in recent months he had seen France offer autonomy to Morocco and Tunisia. Churchill was having trouble in Egypt, and Kenya was constantly in the British press with photographs showing Kenyatta under escort to jail or 'Mau Mau suspects held under the gun as they await screening'.

Mau Mau were not alone in their belief that times were changing.

10

War Brings Nothing About

'The mugumo tree had fallen; Kimathi was gone.'
(Ian Henderson, after the capture of Kimathi)

The war in the forest and on the mountain did not end overnight in the first quarter of 1955. There was no clean-cut surrender – it was not that kind of war – but such co-ordinated Mau Mau control as there had been now dwindled, and each gang went its own way. (The fate of two of them is reported later in this chapter.) Large numbers of Mau Mau had been killed, but many Kikuyu who had taken the oath or held some allegiance to Mau Mau were picked up during Operation Anvil and found their way to detention camps where, to say the least, they provided an embarrassment for an Administration which had to shelter, feed and rehabilitate them.

Screening was devised as a way of separating the metaphorical sheep from the goats, and Africans suspected of being members of Mau Mau went through the process either in large camps or, particularly in the early days, in police stations or makeshift holding points. Before Mau Mau collapsed the screeners principally sought intelligence regarding its activities, but as time went by the object was the return of the prisoner to his or her tribe cleansed of the influence of Mau Mau. It was a procedure which was advocated by the Administration, but for the district officers and the Europeans farmers it caused friction with the police, many of whom were untrained and inclined to be brutal.

Screening began in 1953, but in January 1954 Provincial Governor Wainwright wrote to all farmers asking them to co-operate. He referred to the prodigious amounts of accurate information obtained from the interrogation process and to the active opposition to terrorist gangs generated by those who had confessed. He gave assurances that every possible step had been taken to counteract false witnesses and to prevent the use of threats or torture to extract confessions and information. The weapons employed in interrogation, he wrote, were using information already known – psychological fear, doubt, ridicule and religion – and they 'really do produce results'.

Indeed, reference is made below to the apparent ease with which Kikuyu who had taken the Mau Mau oaths and been active in field and forest were 'turned' to become counter-terrorists.

Arthur Thompson, the post-war farmer at Nanyuki who did not want Mau Mau to arrive with the soup and whose farm-workers decided not to strike, was invited by the district commissioner, Bob Wilson, to be a 'district officer screening'. He worked under Wilson and Chevenix Trench at Nanyuki, at a camp 'over the road' from his farm. The object was 'to get the oath out of the chap's system. It's there until they admit it,' he was told. It required patience and the least possible force, but he. did occasionally make them sit on the floor in the office and take their boots off. He found he got more information by doing that than if he'd given them a chair. He knew that by rubbing the head of a safety match between his thumb and finger he could produce smoke and he would warn the African he was screening that if he told a lie to the next question smoke would come from his fingers. He got quite a few to talk that way. Screening teams were allowed to detain suspects for up to a month, after which they returned to whatever they had been doing. Thompson worked at screening for 14 months. He had an escort of a British subaltern, a sergeant and six askaris. No-one he had screened 'came back at him' about what when on in the screening camps, and they were still working for him 40 years on.

Security officer Kitson's view, confirmed by experience,was that that interrogators who 'struck a blow where one seemed necessary' may have saved loyalists lives and shortened the Emergency, but at the cost of Britain's good name. Officers were aware that the leaders of the government and security forces stood four-square against such practices.

His account of his Special Branch interrogations suggests that the most brutal treatment meted out was depriving the prisoner of sleep. Most success was achieved by the relatively few interrogators who had great patience and could think like Mau Mau. His interrogator Eric Holyoak, a 19-year-old sergeant in the Kenya Regiment, would spend hours squatting on his haunches listening. Typically, the prisoner, confronted with more and more evidence of his activities and wishing to get back on friendly terms, would give in.

On one occasion, when traditional interrogation of a leading terrorist made no progress, Kitson's team enlisted the services of a witchdoctor from another district. He was an old man who could not possibly have had dealings with any of the gangsters round Nairobi where the prisoner had operated. When those involved were seated in a circle he started by pulling a small mirror out of his pocket and sprinkling it with white powder from a satchel. He looked into the glass and brushed some of the surface clean with his sleeve before he started to speak.

'You are Nganga, son of Karioki,' said the witchdoctor.

'Not so, I am Chege Wahome,' said the prisoner.

'You are Nganga, son of Karioki, and you have done terrible things.'

'Not so Mzee.' (Respectful form of address when talking with elderly man).

The witchdoctor then 'saw' an incident well known to several of them which involved the hiding of a gun under a hut floor, all of which was contradicted by the prisoner. A visit to the site confirmed the witchdoctor's statements and the prisoner was won over.

Kitson suggests that the witchdoctor was able to pick up the thoughts of the ex-terrorists and their Kikuyu interrogator and work out the story from them. He is convinced that the whole business was absolutely genuine. National serviceman Robin Grant, serving in the KAR, recalls an incident involving theft of a watch belonging to one of his askaris, which was resolved with the assistance of a witchdoctor.

Special Branch officers used teams of hooded loyal Kikuyu and convicted terrorists to identify terrorists among the thousands of Africans who had been detained during security sweeps. Procedures and cross-checks were introduced to prevent malicious false identification by the hooded men. Kitson's interrogations were generally conducted through Eric Holyoak, who spoke Kikuyu fluently. It was a long, tiring process which was only moderately successful, so they sought alternative methods. By March 1954 Holyoak had formed a team of seven reliable Kikuyu field intelligence assistants. An exercise book containing names of Mau Mau members, their dates of joining the society and weapon numbers was discovered in the pocket of a dead terrorist. It enabled interrogators to cross-reference statements given by prisoners and build on their knowledge. One terrorist, who proved a reliable convert, became a member of the team and taught them Mau Mau ways, slang and handshakes. With experience of using the inside knowledge of willing captives, Kitson developed the concept of the counter-gangs referred to below.

The screening of women detainees began in 1954. European members of the East African Women's League acted as gazetted prison visitors and advised the ministry of community development on prison and detention camp conditions. All prisons and camps were visited from the beginning of 1955. One visitor noted in the EAWL Bulletin that Kamiti prison camp, originally a prison farm, 'even in the worst days of 1955, seemed, miraculously, to have retained the atmosphere of a farm rather than a prison'. The women were either convicts or detainees. Some were hardcore Mau Mau activists and others were women who had been forced to take an oath. 'The most brutal', wrote the visitor, 'were those Mau Mau adherents who had formed a women's court which imposed and carried out shocking sentences themselves.'

But conditions for prisoners in Kamiti Prison were poor in 1954 and 1955. Eileen Fletcher, a Quaker who worked there, described the conditions under which girls of 11 and 12 were held, some on long sentences. Her report led to questions in the House of Commons, and investigations were ordered by the secretary of state for the colonies. Lady Baring made a tour of the prison, and in June 1956 the colonial secretary was forced to admit that harsh treatment had occurred, although conditions had improved.

Women undertook screening, which was put in hand as soon as possible after the detainees arrived in order to prevent the hardcore Mau Mau from victimising the innocent. In the early days, a team comprised a European screening officer who had spoken Kikuyu from infancy and managed teams of Kikuyu elders. The numbers increased, and at the peak there were more than a thousand prisoners and 200 children in Kamiti camp. The detainees responded to the screening. Contact was maintained with the screened women after they had been released. Administrators admit there were some abuses by screening teams, but never by a nod or a wink did the authorities connive at them.

On one occasion Chevenix Trench was instructed by Gen Hinde to see what was going on in a screening camp run by two missionaries in Kenya police reserve uniform. He found that, by third-degree methods, the missionaries had 'uncovered a conspiracy to end all conspiracies', summarized in a 30-page report which revealed that Mau Mau was the joint creation of Stalin, Chairman Mao and Emperor Haile Selassie of Ethiopia. 'Kenya would be invaded by Chinese paratroopers and all Europeans murdered by their servants.' Trench took the report to Hinde, who disbanded the camp within hours. The missionaries 'returned to their spiritual duties'.

The missionaries were not alone in mistreating prisoners during the course of screening. Lorry loads of detainees were sent to DO Terry Gavaghan at Samburu from Campi ya Simba, a camp on a farm between Rumeruti and Nyarahuru, where they had been interrogated. 'There was,' he says, 'no question but they had been roughly handled, [but] the motivation was not the desire for cruelty but to secure information.'

Government offices were by no means exempt from scrutiny. Hugh Sansom's diary for the 24th April records that Africans in the meteorological department were subject to a 'big screening operation' which kept them at the office throughout the weekend, making it necessary for him to organize food for them. And in May Kikuyu staff were issued with pass-books. The Sansoms must, however, have had confidence in their future in Kenya because their principal concern was acquiring a plot of land on which to build a house.

There is ample evidence of abuse in addition to the incidents, mentioned above, from numerous Africans and from reliable, objective Europeans. Governor Baring acknowledged in 1964, after Independence, that 'no doubt there were abuses', adding however, 'I do not believe they were very bad'. In support of that statement he pointed out that the chief screening officer in Kiambu was later appointed as a permanent secretary in the independent government: 'This could not have happened if he had been a really dishonest villain.'

By no means all intelligence was collected through gentle, or not so gentle, persuasion during screening. Much was collected by groups of mixed Europeans and Africans who became known as counter- or pseudo-gangs. These were small groups of government personnel, including former terrorists who had been 'cleansed' of their oaths. Indeed, the co-operation of former terrorists was at the root of the gangs. The principle was that 'cleansed' terrorists led small groups of soldiers, home guards or Special Branch officers into the forest to locate, capture or kill the hardcore Mau Mau.

Campbell wrote that there were, in effect, two types of pseudo-gang. One, comprising police special force teams under Special Branch and intelligence officers, was aimed at eliminating specific leaders and their followers: the hunt for Kimathi by Henderson, below, provides an example of this. The Kenya Regiment's pseudo-gangs, on the other hand, had as their aim 'to eliminate by killing if necessary, all the terrorists in their company's area'.

Kitson, who was involved with Special Branch, did not entirely agree with Campbell's description of its role as an eliminator of specific leaders. It sought to capture leaders, to glean intelligence from them and sometimes to rehabilitate them. The destruction of Mau Mau was certainly the ultimate aim but, Kitson wrote, 'Although most people felt that Mau Mau were better dead, we preferred them alive. You can't get much information out of a corpse.'

What surprised many people of all races was the fact that Kikuyu people who had taken the oath could be, and indeed frequently were, turned against those who had administered it and with whom they had been living and fighting in the forest, sometimes over a period of years. One Kikuyu elder, Mugo Gatheru, explained that the psychological effect of the oath was literally terrifying to the Kikuyu. If a man lied, he lied not only to society but also to the ancestors' spirits and, still more, he lied to the Creator, Ngai, himself. Once taken, it followed that an oath was irrevocable. He added that the 'de-oathing' ceremonies confused the people involved, and that few felt they absolved them entirely.

Be that as it may, numerous oathed Mau Mau terrorists worked closely with government forces. Blundell expressed a view held by many: 'It has always astonished me that the men we used [in the pseudo-gangs] were prepared to go back and kill their comrades-in-arms, with whom they had fought and survived so many trials and hazards, without a flicker of compunction. It was part of the extraordinary schizophrenic psychology of Mau Mau in the Kikuyu mind, which had also been manifested in the real tough oath administrators'. But oath administrators had told Blundell that 'they would just walk back to their old jobs when the Emergency was over'. And many did.

Careful preparation was required if pseudo-gangs were to infiltrate Mau Mau camps. Over a period of time Mau Mau warriors greatly developed their sense of smell and hearing. Njama wrote that their warriors could smell the enemy at more than 200 yards. Soap and any form of tobacco could be detected, he wrote. The Kenya Regiment's response to such sensitivity was to attempt to 'blend with the environment' while on operations. One officer recalled that they weren't allowed to wash or clean their teeth, and they had to grow beards. They smelt terrible at the end of three weeks, but it was the only way to combat an enemy who smelt even worse.

Most pseudo-gang infiltrations were carried out at night, so it was not too difficult for the accompanying European officer to black-up, dress the part in battered hat and ragged clothing and acquire the appropriate odour but, with the exception of Ian Henderson and a handful of others European officers, none could sustain a conversation in Kikuyu which could deceive the terrorists. For that reason the European officer might hold back, leaving one of the Kikuyu to appear to be the gang leader. Skin colour presented serious risks for Europeans on such covert operations. One blacked-up European 'pseudo', offered sex by a Mau Mau camp-follower, refused by saying that he had venereal disease, rather than risk revealing his identity.

Surprise and an ability to improvise were the keys to success, be the aim killing the enemy or taking prisoners. If circumstances dictated a shoot-out, the pseudo-gang could normally rely on greater fire-power, but the close proximity of the enemy generally hindered the use of weapons.

Several leaders of pseudo-gang operations became finely focused on defeating a particular Mau Mau leader, at the same time holding him in respect. In Kitson's case the leader was Waruingi Kurier, who impressed him with 'his aggressive spirit and the hold which he had over his men'. Ultimately Kitson succeeded, but having achieved his object he 'was left desolate'. On the death of Kago, another Mau Mau leader who had been their quarry for several months, Kitson wrote, 'When the news got around, everyone was wild with delight. Kago was by far the most dangerous man in the Mau Mau ranks [but] it was impossible not to admire his skill and daring . . . There were some who felt a sense of loss at his passing. I was one of them.'

An example of the ambivalence of the Kikuyu regarding Mau Mau terrorists is provided by Kitson's description of a sweep involving Kikuyu women who cleared the undergrowth so that the guns had better visibility. He arrived to hear a burst of firing from the line of sweepers and to see the usual gaggle of cutters lunge forward on to something which was struggling on the ground. He was just in time to see a human body disintegrate under the slicing pangas of the girls. They thought the whole thing was a huge joke, and had killed anything that moved for the mere joy of doing so. The day's work had been good clean fun, that was all. 'We all knew that these same people had been sheltering and assisting the gangs for years, and they would probably continue to do so.'

Recruiting and training counter terrorists were matters for careful consideration. Care was taken to keep former terrorists in different pseudo-gangs. Kitson identifies three categories, which he offers as a 'gross simplification' of type-casting. First, those who were fanatically keen on the Mau Mau movement politically; secondly, those who had joined because all their friends had done so; and thirdly, those who had joined from a spirit of adventure. To Kitson's list of categories might be added a fourth, into which Karari Njama might be placed: those who knew that if they did not join they would be killed – a long list of names.

Prisoners in the first category were handed over to the police for prosecution as quickly as possible. The second category, the majority, might be suitable but tended to be feeble and were not generally appropriate material. The third category was regarded as potentially the best source, but candidates from all three categories were given extensive interrogation before decisions were made as to their suitability.

Training took place in three phases. During the first, the prisoner was chained and given a boring diet to 'make him realise that he was not such a wonderful hero'. During the second, those prisoners who satisfied the expectations of phase one were gradually incorporated into the community as a friend, but they were kept under close observation. If he entered the third phase, a man entered the gang without reservation and took part in all its activities. He was encouraged to believe that he was trusted. (Kitson uses the masculine gender in his text: most of the sources consulted referred to women Mau Mau warriors, but none refer to women being taken into pseudo-gangs.)

The Kenya Regiment was not slow to use pseudo gangs but Special Branch or the more traditional regiments were less receptive to the concept. Kitson engineered an inspection by General Erskine, during which he was introduced to the personnel involved. Erskine was supportive, and he continued to take a great interest in the team's progress right up to the time he left the colony. His tour of duty ended in April 1954 and he handed over to Lathbury, who was prepared to continue use of the gangs. Each pseudo-gang was specially trained and armed with rifles and automatic weapons, with European leaders disguised as gangsters. It was recognised by the war council that it was 'a tremendous risk, both to the young Europeans who undertook the task and to the war council's effort if the converts went back to Mau Mau with their weapons'.

As 1954 became 1955, Mau Mau warriors noted that the military had changed its tactics and that there was an increase in what Njama called 'sky-shouting'. Aircraft were used to drop leaflets urging Mau Mau to surrender, and megaphones boomed the message. The Kenya government offered 'all the fighters a chance to come out of the forest and return to the normal peaceful life'. A general amnesty to all who had committed crimes during the emergency up to 'today, the 18th January 1955' was promised. 'Save your life now! Surrender with all your fighting weapons and you will not be prosecuted. You will be detained and receive good medical treatment, food, clothing and general care.' The leaflets were 'signed' by Sir Evelyn Baring as governor and Gen Sir George Erskine as commander-in-chief, East Africa.

A typical Mau Mau reaction to the proposal was to regard it as a sign of the government's weakness. 'It is,' said Njama at the time, 'a fair proof that the government is defeated and instead of yielding to our demands it appeals to us to surrender. If we surrender, we would lose what we have fought for at the last minute of our victory.' However, toward the end of January he found the news from the Mau Mau camps more depressing. From a leader in the Rift Valley, for example, he heard that there was 'no doubt that Makanyanga had fallen into the enemy's hands', but whether dead or alive he didn't know. Every camp in the Rift Valley must have been raided. The Kenyalekalo Memorial Hall and other buildings had been destroyed and all the Mau Mau record books taken by the security forces. He discovered, too, that 'more than half the people in the reserves had become tired and longed for peace. They had experienced dreadful torture, collective punishments (usually at the hands of the Kikuyu home guard). The people were in insanitary camps, near starvation and forced to labour daily without pay or food . . . thousands of our killed warriors were often taken to the villages for the parents to witness the harvest for demanding freedom'. Njama found, too, that the missionaries also challenged the Kikuyu with having 'revolted against God . . . the Kikuyu Supreme Being whom our tribe has honoured and obeyed since creation'. They claimed that 'if the rebels failed to repent . . . God would cause them to be finished off'.

Furthermore, Njama continued, in parallel with fighting in the forest, the government pursued a psychological war for the hearts and minds of the Kikuyu. Radio sets were distributed to all villages in order to spread 'propaganda'. In addition, vernacular papers were freely distributed to all the civilians, even the illiterate ones, and they were forbidden to read any other newspaper. They branded the 'revolution' as Mau Mau, and referred to them always as spivs, thugs, ruffians, gangsters, thieves, murderers, mad outlaws, atavistic barbarians, terrorists, bandits and greedy enemies of peace. They always referred to the government forces as security forces, defenders of the peace, peace restorers, home guards and loyalists. They referred to the civilians as the law-abiding citizens, Kikuyu loyalists or government servants. Broadcast at least three times a day, the propaganda 'defamed and destroyed the good name of our tribe and degraded it to the lowest abyss', wrote Njama.

In parallel with screening and the operation of pseudo-gangs, the Administration had been endeavouring to negotiate a peaceful resolution of hostilities ever since the China negotiations early in 1954. The overtures met with some success. Several Mau Mau leaders (the most notable being General Tanganyika) went to police posts and were taken off to talk with General China. Njama's account is that, after talking to China and representatives of the government, they were given clothing and provisions and driven to the forest in a Special Branch Land Rover. They shook hands with the government representatives and disappeared into the forest. The government waited in vain for the Mount Kenya fighters to surrender. During the talks Mau Mau leaders discovered the government's representatives wanted a surrender and that there were no real negotiations. The government did not reply to their letter suggesting terms for a settlement.

The negotiations had proceeded for several months with delays and alarms, and Ian Henderson had been brought in to negotiate. Early in April it looked as if agreement would be reached but, according to Henderson's account, the Mau Mau leaders were themselves in several minds and did not turn up for an appointment with Henderson and Ruck. Negotiations were called off. It was only after the China negotiations petered out that General Erskine gave Operation Anvil the go-ahead.

There had been settler opposition to the negotiations with terrorists which led Lyttelton to ask Blundell head on, 'Do you want to finish the Emergency or do you want revenge?' Erskine was privately convinced that many of the settlers wanted revenge with a capital R, and Blundell confirmed this. Anti-surrender leaflets were dropped over some areas, and he was the subject of considerable abuse because he was opposed to revenge rather than surrender.

General China was not hanged. This was part of the negotiation agreement, but there was loud criticism from the general public, which would have liked to have seen him punished. However, the negotiations provided a rich source of intelligence for British security.

Almost a year after the failure of the China truce, another opportunity for a peaceful solution presented itself. A letter from Mau Mau was placed in a tree. It contained an offer to surrender all the Mau Mau gangs on the Aberdare Mountains and Mount Kenya. It was decided to follow it up even though many people wanted to annihilate them. The messenger, Ndirangu Kabangu, delivered a letter via Henderson and signed by the chief native commissioner and General Heyman, who fed, clothed and housed him. Kabangu reported on his return that detention camps had been established where surrenderees were given food, clothing and medical treatment. The governor had promised that no one would be prosecuted for any crime committed from the declaration of the Emergency up to 18th January 1955.

Many Mau Mau officers believed that the China negotiations, held the previous year, had lacked commitment on the part of the government. Kabangu was confident that the present overtures were 'a true negotiation', but he recognized that by surrendering to the government he had violated his Mau Mau oath and that he risked execution. On the 13th March 16 Mau Mau section leaders and five members of the Kenya Parliament met to discuss the government's overtures, but Mathenge and Ngara failed to turn up. A letter signed by 'Brig. Gen. Sir Karari Njama, Chief Secretary, Kenya Parliament' was sent to the governor and to Erskine. It welcomed the government's willingness to put an end to the bloodshed and gave assurances of co-operation. It stated that the government's 'request' would be discussed at a special meeting of the Kenya Parliament on the 18th March and suggested that the government start releasing detainees etc and stop bombing the forest as this would disturb their meetings.

The letter was the Kenya parliament's response to the government's overtures, but by this time Kimathi and the majority of the leaders who comprised the Kenya parliament were divorced from Mathenge and his followers, who had set up a separate camp in both physical and metaphorical senses. Mathenge was not so constrained by parliamentary democracy as the parliamentarians, and he was able to act more swiftly. On the 11th February a letter had gone from Mathenge and his followers to the governor and General Erskine. Signed by 'General H.W. Kahinga' (Wachanga), who was Mathenge's secretary at that time, it sought more concessions from the government than the Njama letter had done before the opening of negotiations.

Who, then, represented Mau Mau's intentions and interests – Kimathi and the Mau Mau Kenya parliament or the Mathenge camp and its followers? Whatever the answer to the question may have been, on the 13th March, five days before the Kenya Parliament met, Wachanga, Major Watata King'ori, Kahono Kithii and Mugwimi Gatheru met 10 white men, six African soldiers and four messengers in Nairobi. The Mau Mau leaders had hoped, Wachanga wrote, that Dedan Kimathi would turn up, but in the event they continued without him. The leaders had agreed between themselves that 'no one was allowed to mention the name of Jomo Kenyatta as they did not want the government to know whether or not he was connected with Mau Mau'.

All the negotiation meetings, of which this was the first, began and ended with prayers and included, by Wachanga's account, lengthy recitals by Mau Mau speakers on the failings of the government and instructions on ways in which it might make good its errors. On occasions the Mau Mau negotiators sang hymns. The discussion was lengthy and predictably circular. The government representatives wished to discuss an end to the fighting, while the Mau Mau representatives reiterated that they were fighting for 'land and freedom'. If these were granted, the war would be over.

Wachanga and his fellow negotiators were, in fact, the 'second team' of a minority party. Mau Mau's 'big leaders' (a term used by both Wachanga and Njama) were Kimathi, Muthenge and Mbaria, but because, wrote Wachanga, 'those three leaders had higher ranks than the officials the government had chosen [for its own team] the Mau Mau second team was sent out'. There appears, however, to be nothing to suggest that the Mau Mau leaders knew in advance who would represent the government. After the first meeting the Mau Mau negotiators, wrote Wachanga, reported to Mathenge and Kaniu, who were very pleased with what the Mau Mau spokesmen had said.

In all, eight meetings were held over a period of eight weeks. There is ample evidence that the Mau Mau senior ranks were so divided among themselves that it would have been impossible to field a truly representative team. March had seen the partnership between the Mau Mau big leaders begin to come apart. The Mau Mau parliaments were bedevilled by mistrust and Kimathi was becoming increasingly isolated.

During the fourth meeting, held in the Aberdares, both parties ate a roasted black lamb provided by the government at the request of the Mau Mau negotiators who provided, unbeknown to the government side, 'oathed' water to baste the lamb. The Mau Mau negotiators sang a Christian hymn, in Kikuyu, substituting 'Jomo' and 'Kenyatta' for 'Christ' and the government negotiators returned to Nairobi 'unaware,' wrote Wachanga, 'that they had taken the oath'.

At the sixth meeting Mau Mau leaders asked to be flown to London to meet the colonial secretary, and Windley agreed to put that to the governor. Windley requested a meeting with Mathenge and Mbaria, but Wachanga explained that the three big leaders would not be seen 'until after achievement of our independence'.

The seventh meeting on the 16th May was held in Nairobi and the Mau Mau negotiators met the governor, General Lathbury, General Heyman, Mr Windley and Special Branch officers. 'Their faces were all dark and grim,' wrote Wachanga. The governor and Lothbury left after ten minutes. Windley wanted to know if Mau Mau accepted the surrender terms and Wachanga sought a decision about the colonial secretary. A final meeting was arranged for the 26th May. After the meeting, back in the forest, the Mau Mau leaders agreed that only full independence would suffice, and 'it was clear the government was not going to give it to us', wrote Wachanga.

The eighth and final meeting on the 26th May was held in the Aberdares. The Mau Mau negotiators stated that they would not accept the surrender terms. The meeting broke up. Shortly after dispersal Mathenge was killed. There is no suggestion of foul play by government forces: Mau Mau and government troops were in the forest, and the situation was tense and confused. It is, however, suggested by Field Marshal Musa Mwariama that Mathenge was 'eliminated' by Dedan Kimathi. Muthenge was, Mwariama states, a 'victim of Kimathi's plot to usurp power [from Muthenge who was] his closest comrade'. Mwariama, whose account of the soldier Manley's execution is given on page 193, was shot and wounded in August 1955. He spent much of his time hiding in a porcupine's hole, having been left for dead by British troops. Living was rough, but he survived and he reappears later.

The sky-shouters circled the forest, using their megaphone to announce that Mathenge, Kaniu and Wachanga had rejected the government's surrender terms and that fighting had resumed. Njama did not survive long in the forest after hearing this news. He was minded to escape to Ethiopia, but after numerous close shaves with government forces in the Kariaini Forest, with very little ammunition, meagre food, no tent, blanket or shoes and little sleep in 'the long heavy rain', he began to hallucinate. On the 5th June their resources were almost exhausted. After morning prayers they sought his record books and waited the return of some warriors. He saw Maina, a former colleague, approaching him, carrying a gun with a European close behind. Njama was shot in the ankle but reached cover and bandaged himself. Later in the day he was captured by two Kikuyu home guards. Maina was Njama's closest encounter with a 'cleansed' Mau Mau warrior, a member of a pseudo-gang.

Despite overwhelming odds and declining support, the Mau Mau leaders pressed ahead with their plans for an African government, a democratic parliament. Before the fourth session in March 1955, members of their Kenya Parliament were much pre-occupied with the procedure which might be used to install Kimathi as prime minister. Elaborate ceremonies were designed. Tradition required the initiate to be a married man, but Kimathi's wife was in Nairobi. For some six months, however, he had had as his partner Wanjiru Wambogo, whom Kimathi did not hesitate accepting as his wife. Military promotions were agreed for some members.

Between the 1st April and late May Kimathi and his followers moved through the forest. They made several unsuccessful attempts to contact Henderson in order to open their own negotiations with the government. The Kenya Parliament's 'court' heard cases and dispensed punishments. Many cases concerned misdeeds of komerera leaders, and punishments for those found guilty ranged from caning to strangulation. As time went by 'President' Kimathi tended to 'act for the parliament', and on occasion killed prisoners without trial. A meeting was held in an attempt to restrain him from acting as a dictator, but he became increasingly isolated from even his closest colleagues.

The end of the big leaders was nigh. Henry Kahinga Wachanga was captured in December 1955. He pretended that he had been sent to negotiate an amnesty for '4,000 freedom fighters', but his bluff was called when he was taken to Kipipiri to bring them out and no one answered his call. With Mathenge dead and Wachanga and Njama captured, the leaders were becoming thin on the ground. Njama noticed that Mau Mau warriors, after three months of truce, had become careless, and Blundell observed that '1,000 of the softer gangsters gave themselves up' after the truce.

Which left Dedan Kimathi. His defeat was Ian Henderson's mission during the later part of the war in the forest and his pursuit represents the final phase in the struggle between the government and organized Mau Mau. Kimathi was arrested in October 1956 at the age of 36. He had been in trouble as a boy, but he had attended Karuni-ini school in Tetu, where he did well in poetry and English. He loved traditional ceremonies but chose to be circumcised in the dispensary at Ihururu. He worked, briefly, for the forestry department before spending two years at the Church of Scotland mission school at Tumutumu: he learned fast but was expelled in 1944 for refusing to pay his fees. He had a very brief spell in the army before moving from job to job. He built up a reputation as an activist for, among other things, organizing stewards for Jomo Kenyatta's mass rallies.

In the forest he was soon adopted as a leader. He was well versed in the Old Testament, a copy of which he carried with him. At the end of 1955, three years after he entered the forest, he had 50 of his original 61-strong bodyguard. He was wary of everyone, and there are several accounts elsewhere in this text of his murderous punishments of people whom he no longer trusted.

That said, if Field Marshal Musa Mwariama's account is accepted, it was trust that brought about his downfall. He recounts that Kimathi 'was betrayed by his own men'. Told that he would be protected from enemy aircraft bombs if he took delivery of a sacrificial 'lamb of pure colour, to be presented to him by a pure virgin girl', Kimathi is said to have gone unarmed, as instructed, to 'a certain house' where he was shot and wounded by home guards who received bounty money.

Mwariama's account of this final betrayal of Kimathi involves both Mau Mau and tribal leaders. The Mau Mau leaders, of whom Mwariama was one, knew that Kimathi's plan would not be effective for logistical and communication reasons. They reported this situation to the elders, who assured them that they would make the necessary arrangements. It was they who contacted Kimathi with the promise of protection and informed the home guards of his visit. Mwariama's account concludes that, to save the colonial government from embarrassment, the 'authorities', on learning of Kimathi's betrayal, had the home guards who arrested him 'secretly shot dead'. This 'saddest incident of the war effort would not have happened were it not for his wanting to usurp too much power'.

The British commander-in-chief, Lt Gen Sir Gerald Lathbury, said Ian Henderson, who had pursued Kimathi, had probably done more than any single individual to bring the Emergency to an end. Henderson was the son of a Scot who settled in Kenya shortly before the First World War. He lived on the edge of the Aberdares, where he grew up almost exclusively with Kikuyu children, there being no European neighbours. Their childhood games were in the forest. By his mid-teens he was a first class shot. He did well in the classroom and on the playing field at the Prince of Wales School where many sons of settler farmers were educated. In 1945, at the age of 18, he had the choice of military or police service. As the war was moving to a close he chose the police service. His fluency in Kikuyu and his knowledge of the people led him to be transferred to Special Branch. He led numerous parties into the forest and frequently worked alone when attempting to contact African leaders. He was twice awarded the George Medal and was respected by the terrorists, who named him Kinjanjui after an elder statesman of the tribe.

Many regard him as the creator of the pseudo-gang approach. His hunt for Kimathi had much in common with Kitson's pursuit of his opposite numbers. Kimathi was captured in October 1956, taken to Nairobi, tried for possession of ammunition and hanged.

Henderson records an incident after Kimathi's capture which passes into Kenyan mythology. Henderson returned to the forest to 'unwind' the operation and, in his words, 'to stand down the oddest army that ever fought for Queen and country in the history of the British empire'. He was reminded by Gati, one of his counter-terrorists, of a prophecy that the fight would end in the tenth month before the rain for millet planting began. The prophecy was fulfilled. Kimathi had adopted as his favourite 'prayer tree' an enormous mugumo (wild fig) with a huge trunk and with heaving, hanging branches which reached almost to the ground. It had stood there, probably, since the turn of the century. 'The mugumo tree had fallen,' Henderson wrote. 'Kimathi was gone.'

The pseudo-gangs were undoubtedly a significant factor in defeating Mau Mau during the period 1954–6. Kitson records that in one three-week period his small group of field intelligence assistants with their teams 'completely knocked out the Mau Mau organisation in Kahawa. In all we caught or killed over one hundred gangsters or senior committee members'.

For most of the European farmers the years 1954-6 were not very different from the earlier months of the Emergency. The same pressures, worries and fears continued, and there was growing uncertainty about the future despite Governor Baring's assurances that their future would be secure.

Nellie Grant's letters to her daughter provide a microcosm of small-scale European farming in the Njoro area during the period. By this time she was edging towards 70. Reference has been made earlier to her absent-mindedness with regard to fire-arms security, and this condition persisted. In March 1954 she mislaid 19 bullets, which made her feel physically sick with worry for five days. She eventually discovered where she had hidden them, and suggested that in future it would be safer to give everything to her house servant Mbugwa to look after while she was out. Six months later she left a handbag containing her handgun on the veranda of the Stag's Head. Fortunately it was undisturbed when she returned.

A constant problem was trying to run the farm with Kikuyu labour which might at any time be whisked away by the police for screening and/or cleansing in detention camps. Mau Mau raids on European farms and oathing ceremonies for farm workers were commonplace. In April 1954 she noted 'the last and most horrible murder of a four-and-a-half year old child at Kiambu, who was killed riding its tricycle within a few yards of the back verandah at 8am while both parents were in the house'. Two Kenya police reserve officers in their early twenties were killed, and there was the 'Bruxnor Randall murder'. 'Poor old harmless thing,' Grant commented. Mr and Mrs Gray Leakey (of whom more anon) were murdered. She visited Ingrid Fish, who was deeply depressed. 'She is really,' Grant noted, 'a Mau Mau casualty, I think; she took all the labour defections terribly to heart.'

Grant's Kikuyu workers were not exempt from Mau Mau oathing and she was inconvenienced, to say the least, as they (including household staff) were taken away for interrogation. Her cook, Karanja Kineku, admitted during screening to being clerk to the Mau Mau in the district.

Screening was not necessarily a brutal business. He had been taken away for screening by 'Krueger at Dundari' who, Grant had been told, 'were terribly good'. Karanja was returned by John Dowson, the district commissioner, 'looking relaxed, fat and clean'. Evidently, wrote Grant, 'the camp is a good holiday resort'. She was strongly advised by the police not to have him back but, if she did, never to allow him near the house after dark. She should not trust him an inch. Karanja, at Grant's insistence (and as a condition of his returning to work), made 'a very fine speech denouncing Mau Mau and telling everyone to do likewise'. Dowson warned that, having taken the oath of allegiance to the government, he was at risk of being 'bumped off'. She was 'shattered' by the power Mau Mau had over many Kikuyu, a reality vividly demonstrated when Elizabeth, the mission-educated, highly publicized first African policewoman, who was, she wrote, 'absolutely the best type', deserted from the police and went over to Mau Mau.

On one occasion in November 1954 Grant joined the KPR for the afternoon and, having her van, helped a young policeman transport prisoners and a very bloody corpse to Njoro. After tea, she and a female friend took the dogs to seek the Mau Mau who had escaped. They picked up the line but lost it in the forest.

Grant had pioneered women's clubs at Njoro. These clubs were the beginning of the Maendeleo movement, the aim of which was to raise the standard of living and broaden the education of African women. By January 1954 the movement had grown to the extent that there were 25 clubs with over 1,000 members. She was, however, critical of the Capricorn African Society which, among others, fostered multi-racialism – which the Africans took to mean racial equality. She did not foresee Europeans and Africans having lunch together at the Muthaiga (European club).

Some light relief had been provided by the latest Kenya romance, which was all very 'White Mischief'. In November it was made known that Diana Colville, Sir Jock Delves Broughton's widow, who had subsequently married Gilbert Colville, was to marry Tom Delamere. To make the marriage possible, it was necessary for 'Lady D' to divorce Tom quickly and for Colville to divorce Diana likewise. 'Apparently,' wrote Grant, 'Tom took a great liking to the Colville house, formerly the Errol mansion, and moved in. It is said that Gilbert Colville moved out with joy to his old shepherd's hut.' The well established Happy Valley tradition of partner exchange was thus perpetuated.

By December 1954 Grant's trusted house servant Mbugwa, to whom in March she might have entrusted custody of her firearms, stood accused of 'the blackest of things'. The charges went back years. 'It is heartbreaking about Mbugwa,' she wrote. 'I just don't speak to him anymore except for orders.'

She attended a baraza at the Njoro location, at which loyal chiefs appealed to the assembled Africans 'so prettily'. She felt the days had gone by for that sort of appeal, and suggested in her letter that she would have staged things differently. 'Would have had a gibbet with a corpse descending therefrom,' she wrote, 'with bursts of sten gun fire every five minutes just over the heads of the crowd, and condemned murderers on view in chains. Am scrapping the farm Xmas do's until the end of the Emergency. I have withdrawn from any attempt to foster friendship, understanding etc with the Africans'. Then, on Christmas morning (1954), 'Mbugwa staggered in with my morning cuppa and laid a huge box of potatoes on my bed.' They were special potatoes of the sort she loved, and which Mbugwa had grown 'specially for me'.

Grant's farm was particularly vulnerable to Mau Mau raids, so she was provided with 'non-Kikuyu' farm guards armed with shotguns as protectors. She was a reluctant participant in the scheme, and described her guards as 'bestial'. While she was in Nakuru the shotgun of one went off, perhaps accidentally, hitting a rather simple house boy. He later died of his wounds.

Nellie Grant took a holiday in Europe shortly after the shooting. It was her first for five years, and for the last two-and-a-half she had been living alone save for her dogs, her revolver beside her at night and only the radio for company. Her servants could not be trusted and there had been frequent droughts, machinery break-downs, live-stock tragedies and constant financial worries. Things were no better when she returned in July 1955. The day after she came back two of her Kikuyu workers, a home guard and a woman, were detained by the police for providing food for Mau Mau gangs. Cattle were stolen nightly and African headmen were being murdered.

When 178 'moral rearmers' arrived in Nairobi, Grant was asked to meet them and attend a matinée of their 'awful play'. She declined the invitation. At the end of August she was thrilled by the very high approval of her steers by the 'Meat Commission man'. 'It is marvellous to think the farm may really be coming into proper production,' she wrote. She was successful, too, with her vegetables at the Nakuru horticultural show.

Day-to-day events included the murder of Mrs Milton and her eleven-year-old daughter, mid-morning, in a suburb of Nakuru; cattle poisoning; the discovery that one of the farm guards 'foisted on her' had a tapeworm; her successful replacement of the top of a finger which a boy cut off while using the mower; and a request from a Kikuyu woman for her son to be circumcised in hospital. She was surprised that 'all the glamour, toughness, ritual etc [of circumcision had been] swept away . . . I should have thought it would be the last thing to die.' But she learned that 'the girls on the farm are still being done in traditional style'. The 'local lads', however, 'flocked to the outpatients' department of the local hospital, where it took only a quarter of an hour, and home they go'.

She had been the leader of a project to build Egerton College as a training centre for young European farmers, and in April 1956 she was invited to perform a bridge-opening ceremony at Egerton. It was a modest peak in what was to be a disastrous period.

The blow was the failure of her maize crop, which she recorded only days after the Egerton event. Her only course of action was to sell the cows and try to lease the land. She was not the only grower to suffer. 'What really bites,' she continued, 'is not being able to leave you a tickety-boo farm – that was the mainspring of existence, so to speak.' She sold the cattle, took up weaving and made what she had always longed for – 'a tiny, tiny veg. garden all of my own'. In July she gave a party for which practically all the food was home-grown and home-made, 'so it wasn't an extravagant party'. In October 1956, her daughter wrote, 'she won first at the Royal Show for a beautifully knitted Shetland cape'.

By September 1954, when the fight against Mau Mau had been in progress for nearly two years, Louis Leakey, fluent Kikuyu speaker, tribal elder and acknowledged expert in matters Kikuyu, considered that Mau Mau was losing ground rapidly with masses of the Kikuyu but that it would be foolish to attempt to predict when it would be completely defeated. Furthermore, his view – which was endorsed by many 'leaders of Kikuyu opinion' – was that because 'the masses' were swinging away from Mau Mau an increase in deeds of violence was to be expected. How right he was. In October Mr and Mrs Gray Leakey, members of the long-established family of missionaries and scientists, were attacked in their home while they were at dinner. Mrs Leakey was strangled to death and he was captured: his body was discovered later in the month.

Henry Wachanga described the murder of Gray Arundel Leakey as 'one of the tremendous and marvellous things which brought much fame to Mau Mau'. Wachanga wrote that Leakey 'was led into the forest between Kabaru and Nyona Hills'. He was buried alive, upside down, in a hole 5ft deep by 3ft wide. His feet were left sticking out and thorn-tree bushes were piled around them so that hyenas could not take the body. This was done while his captors said nothing and kept their eyes shut. The reason for the murder was, wrote Wachanga, 'to fulfil a prophecy'. He explained that their 'ago or arathi' (prophets) told them that if they wanted to defeat the European enemy and drive them out of our country, they must duplicate the actions taken against them in 1892', when 'they had taken our great man, Chief Waiyaki, and buried him alive, upside down, at Kibwezi'. The prophets required 'a European elder' as their subject. Gray Leakey, like most of his family, spoke Kikuyu fluently and had been accepted as a member of the tribe 'of the appropriate age-grade'.

By 1954, farm manager Joan Scott noticed changes in the attitude of her African farm workers towards Mau Mau. Previously, they had pretended they knew nothing of it, but now they turned against the society. Her milk boys, leaving the farm daily to make deliveries, must, she believed, have been 'oathed to the hilt', but on returning to the farm one day they reported having been stopped by a Mau Mau gang and pressed for food and money. They told Scott of the rendezvous and the security forces killed the gang. 'Informing on Mau Mau was not,' argued Scott, 'the action of people who were desperately keen to get the Europeans out. They had had enough [of Mau Mau] by that time'.

With the benefit of resources far beyond those of Nellie Grant and Joan Scott, the Seys family at Rhodora were not seriously threatened by the Mau Mau movement and by adverse conditions caused by the weather, locusts and so on. Here, on the edge of the Menengai crater north of Nakuru, they were able to shrug off 'one of Kenya's 20-minute hailstorms' which cost them £23,000.

It was not until October 1954 that the Seys' letters mention contact with Mau Mau gangs – ten months after the commencement of the period covered by this chapter. They did not escape untouched, but in a letter dated 26th June 1955 Seys wrote that the gangs at this stage of the Emergency were not aggressive. They were very much on the run and on the defensive and short of arms and ammunition. They were, nevertheless, still in evidence, and there was an inconclusive encounter in the crater which formed a boundary of the farm with a gang they estimated at more than 20 strong.

In July, General Heyman, the chief of staff, told the Seys over lunch at the Blundells that they had not captured anyone for some time who had been less than six months in the forest. The terrorists, in other words, were not getting new recruits. His forecast was that with Mau Mau casualties running at around 50 a week it would all be over in about a year's time. Heyman's assessments of Mau Mau casualties were very modest when compared with those of Njama.

By this time Rhodora's arrangements at night resembled 'medieval times when all the animals were driven into the castle at night and the drawbridge raised until morning'. All the live-stock was driven in and kept under guard by Kipsigis guards armed with pangas, whistles and thunder-flashes. Communications were by post-medieval telephone. They lacked only a wall and a moat, wrote Seys. Come October he admitted that 'the Mau Mau threat, while still present . . . is diminishing and things have been fairly quiet recently'.

In his 5th December 1955 letter Seys reports a talk they had with 'the almost mythical character, Whately,' who for some months had been operating with the Mau Mau in the district. Whately described the modus operandi of the counter-gangs – how a European, blacked-up and wearing filthy verminous clothing went into the forest for several days at a time accompanied by former Mau Mau fighters who 'co-operate in every way they can in catching or killing other terrorists'. In such ways were the tactics of Henderson, Kitson and the few counter-gang leaders made known to the European settlers.

The October 1955 reference to Mau Mau was the last significant mention insofar as the movement impinged on Rhodora. The 12 months up to the capture of Dedan Kimathi in October 1956 passed quietly. Nevertheless, the Seys began to face the fact that they might have to leave Kenya, and they began to send things back to Europe. During 1955 they bought Hardwick Court Farm in Surrey, 'with a lovely Elizabethan farmhouse'. Seys told Blundell in February 1956 that he would not stand against him at the September elections.

How were lives in the towns affected by this bleak period? Although 1954–6 was to see some unrest and strikes in Mombasa, Mau Mau had no effect on the city. In March 1955 the dock-workers struck for increased pay and the expulsion of some supervisors. This was followed the next month by another strike, in Nairobi. Tom Mboya was closely concerned with both negotiations, and the Nairobi dispute went before a board of inquiry chaired by Mr Justice Windham. He reported favourably on the efficiency of the organization and on 'the reasonable and co-operative manner' in which the case had been presented. Mboya suggests that during the Emergency the trade union movement in Kenya played a political role rarely demanded of trade unions and their leaders. The dock-workers won an all-round wage increase of 33 per cent, which raised the minimum monthly wage from £5 to nearly £7 – quite large compared with the wages then prevailing. There is no suggestion that the trade unions were linked to Mau Mau activities.

In Nairobi the lives of most European civilians were undisturbed and, with one or two notorious exceptions, the life of the Indian population was unaffected. There was a significant demand for safaris in 1954, especially, from the USA. The Kenya economy took in £3.5 million from the tourist trade. An American visitor found that the United Kenya Club had become a community of 'like-minded people' and was helping to break down barriers in the larger outside community. The people members brought to lunch, 'reluctant acquaintances who were racially prejudiced, found to their amazement that people of other races existed who were perfectly civilized and even compatible'. The club suffered, however, during the Mau Mau years. African membership and income dropped from 56 in 1951 to zero in 1955 under threats from Mau Mau activists. As lunchtime speakers such as N. S .Mangat, Oginga Odinga and Chanan Singh frequently 'denounced the pattern of British rule' to the British members, most of whom were members of the Administration, Europeans simply stopped participating in club activities. Membership dropped from 525 to 269.

The intention of the club's founders 'to avoid politics' had disappeared. 'Many members became so political as to make it impossible for some of us government officials to take part,' wrote Tom Askwith, founder member and first chairman of the club.

The club declined despite a 'tradition of pitching in' and volunteer labour provided by members and their spouses.

For the African population in Nairobi, it was to be a stressful time. Kikuyu people were required to carry passes, and people from other tribes took over many of the jobs previously carried out by Kikuyu. Oginga Odinga recalled that as Kikuyu workers were displaced from employment, Nyanza tribes were sent in to fill the vacuum. Nyanza people went into the civil service in greater numbers than ever before, and at this time the status of the civil servants was raised to benefit its newest members. Inevitably, though, the more rapid absorption of Nyanza people in the labour market accelerated the process of their urbanization and the quickening of their political consciousness.

The economy continued to be buoyant, and in October 1956 Princess Margaret made a formal visit which gave a fillip to many Europeans. The Princess's visit coincided with the end of the Mau Mau as a significant disturbance of European life, but the visit was no doubt arranged many months earlier, which suggests that the movement had long since ceased to be a cause of concern for the British government.

Entertaining at Government House was not lavish but continuous, and on a scale that was possible only because the Barings had a considerable private income which they were prepared to spend. At the end of the Princess's visit Baring threw a 'thank you' cocktail party for 700, after which five men were carried out drunk, two husbands rang up the next day to apologize for the behaviour of their wives and one man left his car outside Government House all night because he couldn't be sure which one it was.

The Seys were the Barings' house guests. In a letter home Seys reported that Government House was huge and that their bedroom was nearly as large as the whole house at Rhodora – which was certainly no mean cottage.

The Princess travelled with 14 staff, and the Mason family, who hosted her during part of her visit, had to provide lunch for 52 journalists in addition to the royal party.

Progress on development of the colony did not cease as a result of Mau Mau. While the Emergency operations were still in full spate there was an agrarian revolution which transformed the face of Kenya. Agrarian reform was an aspect of development in which the governor had taken a particular interest and initiative. His biographer linked the transformation to the other profound development which Baring masterminded – the changeover from the rigid colonial constitution he inherited (where a straight colonial administration was confronted by an unofficial majority of settlers within the parliament) to the gradual development of cabinet-style government in a multi-racial polity. This came about through constitutional changes calculated to foster active African involvement in the political life of the country, which before 1952 had been dominated almost entirely by the white settlers.

Baring had persuaded the British government to make a grant of £5 million for African agriculture. It was used to implement a 'master plan' published in February 1954 and largely based on that proposed by Roger Swynnerton, the deputy director of agriculture. Its essence was to concentrate effort where it would make most impact, in the Central Province. Baring identified five main needs: soil conservation, land consolidation (gathering fragmented holdings into viable farms and granting freehold tenure to the owners), the development of cash crops, the introduction of grade dairy cattle and irrigation.

To illustrate the scope of land consolidation, the Kiambu reserves had been divided into over half a million fragments, some hardly bigger than a bathroom. With 'consolidation' these were re-assembled into viable farms or smallholdings. About seven per cent of the land was lost to cultivation in order to provide land for 110 villages, 1,860 miles of new access roads, 285 schools, 225 churches, cemeteries, markets, cattle-dips, tea and coffee nurseries and sports grounds. The average consolidated holding was 5.3 acres, made up of eight gathered fragments. The project was managed by the Administration. The land had to be surveyed, mapped, allocated and fenced, and African staff were trained to carry out the necessary tasks. The land of a few terrorist leaders, about 0.02 per cent of the total, was compulsorily purchased for community purposes. Otherwise it was accepted that Mau Mau were as much entitled to their land as anyone else.'

New owners were given a certificate of title which, once issued, was not subject to litigation. The owner could not mortgage or sub-divide his holding without permission. On the death of the owner the farm went to one son, who must within five years pay each of his brothers an equal share. The project provided useful employment for thousands of detainees and former squatters. It was in progress while the fighting continued.

In 1956 Baring described land consolidation to the secretary of state, Lennox-Boyd, as a very important event which was proving successful, although African nationalists regarded the work of terracing and consolidation as forced labour and were generally opposed to the change. Most of the digging, clearing and general physical work was carried out by the women. This was the Kikuyu tradition, but 'forced' employment of women provided useful publicity material for the Mau Mau cause in the western world.

That, then, was the scenario, the political background and the security framework within which the European farmers carried on; the soldiers from both sides fought to dominate; and the administrators endeavoured to reform peasant farming methods. Meanwhile, in a remote prison in the desert to the north of those activities, a handful of African leaders served their time.

By 1954 there were two prisons in the north of Kenya for leading members of Mau Mau – a small one in Lokitaung for the leaders and a larger one in Lodwar for others. District Commissioner Leslie Whitehouse ('Wouse'), governed the district and became 'Jomo's jailor'. In his memoirs he refers to the part Mzee Jomo Kenyatta played in his life, and the extent to which the 'great man' affected the course of his future. Whitehouse had been instructed to visit Lokitaung at least once a month, and was instruced that the care of Kenyatta was now his most important duty: the British did not want a martyr on their hands, with all the adverse publicity that would bring. Kenyatta was now 60, a great age by African standards, so he was excused hard labour and appointed camp cook for the six prisoners in the camp. It was a light job but it proved too much for him. There was friction among the prisoners, and as the others refused to share a cell with him Kenyatta was given one to himself.

The six principal leaders slept on string mats on the floor with a single blanket for each of them. Their food was no different from that of a 'common convict'. Kenyatta never complained or applied for a special diet. There were no radios or newspapers, and correspondence in and out was strictly limited and censored. 'Mzee did have access to a few books,' wrote Whitehouse. 'In particular I recall he studied comparative religion.'

In July the prisoners' appeal to the privy council was refused, and it was announced that Kenyatta would never be released. He ceased to receive Whitehouse at the prison gate and did not conduct him round the prison. But even then, Whitehouse wrote, 'Mzee himself never uttered a single word of complaint. That was not his way.'

All was not well between the prisoners, and the friction increased after the appeal was refused. In his Lokitaung annual report Whitehouse summarized events during 1954. He referred to the antagonism which had been building up between Kenyatta and the younger members of the KAU intelligentsia throughout their period in detention and which came to a head when Kenyatta was attacked by a fellow prisoner with a knife. Ngei was arraigned for having shouted at Kenyatta that he was a thief and had been nothing but an agricultural labourer in England. Ngei was supported by Kaggia and Kubai, and they alleged that several sums of money sent to them during the trial had never been received by them but had been kept by Kenyatta, to whom they were delivered. The district officer's report made close reference to the tormenting Kenyatta suffered at the hands of the other prisoners regarding his books and academic achievements. 'Perhaps,' he wrote, 'the greatest insult of all was to ask for details of how he had come to write *Facing Mount Kenya*. It is hardly to be wondered at that Kenyatta became almost paranoid and believed the others were plotting against him.'

The only prisoner who was friendly with Kenyatta was General China, who joined the others in April 1954. He was still in solitary confinement when the original prisoners went on hunger strike in protest against what they called the filthy habits of Kenyatta acting as cook. The strike lasted two days.

Turkana, the district in which Lokitaung was situated, received very few visitors in normal times, but in 1954 high ranking officials began to arrive. Whitehouse listed the provincial commissioner, the commissioner of prisons, the director of medical services, the secretary for welfare and development, the principal medical officer and the prison medical adviser. Kenyatta's health gave cause for concern in 1955. Lt Col De Robeck, with whom Kenyatta and China were on very good terms, reported that Kenyatta's heart rate was so high that he was expected to 'snuff it' at any moment. Plans were made for the immediate visit of a high-powered doctor, and an unprejudiced post mortem in the event of his demise. Others became concerned, and 'many important visitors, including the governor, Sir Evelyn Baring, flew into Lokitaung to see the prisoners'.

De Robeck befriended both prisoners and on occasion drove them to his house to borrow books. The Lokitaung annual report for 1955 referred to 'Kenyatta and co' seeming to attract the attention of all and sundry officials who found it their duty to visit Lokitaung. The report stated that the prisoners' egos were done 'a lot of good' by the attention, but that they were not in the least repentant. 'The antagonism between Kenyatta and the others continues', the report concluded. The extra care shown to Kenyatta did nothing to endear him to his fellow convicts and there were several attempts to attack him, but the annual report stated the six Mau Mau convicts gave less trouble than their warders, despite occasional resurgence of their personal feuds.

Bildad Kaggia describes the routine at Lokitaung, where 'there was little variety'. Kenyatta was awoken at three to prepare breakfast for the others, who were roused at five 'by the guard loudly rattling the huge metal padlock on our front door'. There was no furniture in the place, no curtains and no glass in the windows, only bare rooms with bars. Each prisoner had a mug of maize porridge to eat. Kenyatta stayed behind to wash up while the others were taken away to dig trenches from six until about half-past eleven. Then it was back to their quarters for lunch, and a break until one o'clock. They dug from one o'clock until four or four-thirty. Kaggia and Ngei were ordered to dig a trench 10ft long, 4ft wide and 30ft deep. Digging started well, but they struck rock. They were allowed to talk between themselves, but the guards spoke no Kikuyu and were not allowed to speak to the prisoners. 'We were completely cut off from the outside world,' wrote Kaggia. The digging continued for months in the heat of the desert until Whitehouse had rock delivered which the prisoners were ordered to break into small pieces of ballast. That was their work for the year 1954.

De Robeck was popular with Kaggia and the other prisoners, not with just Kenyatta and China. Whitehouse had substituted rock breaking for the arduous trench digging, and de Robeck employed the prisoners on using this material constructively within the compound and around other government buildings. He encouraged them to care for their civilian clothes and cultivate vegetables.

Time passed slowly during these years immediately after 'the war' was over. It would be more years yet before they would be released.

Edgerton, a writer highly critical of the government's handling of the Mau Mau uprising, wrote that 'by 1956 most of Kenya's Africans had repudiated Mau Mau. The rebellion was over, its goals unmet, its legacy uncertain'. Karari Njama, the Mau Mau leader, puts an earlier date on the end of the revolution. 'Around the beginning of 1956,' he wrote, 'the revolution popularly known as Mau Mau came to an end.'

Blundell attributes the failure of Mau Mau to the Kikuyu themselves rather than to the might of the British empire. 'Undoubtedly,' he wrote, 'the movement would have succeeded, despite the evidence of the government and the military support which ensued, had it not met and foundered upon an old and characteristic division amongst the Kikuyu themselves. Since the early years of the century, the tribal leaders had been divided between those who believed that advance was best achieved by close co-operation with the government and the white man in order to embrace his knowledge and learn from his ability as quickly as possible, and those who thought that subversion, non-co-operation and sporadic acts of violence would best free the tribe from the rule of the European. Both sides had the same aim, which was the independence of the Kikuyu people from British rule.'

The end of 1956 provides an appropriate point at which to count the casualties of the Mau Mau uprising, rebellion or fight for freedom.

Precise figures are impossible to ascertain, but reasonably reliable figures are that Mau Mau killed 590 security forces, of which 63 were white, and 1819 'loyal' Africans. The government estimated that 11,503 Mau Mau, 32 white civilians and 26 Indians were killed. Approximately 200 white soldiers and police and 1,000 loyal Africans were wounded. The number of Mau Mau wounded is not known. Many Europeans involved in the fighting expressed amazement at the ability of Mau Mau to keep running in spite of their wounds. Some writers suggest that government estimates of Mau Mau losses were understated. Those referred to above may be compared with estimates made by Njama in March 1955 (*see page 230*) that '22,000 fighters', by which he appears to mean Mau Mau fighters, had at that time been killed. In March 1955 Mau Mau's heaviest losses were still to come.

Over the same period more Europeans were killed in traffic accidents on the streets of Nairobi than by Mau Mau. During a rebellion in Madagascar two or three years before the Mau Mau fighting, French colonists and the army had tortured and killed between 50,000 and 120,000 Malagasy. Edgerton writes that some Kenyan European settlers he interviewed (who remain anonymous) supported the French reaction to rebellion rather than the British one.

11

Politics and Convergence

*'True peace is not merely an absence of tension;
it is the presence of justice.' (Martin Luther King)*

By the end of 1956, some say earlier, Mau Mau was finished as a cohesive force. With the capture that October of Dedan Kimathi, the indisputable leader of the forest and mountain fighters, armed resistance to the government was over – even if a few komereras would make a nuisance of themselves in years to come. This chapter and the next cover events from 1957–9, with chapter 12 concentrating on the resolution of the detainee problem. As the period ends Kimathi is already passing into Kikuyu, indeed Kenyan, mythology while prisoner Kenyatta and the other top leaders are reunited with their families.

These years saw significant changes in the balance of political power between European and African. For the first time in LEGCO history, the March 1957 elections provided eight seats for African members. In 1958 Secretary of State Lennox-Boyd (Barbara Castle's *bête noire*), introduced a constitution that was boycotted by the African leaders, who demanded constitutional changes and the release of Jomo Kenyatta. The following year produced 25 seats for the African members, 15 for Asian, five for Arab and 46 for Europeans. With the end of the war in the forest, the emphasis moved from military force to political negotiation. Debate focused on the possibility of a return to the pure colonial form of government or one of a number of alternatives, most of them concerned with levels of representation to be given to the various groups. As ever, the Europeans were divided among themselves. The right wing had formed the Kenya Empire Party, and as late as 1959 many people denied the existence of African nationalism.

In 1942, during the Second World War, when there was a strong possibility of British defeat, the future of Britain's East African colonies had been debated in the House of Commons (see *page 14*). Harold Macmillan had suggested that the land in the Kenyan Highlands farmed by the Europeans might be nationalized – an uncharacteristic suggestion from a Tory MP. He recognized that this would be expensive but, he concluded, 'less expensive than civil war'. By 1957 few people would have remembered that debate, but in June and July of that year Macmillan, now prime minister, toured the commonwealth and pondered its future. He observed that 'the old *pax Britannica,* which had for so many generations brought to about a quarter of the globe the inestimable advantage of order and good government, and under which social, political and economic development of their peoples could be peacefully pursued, was now being replaced by a new, untried system'. The old commonwealth and empire had, he added, 'been able to maintain a strong centripetal attraction, politically, economically and above all in defence. Now equally powerful centrifugal pressures would begin'.

He traced the changes that were inherent in the policies which had been pursued by successive British governments and which had moved at an accelerated pace from the end of the Second World War. He concluded that since he had assumed responsibility 'the stream of gradual change was now augmented into a fast-flowing river which might soon break its banks through its torrential force'. Astute observers may have noted a consistency in his thinking over the 15-year period. The future form of Kenya was being shaped in Westminster.

The postscript to Mau Mau was written on the 18th February 1957 with the execution of Dedan Kimathi. He defended his cause during his trial, but he died a Christian.

At 1am on the day of his execution he wrote in English to Father Marino, a Roman Catholic priest, expressing his concern over the future of his wife and his mother and for his son's education. His letter concluded, 'I am so busy and so happy preparing for the new tomorrow 18th February . . . I remain, dear Father, Your loving and departing convert'. The letter is displayed in the Kenya national archives.

He soon became a legend. Several towns in Kenya have streets named after him, and two leading Kikuyu writers, Paul Ngugi wa Thiong'o (Ngugiwa Thiongo) and Micere Githae Mugo, wrote an allegory, *The Trial of Dedan Kimathi,* as 'an imaginative recreation and interpretation of the collective will of the Kenyan peasants and workers in their refusal to break under sixty years of colonial torture and ruthless oppression by the British ruling classes'.

Baring was to complete his tour in Kenya in 1959, and his remaining time provided him with new challenges. Among them was Tom Mboya, who joined LEGCO in March 1957. He had returned from a successful 13-month tour of America and Britain the previous October, confident that his most promising route to power was through the trade union movement, his forte. Baring referred to him, in a letter to his wife, as 'the completely indoctrinated man', who spoke very well in LEGCO and who 'partly by persuasion and partly by threats holds his people together'. He complained that Mboya would not co-operate and tried to force the Kenyan government's hand by 'going often for advice to the fountain-head in the UK'. Mboya's advisers were British Labour party members, in particular Barbara Castle and the Bevanites. Baring concluded that Mboya was intensely arrogant and 'a lapsed RC with the morals of a monkey'.

Throughout the summer of 1957 Baring was engaged in redrafting the constitution to increase African elected representation in LEGCO. Blundell, Vasey and the moderates were for it, but both the Africans and the more entrenched Europeans were against. The African members were also divided. Mboya was holding to a plan for independence in 10 years, and he preferred an entirely nominated colonial office government. He did not have unanimous African support for his preference. Others sought an increase in their share of government then and there.

In a letter to the colonial office in September 1957, Baring referred to two roads down which Kenya might go: the common approach of mixed government and the gradual discovery by all groups in Kenya of how to live together in one country and development over a fixed period towards an independent African state. It was decided that Tanganyika would get independence, but not before 1970, while in Kenya and Uganda it was pencilled in for around 1975. Neither Baring nor Crawford, his opposite number in Uganda, were keen for the British government to commit itself too explicitly to such an idea.

During a visit to Kenya, Lennox-Boyd failed to convince Mboya that there was no hope of Kenya going the same way as the Gold Coast/Ghana, the British government's view being that there would be a mixed constitution in Kenya for a long time ahead. He returned to London empty-handed.

Baring now had a legislative council amounting to nearly 80 members, and the first elections were promised for March 1958. His hope for Kenya was to create the general conditions that would be conducive to a mixed economy and a multi-racial society before his departure in September 1959. To that end, in May 1959 he toured the settler areas making many speeches to reassure European farmers that they had no need to worry about the future: Kenya was not going to become independent in the same time-scale as were the neighbouring colonies of Uganda and Tanganyika. He concluded that Kenya would be what he called a 'fortress colony', containing an army base essential to Britain's global defence network.

Baring's speeches reflected an attitude agreed only a few months previously at a conference at Chequers attended by Lennox-Boyd, his junior ministers and the governors of Tanganyika, Uganda and Zanzibar. The governors had agreed that the three main British interests in Kenya were the military bases essential for British global strategy; the need to ensure that the area remained economically friendly to the west; and the need to secure the area as a stable home for those people of Asian and European stock who over the years had been encouraged to settle there by successive British governments. The order of priorities is interesting.

Several events were to upset Baring's expectations during the summer and autumn of 1959. More importantly, they almost certainly influenced the British government. These events were the uproar over atrocities at Hola Camp (described below), the decision of France to give up her African empire and the sudden announcement by the Belgians that they were going to grant independence to the Congo in July 1960.

Michael Blundell was among the first Europeans to see the need for change in European attitudes and representation. In a letter written early in 1957 he noted that a number of Africans and young Asians could truly be said to be capable of maintaining a civilized outlook. He believed it was necessary to educate the European community to the concept of qualitative and selective common franchise based on standards and education. He suggested the appointment of a commissioner to examine the whole question of a common roll, with a view to seeing how this could be achieved without disenfranchising the racial minorities. He believed that African farmers might one day be farming as tenants in the European Highlands. His statements were not, he admitted, well received by the European electorate, but he believed that Africans, who had differing views and outlooks because of their tribal origins and needs, would find one easy meeting point – the elimination of the concept of the European Highlands. He recognized that one day the Africans must have greater influence and responsibility in running the country. He urged 'taking the initiative now' regarding land barriers; some form of common franchise upon which Europeans could vote for moderate Africans and moderate Africans for Europeans; and some opportunity for as good an education as 'our own people' can get.

Other European views were demonstrated by Wing Commander Briggs' political group which canvassed that no African would have an executive portfolio 'except on the mysterious basis of merit and ability'. Such proposals had, Blundell noted, so infuriated the Africans that they were considering leaving the government.

Oginga Odinga was one of eight Africans who entered LEGCO in 1957. He looked on it as going into battle against white domination and British imperialism. In the face of some opposition from the 'settler press' he wore traditional African dress in council, and others followed his example. These African members of LEGCO were for the most part strangers to one other, representing several tribes. Odinga's maiden speech received, in his words, 'the opposite of the traditionally courteous considerate treatment accorded maiden speakers'. He was highly critical of the development programme for 1957, and attacked the workings of the ministries and the chief native commissioner. He was more than once ordered to his seat. He and others, termed by Sir Charles Markham 'the Nyanza clique', were accused of trying to upset everything stable in Kenya.

Odinga remarked that an Indian member of the House, Mr Mangat QC, 'voiced the general disquiet at our speeches', which he said were 'hell-raising' and were not the right way to proceed. Although African members did not agree with Mangat's assessment, they appreciated that African representation could change nothing. 'We could,' wrote Odinga, 'make brave speeches, but the solid benches of white members brushed aside our motions. The constitution had been deliberately and carefully loaded against us. Our most urgent immediate need was to win increased African representation. Our eight representatives had a toe in the door; we had now to exert pressure and fling it open.' The African members of LEGCO formed the African Elected Members Organisation (AEMO) in order to provide a united front and to put pressure on the council.

The Lyttelton Plan was in place but still new. It provided greater representation on LEGCO for Africans than had existed previously but nothing like the representation they sought – indeed, demanded. After attending the second meeting of the legislative council, the eight African representatives issued a press release stating that they did not consider themselves or those they represented a party to the Lyttelton Plan 'nor the standstill agreement contained therein'. They declared the plan null and void, said they would not accept a ministerial post or the position of parliamentary under-secretary and asserted that the most urgent and immediate need was to secure constitutional reforms in the legislature, giving everyone effective and real representation. That was where they intended to direct all their efforts and energies in order to 'build a government and society in which all enjoy equal rights and opportunities and no one enjoys privileges or a privileged position'.

As there was no proper African political party in existence, and as public meetings were forbidden, the African LEGCO members used the legislature as the main platform for African demands – they moved motions such as a vote of no confidence in the Kenya government, well knowing they would never win the vote. Blundell observed that after their election the African members refused to discuss issues with anyone but the governor. 'The wall protecting us from the sea was breached, and the waters of African nationalism were pouring in around us, 'he wrote.

The first riots in the Congo had just taken place, and in October 1956 Britain and France had failed to retain their control of the Suez Canal. Their invasion of Egypt succeeded, but they were shamed into withdrawing. The USA, largely out of self-interest, had failed to give Britain the backing she expected. It was a significant moment in the decline of the British empire.

The government's response to the African members' demands was a suggestion that negotiations should be held with all the racial groups regarding increased representation for Africans. The Africans, however, were looking for an entirely new constitution. They had flexed their muscles and successfully persuaded Lennox-Boyd to visit Kenya to negotiate, but they were disappointed with the treatment they received.

'By the time he arrived,' wrote Odinga, 'the settlers had laid their plans carefully. It certainly appeared that plans for the colonial secretary's mission were cut and dried. At the airport where AEMO had gone to greet him on arrival the African elected members were not allowed to meet him. He stayed at Government House which was virtually inaccessible to AEMO, unless they were invited. Blundell and company, on the other hand, saw him frequently, complained Odinga. There was no round-table negotiation. The groups were interviewed separately. On the one occasion they all met together, Sir Alfred Vincent, the settler spokesman, put forward what the settler group would accept and AEMO were 'virtually told to take it or leave it', wrote Odinga. They pressed for the round-table conference, but without success.

Segal, in his *Who's Who in Political Africa*, describes Odinga as an extremely shrewd politician who was often accused of making wild statements which turned out on examination generally to have had a clear and well thought-out purpose behind them. On this occasion, however, Odinga may have overstepped the mark. He admitted that within the AEMO group his language was thought to have been too strong, and he was urged to apologize. He did so without retracting the contents of his statement.

AEMO's demands for more seats were met in part but by no means in whole. They wanted 15 to bring the total of African seats to 23, three more than the white and Asian seats taken together, but they were given 14 elected members seats in total. There were 14 European seats and six elected Asians. 'The whites had an absolute majority. The concessions given did not meet AEMO's objective of democracy and one man-one vote. They decided not to accept the special seats or recognise any African who was elected to a special seat and not to accept positions as ministers.

Tom Mboya and Ronald Ngala went to England in August 1957 'to tell the British public what was actually going on in Kenya and what Africans wanted'. They succeeded in forcing Lennox-Boyd to come out to Kenya in October, but they found him a difficult man to argue with. In the view of the Europeans, wrote Mboya, it meant 'the common roll never, and no Ghana here'.

But the African members of LEGCO were not put down by rejection of their demands for representation. Far from it. The election of six new African members in March 1958 was accompanied, for the first time, by the slogan 'Uhuru' – literally 'freedom', but usually translated as 'independence'.

Blundell admits that the Lennox-Boyd discussions failed to achieve agreement. He recalled, and agreed with, a remark made by Jake Cusack, the minister for internal security defence, that 'the days of imposing constitutions had gone for ever'. It had become, wrote Blundell, 'more than ever imperative to secure African support and agreement to any changes which were being made'.

Outside the council chamber Tom Mboya endeavoured to develop what he referred to as 'the mass movement'. Everyone, he wrote, was 'taught to know the one enemy – the colonial power – and the one goal – independence'. He was aware of the need for the people to be organized, to have discipline and to have a symbol. He appreciated the importance of audience participation at public meetings, of 'the speaker calling on the crowd to thunder back at him' a series of slogans:

'Uhuru!'

'Uhuru!'

'Uhuru na [and] Kenyatta!'

Mboya realised that the English-language newspapers gave little African news, so *Uhuru* was launched as a nationalist mouth piece, a little cyclostyled paper that told everyone what they were doing and what 'the people' were expected to do. They used it 'to bring the name of Kenyatta back into the limelight, to campaign for his release and to restore him as a symbol'. Mboya regarded the banning of *Uhuru* in March 1959 and the arrest of 39 members of the party as the government's way of paying tribute to their effectiveness.

By this time he had established a significant international reputation. He had travelled in Europe and in the USA, and he was a leader of the pan-African movement. At the All-African People's Conference in Ghana in December 1958 he made the speech for one sentence of which he would always be remembered: 'We meet here, in Africa,' he said, 'to announce African unity and solidarity, to tell these colonial nations – your time is past, Africa must be free, scram from Africa!'

Now he was telling them to 'scram from Kenya'.

Many endorsed the campaign by Mboya and other Africans to have Kenyatta released from prison. Another view was voiced by some quite influential African leaders, however – that the only leaders of the African people were the elected representatives and the chiefs, and that Kenyatta *et al* were criminals, not political prisoners. They were, on this issue if no other, at one with the European members on LEGCO.

There were, however, very few issues on which the Europeans and the African agreed. Indeed, as Blundell put it, 'the political scene did not improve, and the differences between European and African thinking deepened and widened'. It was a period of boycotts, and for nearly a year the Europeans and Asians on LEGCO were forced to listen patiently to 'violent racial tirades against them'. And Odinga supports Blundell's view in this respect. Splits had, indeed, developed but eventually AEMO resolved that as a body it would press for Kenyatta's release and his return to normal life. The slogan 'Uhuru na Kenyatta' which had been coined by Mboya's pressure group was amended to 'Kenyatta na [and] Uhuru' in Nyanza, to stress that only with the release of the Kenyatta generation of leaders could the country have true independence. The African members discovered, however, that the British government would not end Kenyatta's restriction order; nor would it be committed to a date for the relaxation of the Emergency restrictions.

By 1958 Britain was committed to transformation from the old colonial empire to the new commonwealth. As we have seen, the USA had demonstrated at Suez that British imperialism could expect no support from Washington. Macmillan referred to the dilemma which would soon be presented: either to allow the rest of the colonial empire to follow the commonwealth course or to attempt to maintain the old system by force. He concluded that Britain seemed certain to follow the former course. 'There could be no going back. We could only go forward, in faith and hope.'

European settlers may have received some assurance of their future in Kenya when Lennox-Boyd announced to the Conservative party conference at Blackpool in 1958 that it would reflect no credit at all to the British government to abandon the people of Kenya to their fate when they had no certain prospects of being able to stand on their own feet. His speech also averred that 'the responsibility of Her Majesty's government is to all the inhabitants of Kenya of all races and communities, both backward and advanced'. He had made similar pronouncements with regard to the Europeans' security a year or two earlier.

Towards the end of that year the African members of LEGCO decided on non-co-operation as a way of obtaining the constitutional changes they had sought without success. They decided to enlist the support of Asian members on LEGCO, and one white member of the council joined them – S.V. Cooke, an occasional correspondent of the *East African Standard* and a liberal ahead of his time. The multiracial group put their case forcefully to the colonial secretary, but in the middle of 1959 the Kenya National Party, which was almost entirely African in its membership, rejected its Asian officials, declaring that its leadership was to be entirely African.

This was period of new political groupings. The more right wing Europeans formed the Kenya Empire Party, the more 'liberal' the New Kenya Group under Blundell: he resigned as minister of agriculture in April 1959 in order to concentrate on political leadership. The New Kenya Group's policy was put clearly before the electorate: a Kenya nation must be accepted which would be largely composed of Africans. It openly faced the fact that they would ultimately rule the country. Perhaps Blundell recalled his meeting with Churchill. This 'liberal' group advocated the 'opening of the Highlands, qualified entry of all races into all schools and a common roll on a selective franchise'. Blundell spoke in his own 'rough and direct' Swahili to large audiences of Africans on the thoughts and ideas of the New Kenya Group. At most African meetings he was well received, but the European chairman of the board of agriculture warned him in a letter that there was a very definite limit to the extent to which even the most liberally minded European people were willing to follow him.

In formulating their policies the group always assumed they had at least 10 years under British rule in which to build the 'non-racial' Kenya, but in the event they had less than half that period of time. The New Kenya Group had much in common with the Kenya National Party founded by African members, and they would, wrote Blundell, have been in the same political camp had it been possible to agree on who should lead. Blundell's group received moral support from Westminster. He had a long interview with the prime minister in May 1959, during which he learned that the only possible policy was a liberal one which attracted the best of the new African thought. No British government could carry the people with it for long on policies lacking a strong moral conviction in issues of this sort. His own conclusion was that a right-wing policy for Europeans in Kenya was completely impractical unless Britain was prepared to support it.

Oginga Odinga agreed that 46 members of LEGCO backed Blundell and the New Kenya Party (as it became), 'twenty-one of them government nominees and all the specially selected men', but, he wrote, the 'multiracialism of the new group was deceptive. The purpose of the NKP was to take the bite out of African policy for a common electoral roll and unrestricted adult franchise. Tom Mboya agreed with Odinga that Blundell's party served a purpose in helping the Europeans face the realities of the change which was taking place, but he maintained that 'there is no real room in Africa for European "liberals" of this sort'.

Odinga referred to a speech Blundell made for unity, in which he said that Kenya needed 'the ability and integrity of the Europeans, the adaptability of the Africans, the thrift and industry of the Muslim and Indian and the tolerance and experience of the Arab'. In other words, Odinga said in a statement, 'Mr Blundell wants a Kenya where Europeans govern, Africans follow, Asians supply the wealth and Arabs sit musing with tolerance.' The African members were sure the Blundell policy was government-sponsored, and they said so.

Reference has been made to the multiracial but African-dominated Kenya National Party, which had much in common with the New Kenya Party. Some Africans, led by Mboya, believed the multi-racial nature of the KNP diluted the 'African freedom' cause, and he launched the Kenya Independence Movement to 'spearhead the struggle for a democratic and independent Kenya'. Its aim was 'one man – one vote, on a common roll'. The well established habit in African politics persisted of meeting any difficulty by forming a new political party.

Tracing the role of the Kenya Indians, Dana Seidenberg concluded that by 1956 the community had experienced repressive measures by the colonial regime against Asian patriots as well as some violent attacks against ordinary Asian citizens by Mau Mau members. At a large gathering, A.B. Patel told his audience that the Asians 'were disliked by Europeans and Africans alike'. But in February 1957 an Asian elected member of LEGCO was reported in the *East African Standard* as saying, 'We Asians can share the African resentment against racial discrimination . . . while as a minority community we can understand the European fear of an excess of African nationalism.' Not surprisingly, the Asians continued to take a middle-of-the-road stand continuing, as Seidenberg wrote, 'to oppose certain settler

273

policies but never fully aligning themselves with the African leaders'. Indeed, N.S. Mangat, in his presidential address to the Kenya Indian Congress, revealed his preference for British colonial rule over that of the African leaders when he said, 'We have often flattered ourselves by claiming that we have supported African aspirations. We started doing this probably before the Africans knew what their aspirations were . . . Good luck to any African tribe which is sociologically evolving itself into a nation. But to aid and abet those who are trying to reduce Europeans to the same level as the Africans is to court our own disaster. It would be a tragedy, for us of all people, if the British lion in Kenya dies of an ass's kick'. The Indian in Africa always had to exercise diplomacy!

In April 1957 the president of the Kenya Muslim League had announced that Muslims would support what he considered the 'legitimate demands' of Africans, but in the same month the standing committee of congress pointed out that it did not agree to an additional allotment of 15 African seats.

By November the Asian response to the Lennox-Boyd Plan was 'a cautious moderation' while they continued to support multi-racial partnership. In December Ibrahim Nathoo accepted the Lennox-Boyd plan, adding that he would support Africans in their struggle for increased representation, but not majority rule 'which might lead the country into economic chaos'. His caution continued through 1958, with a warning against unwise action which was likely to damage the economy of the country and the Asians' future. In 1959 the president of the Kenya Muslim League gave support to the policy statement issued by Michael Blundell's New Kenya Group, which maintained a 'partnership' approach to the future.

As Kenya edged towards round-table negotiations in Lancaster House, London, where other would-be republics had been before, the Asian community was still in a quandary, and Seidenberg's assessment was that 'they had come to believe they were safer under British rule than under an independent African government, the will and direction of which were as yet unknown'.

Continuation of British rule may have seemed safer for the Asian community, but oddly enough Kenya was now on the road to independence. In January 1959 a conference was held at Chequers under the aegis of Lennox-Boyd to discuss the future of East African colonies. A tentative timetable for independence of the territories was: Tanganyika 1970, Uganda 1971, Kenya probably after 1975. The overall pattern was generally agreed by the British government. The only independence date which had changed significantly since the 1957 assessment referred to above was that for Uganda.

In May 1959, at the request of the New Kenya Party, Blundell flew to London to put their views on the future. He spoke widely in Britain, including an address to the Conservative party's Bow Group. He was astonished to find that a memorandum prepared by that group read 'more like the work of [the left-wing MP] Barbara Castle than that of a Tory-sponsored organization'. He read with amazement that the only future for the settler was to be 'shorn of his privileges'.

The Conservatives won the general election in October 1959, and Iain Macleod took over at the colonial office. Blundell observed that a dramatic change was taking place in the policy of the British government. The conclusions reached at the Chequers conference in January were swiftly abandoned, and the decision was taken to withdraw from Africa as quickly as decency would permit.

Yet in many respects there had *not* been a change of policy. In his biography of Iain Macleod, Nigel Fisher recalled that Britain's policy had always been to lead her dependent territories to self-government within the commonwealth, and there are references to this policy in earlier chapters: self-government for the African had been the aim.

Blundell attended a dinner at the House of Commons during which an ex Bow Group Tory MP aptly expressed the prevailing mood by saying 'What do I care about the fucking settlers; let them bloody well look after themselves.'

This was a time of change which was not restricted to Conservative party policy. It was a time for an agrarian reform which had been in the wind for some time. An article in the East African Women's League's news bulletin in December 1957 referred to changes in Kikuyu community development resulting from the endeavours of the community development office and the Red Cross. 'Before 1953,' the article read, 'there were no villages at all in the Kikuyu Land Unit.' The counter-Mau Mau measures had established the new villages, which had a central meeting place with a shelter, communal kitchen, village school (in the larger villages), central school, dispensing facilities, cattle sheds and pens. Nearly 700 villages had been built in Nyeri, Fort Hall and Kiambu districts, each with 100–150 houses. The developments, the EAWL bulletin noted, 'form a neat and totally unfamiliar pattern from the air, surrounded by terraced, well tilled shambas, and slopes from which all signs of soil erosion seem to have vanished'.

The alleged advantages were a reliable water-supply, shared tasks and companionship. There were, however, disadvantages. In a talk to the EAWL Dr Leakey referred to the increased risk of disease transmission and the loss of traditional lifestyle. The next two years saw considerable progress. Late in 1959 Elspeth Huxley travelled much of Kenya, observing what she called 'an experiment in colonization' that had brought about changes revolutionising African peasants. In Nyeri she saw that within three years the countryside had been transformed – every hillside terraced; almost every field lying on the contour; coffee trees; butter-yellow cattle grazing on emerald pastures.

'Gone,' Huxley noted, 'are the mushroom huts . . . the higgledy-piggledy shambas, the goat-browsing aromatic bush . . . the moated guard-posts, the high watch-towers, the armed patrols, the barbed wire barricades of only five years ago.' In Kiambu district, too, she discovered that 'the old Emergency villages are going or are gone: over 300 of them . . . in the process of reduction to 120 permanent towns, each holding anywhere from 2,000 to 10,000 people and to be equipped with water and light. The density has been fixed at eight to the acre. Urbanization is a result of Mau Mau that will endure.'

Plans were in train for the whole of inhabited Kikuyuland, including Embu and Meru, to be divided into small-holdings, fenced and registered before the end of 1961. A 14-stage plan was devised, including provision for objections, hearing disputes and references to an arbitration board should such a resolution be necessary.

Blundell, too, commented on the speed in Central Province with which the old conservative ideas in agriculture were jettisoned and new ones embrace. He regarded the Emergency as a major factor which changed attitudes from those of the formerly 'negative and embittered political leaders who had resisted all efforts to improve their farming'.

Huxley referred to the army of surveyors, measurers and clerks which had launched major schemes in each of the three Kikuyu districts in advance of the enclosure and consolidation movement which 'swept the country almost with the momentum and fervours of a religious revival'. In some districts the agrarian revolution developed earlier than others, and by 1957 it embraced 'community' projects in addition to those of a purely agricultural nature.

In the Kamba district of Kitui the 'political and agrarian awakening', which started in 1948, had been based on District Officer Kelly's creed that 'God helps those who help themselves'. An advantage of this approach was that by 1955 the people were beginning to think for themselves as to how to improve their own country and where the money to pay for it had to come from. Browning, Kelly's successor, ensured that almost every project carried an element of self-help, in that either finance or labour or some other contribution was given by the location concerned.

Huxley had likened Jomo Kenyatta to Adolf Hitler when she recorded that he did everything he possibly could to wreck the land reforms which had brought about Africans' prosperity. She added that the only Kikuyu to suffer loss of land through Mau Mau were a few of the worst terrorists, whose holdings were forfeited. Their land was paid for by the government, and devoted to public purposes, such as schools.

Inevitably, the transformation created problems. Oginga Odinga wrote of the outcry by the Luo against the commandeering of labour, which reached such heights that it proved virtually impossible to organize. Furthermore, although the Luo people had not set their faces against agriculture improvement, the government's plans 'flew in the face of [Luo] most deep-rooted practices'. The government was keen to complete the works, however, and it forced the pace even if, as Odinga noted, it aroused opposition. He was not alone among Africans in believing that 'negotiation, persuasion, and education could have done more than any degree of compulsion'. But after a period of non-co-operation, a delegation of Luo decided to consolidate, seeking instruction and surveyors in order to lay their plots. The European agricultural advisers not infrequently discovered that opposition to land reforms came from the younger, educated men rather than the women and old men. Women were the principal workforce. The agricultural officers, 'agricolas', had recognised their tendency to order rather than advise. They admitted that they had tried to enforce a policy and failed. Now they issued no more edicts. They were ready to advise, but their advice had to be sought. They now had to establish a personal relationship of trust that made people ask of their own accord.

Water was essential for successful farming, and detainees had been used on public works. This had been one of the few benefits of detention. At the opening of 'the furrow' (a canal) at Kitui in September 1959, Chief Timothy Munai spoke of water flowing through a country that had been dry since the beginning of the world. 'Beginning today,' he concluded, 'every homestead between the Thika river and the Thatha Hills, and every homestead between the Tana and the Tiva, will have water close by.' He enlarged on the expectations of wealth and health which should follow.

Huxley was not blind to the risks to which the programme of land consolidation exposed the Africans. The programme gave thousands of African farmers the pride of individual ownership, but it also deprived thousands more of the sense of security which their often indefinable rights in the tribal ownership of the land gave to them.

Teacher training advanced in parallel with agrarian reform. At Siriba, the teacher-training college near Maseno, co-education had reached a point where men and women students were, in the opinion of the principal, completely integrated. They worked, ate and took their leisure together, parting only at the dormitory door. The students believed they had a vocation to teach and that they belonged to an élite. Almost every student teacher was passionately political and meant to have self-rule. 'They wish above all,' remarked Huxley after a visit to Siriba, 'to bite the hand that feeds them, because it is an alien hand and because they believe it to be faltering.'

Susan Wood, née Buxton, provides an objective perspective of the Kenyan political scene as 1959 ran out. Born in Africa, she was married to the president of the Capricorn African Society (one of the earliest societies dedicated to abolishing racial inequalities), and she had stood as a candidate for LEGCO. Her study was issued under the auspices of the Institute of Race Relations, which was an unofficial and non-political body whose aims were to encourage and facilitate the study of the relations between races. Her connections with the Capricorn Society and, indeed, her writing suggest she might be described as 'liberal'. She was writing in 1959 and early1960 as events unfolded.

A complaint of European settlers, Africans and Asians had always been that the government could usually count on six *ex officio* members, 37 nominated members (many of them civil servants) and 12 specially elected members to secure a working majority. Although only six in number, the government members were of great importance. 'In spite of the power of individual groups to oppose and criticize,' wrote Wood, 'the Colonial Office still holds ultimate power in the form of an official majority, which cannot be defeated or go out of office until Her Majesty's Government itself sees fit to allow a transfer of power.'

The 'parties were not well established, disciplined political bodies as one might expect in the House of Commons', Wood wrote. Her observation is supported by numerous references in this book to groups of politicians coming together and forming an affinity group with a title which might change within months or even days. In November 1959 the New Kenya Group was, with 41 members on LEGCO, the largest and, Wood suggests, probably the best known outside Kenya, although it was comparatively new on the scene. The NKP had, Wood wrote, succeeded in uniting a number of LEGCO members of all races. But, she added, Blundell's group was for several reasons unlikely ever to attract any real African support, and without this no political group could have any lasting effect. She described Blundell as 'more liberal than he succeeds in appearing in public'.

With 17 members, the Kenya National Party had the second largest representation on LEGCO. This, too, had considerable multi-racial strength but, as outlined above, the non-African members were shortly to be dismissed. Before this happened the KNP appeared to offer 'a real break through for liberal opinion'. The Kenya Party and the Kenya Independence Movement (KIM) both had six members on LEGCO.

The Kenya Party stood for a common roll, and had behind it the tradition of the ideas of the (liberal) Capricorn African Society. Wood describes the KP as more progressive than the New Kenya Group, adding that the former had a policy which provided for a bill of individual rights to be written into the constitution. Sir Ernest Vasey (often linked with Blundell as a liberal) took a leading part in the KP. The Kenya Independence Movement arose from the split of the KNP. Its aims are discussed above. Tom Mboya was the leader of KIM, which demanded the release of Jomo Kenyatta and the others.

The United Party representation was from four European elected members led by Gp Capt Briggs. The party, formed from the Progressive Local Government Party (formally the Federal Independence Party), 'hoped to divide Kenya into small, locally independent but centrally federated states'. In this way, wrote Wood, 'the party hoped to retain white invulnerability within the unit of the Highlands'. That policy had, she stated, 'no real appeal to many of the settlers, and at the same time its supporters do more damage than their numbers or importance warrant by fanning the fears of the European community'. She describes a confused and confusing scene.

While racial integration was not uppermost in every European's mind, proposals for integration came from what might at first sight appear to be an unlikely quarter – the Kenya Regiment. In 1955, when the regiment was in bloody conflict with Mau Mau, Maj Schuster had proposed that it should open all ranks to all races. Although European and African troops were then living and fighting together against a common cause, however, nothing came of the idea. Now, in 1959, Col Vernon, the newly appointed commanding officer, made similar proposals for a multi-racial regiment, opening the ranks 'to Africans and perhaps Asians'. Unaware of Schuster's earlier initiative, he concluded that if Europeans, Africans and Asians could be made to live together, be treated exactly the same and 'go through it' together there might be created the first truly multi-racial society which could provide real hope for all races after independence. His proposals worked their way up the system, and in 1961, two years before independence, the regiment recruited Asians and Africans and became fully multi-racial.

This brings us to the effect of the above political changes and convergence on the everyday life of the people in town and country during the closing years of the 1950s.

In the towns, the Emergency was not lifted until 1960, but by 1958 the Sansoms had almost forgotten it. Things were quiet in Nairobi, and they, their two young daughters and their friends travelled around the countryside, picnicking and camping 'as normal'. In the meteorological office the stratified nature of employment was becoming less marked. Recruitment was increasingly open to all races, although Hugh Sansom's diary makes no reference to the changes which were taking place. He played tennis with an Asian woman, but he had been doing so for years.

Schools probably led the way in integration. The African Girls High School became the Alliance Girls High School in order to 'twin' it with the boys' Alliance School. They were both Christian schools, principally protestant, but staff were of all denominations and races.

280

Nan Barratt had completed her teacher training course in Northern Ireland, where she had met the man who was to be her husband as soon as she arrived in Nairobi, and her first teaching post was in that city. She taught English as a second language and was promoted to head teacher at the age of 27. In Nairobi and in Naivasha she taught at all-Asian, all-European and all-African schools. In the Asian school, Hindu and Muslim children were taught together without friction of any sort on the part of the children or parents – even when she introduced Christian prayers into morning assembly. She noticed no difference in the intellectual abilities of the African, Asian and European children, although the Asian children perhaps worked harder than the others. Her pupils included a daughter of the first African mayor of Nairobi and a daughter of an African professor at the University of Nairobi.

However, when she visited the town in 1957, Elsa Pickering noticed, that some Africans were stretching their legs both literally and metaphorically. 'They sprawl in the front of the buses,' she wrote, 'where they can travel now amongst the whites, taking up more room than is necessary, talking in a loud voice; when asked to make room they become truculent, and refuse to move their legs aside to allow people to pass. They were much happier in the back section, where at one time they had to sit; it was not necessary to show off then.'

Jenny Baralon, the Scottish railway engineer's daughter, was in her teens as independence approached. When she left school she worked as an apprentice hairdresser, and she had been in the habit of stopping for a chat with the native shoe-shine boy. He had always been affable, but as Uhuru approached he became surly and somewhat aggressive. 'As soon as we get independence you're going to be one of my wives . . . all you white girls will be our wives,' he told her. They went, Baralon felt, slightly over the top. The attitude was, 'You've had your day, now its our turn'. She shared Elsa Pickering's experience of bus travel with Africans, where 'they were not necessarily hostile but not friendly'. And she was aware that it was frowned on for white girls to use buses. She would, too, have been frowned on by Elsa Pickering for her 'impropriety'. There was, she observed, quite a bit of intermarriage, but when she married she was 'cut out of the family, kicked out', for marrying a man with Seychellois blood in him. 'Great big prophecy about me giving birth to a black baby . . . I was not the kind of person [European] people would encourage their daughters to mix with.' Her husband had blue/grey eyes and was no darker than a French or Italian man, but because he had mixed blood, 'a touch of the tarbrush', it was not on. 'My father and stepmother, especially my stepmother, from a farming background, was a very colonial type and definitely did not approve of me going out with mixed blood. I had a very strict upbringing. I had one or two Asian friends . . . I wasn't allowed to take them home though, definitely not.'

Jaynti Pandit saw a future in the building society movement. He had been to London with his brother to study the business and to train with the City of London Building Society. When he returned to Kenya in 1959 he obtained a licence to run the East African Building Society. Business, at first, was slow as people were unfamiliar with building societies and did not have confidence in them. His society decided to concentrate efforts on Africans, because 'this is an African country'. Pandit had identified an opening in which larger societies were not interested, and the society prospered.

That leader in racial integration, the United Kenya Club, which had come near to extinction while the Mau Mau struggle continued, overhauled its constitution in 1958 'in an effort to meet the objections of those taking aim at the policy of multiracialism'. The club was re-formed as a company, alternative membership categories were introduced and entrance and subscription fees were raised. Ernest 'Verry' Vasey, the finance minister from 1952–9, who was knighted in 1959, played an increasingly influential role in the club, becoming chairman from 1958–1959 and from 1970–1980. He had played a remarkable part in the development of Kenya, particularly as a minister. A past mayor of Nairobi, he made friends with Africans at a time when it was unfashionable so to do. He had been severely criticized for saying that for anybody who believed in democratic principles an African majority in the government was inevitable, and he believed that the United Kenya Club had a role to play in the transitional process from colony to independence. Vasey set in train sources of finance for demolishing and rebuilding the club.

In the country, European farmers' reactions to the Mau Mau raids varied. By the beginning of 1957 some had quit and a few had been killed, but most were still in place. Some saw the defeat of the Mau Mau big leaders as the 'light at the end of the tunnel', while others 'read the writing on the wall'.

The Pickerings were preparing to sell their farm and move from Kenya. Elsa Pickering (who, as we have seen, travelled on buses) was well aware that multiracialism was 'being preached in certain quarters'. In her view, however, it was a hundred years too early. She believed that multiracialism would 'lead inevitably to miscegenation, and who wants a race of half-castes? God must have had a purpose when he created the world and made us different colours. There must be a colour bar. It is, in this country, a culture bar as much as a colour bar. When, in about one hundred years' time, we have taught the African a little of what we have learned in nineteen hundred years of civilisation, it may be possible to talk of racial equality'.

The settlers, she insisted, had lived too long among the Africans on a master and servant basis to admit any other relationship so soon. 'It is too early to treat them as equals, to give them high wages for the pitiful amount of work they do in return, to cram their barely awakened brains with book learning . . . They are groping with all the benefits thrust upon them, uncertain how to use them. In their embarrassment they become rude and ill-mannered like the children they are.' She recognized the fact that her views arose from her own experiences and that she was unable to adapt to a new society when she wrote: 'The new Kenya will have to be for the new settlers, for people who did not know the Africa we knew, or the Africans as we knew them. There was mutual liking and respect in the old days; the African has no desire to be the equal of his Bwana . . . for he knows, however dimly, that he is not his equal and will not be for a long time to come.'

Nellie Grant's letters during the three years 1957–9 make no reference to Mau Mau or other terrorist activity, but the disaster of the 1956 harvest was the final blow to her farming hopes at Njoro after nearly 35 years of effort. By the beginning of 1957 she could afford to farm only 50 of her 250 acres. Nevertheless, her letters suggest she continued to lead an interesting life. She was elected president of the Royal Kenya Horticultural Society and was a long-standing member of the East African Women's League. The EAWL was promoting 'guide circles' which aimed to bring together the European, African and Asian communities, and Grant was on the interracial and African affairs committee, albeit that she occasionally disparaged activities which she regarded as 'reaching down to them' in a way she regarded as somewhat insulting.

In November 1957 she had an offer from an Indian greengrocer from Mombasa who wanted her to grow 'huge quantities of veg. for him'. She took up his offer and delivered, but his cheque bounced and 'no amount of effort sufficed to collect the debt'. No other market materialized for the vegetables. Nevertheless, she bounced back, and in July she 'evolved a five-point plan' for her 50 acres, which included 'vegs; spuds; pyrethrum; poultry; rabbits'. Her servant Mbugwa, who had been with her virtually all her years in Kenya, still looked after her and had her confidence. As 1959 came to an end Nellie Grant was approaching 75. On Christmas Day she made her present to old Kariuki – 'those riding breeches' which her daughter, to whom her letters were addressed, had given her. 'He was thrilled and is thinking of buying a horse.'

The Seys family led a well-ordered life at Rhodora. The farm was well managed and adequately financed. They made a significant contribution to the farming community. In September 1957, at Rhodora, they entertained Nicholas Baring, the governor's son, and Jacob Rothschild, a relative. In 1958 it seemed possible that one of the family might move to Southern Rhodesia, and they had 'fervent admiration for Sir Roy Welensky, prime minister of the [Rhodesian] Federation', who was governing Rhodesia as many European settlers in Kenya would wish to see Kenya governed. It was said that Baring did not get on with him, and that Welensky called him 'the Kaffir-loving Governor'.

In a letter home, Seys described the Welenskys' visit to Kenya as 'an unqualified success', adding that 'he showed up some of our lily-livered politicians, whose sole expedient is to retreat with increasing speed before the mounting demands of African nationalism'. In September Seys wrote of definite signs in Kenya of a revival of confidence. He referred to British government and private investment, and to the appointment of Sir Patrick Renison as governor, which 'is generally approved of'. Seys was hopeful.

The second generations of Llewelyns in Timau regarded the country as unstable, but they decided to stay on and were still there 30 years later. They were, however, surprised when in 1958 a relation whom they had discouraged from emigrating to Kenya wrote to say that he had been assured by the colonial office in London that 'there was no possibility of independence' in Kenya, and that he had been given a grant to 'come out and settle'.

Despite pleas for his release, Jomo Kenyatta remained in gaol at Lokitaung with the handful of top African leaders. Visitors during this period would find only marginal changes among the prisoners. During 1957 they continued to be divided among themselves, with Kenyatta and Waruhiu Itote (General China) on one side and Kaggia, Kubai, Ngei and Kungu Karumba on the other. When Kariuki Chotera arrived in March, he sided with the majority group.

In the spring Kenyatta was greatly comforted by a letter from his wife Edna, in Storrington, Sussex. It carried him back in spirit to that village where he had been so happy. In a report, DC Tennent described Kenyatta as 'old and mellowing'. During the year he was visited by the Kikuyu suffragen bishop Kariuki, who had stood against the Mau Mau and was engaged in rehabilitating Mau Mau detainees. Kenyatta and Kariuki discussed 'the state of their country [and] God's love and mercy for the individual'. Kenyatta was moved by the bishop, and learned from him 'how the Christian Kikuyu had met the threat from Mau Mau and loyalist terror with equal courage'. Kenyatta asked to keep the bishop's bible, as he planned to read it 'right through from beginning to end'. The other prisoners gave the bishop a hostile reception. Kenyatta tried to quieten them, but they trooped out of the block, leaving only Kenyatta and China to receive his farewell prayers.

As might be expected of any group of politicians confined together, the majority group formed a political party, the National Democratic Party (NDP). Kaggia was appointed president, Kubai secretary, Chotera, the young recent arrival, treasurer, Karumba vice-president and Ngei assistant secretary. Their regular meetings were formally minuted, and 'discussion became very lively'. They drafted a constitution and designed a gold, black and red flag. Their slogan was 'liberty, equality and justice'. Kenyatta and Itote were not invited to take part in these activities. Although Ngei was the most junior officer in the NDP he was, reported Tennent in his handover report of 1957, the spokesman for the convicts who had given him no trouble. He also reported that there was 'no hope of getting rid of the young murderer and escape artist, Kariuki Chotara'.

Kenyatta and China were not signatories of a letter smuggled out of the camp in 1958, which stated that the 'political prisoners of Lokitaung' wanted the world to know that they were being beaten, inadequately fed and ill. The letter complained of 'the most brutal and inhuman treatment ever', and compared it to that of a Nazi concentration camp. It was a long letter, which was published in the *Observer* and other newspapers in London. Questions were asked in the House of Commons, and Fenner Brockway and other members of parliament became involved. Some of the mud thrown by Kaggia and co. stuck to the Kenyan administration, although the letter was subsequently admitted by the newspaper to be 'a wicked libel'. A complete apology was printed and substantial damages paid. The allegations were the subject of an enquiry by the ministry of defence, which found all the convicts' allegations of ill-treatment to be untrue, but their complaint that the district officer had ordered them to take their water from a polluted well was valid. Kaggia recorded that improvements to the prison followed the questions in the Commons, but the signatories to the letter found that remission of their sentences was cancelled because, by smuggling letters out, they had broken regulations.

During 1958 there were plots to kill Kenyatta. China overheard talk of the first plot, which he reported to the district officer, and China appointed himself Kenyatta's bodyguard. The second attempt, a knife attack, occurred at breakfast. Kenyatta had just enough warning to catch the man's arm and shout to China, who was held back by the other prisoners. Warders arrived in time to separate them.

The assailant was Chotara, who was said to be twice or thrice a convicted murderer, saved from the death sentence by reason of being under 18 years of age. 'Mzee,' wrote Whitehouse, 'was not only ostracized by his fellow convicts but was subjected unceasingly to vituperation and harassment of every kind. The knife attack was the climax.' Whitehouse was aware that it was a planned attempt at murder, incited by the others with the knowledge that Chotera was too young to be sentenced to death. He received 'twelve strokes' corporal punishment. Active harassment now ceased, recorded Whitehouse. Kaggia's book, detailed in most respects, makes no reference to these attacks on Kenyatta, nor does China in his book *Mau Mau General*.

In a letter to his daughter Margaret, dated 4th September 1958, Kenyatta wrote that 'although the attack was planned secretly and craftily it did not achieve its aim. Almighty God brought me out of this great danger . . . I was not badly injured because I managed to get hold of the hand that held the knife which was then snatched from him'. His reference to divine intervention was not evidence of recent conversion to Christianity, since he had always acknowledged Christ while refusing to be drawn into any strict denominational loyalty.

Kenyatta may, however, have experienced another form of conversion while at Lokitaung. Elizabeth Watkins, in her study of Kenyatta and his relationship with his 'gaoler', the district commissioner Leslie Whitehouse, writes that 'Kenyatta went into prison as a self-seeking and irresponsible agitator, over-fond of the bottle, paunchy, over-given to rhetoric, a sick man with a short life expectancy. He came out of prison with his health much improved, a mature, hard-working elder statesman with a breadth of understanding rare in African politics, and a willingness to work with the British to achieve peaceful independence'.

He seemed at this time, however, to be spurned by many Africans. When, in 1959, Oginga Odinga referred to Kenyatta in LEGCO as leader he had been shouted down by both black and white representatives, and some six months later a Kenya intelligence report stated that Odinga was considerably shaken to receive a letter from Ngei and the majority group at Lokitaung denouncing Kenyatta 'as being on the side of the government'. The irony was that Kenyatta was recognised as leader by Odinga, a member of the Luo tribe, rather than by members of his own.

Kenyatta completed his sentence and was released from Lokitaung in April 1959. He was moved to a bungalow in a purpose-built compound attached to the Northern Frontier District headquarters at Lodwar. He had to report to the district commissioner twice each day, but he had some freedom to move about and he was joined by his wife Njina and his family. He was allowed some visitors and he had a small government allowance. It was, however, a very restricted freedom. The missionary Jillian Cossar suggests, not entirely facetiously, that Kenyatta was kept in prison to save him from settlers, and a government official at Lodwar said of him that he was 'the first African I have met with a deep appreciation of western classical music'.

The other prisoners at Lokitaung followed Kenyatta to Lodwar, where they experienced similar conditions. They knew of pressure for their release. 'African nationalism,' wrote Kaggia, 'led by Tom

Mboya and Oginga Odinga, was definitely on the march . . . the colonial government was going under.' Kaggia and the majority group made plans for the future which appear to have excluded Kenyatta. They were, however, reunited with their families, 'which was', wrote Kaggia, 'like coming back to life after being dead for many years'.

The following years leading to independence saw an intensification of political activity and further integration, but a monumental problem still had to be resolved – returning thousands of former Mau Mau adherents, still in detention centres, to the community.

12

From Detention to Reconciliation

Compared with Algeria and some other countries I have seen this
place is like a garden of Eden and you are angels of mercy!'
(Phillipe Junod, Red Cross bearer, during visit to
a detention camp in Kenya, 1958)

Much was happening in parallel with the political activity discussed in the previous chapter. The African population as a whole greatly benefited from the agrarian reforms; Mau Mau influence was fading, almost forgotten, for many, particularly those remote from Kikuyu reserves; and there was the beginning of hope for many of all races as attitudes converged. But for former Mau Mau fighters, still detained, and those thought to have taken Mau Mau oaths and/or to be connected with Mau Mau activities, conditions in the detention centres were crowded, austere and dangerous. Their detention provided a dark backdrop to the years 1957–9.

The stated aim of the government, through the Kenyan Administration, was to cleanse detainees of the Mau Mau oath so that they could return to their former communities and live peaceful lives. The detention of many thousands of Africans, almost all Kikuyu, was costly, and their presence was a constant embarrassment for the Kenya government. The numbers of detainees had escalated in April 1954 with Operation Anvil, and references to screening interrogation and 'cleansing' are made in earlier chapters. It was in no one's interest to keep people in detention. On economic grounds alone, the sooner they could be rehabilitated, the better.

By 1957 and beyond, many of the detainees in their 'compounds' were virtually unapproachable. If by some extraordinary chance a detainee had not taken a Mau Mau oath before entering a camp, it would not be long before one was administered, whether the detainee wanted it or not. Mau Mau Field marshal Musa Mwariama, while recounting the administration of 'repair oaths' in post-1956 years, said most people had had their first oath in jail or a detention camp.

The number of detainees accommodated is uncertain and would vary almost from day to day. At the peak in 1954, over 80,000 were held – one in every three adult Kikuyu males. The construction of camps in a short period of time was a major operation, and accommodation was basic. Terence Gavaghan, whose role in reducing the number of detainees is described below, described Manyani camp as 'a desperate place, a vast bull-pen of humanity, secured by distance, heat and isolation; a place of grinding work at breaking mounds of stone . . . of emptying a thousand latrine buckets daily into seething pits'. Twenty thousand detainees were contained in wire compounds with metal-covered A-frame shelters. Watch towers and guard-dogs completed the scene.

Staff had been recruited in large numbers – Europeans from Britain, Africans from East African territories and a small minority of Kikuyu. Recruitment in Britain was perfunctory. Descriptions of recruitment for the police force, in earlier chapters, apply to applicants for the prison services. Terence Image responded to an advertisement in England in January 1955. He was in his early twenties, had undertaken military service and had had several jobs, one as a cashier. At his interview he was asked a few simple questions. He said he needed a month to put his affairs in order and he 'got a month to the day'. He flew out in the second plane-load of recruits from England. There were six of them in his bunch. On arrival they were not really briefed. 'They were only too pleased to have people, I suppose,' Image added.

He was taken to Kamiti, about 12 miles out of Nairobi, where there was a very large women's prison. His description fits Gavaghan's of Manyani. At the camp they 'got a bit of induction but not a lot'. They learned 'by listening and watching and seeing what went on around [them]'. Then 'the authorities' sounded the recruits about their abilities and most were sent to the big camps like Manyani and Mackinnon Road. Image was posted to a small, distant prison on his own at Kericho, which had been run until then under the district commissioner's aegis. He was thrown in at the deep end, taking over from a warder/clerk who had been running the camp, with one of the district officers popping in now and again. Image learnt how to run the prison by reading the book of regulations and by asking the chief warder to explain what all the books were that he was filling in. It was quite simple. His knowledge of book-keeping and experience of administration and discipline in the forces stood him in good stead. He was at Kericho for two years before a posting to Mageta on Lake

Victoria, where they had some 'hard cases'. Image learned that the prisoners had their own 'command structure' and their own regulations and discipline set-up. One regulation referred to non-co-operation with European officers. All co-operated to some extent, but if anybody went too far out of line he would be fined so many goats, to be paid after Uhuru and once Mau Mau had won the battle.

Prison officers were armed at all times, taking their arms with them even when they bathed in their secure quarters. Image had heard of some harsh prison officers but had no personal experience of brutalities. His experience was that the prison service was particularly vulnerable to being staffed by uneducated, untrained people. European staff were in short supply and few, if any, checks were made on their suitability for such appointments. Many of the 14,000 (mainly African) prison guards were virtually untrained. Many were military pioneer labourers brought back from Egypt. One district commissioner dismissed 35 prison officers in his area.

The treatment of detainees varied to some extent from centre to centre. Karari Njama refers to Ihururu centre in North Tetu location, Nyeri; to Kambi ya Simba in Thomson's Falls district, and to another camp in Bahati area of the Rift Valley as being the centres of 'the worst in torturing'. Administrators – Terence Gavaghan and John Dowson in particular – recall seeing badly injured detainees *en route* from Kambi ya Simba to other centres. Conditions at the Athi River camp, managed by Moral Re-armament, were observed by Nellie Grant and her daughter Elspeth Huxley. 'There are,' Huxley wrote, 'about 1200 of them in this camp and they are not obligated to do any work. Those who wish to "co-operate", some 250, volunteer for work, the rest sit around in compounds and do absolutely nothing all day. They are fed on a Geneva ration scale for POWs [prisoners of war], about four times as heavy as the normal Kikuyu diet.'

What motivated the people who undertook the screening? For the administrators, European and African, it was part of their duties. Kikuyu chiefs and European farmers such as Arthur Thompson at Nanyuki, mentioned earlier, saw screening as a way of restoring order to their communities. For some it was a Christian duty. At Athi River Camp 'moral rearmament' was the mission. Reference is made on pages 236–7 to two Christian missionaries discovered by Chevenix Trench to be using 'third degree methods' while screening, and Gavaghan's experience was that the Buckmanites were 'decent God-fearing people . . . One of the things I've observed of God-fearing men is that when they are confronted with resistance to righteousness they can be more violent than many others . . . There was a tendency when people did not respond to resort to locking people in corrugated iron lavatories, sloshing them with water throughout the night and so on . . . there was certainly a great deal of unintended violence in the detention camps . . . not as much as has been said, but certainly it occurred, without any doubt at all.'

By 1957 screening had become more sophisticated. The approaches used by Kitson *et al* were appropriate for relatively small groups of Mau Mau associates whom it was hoped to 'turn' and use against their former colleagues, but some measure of streamlining was necessary where the aim was rehabilitation of thousands .

One of the most successful screeners, who had particular affinity for the Kikuyu, described some aspects of his methods. He regarded selection of the team as the most important consideration, and he recruited as his no. 1 a 'fearless heathen headman with experience as bearer to a hunter'. The two of them then recruited no. 2, a deeply religious Kikuyu church elder whose trade was selling clothes from farm to farm, which gave him local knowledge. No. 3 was an elderly farm headman, deeply religious and very strongly opposed to Mau Mau, no. 4 was a woman of strong character, married to a man of another tribe and no. 5 was the clerk, who offered his services free because his building business had collapsed.

The team screened some 7000 Kikuyu, gave talks and services to thousands more and trained five other teams. They decided that as screening was directed to capturing the hearts and minds of their subjects, and as Mau Mau was built on fear, the screeners should create a greater fear of their camps than that of Mau Mau. They started rumours of atrocities they had committed in the camp, which spread, and they staged mock atrocities. One such was to walk into the camp at dead of night with a hurricane lamp, handcuffs, rope and gun, select a prisoner who had been difficult to screen, handcuff him and march him out, 'all without a word'. Shortly afterwards there would be a series of screams and shouts in the forest, then a shot followed by complete silence. In the morning he would walk into the camp dangling a pair of handcuffs, rope and gun, throw them on the office table, say nothing and start the day's screening. The prisoner had been transferred to another camp, but after the charade there was 'a remarkably improved atmosphere amongst the Mau Mau prisoners'.

The screeners filled the void created by 'de-oathing' with Christianity. Services were held twice daily in the camp, and it was not uncommon for prisoners to add to their previous confessions. Only two of the first 3,000 the team screened and returned to their previous employment let them down, and even those in relatively trivial ways. The majority of their screening was, however, 'intensive and sustained interrogation, using every possible trick . . . questions, questions, questions, the answers being written down, the next day more questions and usually different answers'. The team built up an index file until, eventually, most of the wanted people were picked up.

Their experience of screening, generally, was very similar to Kitson's, but their aim was directed more towards rehabilitating the subjects into the Kikuyu society than using them for military purposes. 'Winning the hearts and minds' of the former terrorists are words which occur regularly in texts on this subject, although Elkins (*see below*) records that during conversations with Gavaghan he denied the existence of a 'hearts and minds campaign' and described it as 'idealistic rubbish'. For some administrators a 'policy of retribution' was necessary before 'palliative measures' were introduced. Elkins refers to F.D. Homan (DC Meru), who wrote that 'Mau Mau must be crushed' so that the Africans could be 'led from strength'.

There are references in earlier chapters to Josiah Mwangi Kariuki. Born in 1929, he was the son of a squatter family on a farm in the Rift Valley. He worked as a kitchen boy, was educated to school certificate standard and learned English. He was impressed by Kenyatta, was caught up in the cause, took his first oath in December 1953 and was detained in 1954 in a camp at Kowop in north Kenya. From there he went to other camps. His account of his experiences, *Mau Mau Detainee*, has been the subject of considerable controversy and has provided a platform for critics of British imperialism.

J.M. Kariuki was detained for more than five years (October 1953–December 1958), during which period he was moved 11 times. He was a subject of 'the pipe-line', the method of rehabiliation to which reference is made below. His account of his time in detention occupies 96 pages, on 14 of which he records incidents of beatings or 'suicide' hangings in which he was not directly concerned. Some deaths were the result of the detainees' own 'command structure'.

Kariuku was, he wrote, classified 'Z', which was the most 'hard-core' of the four Mau Mau grades. It was he who was, in most of the camps he occupied, elected leader or spokesman for his compound. He admits that on one occasion he physically assaulted the officer-in-charge of his compound, and in several camps he refused to work. He was wont to have letters smuggled out of the camp addressed to, for example, the colonial office in London, the local district commissioner or chief secretary to the Kenya government. At least eight such letters were dispatched, some to more than one destination. The House of Commons and Labour party members were his prime targets.

Kariuki tended to court punishment. He was aware that The Emergency (Detained Persons) Regulations 1953 set out forms of punishment for disciplinary offences. For minor offences such as spitting, malingering, shouting and stealing from the camp or other detainees, and for false accusations against camp staff, the offender could be sentenced to solitary confinement and a reduced diet. For more serious offences such as mutiny or attacks on prison staff the sentence could be 12 strokes and/or solitary confinement on bread and water.

He writes with confidence of his knowledge of the law and of 'the power of a letter, especially if copied to politicians in England'. He was aware of the possible consequences of his actions and he writes almost philosophically about the punishments he suffered. Excluding random 'hurry up' blows from battens meted out by guards, he received seven what might be described as official punishment beatings totalling 168 strokes. He was awarded solitary confinement with reduced diet on five occasions. One of the beatings, of 12 strokes, he describes as 'very painful', but after another (of 60 strokes when his clothes were not removed) he writes, 'the pain was not as bad as it might have been'.

On one occasion, after he and another detainee 'decided to have a showdown' over detainees' meat which, he wrote, was being purloined by the guards, he was given 40 strokes as an unofficial punishment from the guards who had been purloining the meat.

On another occasion, after detainees refused to work, as their 'most effective way of embarrassing the government', a team of 'European Special Branch officials' was sent in to investigate the troubles. Forty-two detainees were 'questioned and scientifically beaten up with sticks and punches', after which five agreed to co-operate. He and another were thrown into a small cell almost naked and without blankets. 'It was very cold . . . on the cement floor,' wrote Kariuki.

At Lodwar, where Jomo Kenyatta and the five top leaders were detained from 1959, Kariuki met the camp commandant 'Buxton' (not his real name) whose opening remarks were that if they refused to work they would 'see what will happen'. He assured them that his word was law. 'I was,' writes Kariuki, 'impressed by this man, whose tough and uncompromising words were those of a straight and honest man doing his duty. We liked this kind of man, who says what he means and does what he says, which is why most African politicians perversely prefer Briggs and Cavendish-Bentinck [recognised as uncompromising European settlers] to [the liberals] Blundell and Havelock.' Kariuki was so impressed that he persuaded his fellow detainees to co-operate with Buxton rather than incur his wrath.

Kariuki was to meet Buxton again the following year in the Kitale camp. On this occasion he was being screened as a step towards rehabilitation. He refused to 'confess', and Buxton and three European officers beat him with clubs and 'a truncheon with nails in it'. His face 'was puffed up and split open, [my] right knee was fractured . . . [and my] chest was pierced'. He was thrown into a small cell for two days without food, having first been paraded in the compound.

Kariuki suggests that Europeans undertook beatings themselves because they 'thought they could do it without going too far and they were frightened the Africans would deliver a fatal blow'. The beating was, presumably, carried out in the open because, writes Kariuki, 'many of the detainees working nearby could see what was happening'.

He 'confessed a whole pack of lies, embroidered with pieces of the truth', and afterwards he was returned to the compound. The following day he wrote a lengthy memorandum to everyone he could think of (to the colonial secretary, Barbara Castle, John Stonehouse, Tom Mboya, Argwings-Kodhek, the commissioner of prisons and the attorney general) and a commission of inquiry from Nairobi ensued.

To what extent is Kariuki's account credible? Margery Perham, whose debate with Elspeth Huxley in the 1940s and her subsequent stance establish her as an opponent of colonialism, wrote the foreword to Kariuki's book. She believed it to be 'a substantially true account of his experiences'. She referred to official reports as evidence that some of the authorities concerned were guilty of acts of negligence, harshness and cruelty. She had visited camps and been otherwise informed of conditions in them. Gavaghan, architect of the system which Kariuki describes, had the greatest respect for her.

Various estimates suggest that some 20,000 Kikuyu detainees were still closely incarcerated in 1957 and were 'virtually unapproachable'. Terence Image referred to the 'command structures' which detainees operated within Kericho, under which they held kangaroo courts and awarded punishments. C.M. Johnston, the responsible minister, initiated, wrote Chenevix Trench, 'the dilution of this indigestible mass' of detainees by separating 'greys' from 'blacks'. Their movement through rehabilitation camps to work camps in their own districts was to be speeded up to keep pace with political advance, 'even if discipline were imposed by force'.

The permanent secretary for community development, Tom Askwith, had previously been made responsible for the 'rehabilitation' of detainees, and to assist him he had selected a staff of devout Christians who shared his liberal views. Askwith, however, formally protested at the nature of the pipe-line project, and he was not surprised when he was replaced by Gavaghan. The government sought a dynamic approach to the problem in order to achieve the proposed reduction in number of detainees within a sensible period of time.

As the officer in charge of rehabilitation Gavaghan was at the centre of the rehabilitation network, responsible to the special commissioner Carruthers Melville 'Monkey' Johnson (who held three posts in one officer) and through him to the governor. Gavaghan had as staff two main elements, a Kenya prisons department complement of camp commandants under a senior superintendent, with some hundreds of non-Kikuyu warders, and a team of European rehabilitation officers, under a senior community development officer, with three Kikuyu rehabilitation assistants and a considerable number of Kikuyu elders as screeners or verifiers of evidence. The briefing was 'minimal to the point of folly or negligence', and his relationship with the special commissioner was 'one of trust'. Nothing was put in writing.

Trench's précis of Gavaghan's project (similar in many respects to Gavaghan's own) is that in order to reduce the detainees' fear of Mau Mau oath administrators and executioners, who held sway in the camps, regular warders sub-divided the compounds into manageable units, mostly non-Kikuyu, with a corps of young, educated Kikuyu trained in unarmed combat and armed only with short belt-slung truncheons. Mau Mau oaths were purged by public declarations before traditional elders. Detainees who co-operated were offered early release to their consolidated farms and a part in the progress towards independence. Prison staff were allowed to use 'necessary and compelling', as opposed to punitive, force. In order to succeed, Gavaghan sought 'control, absence of fear, some kind of shared objective and sufficient obedience to secure the movement, and resources', a mantra which he later reduced to 'control, convergence, co-operation, community'.

His assessment was that Mau Mau's stated objectives included land and independence, and he argued that the government's and the prisoners' objects should be put on converging courses. The prison staff (as representatives of the government) had in train a detainee-manned rice development scheme which was congenial to the Kikuyu as it provided contact with the land. But, and more important, the prison staff held the key to independence. 'We ourselves,' said Gavaghan to his staff, 'are hired on the basis that we are trustees for movement towards independence with African paramouncy as the lodestar. If we have got that and we are developing the political system of the country in that direction there is a convergence. And if we can treat it as a triangle, with both aims moving towards the same point, what is the point of running in parallel? We must, of logic and good sense, converge with a common objective. And if we can persuade [the detainees] that [convergence] is the alternative to the oathing we are in business.'

By the time Gavaghan became involved the original total of more than 80,000 detainees had been whittled down to some 20,000 who were not regarded as amenable to conversion and cleansing. The government had decided that rehabilitation should be induced by one means or another, not in a menacing sense, to change their ways sufficiently to be released home without further disturbance and reversion to the period of war-like violence. In *Corridors of Wire* he recounts his personal experiences and his perceptions of the part he played in accelerating rehabilitation. His initial approach was to sub-divide the detainees in the large compounds into smaller units separating, where possible, those who were dominant intimidators from the rest, so that fear and intimidation were dispelled. He initially re-established full control in one camp.

The large compounds, each with 1,000 detainees, were divided by means of post and wire partitions into four. In order to facilitate this, Gavaghan and senior staff first marshalled the detainees (who did not move voluntarily) to the football pitch. They were later returned to the new, smaller compounds formed by the partitions.

Detainees were subsequently transferred by rail and road to further, smaller camps where they were provided with new clothes and had their heads shaved: previously their hair had been allowed to grow. Some detainees had to be restrained while being shaved, but resistance diminished with time.

Gavaghan was advised orally by his superior officer that it would be reasonable to use minimal compelling force to compel movement provided it was directed to the fulfilment of reasonable and necessary instructions. He was, physically, in the front line when moving detainees around the camp and from one camp to another, and there were letters of complaint from detainees (Kariuki's no doubt among them) to the press and to Westminster. But, Gavaghan writes, there was need for the exercise of punishments for offences. The only punishment he countenanced was 'bucket fatigue', which he considered clearly skirted the edges of the quasi-legal concept of 'compelling force'. Wearing woven grass caps, unco-operative detainees were required to half-run on an elliptical path carrying galvanised iron buckets filled with mud and stone on their heads. It was a long-practised form of punishment, reserved for the specific purpose of publicly counteracting the influence of those who had held their comrades in fear and were seen to have tried to carry forward their dominance. It was held by the prison officers to be both necessary and effective. 'No harm was done to anybody, but it was bloody unpleasant for both detainee and observer,' he recalls.

There were four 'pipe-line camps' through which detainees passed. Initially, movement was, in Gavaghan's word 'messy', as the staff attempted to move too many detainees in each batch, but over the months a progress rhythm was built up, making the fortnightly incursion almost a routine affair. Smaller camps meant that the newest arrivals soon looked forward to moving up the ladder towards repatriation. A man had a good chance of working to the top of the waiting list in six months.

As they progressed, the detainees made overcoats from blankets and sandals from old lorry tyres, and they ran up trousers from khaki cloth on camp sewing machines. In the carpentry shop they fashioned leather wallets to hold their modest savings from paid work in the rice fields, to which many hoped to return as smallholders. 'In a curious way,' wrote Gavaghan, 'the changes which had taken place in the detainees were now reflected in the relationships between them and the rehabilitation staff, and among the staff themselves.'

The pipe-line was subject to visits by members of the Red Cross, the church, the press, Barbara Castle, Margery Perham and Elspeth Huxley, among others. Phillipe Junod, a Red Cross bearer who had wide experience of other counties, commented to Gavaghan, 'Compared with Algeria and some other countries I have seen, this place is like a garden of Eden, and you are angels of mercy! I speak in relative terms, of course. Let us all thank God when it will be over.'

Gavaghan completed his duties in connection with the pipe-line project in 1958, by which time the detainee population had been reduced to less than the 6,000 target which he had been set. He was made a Member of the Order of the British Empire, and in June 1958 congratulated by Governor Baring on his 'accomplishment', which was 'one of the outstanding successes of the Emergency'. Gavaghan was posted to other, different duties. Many recalcitrant detainees had been rehabilitated by the end of 1958. 'The detainees wanted out – they were not converted,' says Gavaghan

Outside Gavaghan's domain were the women detainees. Kamiti camp was the camp through which most of them passed. In 1957, 4,220 were released and 174 remained in detention. Some, the hardcore, were not released until 1960. But, notes Cora Ann Presley, 'the rehabilitation efforts among women were so successful that by 1957 Mau Mau detainees were processed straight to their homes on release. This is a tribute to the thorough and successful rehabilitation work undertaken at the camps'. Presley does not give compliments lightly.

Beyond the camps, return to the reserves required reconciliation, which was often difficult to achieve. The Administration relied heavily on the Kikuyu home guard to assist with policing, and there are many reports of brutality in the execution of their duties. Caroline Elkins provides evidence from un-named interviewees which refer to Kikuyu home guard posts being centres notorious for sexual assaults and rapes. Sodomy with bottles, snakes and vermin were common-place, as were beatings and verbal assaults. Such brutality was not, she writes, undertaken solely by African police or askaris. She refers to mixed-race infants as evidence of miscegenate rape, adding that oral and archival evidence supports the contention that those in detention routinely lost out in land consolidation in spite of the best efforts of their wives, who remained in the villages. 'It was not unusual,' she suggests, 'for detainees to return to the reserves only to find that loyalist kinsmen or neighbours had expropriated their land.' Furthermore, 'when they were released, they were brusquely treated by the land consolidation officers and the demarcation committees if they persisted in their requests'.

Such comments are consistent with those made by Njama in earlier chapters, describing the disillusionment of the Mau Mau warriors when they discovered that their wives and families had had enough of the suffering they had endured because of the Mau Mau fighting and had pleaded with their warrior husbands to give up the cause and accept the truce offered by the 'sky shouters'. Inevitably, in a tribe where land ownership by individuals was an integral part of tribal law, custom and culture, temptation was not always resisted when loyalist members of the home guard were presented with the opportunity to acquire land from discredited formerly Mau Mau neighbours who had been out of the reserve perhaps for years.

In 1959 an incident at one camp became known as the Hola Massacre. It ranks with the massacre by Mau Mau at Lari in its influences on public opinion, although far fewer people died in it. Blundell wrote that 'eleven detainees in the remote camp of Hola, to which Mau Mau irreconcilable were sent, had died suddenly in what appeared mysterious circumstances in that the medical report which was first received stated that death was due to the sudden drinking of water. Subsequently it was revealed that ill-treatment had been the cause, and a political storm burst around the head of Lennox-Boyd'.

Terrence Image, a prison officer in another camp, provides an oral account of the incident which circulated: 'Spike Sullivan was an ex-naval chap. He was selected to run the Hola camp. The detainees wouldn't work. Part of their oath was non-co-operation. Someone devised the idea of physically making them work. A couple of wardens would grab hold of them, put a spade in their hands and bend them through the motions of shovelling up some dirt. The idea being that once they had done that they had broken their oath and they were free of it . . . Spike, instead of taking out small groups, turned the whole camp out in this long column with himself at one end in a Landrover where he couldn't control anything. When the trouble started he couldn't get back because there were groups of Kikuyu rioting. The wardens got out of control. They drew their batons and set about the prisoners. They killed them. Everyone killed was beaten to death by African wardens. The few white officers there were physically pulling them off the detainees . . . It was misjudgement by Spike in turning the whole camp out in one go instead of in small groups.'

The Government Reports to Parliament (commands 778 and 795 dated June and July 1959) occupy 248 pages, of which 31 are findings with annexures. The record of proceedings includes statements from 65 witnesses. References, below, to 'evidence' are made with *E*, followed by the page number. Reference to 'findings' carry an *F*.

One Turkana and 10 Kikuyu detainees were killed and some 50 injured on the 3rd March 1959. Contaminated water was not the cause of their deaths. R.N. Lindsay, the chief press officer, explained that he was left 'with the emphatic impression on the information then given . . . that a possible cause of death was the drinking of large quantities of water in the extreme heat'. (When senior resident magistrate W.H. Goudie visited Hola the temperature was 120°F). Lindsay later learned of 'serious rioting, absolute refusal by detainees to go to work and the reported use of violence'. He suggested that, initially, his office was given an incomplete picture by Government House (*E* 75–7).

The inquiry disclosed that Hola camp contained 'the inner core of the hardcore of Mau Mau, hostile to and contemptuous of, any form of authority'. The camp staff had a most difficult, unpleasant and provoking task to perform. There was no evidence of ill-treatment prior to the 3rd March.

In November 1958 Lewis, the commissioner of prisons, had visited the camp and had 'been disturbed at the lack of discipline'. His visit was followed in February 1959 by another, from Acting Assistant Commissioner Cowan who had 'some experience in other camps of persuading recalcitrant detainees to work'. Clearly, it was essential to work within the relevant regulations. Prison regulations read that detainees 'may be usefully employed in work'. Other regulations provided 'punishment for disobedience'. The 'Cowan plan' was put it into operation. The plan was 'designed to compel 66 recalcitrant detainees to work'. It gave, 'intentionally or unintentionally, *carte blanche* in forcing detainees to carry out the task'.

The Cowan plan, dated 11th February 1959, and headed 'Discipline – Hola Camp', referred to a short- and a long-term problem regarding discipline. Two solutions were proposed:

a. An immediate effort to control and ensure absolute obedience from the 66 recalcitrants.
b. Having succeeded initially with (**a**) to enforce and maintain a higher standard of discipline.

The first solution was to be implemented by dealing with the recalcitrants who refused to work in 'four small separated groups', taking them one at a time. If a group refused to obey the order to work, 'they would be manhandled to the site of work and forced to carry out the task'.

The plan stated that 'discipline among the detainees [had] been allowed to deteriorate', and that 'a higher standard of discipline and obedience must be maintained by more firmness on the part of the staff', but while there must be 'insistence always on immediate obedience . . . this does not imply a brutal and harsh regime' (*F 27–8*).

What occurred on 3rd March was the result of Sullivan's unsuccessful attempt to put in hand the Cowan plan. In summary, the inspector's opinion was that there were defects, ambiguities and omissions in this plan, that it was not executed as had been intended and that there was grave lack of European supervision of the African wardens in the main charged with the execution of the plan. The situation created by this lack of supervision was seriously aggravated by the orders given by Mr Sullivan regarding the use of force which, however, appear to have gone no further than the order of the plan itself; that the detainees would if necessary 'be manhandled to the site and forced to carry out the task' (*F 17*).

Sullivan was, then, carrying out orders on the morning of the 3rd March when, in the words of the inspector's 'irresistible conclusions', there was 'a very considerable amount of beating of detainees by wardens with batons solely for the purpose of compelling them to work or punishing them for refusing to work'. As one reads the conflicting witness statements one finds it difficult not to sympathize with the inspector when he wrote, 'I have had the misfortune in this Inquiry not to be able to feel that a single witness of the Hola prison staff wardens or the detainees, was making any real attempt to tell me the plain unvarnished truth' (*F14–5*).

Terence Image's oral recollection of events, as he heard them, no doubt on the prison services' grapevine, probably provides a reasonable account of an incident which was to have a significant influence on future events – indeed, of the colony of Kenya.

Both Sullivan and his deputy Coutts were suspended from duty when disciplinary proceedings were started against them. Sullivan was found to have 'put the detainees to work in such a way that he was unable to exercise control over them and in a manner contrary to the Cowan instructions'. It transpired, however, that Sullivan had never actually seen a copy of the Cowan plan. Sullivan was also found to have 'failed to supervise the wardens adequately' and to have 'misled the three officials who visited him the day after the affray by minimising the extent to which batons had been used'. The charges against Coutts were dismissed.

Labour MP Barbara Castle referred to 'one of the most blatant cover-ups' when she heard stories of the detainees dying 'after drinking water from a water cart'. She was informed by telephone by 'D.N. Pritt. The left wing QC' (her description), who had represented Kenyatta at his trial, was in Kenya when the men 'were flogged to death by their wardens'. She reported what she had found in the House of Commons in March. She was 'trembling so much from anger I could barely get out my facts', she wrote. She was followed by Enoch Powell, who was equally outraged. Powell carried considerable weight in the House, particularly as he was a member of the governing (Conservative) party. Castle's report was given in March shortly after the event and taken up by the quality press.

Prime Minister Harold Macmillan's diary entries in June and July, at the time of the Inquiry, indicate the effect of the 'Hola tragedy' on the British government. His autobiography records that 88,000 members of the Kikuyu had been detained, but by early 1959 all but 4,000 had been released and were serving prison sentences. There were 1,000 'hardcore' and 'incorrigibles' in special camps. He felt 'particular concern for Alan Lennox-Boyd, the colonial secretary, whose deep sympathy for all African peoples had won him not only their respect, but their affection'.

Macmillan's 9th June diary entry records, 'We are in a real jam.' He foresaw ' a serious split' in his own cabinet, and he set up an African committee which was to endeavour to keep a grip on the situation. Macmillan had recorded in March, shortly after Hola, 'I must . . . take a hand in this affair, or it may prove really difficult as well as politically damaging at home.' He recorded on the 16th June 1959 that the colonial secretary 'frankly admitted the mistakes and the muddles of the Hola tragedy. But by giving the whole story of Mau Mau and particularly by relating a vivid account of how the 80,000 detainees had been brought down to under 1,000 by the "rehabilitation" work, he succeeded in putting the incident in its proper perspective'.

A few days later (22nd June), after Lennox-Boyd had offered his resignation, Macmillan wrote that he had kept telling him that 'it would be a fatal mistake, and quite uncalled for, to resign over this affair. It would be a great blow to the government; would be a very sad end to his splendid career as colonial secretary; would upset the whole colonial service; would have very bad even dangerous effects in Kenya and Africa; and would involve Sir Evelyn Baring's resignation'. The prime minster met the colonial secretary on the 23rd June, during which meeting they discussed Hola and a plan of action. Macmillan proposed that the colonial secretary should write to the governor when he returned to Kenya in a few days, giving his reflections on the affair now that the debate was over, laying down certain principles and asking what the governor was going to do. Then, when the disciplinary trials were over, the governor could reply and set out the organizational changes he proposed. In the course of these structural changes in the government 'the most notorious figures can pass on or be transferred to other jobs or colonies'. All this was accepted.

The part played by Baring in the Hola affair, and the effects it had on his closing weeks as governor, are discussed by his biographer, Douglas-Home. Baring recommended that in view of Sullivan's good character and past record he should be returned for the service without loss of gratuity. The commissioner of prisons announced that he wanted to retire as soon as a successor could be appointed, and the minister of defence, who was due to retire, left before the findings were published.

Baring 'was almost continuously having to provide material with which the colonial secretary could defend himself in the Commons'. He argued that constructive work had been seen as 'an essential part of the rehabilitation process, and that unless hardcore detainees could be got working, their rehabilitation was impossible'. The attorney-general wound up the debate by saying that 'it was not possible to establish any responsibility for any injury', and that there was no evidence of a common agreement to use illegal force – no 'conspiracy'.

It may be argued, suggested Douglas-Home, that prosecutions would have undone all Baring's work of 'fostering loyalty and co-operation of his colonial administration, and bequeathed to his successor a sourness which might in the long run have been more damaging than the effect of not being seen to exact judicial revenge for the scandal of Hola . . . He had thrown his whole mind into the overall objective of Kikuyu rehabilitation'.

The Hola affray was not the only incident of its kind, but it was the most serious and most publicized. Baring wrote home to his wife 'about a number of other cases' which included a Kikuyu loyalist who was sentenced to two years for maltreatment involving the death of a detainee, and an administrative officer who caused a man to be beaten with a kiboko (a hippopotamus-hide whip) instead of the regulation cane. He had given the regulation number of strokes.

The administrators to whom Baring referred were in day-to-day close contact with events, and they saw the human face of 'atrocities'. Sam Githu was almost certainly one of the cases about whom Baring confided in his letter. He was a 'loyal' Kikuyu district officer charged with the murder of a detainee who died after being beaten up at a camp of which he was in charge. Githu had previously been awarded a George Medal for his service, and his fellow administrators' opinions were divided on whether or not he deserved their support or whether justice should simply be allowed to take its course. In the event, Tom Askwith (who had been replaced by Gavaghan on the pipeline project) passed the hat around for the defence, 'but the best lawyer could only get the charge reduced to manslaughter, for which Githu was sentenced to three years' imprisonment.

'To the Kikuyu,' wrote Chenevix Trench, 'his prosecution was quite incomprehensible.' What had he done wrong? To Terence Gavaghan the affair smacked of hypocrisy. He suggested that 'every DC and DO who suspected that violence was sometimes used against prisoners should resign'. In his closing minutes on security Baring praised his administrative officers but referred to a tendency for some to become emotional and to 'break the law, put the government in a difficult position and damage the policy they are eager to put forward'.

Baring used Hola as a reason for hastening a formal ending to the Emergency, 'which would encompass legislation allowing an amnesty for persons guilty of crimes on both sides of the line'. Sam Githu was one who benefited from the amnesty. He returned to his shop and, wrote Chenevix Trench, 'no doubt had mixed feelings about the government he had served so faithfully'.

Both the colonial secretary and the governor had offered their resignations after the Hola affray, but the second Hola debate in the Commons, on the 27th July, was not as disastrous for the government as it might have been. Macmillan's diary entry records that 'The opposition muddled the attack in two ways . . . .and they got no press'. He wrote to the queen, explaining why he did not accept the resignation of the colonial secretary.

Nevertheless, from the government's standpoint the debate had been a close-run thing. Macleod and Hailsham, two Conservative senior ministers were, wrote Douglas-Home, 'out for blood', and a 'brilliant back-bench speech from Enoch Powell' opined that even if there was no cover-up going on 'someone had to be held responsible'. Yet nobody was. Douglas-Home suggests Baring's imminent departure at the end of his governorship period was a factor which influenced actions, particularly as his 'governorship had been outstandingly successful'.

Blundell's impression was that the violent disagreement over the Hola affair was mainly in the political world and raged largely at Westminster. At that time he had spoken to a number of meetings in England and Scotland, covering an area from London to Edinburgh, and only once had the issue been raised by the ordinary listener interested in East Africa. Blundell's view was that 'the minister concerned in Kenya, although a civil servant, should have tendered his resignation', which would at least have demonstrated the concern with which the affair was regarded. He added, however, that Lennox-

Boyd 'defended the officers concerned with all his great loyalty'. Blundell felt that the affair had 'in an indefinable way, increased the moral unease which was always present in the minds of many people in Great Britain over the whole colonial issue'.

Oginga Odinga made much of the Hola Camp 'killings'. He found his public meetings banned by the government on the grounds that he was glorifying Mau Mau. Tom Mboya was pleased that the Tory party was shaken by the Labour attack during two debates in the Commons.

J.M. Kariuki recorded that several of his friends 'went off to *Galole*'. (Kariuki's emphasis). 'The government,' he wrote, 'recently issued a circular changing the name of Hola to Galole. They realised that the word Hola would remain a deep reproach to their reputation for all time'.

Writing his biography of Baring some 18 years after the Hola affray, Douglas-Home stated that historically it had come to be seen as one of the major blights on Britain's colonial reputation.

It had been a miserable period for all concerned, and there were still several thousands of seemingly irreconcilable terrorists to rehabilitate. The administrators' understanding was that the relatively few hard-core Mau Mau who remained in detention would not be released, at least not for the time being, but after the Hola camp affair they were even more of an embarrassment and were, in Chenevix Trench's words, 'shovelled back home come what may'. One way out of the embarrassment would have been for DC Hola/Galole to have accepted offers for the remaining detainees from Arab dhow captains who were keen to purchase them to satisfy the needs of the Arabian slave market, but the DC declined the offers.

There had been predictions that fighting would be renewed when the unrepentant detainees went home but, continued Chenevix Trench, 'nothing very awful came of their return: some dropped into the criminal world of Nairobi; most settled down on their farms, consolidated in their absence, and realised that the party was over'. Inevitably some ex-detainees, returning to their villages, 'decided to have a go at the loyalists who had brought them to book', and there was, recalled DC Wilson, 'an epidemic of assaults, illegal imprisonments etc – some,' he added, 'probably justified'.

Travelling around Nyeri in 1959, Elspeth Huxley remarked on how quietly so many oath-takers and gangsters had settled back into normal life and how little open friction there had been between them and the loyalists. A number of 'irreconcilables' with whom Blundell spoke told him quietly and confidently that they intended to go back to their old employers for their former jobs. 'That they might not be wanted,' wrote Blundell, 'or that their jobs might have been filled by others, or even that their employers might no longer be in Kenya, did not occur to them.' European farmers interviewed more than 30 years later had in their employment former Mau Mau warriors who had returned to their farms as soon as they were released.

Inevitably some former warriors remained in the forest after their 'big leaders' were captured or killed. Organizations such as Kiama Kia Mwingi (KKM), the Land Freedom Army, the Kenya Liberation Army and the Kirimara Kenya Liberation Army were formed. Some were reconstructed Mau Mau units and others were new groups. The KKM became sufficient of a force in parts of the Kikuyu and Kiambu areas for the Kenya Police Reserve to be, for a while, resurrected. There were occasional attacks on European farms, but after a while the new organizations died the death. Bill Furner, a Kenya police officer recruited in Britain and involved in the aftermath, had no recollection of Europeans being killed, 'but perhaps some Africans were'. Blundell suggested that these new organizations included many of the ultra-hardcore Mau Mau, former detainees, who had been released after the embarrassment of Hola.

Field Marshal Musa Mwariama's biography, referred to below, supports Blundell's suggestion. It also provides a picture of post-Mau Mau life in the forest. By 1957 Mwariama was a senior officer in a force which lacked a military structure. He recalled how oaths of loyalty to the new group were taken and remembered administering the 'repair oath' to three who had previously taken Mau Mau oaths but had subsequently been 'cleansed'. Candidates who had taken 'oath grade one would be given oath grade two; those who had grade two would be given grade three', so making good oaths subsequently damaged by 'cleansing'. Mwariama lists a number of Mau Mau leaders who were in the forests between the end of the fighting and the lifting of the Emergency – people like Gachienja, Karanji, Gakengere, Gakoni, Kibaru and Mwangi. He mentions, too, 'a meeting of 1,800 people near Mount Kenya, during which they made 'elaborate plans'. He refers to recruiting hardcore fighters, 'those who had been released from detention and jails' and were currently in

Nairobi. About this time, he writes, he was promoted to field marshal and was involved in 'a big battle' with white soldiers in the Kina area, near the river Tana. He makes no mention of the outcome of the battle but says that he fled across the river. On reorganization, they embarked on oathing 'everyone including children', car thefts, buying bhang in Kisumu 'so that they would be able to fight without fear', stealing dogs to train to work for them and cattle stealing. Mwariama was banned from smoking bhang, although he doesn't say by whom. He was banned, writes Njagi, because 'after smoking he would start shooting in the air, thereby betraying their position to the enemy'.

The impression Mwariama gives of life in the forest for the post-Mau Mau war 'freedom fighter' is of primitive conditions, constant theft, poor food and an outlaw's existence without a positive plan. Their main concern was with personal survival.

As 1959 came to an end the transition from arms to politics was almost complete. The African members on LEGCO had high hopes for 1960. For some months in 1959 they had walked out of Government House in protest at the government's failure to end the Emergency. Their point was made, and they ended their boycott of the legislative council.

On the eve of his departure from Kenya, while 'resting' on the coast, Baring became the local hero of the hour by saving a young Asian girl from drowning. Two girls had been cut off by an incoming tide and were struggling in the water about 150 yards out to sea. Baring, who was nearly 56 and not a strong swimmer, ran down the beach and plunged into the sea. He managed to bring both girls near to the beach but one panicked and drowned. The other he saved. He was himself so far gone that the rescuers concentrated on saving the girl, leaving him to die, but he defied them and lived.

There appears to be no clear consensus on Baring the man. Michael Blundell described him as 'one of the most complex human personalities which one could wish to meet . . . [with] an extremely imaginative, far-seeing mind'. He agreed with the majority that Baring rarely gave firm, concise instructions, but he considered that Kenya owed Baring a great deal. Lady Pamela Scott referred to him as a devout Christian, rock climber, keen farmer, bird watcher and good linguist but, his biographer admitted, 'to the outside world . . . he could appear to be something of a 'grand seigneur'. Until, he wrote, 'one had heard that extraordinary nasal grunt/foghorn/goosehonk which signalled the arrival of mirth or observed the boisterous tomfoolery which characterized Evelyn's family affairs, he appeared to typify the remote aristocratic proconsul in the most superior British tradition'. He was inclined to joke, at Blundell's expense, with one or two other ministers, sometimes passing them notes across the table during cabinet meetings, often about 'Blundell's malapropisms', which Baring found uproarious. Tom Mboya considered that Baring did not seem to understand African nationalism at all clearly, nor did he appreciate the determination of the African elected members.

For years he had been accused, particularly by European settlers, of having no guts and of being remote. Following his rescue of the girl, the *East African Standard* described him as 'the governor who led Kenya out of the shadows'. There was 'an explosion of emotion in his favour', and he was given the Queen's Commendation for Brave Conduct. Later he was created Lord Howick of Glendale.

The British general election in October 1959 had provided a new colonial secretary, Iain Macleod. Prior to his appointment to that post Macleod had, wrote his biographer Nigel Fisher, 'taken little interest in colonial affairs'. He was aware of the Hola camp killings and of the description in the Devlin Commission report of Kenya as a 'police state' (with other ministers, he was outraged by the findings), but that was the extent of his interest. Fisher suggests that in appointing Macleod, Macmillan was in effect issuing a directive to 'get a move on' in Africa. Policy had not changed, but Macleod recognized that independence could not be withheld simply on the grounds that a white settler community had become established there: he took the view that the transfer of power must come swiftly. He believed passionately in his policy and became emotionally as well as intellectually involved in carrying it out.

In an article in the *Spectator* Macleod wrote: 'It has been said that after I became colonial secretary there was a deliberate speeding-up of the movement towards independence. I agree. There was. And in my view any other policy would have led to terrible bloodshed in Africa. This is the heart of the argument.' Macleod was the new broom in the colonial office. In November 1959 he lifted the emergency powers in Kenya which had lasted since 1952. By the end of the year three-quarters of the detainees had been released.

An article in the December 1959 issue of the East African Women's League's news bulletin identifies the achievements of

European settlers as seen by a member, Susan Wainwright, and the disappointment felt that such achievements never made the headlines. She had fears for the future. She was well aware that European settlers in Kenya were not the subject of sympathy in the world press. Her article referred to the achievements of the Swynnerton Plan with experimental farms, research into plant and animal diseases, pest and plague control, 'new lands' schemes involving extensive irrigation of some 40,000 acres, a canal across the Yatta Plateau and the Barringo District scheme, farm schools and institutes, improved live-stock, coffee and tea improvement and marketing initiatives. It listed educational provisions for children and adults, hospitals, health centres and the various clubs and charitable organizations which the Europeans ran for the benefit of Africans. Clearly, the EAWL felt hard done-by and under-appreciated. The article concluded with the question, 'Will the Europeans lose their lands?'

As 1959 came to its end Peter Poole, a European settler, was in prison having been found guilty of murder of an African for which the sentence had been death by hanging. Poole had shot and killed the man during the course of an argument. He had appealed against the sentence.

Elsewhere in the world other 'imperialists' were experiencing similar and, often, more serious problems with their colonies. By the end of 1959 12,000 French people and nearly 150,000 Algerians had died in their independence confrontations. In the USA, 1957–9 were years of extensive race riots, as Washington attempted to integrate whites and blacks in state schools. Martin Luther King was stabbed in Harlem. Daniel arap Moi, one of several future leaders to visit both western block and communist eastern bloc countries, was refused service in a restaurant in Atlanta, Georgia, because of his colour.

ABOVE: Jomo Kenyatta (left) with Field Marshal Musa Mwariama, former Mau Mau leader, in December 1963.

BELOW: The prison at Maralal in which Kenyatta and several other Mau Mau leaders were held before independence.

13
Conferences and Speeches

'The wind of change is blowing through
the continent . . . whether we like it or not.'
(Prime Minister Harold Macmillan, public address in South Africa)

In January 1959 the Chequers conference under the aegis of Alan Lennox-Boyd, then secretary of state, suggested that independence for Kenya would 'probably' be after 1975. At much the same time the Llewelyns' relations were being encouraged by the colonial office to come to Kenya to farm as 'there was no possibility of independence'. Now, in 1960, that rock-solid headmaster Carey Francis referred to 'the wild rush to Uhuru' as madness and, in a letter to the newly appointed colonial secretary, Michael Blundell wrote of the Europeans' 'fear and insecurity'. They wanted to know how 'firm and sincere' the government would be if African members did not accept its proposals for a new constitution. He warned that 'a section of the European community' would seek compensation for the investment they had made in their farms, having been 'induced to come to Kenya by successive policies of the Kenya Government and Her Majesty's Government to develop and farm'. He also referred to 'the small element' who would not accept multiracialism and hated 'the whole march of events'.

All members of the legislative council, not least the African members, were aware of changes which were continuing to develop in the British empire. Indeed, by 1960 the word 'commonwealth' was replacing 'empire'. Odinga, that shrewd politician, provides a summary of the state of play elsewhere in Africa: 'Constitutional advance was granted to forestall victorious national revolt', and a 'process of decolonization was set afoot that would obscure the political controls, yet guarantee the retention of economic influence'. This was because Britain would continue to provide economic support in order to prevent herself 'being eclipsed in competition with the United States of America for spheres of control and influence and to repel the attraction of socialism and the socialist countries, especially the Soviet Union, to Africa nationalists'. There

313

was another factor, too, in his opinion: 'British policy rested squarely on the retention of white privilege in Kenya'.

Inevitably the Africans entered the 1960s with different aspirations among their ranks, and Tom Mboya considered the gulf between 'loyalists' and 'terrorists' to be one of the biggest problems Kenya had to overcome. This rift was beginning to narrow, but it undoubtedly existed.

Kenya was by no means the first colony to leave the British empire, and the colonial office had developed a system for processing independence, part of which included meetings of delegates in Lancaster House, London, not far from Buckingham Palace. A conference at Lancaster House was almost a rite of passage for colony wishing to leave, and what was to be the first Kenya conference took place in 1960.

The conferences were intended to be the keys to providing a new constitution for Kenya which would be acceptable to all the people. By the time of the first one, Blundell was no stranger to Westminster and he was quick to sense change from his earlier visits. It was brought forcibly home to the delegation that changes had taken place the moment they flew into London. The press greeted them with dissertations on the 'wind of change' in Africa, on the number of African countries which already had achieved independence and on the inevitability of others achieving it. It was almost as if the decisive alteration in the policy of the British government made some time between October and December in 1959 had been judiciously but very adequately conveyed to the press, and that everyone in the Kenya delegation, not excluding the Africans, was being quietly softened up in the process.

The conference began a week late, with Macleod in the chair. It was his first colonial conference and it lasted five weeks. He stated that the time had come to recognize that majority rule would come to Kenya and that the Africans were the majority race. Macleod's message was that 'the African's voice must in time predominate', and Odinga's rhetorical question was 'How long a time?' During a television interview Macleod had said that he very much wanted to see moderate policies developed. People could not be compelled to be moderate, but the constitution could be drafted to encourage it.

Odinga's summary of what the opposing delegates sought from the conference was that the Briggs Group of four members wanted a return to colonial office rule and a reversion to an advisory council. The African delegation, led by Ngala with Mboya as secretary, demanded responsible government in 1960, a common roll with universal adult suffrage, the right of the majority party to form the new government, the abolition of nominated and specially elected members, the release of Kenyatta and the opening of the White Highlands to landless Africans. The group which most closely matched Macleod's preference for 'moderate policies' was the New Kenya Party led by Michael Blundell: it wanted a half-way scheme for command, and common roll elections.

The conference opened on a dramatic note with everyone sitting at long blue tables, 'smiling with enthusiasm and amiability under the eyes of the press and the lenses of the TV camera'. Macleod arrived looking worried and ill at ease. An important part of the conference was missing because the African elected members had boycotted the opening ceremony over the status of one of their advisers. Each delegation had already nominated the name of its adviser in advance, but the Africans wished to add Peter Koinange (the former chief's son) after their arrival in London. His presence at the conference was initially unacceptable, not only to the British government but to many other participants. This caused the talks to be deadlocked for five full days until Macleod found an ingenious compromise solution. It involved giving the African delegates a blank pass into Lancaster House for Koinange, who would not be allowed into the conference room. Blundell was given what almost amounted to an ultimatum that unless he agreed with this he would go back to Kenya 'a discredited political leader'. Quite early in the life of the conference, therefore, Blundell came to the conclusion the Africans already knew from the colonial office that 'they were batting on a wicket specially prepared for them'.

Every delegate who wished to do so made a prepared speech, after which it was possible to get down to serious negotiations without anyone feeling frustrated. When tempers were rising Macleod divided delegates into committees, and when opposition to his first proposals grew, he had the delegates working late into the night so that anger simmered down in weariness.

Macleod was patience itself. He told the Africans man-to-man that they were at a constitutional disadvantage and that they should assist him in dealing with the settlers, who were not prepared to give an inch of the way. They had been worn down over the weeks of talking and softened up one by one. After all this time they could not go home empty-handed. Blundell found him a most difficult man to assess. He was 'quite impervious to unpopularity and prepared to change the details of his approach overnight to secure his objective'.

From his talks with Macmillan it was obvious to Blundell that the right wing views of the Briggs Group had been completely discarded, and from then on they might as well not have attended for all the attention which government representatives paid to their views. Blundell's New Kenya Party 'almost became the right wing of Kenya thought overnight', he wrote.

Macleod's proposals for the new constitution at the end of the first stage were unacceptable and were rejected by all. The conference was in danger of collapse. The New Kenya Group was convinced that this would lead to increasing tension in Kenya and suggested informal talks between African members and themselves. The discussions were not important in detail, but they created a more friendly atmosphere. The NKG began to see the sincerity of the African members and to appreciate the emotional forces behind them. African members as individuals began to understand the fears and doubts of the Europeans and Asians.

The African delegates sought a bill of rights as part of the constitution, and Blundell sought specific guarantees for land ownership as part of any bill. Macleod persuaded them to postpone the issue until the next meeting of LEGCO.

Negotiations continued, and after some five weeks Macleod produced a document for acceptance or rejection by conference. His biographer records that although he achieved his main objective, which was to reach agreement between Blundell's group and the Africans on a constitution, the United Party of right wing Europeans did not accept the new constitution, and the land problem was left unresolved.

Macleod conveyed his proposals to the parties at separate, private meetings with each group of delegates on the 13th February. At the end of each meeting, having conveyed his proposals, he said nothing but 'Thank you very much, gentlemen'. The proposals were rejected by all parties, to which Macleod replied, 'Gentlemen, I did not ask you to comment on the proposals I have put to you. I only asked you to accept them or reject them. I understand that you reject them. In the circumstances I propose to withdraw the proposals and send a commission to Kenya in six months' time. It will report to me maybe in a year's time, if that is what you would like.' He obtained guarded acceptance of the formula and ten days later the conference was over. 'Macleod was a master in the tactics of running a conference, and it was a pleasure to watch his skill,' said Mboya.

On the eve of leaving Lancaster House, the African elected members presented a paper to Macleod and the government which suggested that the new constitution had arrived many years too late and would be out of date before it was implemented. The aim was, wrote Mboya, to draw Macleod's attention to the fact that the Africans' struggle was still going on. Mboya believed Macleod understood their motive better than the people in Kenya. He told them the issue was by no means closed, and he would, at the appropriate time, be happy to receive further representations about another constitution.

None of the major delegations was pleased with the outcome. Blundell consulted all his delegates and some influential back-bench members of the British Conservative party, who promised support. Finally, however, as 'tough and almost harsh as Macleod's decisions were', they accepted them, believing they were wise to do so. Odinga recalls the African group's expression of its 'bitter disappointment' with Macleod's proposals for representation on LEGCO, which increased African membership but which made no provision for universal adult franchise.

Late one evening, after Macleod had presented his proposals, the prime minister, recently returned from his African tour, invited Blundell and some others to 10 Downing Street, where he urged them not to let the emotions of the moment deflect them from their ideas and ideals. He attempted to put the conference in perspective.

Macleod's biographer writes that Michael Blundell was the bridge between white rule and black, and that without his help in the transition period African advance might have been dangerously delayed. In fact, he suggests, much of the credit for the success of the conference was due to Blundell and his colleagues, who were regarded as traitors and renegades, and were ostracized by their friends.

Blundell's initial reaction to Macleod had been that he was deceitful and evasive, economical with the truth and, on occasions, that he 'had not even the truth within him'. He remarked that 'Not once did

Iain Macleod or his senior officials indicate to us the decision [for the Europeans] to go as soon as possible had already been made'. Some years later Blundell discussed Macleod's deceit with Lord Chandos (formerly Oliver Lyttelton). Chandos commented, albeit 'with a twinkle in his eye, 'But surely, Michael, you realize that Iain is not the first British minister to have lied.'

Prime Minister Macmillan's diary for the 21st February, a week after Macleod conveyed his proposals to the delegates, records 'Iain Macleod came in after dinner to tell me that the Kenya conference – after many difficulties – has reached a successful conclusion, everyone (except Group Captain Briggs) being in agreement. This is certainly a great triumph for the colonial secretary.'

In addition to the main Lancaster House conference, Macleod held a number of 'side' meetings with the groups of delegates on matters of particular interest to them. The African delegates had as their primary aims Kenyatta's release and the freedom of political parties to operate nationwide. 'In a private meeting with the African delegates,' Odinga recalls, 'Macleod said the British government would be prepared to let political parties function on a national basis, and to relax restrictions on political meetings. But there would be no release of Kenyatta.' On the positive side, Mboya noted that Lancaster House not only brought the declaration that Kenya was to be 'an African country', it also reversed the whole constitutional process. Now 'the Africans would have a majority in the legislature and a four-to-three lead in the Council of Ministers'. Odinga added, 'By some superhuman effort (or so it seemed at this time of splintering and antagonism) we had achieved African unity in time for the Lancaster House conference and that had won us the day.'

Blundell had reason to remember his return to Africa. 'As I stepped out of the aircraft at Entebbe,' he wrote, 'I was called to the long-distance telephone to hear Wilfrid Havelock warning me that there might be demonstrations at the airport in Nairobi. On our arrival in Nairobi I was greeted with a barrage of loudspeakers mounted by an extreme section of the Federal Independence Party, blaring out that I had betrayed the Europeans; counter shouts from a large African crowd arose into the air with the cry "Never mind Mr Blundell, we will vote for you." I was met by my wife and daughter and we were pushing our way through the crowd to the cars at the entrance, when a small group of hot eyed, angry men ran up to me shouting and hurling abuse. One of them, with a thin, lined, sunburnt face and bitter questing eyes, raised his hand and threw something at my feet. A small white bag burst open, and thirty East African simunis, or sixpences, flew in all directions across the hard pavement of the hall. He cried out "Judas, you have betrayed and left us." In the surging crowd of Europeans, Asians and Africans, which were milling around us, some crying encouragements and others cursing, I managed to get near enough to tell him that I would be in Kenya long after he had gone, and an African voice interjected in English, "Yes, and taking his compensation with him." '

For the next two years Blundell, his wife and daughter were almost ostracized by people he had come to think of as his friends. Cavendish-Bentinck greeted him angrily in the parliament building and resigned from speakership of LEGCO. 'The European community was rent in twain,' wrote Blundell, 'between those who could only think of going and those who were determined to stay.' Blundell recognized that the result of the conference was a great, indeed a stunning, blow to the European community. Sir Peter Tapsell told him many thought he had betrayed them. He had been elected as a European leader to look after their interests and had sold out to the Africans.

However, not all Europeans denigrated Blundell. The Earl of Portsmouth, a member of LEGCO, saw something of the first Lancaster House conference from the sidelines and felt bitterly sorry for the way he was mistreated for it in Kenya. Portsmouth found it hard to have sympathy for the die-hards. Later he joined Blundell and others in forming the New Kenya Group.

The constitution derived from the agreement reached at Lancaster House provided for a legislative council comprising:

- *ex officio* members, members of the council of ministers not otherwise members of LEGCO.
- 65 elected members.
- Governor's nominated members.

The elected members comprised:

- Fifty-three constituency members elected by votes on a common roll, who were to be British subjects or British protected

319

persons, 21 or more years of age, possessing 'certain literacy or property qualifications'. Ten European, eight Asian (three Muslim and five non-Muslim) and two Arabs, all to be subject to primary elections.

• Twelve national members elected by constituency members: four Africans, four European one Muslim, two non-Muslim Asians, one Arab.

The Council of Ministers was to consist of the deputy governor and 'such number as may be prescribed by His Majesty'; parliamentary secretaries, twelve ministers (three official and nine unofficial) and nine unofficial ministers.

The bill of rights was to be drawn from a Nigerian bill.

On the 3rd February, while the Lancaster House conference was in progress, Macmillan had addressed a joint meeting of 'both houses' in South Africa. It was his 'Wind of change' speech, the most significant (and most widely quoted) speech of his African tour. In it he declared, 'The wind of change is blowing through the continent, and whether we like it or not this growth of national consciousness is a political fact. We must all accept it as a fact and our national policies must take account of it . . . We reject the idea of any inherent superiority of one race over another. Our policy therefore is non-racial. It offers a future in which . . . all play their full part as citizens . . . and in which feelings of race will be submerged in loyalty to new nations.'

Michael Blundell might have been forgiven for feeling downcast. Lancaster House had not gone as the Europeans would have wished, his return had been greeted with contempt and the future looked, to say the least, uncertain. It was time to take stock. It would be a gross understatement to say that the formula for a constitution which came out of Lancaster House merely concentrated minds. From his talks with Macleod, Blundell was convinced that the decision had already been made to clear out of Africa as soon as possible, but his impression was that Europeans had at least 10 years before a complete transfer of power took place. He was, nevertheless, aware of the immense increase in the emotionalism of the African, and he had a firm impression that the government did not want to face a series of riots, detentions and arrests in the multiracial communities. Blundell got small change from Macmillan when he sought finance and security for the European community. Macmillan told him Britain was today 'a poor country', and that with the threat of the nuclear bomb hanging over their heads the people of Britain, too, felt insecure. Blundell concluded that Kenya was 'destined now to be an African country'.

Sir Ferdinand Cavendish-Bentinck resigned as speaker of LEGCO, telling Blundell that he had destroyed everything for which he had worked – 'a white Dominion in East Africa' – and Group Capt Briggs wrote in the *East African Standard* on 22nd February that he regarded the outcome of the conference as the death-blow to the European community in Kenya. But 10 days later he suggested all was not lost.

The bitter fruits of the Lancaster House conference convinced many of the settlers that, as Jock Dawson put it, 'the end was nigh'. It was, commented John Carver, 'a question of when [independence] happened. People who thought we could carry on indefinitely were just imagining things. There was no way we could hold on.' Jillian Cossar, working for a missionary society, returned to Kenya from England in 1960 after Lancaster House. She was a relatively independent observer of the scene after an absence of years. She observed how its settlers suddenly realized that the government, which had encouraged them to come to Kenya, to develop and settle, was now going to desert them and hand the country over to the majority – and they would be a minority with next to no voice. Their spirit had gone out of them. A lot of settlers left at that time, disillusioned. The Seys family at Rhodora believed the Lancaster House agreement had virtually disenfranchized the Europeans. 'Is it not wonderful that the Europeans, who contribute 90 per cent of the country's exports, will have no effective say in the country's government?' They thought it a curious conception of democracy.

On some European farms, however, little thought was given to approaching Uhuru. The Murrays at Timau noticed no changes in African attitudes in field or kitchen, and at the time of the 1960 conference they were replacing the wooden house on stilts in which they had lived for many years with a larger permanent house with brick structure and tiled roof. In 1961, as it approached completion, they asked themselves whether they had made the most horrendous mistake, but they went on working and ignored what was going on beyond the farm. They had put everything into it, and had 'no contingency plans, no Swiss bank accounts'.

For some European settlers, particularly the older ones, the prospect of African rule was unacceptable and, like John Carver's ageing father, they left as independence approached. The Carver parents had spent their lives in Kenya, so their reluctance to accept change was understandable, but post-war settlers went too: Ray Terry's parents and brother, all post-war settlers, sold up and moved back to the UK. Many European settlers felt let down by the 'Conservative' government. There had been an expectation that the Labour party would give the British empire away, but not the Tories, and it was they who were in power. After Lancaster House it was obvious for all to see. 'The Conservatives were the biggest traitors of the lot,' recalled George McCall with considerable bitterness some 30 years on. The assessment of Carey Francis, the pro-African headmaster, was that 'Uhuru, good or bad, is clearly coming. The fact that I consider it an unmitigated disaster and that I shall be able to say "I told you so" from the ruins does not ease us through the difficult transition.'

Early in 1960 two African parties were formed, the Kenya African National Union (KANU) and the Kenya African Democratic Union (KADU). Mboya suggests that the essential difference between the parties was that 'KANU set about eliminating tribalism [while] KADU were busy building up tribal organizations and seeking regional assemblies' – majimbo. KANU had the greater support from the large tribes, the Kikuyu and Luo, whereas KADU was preferred by the smaller tribes who hoped to keep their tribal identities in their regions and avoid domination by the Kikuyu/Luo combination of politicians. The European settlers also preferred the less powerful regional government on the principle of 'divide and rule': they had significant influence in some areas. The perception of John Cumber (formerly administrator, but now private secretary to the governor), was that a fundamental difference existed between the two parties: KANU represented the Kikuyu *per se* while KADU represented just about every other tribe in Kenya. There is contradictory evidence as to the people who led the parties during their formation, but as there appears to be agreement that Mboya and Odinga, both members of the Luo tribe, were founder members of KANU, Cumber's perception of the parties' stances may not be reliable.

Inevitably, the quest for political power, regardless of tribal roots, influenced the actions of individuals. In Michael Blundell's analysis they represented two markedly different streams of thought in their community. Mboya wanted and represented a modern Kenya, while Odinga represented African traditions, old customs 'and the bewilderment which the impact of western values brought to these simple, unsophisticated and often remote people'.

From shortly after their formation, KADU and KANU had little in common. Kenyatta asked for consultation with the leaders of both parties and they travelled to Maralal where he was detained. Out of their talks came the formal Maralal Agreement, which defined common objectives and set up a working committee charged with the task of sending a joint delegation to the governor and the colonial secretary, demanding Kenyatta's release. They also sought a new constitution and full independence in 1961. With the 'winds of change' blowing, the African politicians were eager to see the arrival of independence. 'Uhuru Sasa' ('Independence Now') was the rallying cry. Blundell regarded the British decision to 'clear out of Africa' as quickly as it could as an act of great irresponsibility, but it was in keeping with Macmillan's pragmatic approach to political problems. It is estimated that after January 1960 capital flowed out of Kenya at a rate of £1 million each month, and none came in.

Writing some 30 years after the events, Blundell opined that Kenya was 'singularly unfitted for independent African rule', as there were virtually no Africans trained to take over government. But he gave Tom Mboya credit for his contribution to the future of the country by encouraging crash programmes to give promising civil servants higher education overseas. Blundell suggested that the disagreement among African leaders which resulted in the formation of KANU and KADU delayed the declaration of independence for nearly three years – from February 1961 to October 1963. In this period the Kenya government initiated intensive training, primarily in the administrative, military and police organizations and, whenever possible, in the technical divisions of government, but John Cumber was impressed by the 'atmosphere of great goodwill, letting bygones be bygones', which prevailed at all the meetings. He observed, however, that there were 'stern attempts at negotiation going on all the time. Nobody really gave any ground'.

On the European settler front, Cavendish-Bentinck headed a political group called the Kenya Coalition, which was launched with the object of protecting all minorities and achieving an orderly transition to independence, with compensation for those who wanted to go. It was a non-political organization open to all races. Members of Blundell's New Kenya Group came under pressure to join it, but they did not do so.

By August 1960 the Seys family believed that the British government 'cynically' aimed 'to divide the Africans amongst themselves, so that some of them may conclude that they cannot get along without European help'. He believed, too, that the aim was to keep the Europeans divided, and he identified those he regarded as the stooges of the British government – the New Kenya Group led by Blundell, the right wing United Party led by Briggs and a middle group, the Kenya Coalition, led by Cavendish-Bentinck.

There was activity on the Asian front, too. In January 1960 the Kenya Indian Congress and the Kenya Muslim League were joined by a third political organization, the Kenya Freedom Party. Membership was unrestricted, but the founding officers were predominantly Asians: Chanan Singh, a former member of LEGCO, I.T. Inander, A. Rauf, K.P. Shah and I.K. Mehta. All were established in politics and commerce. The central aim for the Kenya Freedom Party was to represent and educate Asian public opinion. Its published 'policies' included working for independence, with a constitution similar to that to that of the United Kingdom, the introduction of legislation guaranteeing human rights and the establishment of equality of opportunity. They were similar to those of KANU, and 'rights of residents' were written along the lines of the Universal Declaration of Human Rights. The party became involved in disputes with the older Asian/Indian parties. It put up candidates for the 1961 general election and lobbied for Kenyatta's release. A six-man delegation visited him at Maralal, where he reassured them that the future of the Asians in Kenya was secure. During 1960, wrote Seidenberg in her study of Kenya Indians, the Asian community had become increasingly fearful for its future as anti-Asian feelings were spread by Europeans and Africans alike.

Seidenberg may have been aware of a public meeting in Nairobi in March at which A.T. Culwick told Asians that they should 'stop sitting on the fence' and pull their weight. He warned that if the European farmer left the country, the source of Asian wealth would be removed and he would have little alternative but to eke out an impoverished existence as part of a downtrodden, intimidated, persecuted community. And in October 1960 Tom Mboya, secretary-general of KANU, remarked that resolutions, statements and ideas of support from the Indians in Kenya were not of much interest to the African people who were asking 'just what these people have done and what they intend doing to assist in the struggle for independence'.

Police officer Douglas Walker, whose work of registering and controlling European firearms brought him in close contact with the community, recalled that 'Africans and Europeans didn't seem to like Asians'. An Asian or an African would invariably prefer employment by a European, and employment of an African by another African was no more attractive because the Africans had the reputation of not paying their staff.

One of the few Asians to receive a warm word from Africans involved in Kenya politics was Pio Gama Pinto, of whom Odinga wrote, 'Pinto might have been a Goan but he was as African as the truest Kenyan nationalist. There is no phase of our struggle in which he did not play an invaluable part.' During the post-war years he had tried to get Asians to throw themselves fully into the African liberation struggle. He maintained political liaison and supplied arms and money to the fighters during the Mau Mau period. During the three or four years before independence he threw himself into helping KANU.

Susan Wood, a local, informed and liberal commentator, wrote that Asian politicians were logically led to take a moderate course. She regarded S.G. Amin, the president of the Indian Congress, who was not a member of the LEGCO, as a moderate who took pains to try to bring understanding between the opposing groups. Her appreciation of Asian politicians' attitudes was that most would be prepared to see a common roll, and all would like to see increased representation.

Some Asian members of LEGCO were openly in the African camp. Others sat on the fence and were unlikely to take a course which would be unpopular with the African leaders, clinging as Wood put it, 'to whatever seemed to provide an immediate insurance'.

The three Asian organizations continued their activities until, in November 1962, KANU threw open its membership to all races. The Kenya Indian Congress and the Kenya Freedom Party then both decided that there was no longer any justification for continuing as separate organizations, and their members were encouraged to join KANU. Some, such as K.P. Shah, became officers.

Other affinity groups which blossomed briefly were the Masai United Front and the all-white United Party, which appealed to the minority tribes to combine with it against the 'Luo-Kikuyu combination of politicians'. The reasoning was that the smaller tribes and the whites were in the same predicament: they were all minorities. Cavendish-Bentnick was invited to lead a delegation to London to plead the cause of the whites and other minority communities, but in the event the Europeans sent a number of delegations to London to interview the secretary of state and other responsible bodies, with a view to getting compensation to enable many of the settlers to leave. They were spurred on by the events in the Congo, and the stream of Belgian refugees who passed through. Blundell was invited to take part but he declined.

August arrived, and Peter Poole was in gaol (*see page 311*) while appeals against his death sentence went to the court of appeal and to the judicial committee of the privy council. Muriel Buttery, a district officer's wife stationed in a boma between Embu and Nyeri, had arrived in Kenya from England in 1951, so she was relatively new to the country. She travelled around with her husband when he went on safari and was therefore in a position of observe customs and attitudes. 'If,' she remarked, 'a European shot an African, that was it, no one would go and inform the police, no one would stand up in court against a white man, they just wouldn't do that.'. Her observation was not unique. Nevertheless, Poole's appeals were dismissed. A petition for mercy to the Queen was unsuccessful, on the advice of Macleod. The irony was that Macleod was a convinced capital punishment abolitionist. There had been rumours of Europeans storming the prison. Some 300 waited outside on the day, but there was no violence. Poole was the first European in Kenya to be hanged for murdering an African.

Poole's execution marked a significant change in attitudes and expectations. The law had not and did not distinguish between the rights of the European and the African, but the reality, as the Buttery observation indicates, had favoured the white man. Yet again bitterness arose between the European settlers and the civil servants. Generous compensation terms were announced for the latter but the settler, Blundell wrote, 'was left to fend for himself'.

On his return from a visit to Macleod early in May the governor, Sir Patrick Renison, called a press conference at which he made the

statement by which his term as governor of Kenya will most be remembered. He referred to Kenyatta as 'the African leader to darkness and death who had been sentenced by due process of law to seven years' imprisonment'. That was the official view of Kenyatta. Renison was responding to the calls by Africa leaders to free Kenyatta, and he made it clear that he did not intend to react sympathetically. Murray-Brown, Kenyatta's biographer, suggests that Renison's statement can only be described as 'official blackmail' since Renison said that 'self-government according to the Lancaster House formula depended on the co-operation of all races in Kenya, that Africans must be ready to accept the government's view of Kenyatta and that their readiness for self-government would be measured by the readiness of their leaders to acknowledge those facts' and their ability to carry their followers with them. 'I have at present,' Renison's statement continued, 'no evidence whatsoever that Jomo Kenyatta will help Kenya in these aims. I have much evidence to the contrary.' Renison relied to a significant extent on evidence from the Corfield Report when making his statement. Corfield was convinced that Kenyatta was rightly found guilty of managing Mau Mau, from which it followed that he was the man primarily responsible for all that had happened in Kenya during the Emergency.

Renison's stance had the support of virtually all Europeans in Kenya, and presumably of the colonial office. Murray-Brown suggests, too, that the 'overwhelming weight of African "loyalist" opinion was against Kenyatta', as were many of the younger African leaders'. Macleod had strongly advised the governor against describing Jomo Kenyatta as 'the leader to darkness and death'. He recognized that sooner or later the British government would have to deal with Kenyatta, and Renison's description would not be helpful when that time came. Macleod did not, however, wish to call for Renison's resignation, so he did not veto the speech. To have replaced him at that time would have intensified European antagonism.

From Rhodora, Seys referred to Renison's speech as 'the great event here in Kenya' – a firm declaration of policy to which reactions were 'very favourable, except from African nationalist politicians', who described it 'as an indication that the British intend to keep the Africans down by force.'

There was some jostling for place among the African leaders. Odinga wrote that 'British and the United States strategy seemed to

converge on the grooming of Mboya for leadership in the place of Kenyatta', and with the help of Gichura, himself a Kikuyu, Mboya hoped to rally Kikuyu support for Kenyatta. The irony was that Mboya, a Luo, should be rallying support for Kenyatta from members of Kenyatta's own tribe.

There was strong pressure for the release of Jomo Kenyatta. Renison was not alone in resisting it, but the pressure increased as 1960 progressed. With the prospect of a general election in February 1961, KANU and KADU developed their aims. KANU's objective 'was to work for a predominately African government' while the KADU leaders 'hoped to win enough seats to form a multi-racial government together with the small political groupings of settlers and Asians'.

Both KANU and KADU stated that they would not form a government unless Kenyatta was released. Odinga was convinced that Kenya could not attain self-government or independence while its foremost political leaders were imprisoned by government decree or Emergency measure. Pressure was not restricted to African leaders. The majority of Asians sat on the fence but some, such as V. and A. Patel, served with Odinga on the Release Jomo Kenyatta Committee, and K.P. Shah, among others, continued to write to the press (as he had done for some years), urging his release on the grounds that 'it is he alone who could change the African mind'.

In Britain, Fenner Brockway was 'of course in favour of the immediate release of Mr Kenyatta', and Hewlett Johnson, the 'red dean' of Canterbury, 'regretted the intolerable position which still pursued him'. Chou En-Lai, whose country was in political and economic chaos (having lost some tens of millions of its subjects to starvation and, worse, losses caused by political strife), claimed that 'six-hundred and fifty million Chinese resolutely support the noble cause' to which Kenyatta was dedicated. Indira Gandhi, daughter of India's prime minister, added her support. Early in 1961 KANU sent delegations to Nairobi and London, demanding Kenyatta's release in time for the approaching elections. Macleod would not see them, and Renison made an official 'nothing to say' statement. 'The British Government tactics,' wrote Odinga, 'were to keep Kenyatta out of the political arena while a last-minute search was conducted for more malleable leaders.'

Elections for seats on LEGCO were held in February 1961. KANU won 67 per cent of the votes and 19 of the 32 open seats. In a

'personal and confidential' letter to Macleod, Michael Blundell admitted that the New Kenya Group had taken 'a bit of a knock in the parliamentary elections'. He attributed this knock to, among other things, the European community's desire 'to hit back at Lancaster House and the British government'. He also referred to the poor tactics employed by the New Kenya Party. Nevertheless, he added, 'We intend to go forward unhesitatingly to the common roll and will attempt to win our common roll seats'. He then went on to seek finance for general development of the country, especially in agriculture and in education. He concluded by saying he was convinced that there was no other policy ahead but one of steady evolutionary advance.

The feelings of the Europeans were on occasions demonstrated at meetings Blundell attended during the hustings. At one meeting in Londiani a European invited him to agree that he was a traitor to the European community. After this question 12 men and women bombarded Blundell and the chairman with eggs and tomatoes. The meeting broke up in disorder. And during a meeting at Sotik a European woman 'of Danish origin' asked him when he was going to have his daughter circumcized by the Kalenjin. This was, wrote Blundell, intended to indicate how much his views would drag down the European community.

Former Mau Mau fighters took an active part in the elections but they were in disarray. Towards the end of the campaign they fought among themselves, and on polling day they locked each other up, 'so great was their mutual distrust'. Blundell discovered that an African he had never met had given up his 10-day holiday to electioneer for him, and at a polling station he found that an immense crowd of Africans had gathered to cheer him. But a European woman confronted him on the outskirts of the crowd and spat in his face, 'rasping out, "Why don't you let them kiss you, Judas Iscariot?" '

Blundell admitted that he learned a lot about the black man's outlook on his white counterpart during the hustings – 'how he resented the arbitrary way in which many farmers turned off their land as trespassers innocent visitors who were coming to see or stay with relatives; how once more this overwhelming desire to be recognized as a fellow human being filled their minds; and how many of them wanted the white farmers, who they knew and trusted, to stay in the country'.

Once the elections were over, KANU, with a significant majority, were prepared to form a government only if Kenyatta was released immediately. Renison refused to accept the condition and began to make the necessary preparations for government by decree. Blundell describes Renison as 'one of the most sincere, honest and likeable of men'. His background was the civil service, in which he had reached the top of his profession. He had only one idea, Blundell said, and that was to serve Kenya to the best of his ability. He believed, however, that Renison was never really at ease with the political leaders of Kenya. In official correspondence, Blundell noted, Renison always referred to 'my [colonial] service' and 'you politicians'.

Renison's action with regard to his radio broadcasts illustrates Blundell's observations. In February 1961 he invited James Gichuru, Mboya, Ngala and Muliro (leaders of KANU and KADU) to Government House to hear him broadcast a statement on local radio. He said that in his view Kenyatta should not be kept in restriction indefinitely, but that he did not propose to release him until the new government was working well and he thought that the security risk could be accepted and contained. He was, in effect, reiterating the statement he made the previous May.

With the benefit of hindsight Tom Mboya suggested that Renison mistook the mood of the African people. Instead of calling together the newly elected members and discussing future plans with them privately, he took it upon himself to make his national broadcast re-emphasizing Kenyatta as the 'leader to darkness and death'. Mboya's thought this single broadcast ruined the chances of forming a popular and stable government at that time. He wrote that Renison kept telling them he did not know what was on Kenyatta's mind, but even when pressed would not visit Kenyatta to find out for himself. 'Perhaps,' mused Mboya, 'Sir Patrick lacked confidence in Kenya.'

KANU and KADU may have been united in their lack of confidence in Renison, but the parties had little else in common. Nor were the leaders of KANU united. Mboya and Gichuru had had discussions with Macleod in London. They had not reported the contents of this meeting to KANU's governing council, whose officers read in the *Guardian* newspaper that Macleod was 'on the best of personal terms with Mr Gichuru'. The signs pointed to Macleod sounding out Mboya and Gichuru on their willingness to take part in the formation of a government without Kenyatta, and the KANU

330

governing council felt it was increasingly being bypassed by Mboya and Gichuru. 'We vetoed Mboya's and Gichuru's participation in a joint deputation to Kenyatta,' wrote Odinga, and 'once again we confirmed that KANU had irrevocably decided not to join the government until Kenyatta was freed.' Meanwhile KADU, under Ronald Ngala (from the coast), seized their chance and formed a government with the support of the New Kenya Party, which had campaigned on a programme of forming a government in an alliance with one or both of the African parties. They proceeded to negotiate with the British government a federal constitution in which Kenya would be divided into eight regions, each with its own administration and other services. Nothing came of it, but Macleod suggested the move helped allay European anxieties. A year later a KANU/KADU coalition took office, to be replaced ultimately by a KANU government led by Kenyatta.

The tensions between KANU and KADU spread from council chamber to countryside, and 1961 in particular saw inter-tribal strife. The Masai and Kamba fought 'several bloody battles', the Kipsigis swore they would keep their lands 'tribal' and 8,000 Luo working on estates in Kipsigi lands were threatened with violence if they did not leave. There were numerous inter-tribal raids for cattle, which harked back to pre-colonial days and led to severe loss of life. Only the intervention of British troops, Edgerton suggests, prevented outbreaks of large-scale violence.

Where to go now? KANU and KADU decided to invite Kenyatta to advise them on action to take that would mediate their differences. Representatives of both unions travelled to Lodwar for a meeting which was held on 23rd March. Bildad Kaggia, who was still in detention with Kenyatta (but was one of those at loggerheads with him) made a record of the meeting. It must have been like old Mau Mau times in the forest.

Jomo Kenyatta took the chair of the 'Lodwar Conference' by unanimous agreement. The language of the conference was English, and Kaggia recorded those present in three groups:

• The Lodwar Group: Jomo Kenyatta, B.M. Kaggia, P. Ngei and Petro Kigondu.
• KANU: J.S. Gichuru, T.J. Mboya, O. Odinga, Ngala Mwendwa, and J. Nyagah.

• KADU: D. Moi, J. Tipis, W. Murgor, F. Khamisi, S. Matano and A. Kilelu.

Kenyatta found the policies of KANU and KADU almost identical. He wondered where disunity came from and blamed 'selfishness among the leaders, each hoping to dominate, to be praised and to achieve fame'. He condemned this attitude and accused the leaders of undermining each other to the detriment of African interests. He told them they were 'contributing to his continued restriction by their disunity. This had to be brought to an end'.

Following discussion, KANU and KADU agreed that unity between the two unions was possible. The main issues were the immediate and unconditional release of Jomo Kenyatta and full independence of Kenya before the end of the year. They recommended setting up a joint consultative committee of the two unions' councils. Kenyatta advised that KANU and KADU should try to create conditions to enable Africans to form a government.

Oginga Odinga noted that there was concern over the prospect of friction between those who were in the forest and camps and the loyalists – each faction claiming that it had Kenyatta's support. Kenyatta's response was typical of many which he would make in the next year or two. 'I am not,' he said, 'for those who have been in the forest or detention camps, I am for the African people. All of them. I do not support or fight for any particular individual, race or tribe, but for all the people.' Odinga observed that many of the KANU leaders, including Mboya, had never seen or met Kenyatta before the meeting.

Motives are difficult to assess, but KANU's parliamentary group put a motion for the release of Kenyatta 'now and unconditionally'. Odinga suggests that their aim was to embarrass KADU, but whatever the motive the motion was debated for six hours and defeated by 43 votes to 26 – 'KADU and its allies voting against,' wrote Odinga.

Support for Kenyatta's release from Lodwar came, too, from a number of European members of LEGCO. Blundell, R.S. Alexander, Wilfrid Havelock, Humphrey Slade and Norman Harris were represented by Blundell and Havelock at a meeting with Renison, but he resisted the idea on the grounds that public opinion and his own stand on the matter made it impossible. The petitioners suggested a release in stages, and this approach was later adopted.

At Kenyatta's request the political leaders of KANU and KADU again met with him, this time at his new, restricted 'home' in Maralal. Out of the talks came a formal agreement for joint action by the two parties. The aim was a new constitution and independence in 1961. The agreement between KANU and KADU was for improved relationships between them; the immediate release of Kenyatta; immediate independence; a delegation to the government calling for Kenyatta's unconditional release; and a study of the 'land problem'. But by August, Odinga wrote, KANU's and KADU's attempts at co-operation had to be suspended.

The release of Kenyatta came in two stages. The first was to move him from complete inaccessibility to a place where people could see and consult him. If this was successful, his final release would follow. There was no rigid timetable, but it was to take place in the summer of 1961: the date would be announced simultaneously in the House of Commons and in Kenya. Although by then the idea of Kenyatta's release had become accepted, it was still a blow to many Europeans and had to be clearly seen as a joint decision by the governments in Nairobi and at Westminster.

On 4th April 1961 Kenyatta was flown from Lodwar to Maralal, 'an attractive hill station'. He met 'the world's press' on the 11th April, some eight years since Thacker's judgement at Kapenguria. He wore his leather jacket and his face was thin, almost harsh, his voice slow but controlled. He dismissed the Corfield Report as 'a pack of lies, collected from needy informers', but he said he bore no grudge. He considered the governor to have been 'poorly advised', but he asked that they be forgiven, 'for they know not what they do'. He claimed he had never been a violent man. 'My whole life has been anti-violence' and would continue to be so. He sought immediate independence, and vowed that he would remain an African nationalist to the end. He denied any communist affiliations. His visits to Russia had been 'for educational purposes', he said. In the cold war between east and west Africans suffered 'as grass suffers when two elephants fight'. As to the future, no one had reason to fear. All citizens of an independent Kenya would be protected in their persons and their property by an African government – both forest fighters and loyalists, 'since they are all of them brothers and sisters' – and the Europeans who chose to stay in the country, provided they gave up their 'big boss' mentality.

The *East African Standard* described the scene as 'a publicity circus' second only to that in which Adolf Eichman (the notorious Nazi war criminal) was the central figure in Jerusalem.

Odinga recorded that 'the largest crowd he had seen in Kenya gathered to see Kenyatta, to greet the father of the nation back among the nation'. Odinga took the chair in LEGCO, introduced Kenyatta to all his colleagues and read the KANU/KADU agreement 'to press for independence by 1 February 1962'.

K.P. Shah, a businessman cum politician, was one of a group of Indian politicians to visit Kenyatta at Maralal. They talked with him about 'the usual things', but they were surprised when they were provided with a meal before leaving. Shah had met Kenyatta on previous occasions but he did not expect him to remember that he and one of his colleagues were vegetarians and to provide accordingly. 'Such small things,' he remarked, 'make a great man.'

Blundell, too, made the journey to Maralal to visit Kenyatta. It was the first occasion on which their paths had crossed. Their talk included land problems of the poorer Kikuyu. In reply to a direct question, Blundell told Kenyatta that the Europeans disliked him because they associated him with 'the evil side of Mau Mau' and considered that he had planned and initiated the movement. They felt that he hated them and would not treat them fairly if he ever achieved power. Kenyatta said this was 'a wrong analysis of his feelings, although he was determined to see that Africans were the leaders and first class citizens in their own country'. Kenyatta seemed to Blundell to be one of the ablest and most intelligent Africans he had met. Above all, he was conscious of being a leader of the Kikuyu people. 'Every time we mentioned their problems his eyes appeared to light up and his manner became more animated.'

Murray-Brown referred to Maralal as 'an African Delphi' which attracted representatives of 'different political parties, of Christian denominations . . . of racial communities, world powers, lawyers, photographers.' They came to see Kenyatta. On the eve of his release he broadcast to the people of Kenya, appealing for calm. He was allowed to return to Kikuyuland on 14th August 1961. A new house had been built for him at Gatundu, and his family and retinue awaited him. So did 150 police who were on duty, and some 10,000 Africans who were in festive mood. His text on this occasion was 'Love thy neighbour'.

Renison first met Kenyatta in the district commissioner's office at Kiambu. 'Renison was tense, unsmiling; Kenyatta inscrutable.' A brief communiqué was issued to the press. Numerous public appearances followed, and a 'crowd of many thousands' saw him drive to the LEGCO office in Nairobi on 25th August. There had been voices suggesting that the coastal strip should be separated from the rest of Kenya (as it had been before becoming part of the British protectorate), but Kenyatta visited Mombasa on 3rd September and opposed the idea of such autonomy. He appears at this time to have structured his speeches to suit his audience. He was, after release, a minister without portfolio under the chairmanship of the governor, Sir Patrick Renison. Blundell refers to 'a most unpleasantly racial speech' which Kenyatta made in the Murang'a District. As he would almost certainly become president of Kenya after independence, and would need the co-operation of Europeans and Asians, Blundell felt that 'it was not sensible to build up emotions against them'.

At that time the BBC television series Face to Face screened 45-minute celebrity interviews and was among the earliest programmes to encourage penetrating, indeed embarrassing, questions. Kenyatta appeared on 26th November wearing a Luo hat ('to symbolize his national status'), his rings and his carved walking stick. 'He carried the interview well.'

For a short time Kenyatta's release from detention led KADU and KANU to agree that their parties would work together. They took a joint memorandum to the governor, pressing for Kenya to move immediately to full internal self-government. The parties pushed for Kenyatta to be made a member of the legislature, and before long a seat was found for him. There was a KADU-supported government proposal for 'regionalism' (Majimbo), which was unacceptable to KANU and once again, Odinga wrote, 'KANU/KADU relations were acutely strained'. Kenyatta attempted to act as conciliator, and he threatened to form a third party if KANU and KADU did not find a way to co-operate. By the end of the October, however, he decided to join and lead KANU. 'KADU,' wrote Odinga, 'let fly.'

The Seys at Rhodora quoted page 170 of the Corfield Report when writing home about Kenyatta's release, wondering how long it would be before he danced with a member of the royal family at a ball at Government House and was invited to stay at Buckingham Palace. 'How humiliating can appeasement be?' Seys asked.

Reginald Maudling had succeeded Iain Macleod as colonial secretary in October 1961. He was aware that Macleod had come under a great deal of wholly unjustified criticism from the right wing of the party. The government's policy of progressively granting independence to colonial territories was, Maudling commented, as wise as it was inevitable. 'The truth is that Iain was a man of integrity and vision whose only fault might have been that he was a little ahead of what the right wing thought should have been his time.' Macleod's diligence may have cost him leadership of the Conservative party, but during a television interview in 1970, when asked what he would do if he had to make a choice between acting as he did in Africa or becoming prime minister, he replied that he would have stuck by the course he had taken: 'You must just take the consequences of the actions you believe to be right.'

During 1961 more than 6,000 Europeans left Kenya, including Colonel Grogan, doyen of the settlers and their most tempestuous spokesman, who announced that he had given his life to developing perhaps half a million acres in Kenya, Tanganyika and Uganda but was selling his large sisal estate. 'Only a damn fool wouldn't sell,' he said. The Nairobi stock exchange recorded deep depression.

The second Lancaster House conference was the show which ran from February to April 1962. Maudling had taken up his appointment as colonial secretary and the purpose, he wrote, was 'settling an agreed constitution for self-government, which would in the normal course of events be followed shortly after by full independence'. He considered Kenya to be the greatest problem he had inherited from Macleod. 'There were,' he wrote in his autobiography, 'deep suspicions and fears. The African nationalists were divided between KANU and KADU. The Asian community, though relatively small, were fearful of the possibilities. The European population were deeply alarmed at the prospect of independence . . . People genuinely feared, as I knew from letters I received, that independence and African rule would lead to atrocities on a large scale against the whites. More real was the danger of struggle between the various tribes . . . it was essential to grapple with the problem. Independence for Kenya could not long be delayed.'

The list of conference members included 65 elected members, made up of KADU (27), KANU (31), Kenya Coalition(3), Mwambao United Front (2) and cross-benchers (2). There were four advisers (two KADU, one KANU and one Kenya Coalition), five representatives of the Kenya Government (including the governor, Sir Patrick Renison), 14 United Kingdom representatives (headed by Maudling), a 'constitutional adviser to the conference' and 10 members of the seretariat. Delegations were received from the Masai (10) and Northern Frontier District (8). Blundell hoped this would be 'the final conference on Kenya before independence'. He recorded that 'Lounge suits, sports jackets, ostrich plumes, black and white colobus monkey skins, fly whisks and gaily coloured bead hats poured down the steps of the aeroplane into the snow and slush of London Airport'. As Blundell saw it, 'this time . . . the struggle over ideas was between two African parties supported by European and Asian thought, rather than between liberal white and nationalist black leadership'.

The conference was to run from 14th February to 6th April. It was originally intended to have short opening statements by Maudling and the leaders of the various groups and then get down to the business of detailed discussion, but one of the African delegates asked Blundell to tell Maudling that 'they must be free to express the emotions of the people'. Blundell conveyed the message and, he wrote, 'We were almost locked for the next three weeks in the main conference room listening to them.'

Whether or not Blundell's message got through is unclear, but Maudling decided that 'the only possible tactic' (which Macleod had adopted previously) was to let the participants talk themselves to a standstill and then produce a British solution in the hope that they would accept it. He listed the main forces as KANU, represented by Jomo Kenyatta and Tom Mboya, KADU, represented by Ronald Ngala, and the Europeans, 'whose natural leader was Michael Blundell'. He stated the underlying problem as being tribal antipathy. 'The smaller tribes,' he wrote, 'feared that the Kikuyu, with their substantial numbers and great ability, would dominate an independent Kenya.' Blundell, in the KADU camp, wrote that KADU members feared 'the authoritarian rule and personality cults' that had developed in other, now independent, African countries.

Oginga Odinga, vice-president of KANU, was in no doubt that the government favoured a regionalism which would create autonomous regions. The principle of regionalism could be extended to apply to Uganda, Tanganyika, Nyasaland and the Rhodesias. The *Times* of 6th October 1961 hoped for 'a large state consisting of anything up to 30 or 40 regions and to be known as the Federate States of Africa'. Such a federation would not have a head of state or prime minister but a rotating chairman. KANU was accused of being in favour of a unitary system of government which meant dictatorship under Kikuyu/Luo domination. Britain and the USA feared that such a dictatorship would be vulnerable to communist infiltration. Odinga found himself increasingly isolated. The press in Britain, the USA and Kenya painted him red and accused him of using large amounts of money received from communist China to build a sizeable personal following. The *New York Times* described him as 'a threat to both Mr Kenyatta and Mr Mboya as well as a disruptive force'.

Maudling recalled that the conference was long and hard. It was certainly not helped by Odinga, the only man Maudling had ever seen actually frothing at the mouth in a moment of excitement – and, Maudling wrote, 'his moments of excitement were many'. Blundell watched Kenyatta, who was sitting next to Odinga, continually ducking and bobbing as an expansive arm would swing out in a wide gesture. Julius Kiano, on the other side, finally withdrew his chair from the field of Odinga's fire. At the conclusion of one speech Odinga 'strode angrily from the room shouting at Ngala (leader of the KADU delegation), 'as for you, you were only my karani [clerk] once'.

The meeting was adjourned. Blundell wrote, 'We rose stiffly and slowly from our chairs and adjourned, blinking our eyes, thoughtful like men who have watched some tremendous human drama on the screen in the dark of the cinema.' He was impressed by the depth of tribal feeling. When Kenyatta was speaking, the nomadic Hamitic representatives moved uneasily in their chairs and had difficulty in restraining themselves, whereas when they in turn were putting their views, a look of dislike and almost contempt passed across the faces of the Bantu Kikuyu. 'It was as if the age-long conflict between the people of the plains and the secretive people of the forest were being enacted across the blue tables in the guilded rooms of Lancaster House.'

Oginga Odinga admitted that in a month of talking they made virtually no progress and that the colonial secretary 'sat patiently waiting, letting everyone speak, waiting; seemingly, for us to reach a state of physical exhaustion as well as policy deadlock'. He was well aware that he was regarded by the majority of people as a subversive. He refers to a 'press slander campaign' which insisted repeatedly that he was the 'grave danger to Kenya'. It referred to him using communist funds to make the first serious attempt to undermine the position of the prime minister of Tanganyika. He was accused by the *East African Standard* of being the leader of a powerful faction within Kenya and a 'supporter of Mr Kenyatta and the Old Guard' who was accused by colleagues of being 'the chief architect of the alleged revolution plan'.

Maudling recorded that they reached agreement on a constitution for a self-governing Kenya, with Kenyatta and Ngala as joint premiers, which would pave the way for independence. 'My relief at this result was profound.' Odinga's impression was that Maudling delivered a virtual ultimatum to KANU and KADU to form a coalition government.

The 'Framework of the Kenya Constitution', set out in the Appendix II report comprises 23 clauses under 14 headings. The objective is stated as 'a united Kenya nation, capable of social and economic progress . . . in which men and women have confidence in the sanctity of individual rights and liberties and in the proper safeguarding of the interests of minorities'. The framework includes an impartial and independent judiciary, a bill of rights guaranteeing the proper protection of individuals, a two-chamber parliament, an executive, six regional assemblies with administrative powers and powers to make enactments regarding agricultural land, education up to intermediate level, local government and public health. Central government would assume the responsibilities of the public services, law and order, finance, constitutional change, emergency powers and national government.

A problem remained, however, in the person of Odinga. Kenyatta was invited to Maudling's office as the conference ended. Maudling told him that he should pick his own team for his share of the government, but that Odinga would not be acceptable as a member of any government under the British Crown. With tears in his eyes, Kenyatta told Maudling he was asking him to desert his oldest friend. But later in the day he signed, and Maudling believed that his own judgement 'had not been all that wrong'. Odinga blamed the colonial office for the veto of his appointment, adding that the British government refused to give a reason. He had no doubt that Renison had persuaded the colonial office (if persuasion were needed, he added in parenthisis) 'that my visits to socialist countries made me unfit to take cabinet office'. He continued, 'I also know of behind-the-scenes discussions in London in which some KANU men hinted that I would be unacceptable not only to KADU but even to some groups in KANU.' And he concluded his comments on this incident by recalling that Kenyatta 'removed me from his list. I was neither consulted nor even informed by Jomo'.

'Kenya seemed,' Maudling wrote, 'to be set on a course that might not have seemed possible a bare year or eighteen months before.' Blundell referred to reaching a general agreement on a federal type of constitution. He considered Maudling to be an outstanding success as secretary of state and chairman. John Cumber, by now private secretary to the governor, was also impressed by Maudling, who 'could sit, leaning over the table starting at 8 o'clock after breakfast and I noticed that his staff never took a note. At tea-time, 4:30 or after, when the delegates finished speaking he would turn to a delegate as if he were reading it from a paper and say "Mr X, this morning you said A,B and C". He had a phenomenal photographic memory'.

In July 1962 Maudling visited Nairobi. He announced new proposals for the distribution of powers between the central and regional government in a new Kenya constitution. There was a need for elections as soon as possible. He also announced the tripling of the land settlement measures which improved prospects for 70,000 landless African families in the one million acre-scheme which is described below. It was designed 'to avoid the danger of tribal warfare and possible bloodshed – African and European alike – on a large scale', wrote Maudling.

Speeches from African leaders became the order of the day. Kenyatta made one in 1962 which suggests he appreciated the need to get to grips with the outlaws in the forest. 'We are,' he said, 'determined to have independence in peace, and we shall not allow hooligans to rule Kenya. We must have no hatred towards one another.' Mau Mau was a disease which had been eradicated, and should be forgotten.

Tom Mboya addressed groups of Europeans and Asians on the issue of citizenship. He told them that he believed 'dual citizenship' to be an unwise move. The test of sincerity was, 'Has the citizen given up everything else to become a Kenya citizen?' KADU simply asked that people investing in agriculture in Kenya be obedient and loyal to Kenya, but Mboya maintained that the country should look for greater commitment. 'The best way to ensure they are loyal,' he said, 'is to stipulate they should become citizens.' He noted that after a year's independence in Tanganyika only 40 Europeans and 2,500 Asians had applied for citizenship. This must lead Africans to doubt the sincerity of immigrants who continually talked about being Tanganyikans, he wrote. He admitted to putting 'a cat among the pigeons' by telling the Indian congress to revise long-established conceptions and recognize that an integrated community can lead to intermarriage between members of that community – 'and why not?' he asked. He was not disappointed by the widespread reaction against these remarks from Asians. 'We have,' he said, 'to break the myth that there is something wrong with the different races marrying each other. On the other hand intermarriage cannot be treated as a policy, as something to be legislated for.'

And so to a new governor. There are very few references to Sir Patrick Renison's departure, but he is reported as being 'abruptly retired' late in 1962 by Duncan Sandys, who replaced him with Malcolm MacDonald – who proved to be Kenya's last governor. MacDonald was the son of Ramsay MacDonald, the former Labour prime minister. He was a small, cheerful politician turned diplomat who had earned distinction as 'a chairman and unconventional decolonizer of Britian's possessions in south-east Asia'. He took over the governorship early in 1963. He was a man who mixed easily with members of all races, and 'he brought to Kenya an open mind and an optimism in the future'.

KANU's victory at the May 1963 election 'became in effect absolute', to use the words of the *History of East Africa*, but KANU's share of the votes was about the same as in the 1961 elections – two-thirds of the total. KANU secured 68 out of the total 112 seats and four Independents declared themselves for KANU immediately after the election. KADU and their allies were unable to field enough candidates to promise a potential majority: they won 32 seats, and Paul Ngei's African People's Party, eight.

Oginga Odinga, reviewing the elections, was satisfied that 'the youth and women wings galvanized the people on whose support we rode to victory; they were never afraid of bullets, tear gas or jail'. He named many of the 'mamas' who created 'the political consciousness' that sent the women to the polls and 'swept our first independent government into power'. Tom Mboya shared Odinga's view of the women's contributions and wrote of their 'undying loyalty and confidence'. He found that when youths failed to get donations for KAU the women invariably succeeded as fund-raisers. He believed they had a role in the preparation for independence in education, in agricultural development, in business, in the taking over of the civil service and in the trade unions, not to mention 'the task of creating an enlightened family and community'.

Jomo Kenyatta was appointed prime minister and was increasingly addressed as 'Mzee'. His government included a Kamba, a Kisii, a Maragoli, a Taita and a European of South African origin, while his parliamentary secretaries included another European, an Asian and a Masai. Old KAU leaders and men who stood trial with Kenyatta in 1953 were balanced with the new KANU men who had gained prominence in their absence. KANU had won over many members of the opposition parties by the time independence arrived.

Odinga writes of the period of coalition cabinet government which followed the election as 'a crucial one for the country', although he was uneasy about many aspects of it. The joint KANU/KADU cabinet was 'a thoroughly uneasy coalition'. He noticed, too, a great change in Kenya's legislative council with the entry of the African representatives: 'The council chamber was charged with issues, antagonisms, battle'. As African representatives were 'sucked into the process of parliament and constitutional conferences', a change came over them. The more adept they became at parliamenteering, the more remote they became from their own people'.

Blundell, too, observed that members of KANU were in a dictatorial and difficult mood during a meeting held in the autumn of 1963 to discuss further changes in the constitution. 'They seemed to be obsessed with the fact that they were the majority party, and arbitrary demands were the order of the day,' he wrote. He suggested that the result of KANU's intransigence was that KADU turned its mind to a federal type of constitution with the object of limiting the power of central government and of the Kikuyu over the remainder of Kenya. He noted, too, that regionalism was attractive to the smaller tribes in rural and remote areas of Kenya, as it offered them a measure of control over the issues about which they were most apprehensive, such as land, education, the police, and the composition of the civil service. Mboya believed that regionalism as conceived by KADU 'could never have worked'.

In 1963 Kenyatta became more conciliatory towards the European community. The *East African Standard* of 24th April recorded a speech in which he admitted that he had himself suffered for a long time but was not bitter. He was aware of the fear and hatred on the part of many Europeans, and he asked those who still had hatred in their hearts to cast it aside. 'We cannot build a happy and progressive nation as long as men harbour ill-feelings about the past.' He offered 'forgive and forget' as a slogan for the future. Then on the 12th August 1963 at Nakuru came the speech which made the greatest impression on the European community. Some 300 settlers heard Kenyatta make it clear that his speech was policy, not platitude. 'I am,' he said, 'a politician, but I am a farmer like you . . . I think the soil joins us all.' The most disturbing point among them was suspicion, fear. 'We must also learn to forgive one another. There is no perfect society anywhere. Whether we are white, brown or black, we are not angels. We are human beings and as such we are bound to make mistakes. If you have done harm to me, it is for me to forgive you. If I have done harm to you, it is for you to forgive me.' It was the government's policy that everyone should work together for the benefit of Kenya. 'Many of you . . . are just as good Kenyans as myself . . . Some of you may be worried what will happen . . . Let me set you at rest that Kenyatta has no intention whatever to look backwards . . . We are going to forgive the past and look forward to the future.'

During interviews 30 years on, Europeans still living in Kenya who attended the meeting or who heard reports at the time reaffirmed that his speech provided them with the confidence they needed to stay on. Jasper Evans (who in 1953 had believed that giving the settlers a free hand to recruit Masai levees and eliminate the Mau Mau and all their followers was the only course for the Europeans to follow), was now reassured. He stayed. Up at Timau the Murrays had already committed themselves to stay on when, in 1960, they converted and extended their home from timber to brick and tile, but the speech gave them encouragement and, George speculated, produced a more peaceful handover. 'We were,' he believed, 'incredibly lucky having Kenyatta, no shadow of doubt about that.' Farmer John Carver recalled a friend 'who was very, very right wing' and was involved politically. 'He went up to listen and came back a changed man.' He had planned to leave Kenya, but he stayed on. The speech was, said Carver, 'a wonderful thing'. Blundell confirmed that the apprehensions of European settlers were allayed and the atmosphere created by it enabled the land transfer programme to be carried out over several years without tension or fear. And an 'influential Indian' noticed a new element in Kenyatta's reception: 'As he appeared in the hall people stood up in thousands in reverence, as one would expect royalty to be treated . . . he had become more than just a political leader.'

A few months after his August speech at Nakuru, Kenyatta made a similar speech to an African audience. 'Forgive and forget' was the message he gave to his own people, who were divided among themselves. He suggested 'ignorance, sickness and poverty' as the true enemies, not the Europeans.

The reassurance Kenyatta gave the European and Asian populations was not given for entirely altruistic reasons. Kenya's immediate future depended on the contribution of the immigrants, Asian traders, clerks and craftsmen. As independence approached Odinga made a 'nation-wide tour to explain our policy to the people'. He spoke of the need for everyone 'to re-orientate themselves to a changed condition', and he explained the principle of 'harambee' – working together – which had to be carried out in local government. Jock Dawson recalled that Odinga hosted several informal lunches during which he encouraged European farmers to stay on after independence. During a formal luncheon at the British embassy in Addis Ababa, Ethiopia, the emerging statesman proposed a toast to 'the Queen'.

Tom Mboya also spoke. He sought inspiration from the poems of a writer often regarded as the epitome of the British imperialist, Rudyard Kipling. When addressing a great crowd on the challenge of nation-building Mboya read out the whole of Kipling's poem 'If'.

'Nobody,' he told them, 'can claim to have played a manly part if he or she has not filled the unforgiving minute with sixty seconds' worth of distance run.'

Mboya must have recited the closing lines of the poem:

> *Yours is the Earth and everything that's in it,*
> *And – which is more – you'll be a Man, my son!*

The politicians had provided a framework. It now remained for mere mortals to clad the frame.

14

From Colony to Nation

'It was as if a new era had started.' (Enid Dawson)

The mere mortals who realised the politicians' dreams were the administrators, whose skin pigment became increasingly dark during the four years of change from colony to nation. Blundell had referred to the years of training that would be needed before Africans would be ready to take over when independence arrived. The end of the Emergency period saw the beginning of decline in the status of the British administrators at district level, and their lack of confidence in their new status did not assist the transfer of power. The district commissioners had always regarded themselves, and had been regarded by most other departments (albeit sometimes grudgingly), as firsts among equals, but now they were, in the words of one of them, downgraded to the amorphous status of 'regional government agent' – stripped of the responsibility for law and order, and even of their status.

After the 1960 Lancaster House conference European district commissioners and district officers trained Africans to take over European jobs. 'It was not very enjoyable,' wrote Chevenix Trench, because 'however they might intellectually agree that it was time to go, they were being thrown on the job market while still quite young and with no skills or experience which would be of much use in Britain in the 1960s.'

To co-ordinate efforts, Terence Gavaghan was appointed a 'localization and training officer', his target being to 'Africanize' a third of the top 10,000 jobs in all departments in time for independence, whenever that might be. It was ironical that Gavaghan's previous commission had been to reduce the number of Mau Mau in detention camps; now he was to reduce the number of British administrative officers in post, albeit with the additional task of replacing them with Africans.

In a memo to the governor, Sir Patrick Renison, Gavaghan suggested that the government should 'try something new about independence'. Recalling the British reason for colonizing Kenya, he wrote that 'it was in our imperial interest to keep other European powers out'. He argued that the colony had reached the point where the Africans considered they were ready for independence. 'OK, lets make a contract [with them]. "We go, you take over. May we suggest a date?" . . . faster than we think they will want'. He recalled that Kenyatta had said in a speech in Cairo that if he had not been in prison for 'seven plus two years' he would not have been able to form a government, because he would not have had the resources. Without Kenyatta the Africans could not have done it, Gavaghan suggested. His proposal was that the government should reduce the traditional formalities associated with granting independence to colonies and 'constitutional instruments'. Let us, offered Gavaghan, make a contract with the Africans: 'Willing buyer, willing seller and go'. And say 'Until the moment we go we shall maintain law and order. We are going in order to keep communism out. We came in, in our own interest, and we go in our own interest. All we have to agree now is the time'. Gavaghan's assessment of the situation was that a third of the top 17,000 posts in the colonial service should be Africanized by the time independence arrived. In the event the British administrators were persuaded, and his assessment proved accurate.

In 1961 the Kenya Institute of Administrators was set up in the Jeanes School, Kabete, to train African district commissioners and district officers. The syllabus was similar to the Oxford and Cambridge colonial cadets' courses. Administrator Frank (Dick) Wilson's African staff were mainly drawn from the Kikuyu and Kamba tribes, whom he considered to be suitable and capable people. Some became permanent secretaries. The Administration had, however, needed more time to train senior staff, and by the time independence was finally achieved they were a long way from providing all the African technical staff such as doctors, educationalists and so on. The secretary of state was saying that white government would continue for ever in Kenya. Nobody knew when the end was going to come, and certainly few expected it to come as soon as it did.

The first four African DCs took up their posts in September 1962, and by independence a third of the senior administrative posts were held by Africans. Nearly all the remaining European officers left within the next two years. Geoffrey Karithi, who had been a district officer in Embu, succeeded Wilson. He had done the Oxford course, and he became head of the civil service and secretary of the cabinet.

There is a reference above to the regional form of government which was set up when rivalry between KANU and KADU was at large. It proved, as Wilson had predicted, disastrous. It was too complicated to be workable, and both Kenyatta and Odinga 'ditched the whole of the regional idea'.

Although a significant body of senior British staff stayed in post after independence, others, particularly those at Government House, left with the governor. John (later Sir John) Cumber was one of those who left at least a month before independence: 'We doffed our caps, said "kwa heri" [goodbye] and left Kenya for good as far as our jobs were concerned – a country that had given us so much and which my sons, who were babes in arms there, still think of as home.'

In order to maintain the morale of the European officers they were given 'fair compensation'. This led to further grumbles among the European settlers who believed they had more to lose through Britain's rushed withdrawal. Governor Renison was, Michael Blundell wrote, 'obsessed with the idea of fair treatment' for what he called "my service" '. Blundell thought it strange that Renison made a distinction over 'a change of employer' for 'his service' while oblivious to the vulnerability of farmers whose leases would now be held from the Kenya government rather than the British Crown. He left the governor's room 'feeling like the president of a local association leaving the office of the district commissioner, rather than a minister talking over a problem with the chairman of the council of ministers. Administrator Gavaghan, on the other hand, viewed the governor as 'the epitome of simple unassuming virtue . . . warm, vigorous, shrewd and decisive, but professional enough not to upstage or overbear those around him'.

Although the speed of transfer from British to African government may have been too fast, the transfer of power was managed with much less trauma and bloodshed than in Belgian Congo 'next door' where, recalled police officer Douglas Walker, 'they upped and off one night. It was a disgraceful state of affairs. In Kenya there were British district commissioners, district officers and policemen kept on for several years until they chose to leave. The gradualness with which everything occurred was I think the best thing that happened to Kenya and made it become a good example – the jewel in the African crown.' The Walkers stayed on as officers of the new government and experienced no difficulties adjusting to the change.

Colonel Sir Guy Campbell, former commanding officer of the Kenya Regiment, gives the regiment credit for 'peaceful handover at independence'. He suggests that the co-operation which developed between the young Kenyan settlers in the regiment and the loyal Kikuyu and trackers led to a better understanding between the races when the Emergency ended. 'It showed the way to a peaceful handover at independence, and the eventual development of modern Kenya under African leaders. It was an achievement almost unique on the African continent, something that most considered impossible; but to those involved in the Emergency, this co-operation which developed between races, initially out of necessity, was soon to flourish in goodwill and respect'.

Kikuyu demands for land were a major, perhaps *the* major, cause of their push for independence, and some provision was made for land settlement. In 1960 a plan was devised to buy out a million acres of the White Highlands which had been farmed exclusively by Europeans, using mainly African labour. The project is described in a booklet by Nottidge and Goldsack, *The Million-Acre Settlement Scheme 1962-6*, the title referring to an order in council at the end of 1960 which 'ended the reservation of the scheduled areas'. Ownership in these areas was made open to all races. Speed was essential because African hopes had been raised, and European land owners foresaw little security of land title. Investment by Europeans and Asians had virtually stopped. The scheme intended settling 12,000 families and the purchase of 200,000 acres of land a year over a five-year period.

The scheme was introduced in 1961 with the creation of an agricultural settlement fund for the purchase of the land which was administered by the Land Development and Settlement Board through a structure of trusts and committees. The problem was to organize 'the switch-over from a large-scale farming economy to small-scale peasant farming'. Provision was made for small holders, large-scale farming units, assisted owners, the 'Nandi Salient' and 'compassionate' farms.

The need for provisions for small, large-scale and assisted owners is obvious. The aim of the Nandi Salient was to hand back to the Nandi tribe land which had been purchased as unoccupied but which was, in fact, their tribal land. For 'compassionate' farms, 129,749 acres of land was purchased by the Central Land Board from aged or disabled European farmers who, 'by reason of their age and location, were regarded as security risks, and who, due to the absence of a free land market, had been unable to realise their assets and retire'.

The British government provided both grant and loan funds for the purchase of land, development loans and the administration of the schemes. The land board's valuers used 1959 valuations as a yardstick to determine the value of a farm, as that year was the most recent in which a reasonable volume of transactions occurred. Permanent improvements such as buildings, fencing, soil conservation, water supplies, grass lays etc were taken into account. The value of a dwelling house was limited to a financial maximum of £1,300, except in certain cases where it may have been raised to £2,500.

There was, inevitably, a delay between hand-over of a property to the land board and the actual settlement. As it was important to maintain production from the land, a settlement officer was appointed to ensure that the land was well managed. Some 25,000 plot-holders were settled. Aerial photographic and ground surveying methods were used to mark out boundaries. Provision was made for village centres, schools and roads. A village centre of 30 acres was provided for each 10,000 acres (15 square miles) which accommodated about 4,000 people. Each village contained a market, shops, a school, housing, playing fields, churches etc. Farmers were encouraged to form themselves into co-operatives, which arranged for the purchase of seeds, fertilisers and other requirements and for sale of produce. Finance, credit loans and banking facilities were available to members on long-term loans. Training was provided for members and staff. Courses were arranged, usually of one week's duration and covering specialised aspects of agricultural economy and administration. Settlement rules were drafted to facilitate plot transfer, sale and lease, evictions and post settlement disputes.

Alexander Storrar, the deputy director for agriculture, was dispatched, with another officer, to Whitehall to sell the scheme to the government. It was accepted without demur. Storrar comments that the Land Development and Settlement Board bought land which was suitable for mixed farming, and that approximately 75 per cent was sold to members of the Kikuyu tribe.

The million acres scheme came into being as a result of political pressure, but the government was, Storrar insists, anxious to be fair to the vendors. The reason for selecting 1959 as the valuation year was that at that time farm values were by no means at their peak, since too many Europeans were uncertain of a secure future in Kenya. Nevertheless, some European farmers were more than happy with the prices they were offered. Storrar refers to a farmer who sold the board his 10,000 acre farm at Timau, remarking that it was the best thing the happened to him. But the Timau farmer was almost certainly an exception: Storrar admits that some, perhaps many, lost a 'life style', as such intangibles did not come into the valuation.

For their 4,500 acres at Timau the Llewelyn's were offered enough to buy a house in England but not any sort of business. They stayed on. Many settlers considered the maximum valuations for 'dwelling houses' (£1,300, exceptionally £2,500) as quite inadequate. Donald Robathan was one such. His house, 'one of the best houses in the country with beautiful garden and swimming pool', was valued at £1,500. George Murray, too, considered the terms 'were pretty unfair. The valuations were very, very low' – an opinion endorsed generally by European farmers.

George McCall felt strongly about the buy-outs. The settlers were treated in an 'exceedingly dirty way', he recalled. 'They did everything they could to demoralize us, so that when the buy out came you'd be frightened off. "Oh well, this is the last offer; and one had seen what happened in the Congo". . . It was organized theft by the British government, the crumb-bums in England'. His estimate was that it was not unusual for the government to offer the European farmers 10 per cent of the real value of the farm. Perhaps Robathan's comment that 'generally speaking the prices [stated by the valuer] were far below what the owners expected to receive' summarises the settlers' view and the reason for their discontent. Property values, generally, are determined by the price a purchaser is prepared to pay and are notoriously mercurial.

The farmers' views of undervaluation were, however, confirmed by some who stayed and, later, sold at much better prices than the government had offered. But it took courage to stay on with, as Robathan put it, 'farms going and your neighbour going and your social life disappearing'. Many, like the Robathans, thought they would be wise cut their losses and go.

The European settlers had resisted the principle of Africans farming the highlands. Blundell recalled speaking at a meeting during which he advocated changes in the Europeans' outlook when one of the audience sprang to his feet and moved a resolution to the effect that the maintenance of the White Highlands was an idea for which they were prepared to die. 'It was,' commented Blundell, 'no good pointing out that the age of many of the people in the audience made nonsense of such a resolution; it was passed with acclaim and by a large majority.'

Lady Pamela Scott, whose family had farmed at Deloraine, Njoro, since 1920, describes the dilemma which faced many Europeans. 'Some had children to be educated and they felt it too big a risk to stay where they were. Others felt more confidence in the future and decided not to sell. People were divided into "stayers" and "goers". If the majority of people in a district decided to sell, even those who wanted to stay felt it would be very difficult if they were to be surrounded by small peasant farms. The facilities they had previously enjoyed would no longer continue; clubs would go, certainly; perhaps telephones, water and roads; and they would be forced to sell.' In some cases they were already harassed by Africans who stole their cattle and fencing wire, and chopped down their trees. 'Many Europeans felt it was no good staying on under such conditions.'

For the Kikuyu, the land settlement programmes represented a major achievement. Land ownership meant more than just a place to farm. Blundell 'was immensely struck' by the way in which Kikuyu in good positions, earning high wages, would almost beg to be included, 'so concerned were they with even the smallest stake in land'.

European roots in the land were not as deep as those of the Kikuyu, but many had invested their past and were investing their futures in it. By no means all the European farmers were affected by the scheme, and for many it was business as usual. But uncertainty in the future increased with the arrival of European refugees from the Belgian Congo, who came pouring in by road and rail. A letter from Rhodora Farm in July 1960 referred to a thousand Africans gathered at Nairobi station to meet the trains, shouting 'Go back! We don't want you. The same will happen to the Europeans here when Uhuru comes.' Seys recalled that just after independence in Congo the Congolese had disarmed the European population, leaving them vulnerable, and the same might happen in Kenya. His letters record that Kenya took in some 2,500 refugees from the Congo, from whom came accounts of 'rape, murder . . . and, of course, of the majority losing everything they possessed'.

Nellie Grant wrote in a July letter that, as Congo stories increased in horror, plans were made for escape by air should conditions become desperate. Airstrips were prepared in strategic places and, for a modest charge, some 'iron rations' were banked where those under threat were to assemble and wait until flown out. Such an emergency was not anticipated, but it was thought that it might happen after independence if the army did not get paid and mutinied. The Solai Association of Farmers met in July to prepare a plan for the district in the event of law and order breaking down as in the Congo.

In January 1960 Nellie Grant had just celebrated her 75th birthday, almost 50 years of her life having been spent in Kenya. She had lived there for the greater part of Britain's 68-year colonial span. The four years leading up to independence saw her fortune fade as the weather vacillated from drought to floods and back again. In May 1960 a letter described the drought, which 'had got simply terrific'. Then, on a Friday morning, she woke up to very low cloud, quite a fog, 'bone dry like dry ice. Never seen it before', which culminated 'with a flash and bang' overhead, with torrents of rain and lots of hail which produced 2.7 inches of rain in an hour. But that was 'just a flash in the pan', and the drought continued.

In February 1961 she wrote of the continuing drought which lasted until the middle of the year, by which time it had been the driest period for 40 years. Then came floods which 'ruined crops, paralyzed transport and killed thousands of cattle. Whole districts were cut off, and their inhabitants would have starved had it not been for air-drops by the RAF'. On the 18th November her letter reported 'the floods get worse and worse', and they continued to do so until 'everything is so soggy it is one vast quagmire . . . The damage . . . must run into millions'. A woman and child drowned fording the Njoro river, and by the 3rd December she reported that Meru had had 88 inches (2.2 metres) since 1st October. It was mid-December before the rain cleared, leaving house timbers and earth sodden and cold. The cycle continued and in October 1963 'the real worry' was the drought and maize, 'which was not pollinating properly owing to hail'.

As if the weather were not enough, the Lancaster House conference in 1960 left everyone 'in the deepest gloom' and with feeling running 'very, very high against Macleod'. Her 6th February 1960 letter read: 'We settlers have had it.' People started to shut down on development and get their money away. One of her neighbours predicted that times 'far worse than Mau Mau were ahead and the settlers would all without doubt be got rid of by murder'.

Some racist speeches by African politicians did not allay Europeans' fears of murder and mayhem. They were probably made to the gallery, but Gichuru's Naivasha speech, which referred to the white man having to 'go down on his knees' after independence, led Grant to write in November of things being 'all pretty hopeless'. From July 1960 until June 1963 her letters are occupied with news of this and that neighbour selling up and leaving Kenya. The Hawes 'decided to go home for keeps' (17th July 1960), and (in May 1961) 'the Purvii [Purveys] decided to clear out leaving everything, that lovely little place just abandoned, animals put down etc'. 'The old Mervyn Rays . . . are off too. And masses more'. A neighbour reported 'a mass flight mostly to S. Africa' (April 1962). 'Poor Arnold Thornton shot himself on Thursday night . . . they were terribly worked about the future, their savings were bringing in nothing . . . A casualty of Lancaster House?' (June 1962). The exodus continued, with Hans 'off today week', 'Nils [who] dashed in to say goodbye', 'Charles and Kit Taylor off to Somerset for keeps in April' and 'Donald trying to sell the farm to follow' (November 1962), to mention only a few of Nellie Grant's friends and acquaintances who upped and left. Her letter on the 12th May 1963 provides examples of the financial losses suffered by some European farmers who opted to leave. 'The Englands,' she wrote, 'spent £6,000 on their place and are getting £2,500 for it and going,' and 'Rebecca spent more than that on her really excellent house at Gilgil and has sold for £1,600.' Her letter concluded, 'Viveka is definitely going in October. It is horrid when people go for keeps'.

The sale of farms based on the official valuer's assessment gave rise to misunderstandings, particularly, when the European vendors were under emotional stress. Grant's 24th August 1963 letter refers to 'a large car full of Nandi [who] drove to buy [Ingrid's] farm'. Ingrid 'kept on bleating both to the Nandi and the valuer that the farm wasn't for sale'. The valuer was, she said, 'quite beastly', and 'the valuation was £10 per acre, which would pay her debts and leave her with £2,000'. 'But,' questioned Grant in her letter, 'where would she go?'

Throughout the whole period there were random attacks on European farms. Tom Petrie was slashed on the face (and 'may lose two fingers') when one of his own Kipsigis together with two others burst in on him while he was finishing his supper. 'Tom fired and the chaps went off. One was found 'stone dead in the chicken-run' (September 1960).

In May, Grant wrote of the 'ghastly murder at the Osbournes [close by] which looks horribly like a really typical Mau Mau murder as it wasn't for food or money'. David Osbourne and his wife went to sleep 'with an open door and no weapon'. The only non-Mau Mau aspect of the attack was that the two babies upstairs were not killed. The 'Osbourne affair' led to an emergency meeting attended by over 200 people. 'We are,' wrote Grant, 'all back practically to Emergency conditions and it is a dreary, dreary thought.'

The closing months of 1961 saw 'lots of daylight attacks going on these days on Europeans'. On the road near Naivasha a European farmer, his wife and four children were attacked and wounded by a masked gang which went off when they found that the farmer hadn't got the payroll money. There was a similar attack near Kitale, and Ingrid had 'the most awful thieving' involving lorries arriving at night to steal an acre of maize cobs, three sheep and endless ducklings, and petrol'. 'The gloom is very deep and real these days,' wrote Grant in her 6th January 1962 letter, adding 'but the country is so lovely.'

It was not until September 1963, some 20 months later, that her letters mentioned a further attack on a farm at Ol Kalou, which left 'sixty-seven sheep, dead or dying, strewn about'. To what extent the 20-month gap between reports reflects a reduction in crime one may only speculate. The lack of reports may simply have reflected the fact, as Grant wrote in her 1st September letter, that 'they just don't put these things in the papers any more'. Her letter concluded, 'People really are abandoning their farms and just leaving that district.'

Her concerns were mainly with her farm. She had built a school on the farm for the children of her squatters when she had a thousand acres and quite a large labour force. Now, with only 50 acres, the cost of maintaining the school and paying the teachers could not be supported – and there were, in any case, lots of other schools around. In June 1960 it was, however, proving difficult to close it. The 'education man' who arrived in September informed her that no one would have a school on their land. 'I can't cut off the education, bang,' she wrote. She considered alternatives, and eventually decided that the school could continue on the strict understanding that it was to go the moment it could, with absolutely no lien on the farm. An official census of the farm's population revealed that there were 15 adult males, 18 females, 29 male children and 43 female – a total of one 105 on 50 acres. Old Nganga the gardener had a family of 13. Very few of the population were on the Grant payroll.

In April 1961 Nellie Grant had been in two minds whether to pack up and leave or hang on. By hanging on, one might get better compensation when the blow up came, and it would give the dogs a bit longer to live. She was at a loss to understand why the banks were so keen to help people on, but although clearing her overdraft was a matter of concern she was not under pressure in that respect. She investigated various countries to which she might move, having rejected her daughter's offer of a home. She discovered that there was no quarantine for dogs in Portugal, which made it attractive to her.

A year later, in April 1962, her greatest causes for concern were the futures of her retainers and her dogs (and getting rid of the overdraft). For much of 1962 and 1963 she struggled with solutions to the retainer problem. The resettlement board's scheme for 'compassionate' cases, referred to earlier in the chapter, was one solution, but at that time it was 'all very vague'. By November she had decided that once the old retainer problem was settled she would 'sit back and live as cheaply as possible and see'. The farmhouse was in poor condition, but by May 1963 the 'cubby-hole' she intended to use as her kitchen was ready to move into at any time.

Yet again she told Kananja to find a job. She explained that she had no money at all for the moment to help him, but would try to help later on. He at once mentioned several friends who had been given lorries by their ex-employers. She taught herself to cook, and invented an excellent gadget for heating up a single plate: she refused to light the oven or grill just for one. She wished to be a good cook but could see little chance of achieving that wish. She loathed the changes in her lifestyle and missed Muchoka, who left her in June, 'more than words can say'.

That month Mr Hamisi, a Muslim, and his partner became her neighbours. They first met at dusk as she returned from walking the dogs, which charged the 'two seedy-looking Africans' who were 'hanging about'. They had come to look at her house-cows, which Grant sold to them for £50, throwing in her very old, very small and not very efficient separator. They were, she wrote later, 'nice chaps'.

Her nature prevented all life from being doom and gloom. She was given a generous 75th birthday present by 35 friends; she attended the Nairobi and other shows, where she invariably won prizes for her vegetables; she played 'with great delight and satisfaction (and practically no expense) with a new form of gardening'; and in July 1963 she and Betty Roche set up 'a very modest goat enterprise between [us], partly to be able to keep old Karanja (herd) on, partly to have some animals that you don't have to bring up to kill (though we may have a roast kid every so often), and partly for fun'. She had, she ended the letter, 'always adored goats'.

Shortly after the 1960 Lancaster House conference she had reached the conclusion that the more one thought about it the more unlikely it seemed that 'our settler sort' would be able to make out in Kenya. She recognized, however, that other Europeans would doubtless come, and 'farms would be turned into companies and so on, but quite a different sort of country, that's all'.

Nellie Grant stayed on.

The letters from the Seys family at Rhodora begin with concern at the plight of the European refugees from the Belgian Congo, which coincided with interest from prospective purchaser for much of the Seys' farmland. Seys had been invited to become even more closely involved in political and national farming affairs, but he declined most offers. In January 1961 they sent some of their furniture and paintings back to England, as they had decided the outlook in Kenya was so bad that they must rearrange their lives and concentrate on how they could expand their farming in England. They, too, had experienced 'an extraordinary year', which had seen drought, plague of army worm (black caterpillars), torrential rain, famine, political chaos, national bankruptcy, indecision and a 'growing threat of Mau Mau'. The army worm, mentioned by other farmers, had cost Rhodora dear, but they had reserves of 'keep' and could stand the £30 or £40 a day which it cost to spray. Less substantial farmers, without keep for their animals, had been forced to sell them.

The famine caused by the series of 'biblical' natural disasters would, in pre-colonial times, have caused starvation and massive loss of life, probably almost to the point of extinction. At the time of Seys letter there were 400,000 people in need of, and being given, famine relief, and the Masai were said to have lost half their cattle. Rhodora continued to sell livestock during 1961, but prices were 'somewhat lower' than those in 1960. They expected the date of independence to be some time in 1962, and they were taking steps to make it possible for them to move to a farm in Surrey, which they had purchased in 1956. They considered the Africans insufficiently educated and too irresponsible to run a modern civilized country.

The last of the Rhodora letters is dated 27th February 1962. It discusses a visit to the cinema to see the film 'Spartacus', to which they took Kiberengi, their driver, who described the 'great armies locked in bloody combat' as 'exactly what it is going to be like in Kenya after independence'. The Seys left 'for good' at the end of 1962.

The Scotts regarded the 'infestation of army worm' in 1960 as even worse than the drought and floods. 'Everything was covered with them; they ate up all the new grass . . . the cattle had virtually nothing to eat . . . and a number of them lay down and died.' In despair, Lady Pamela Scott would climb up the hill at the back of the farm and sit on a rock. 'My mother had done the same when she was depressed, forty year before'. From the rock it was possible to see the extent of the European farming and engineering achievements, and she would 'take courage'. In 1962 her elderly neighbour decided she would have to sell her farm. She had been widowed some years earlier and it made sense for Scott to run the farm, Fintry, with Deloraine but, she wrote, 'everybody told me I was mad and nobody would help me'. At a time when most Europeans were moving money out of Kenya she invested in Fintry the little money she had been left by her father. This money, together with a 60 per cent government loan, enabled her to buy it. The combined farm ran to about 5,000 acres. She took on Fintry's labour (most of whom were related to her own), built a dam, acquired a big financial burden and discovered that the farm was littered with archaeological sites. She stayed on.

Jock Dawson, one of several children of a British farmer in Kenya, had managed and owned farms. He had served 25 years as soldier or policeman. 'People like myself,' he remarked, 'had been promised by the British government that we would remain in this country as part of the British empire forever . . . suddenly it was cut, just like that. One doesn't love the British government all that much for doing that.' He stayed on.

Between them, Nellie Grant and the Seys, Scotts and Dawsons provide some indication of European farmers' experiences and responses during these uncertain years.

Field Marshal Musa Mwariama's outlaw life in the forest continued with little variation from the end of the Mau Mau war in 1956 until Kenyatta's release in 1961. Mwariama and his fellow post-Mau Mau outlaws had administered the repair oath to many members of the population who had been cleansed of their Mau Mau oaths. The much oathed, cleansed and repair-oathed population was now under pressure from the colonial government to 'confess the repair oath'. The civilian leaders told Mwariama that the best alternative would be for him to leave the area because, as things stood, people might be forced to expose him and his followers. He sent four 'emissaries' to Kenyatta in Nairobi, and he and his 6,000 people 'went far away into the wilderness'.

Mwariama's message to Kenyatta sought 'help to end the military harassment'. The emissaries returned with a message from Kenyatta that he wanted to see Mwariama in person, unarmed. It was August 1963 when Mwariama met Prime Minister Kenyatta during a 'top secret mission to Jesse Kariuki's office in Nairobi'. Mwariama and his brigadier, Joseph Mwenda, denied reports that Mwariama had sworn to kill Kenyatta 'if he ever stepped in Meru'. He, Mwariama, had been 'fighting to attain freedom for the African' and, Mwariama said, 'Kenyatta was most suitable to lead the government'. All were agreed that they had been fighting for the same cause and that they had achieved it. Kenyatta asked Mwariama to 'go back and organize [his] fighting forces in preparation of leaving the forest on attainment of Uhuru'. Kenyatta pledged that the government would make arrangements as to how they should live thereafter. Many photographs were taken. Kenyatta ordered that Mwariama's warriors should be supplied with military uniforms, and they were entertained around Nairobi before they returned to their bases.

Mwariama's people 'welcomed the good news' that they would be leaving the forest, and arrangements were put in hand for their 'march out of the forest in glory and of laying down [their] arms under the free Kenyan flag'. Civilian leaders were to take part. Much celebratory honey beer was consumed and they slaughtered many rams. The leading fighters 'went to Nairobi to see the new government'.

General Muthoni Kirima, the longest surviving female Mau Mau fighter, has recollections of the years before independence which have much in common with Mwariama's. Her group lived very austere 'hunter-gatherer' lives in the forest during the 1961 floods. Their morale was boosted by the release of Kenyatta and rumours that 'freedom was near'. In 1963 she had been told that people who were faithful to the Mau Mau movement had arranged for her to travel to Nairobi to meet Kenyatta, and after several alarums and excursions she came face to face with him. In response to a question, she told him that there had been many of them in the forest but that now she was one of only two. 'Some died and others surrendered,' she said. When she came out of the forest she could not at first look at the sun because the light burnt her eyes, but people calmed her.

The Northern Frontier District was remote from Mau Mau, but the local tribes had always provided a challenge for British administrators. In 1963, shortly before independence, tribes on the northern frontiers became restless, and during 'a full-scale rebellion' Somalis murdered Neville Judge, a district officer who had recently taken office. The rebellion ran over the independence until, wrote Chenevix Trench, who served many years in the north, 'the Kenya army (under African command) entered the district in force and suppressed the rebellion with far more severity than the British had ever used'.

In the towns, opinions on the future were divided. Meteorologist Hugh Sansom and his wife Susan found that some Nairobi settlers said, 'I can't take this, I must go', while others were keeping their options open and a few, who included the Sansoms, were becoming optimistic, even quite excited: 'It was going to be their country.'

In 1960 Nan Barratt was posted to Westlands primary school in Nairobi. Formerly exclusively for European children, it was to change over the years to become 'all black' having passed through European and Asian stages. She found that all races had similar abilities but, as she had discovered at her previous school, the Asians tended to work harder. The 'common room' was indeed common to African, Asian and European staff. 'Education has,' she remarked, 'probably been the most integrated part of the society,' but elsewhere 'discrimination was there. There was definite racial segregation'.

Teenager Jenny Baralon, the Scottish railway engineer's daughter, noticed that as independence approached attitudes changed. 'A lot of the white settlers were afraid of upsetting the Africans so they relaxed their attitudes a lot more but, still, at the railway club they weren't allowed to come in and drink with us. So we [teenagers] used to buy our cans or whatever and go off in cars a whole group of us . . . up to Nairobi dam or somewhere . . . but it wasn't approved of by the white settlers.'

Aided by legislation, attitudes began to change. Steps were taken to outlaw racial discrimination. In 1960 a law was passed which named many places or occasions where a colour bar would be illegal. The law was set out in circular no. 2, headed Membership of Clubs, and was part of a wish to create a new national atmosphere in the country against any discriminatory constitution the clubs might have. It suggested that any constitutions which barred membership solely on grounds of race, colour, or creed were out of step with the times. The circular gave advice in order to avoid further unpleasant incidents, and wished this advice to be accorded immediate attention. But 'race, colour and creed bars' were easily broken. Edgerton observed that the Kitali Hotel professed to have no colour bar, but in 1961 and 1962 he saw African guests turned away on the pretext that the hotel was fully booked when in fact it was half empty, and Odinga wrote that 'bars, hotels and clubs . . . tried to wriggle by claiming that their exclusiveness was based not on colour but on interest'.

Ever adaptable and industrious, some at least, of the Indian/Asian community prospered. Jaynti Pandit, the Indian building society man, having decided to concentrate on Africans, 'started propaganda and advertising in African languages and got a lot of money from the African community'. They were to prosper after independence, when European and Asian money left the country and other building societies failed.

The barrister T.R. Johar observed that as independence approached people became more liberal. They came to the conclusion that things were going to change and that a new order had to come in, and the White Highlands were officially done away with. In the city many of the properties were owned by the Asians, so the Africans started to buy them. Some of these properties the Asians held as investments, so they brought other properties elsewhere.

Conditions for Africans in the towns still left much to be desired. In 1963, in the course of his professional duties, Carey Francis, the headmaster of Alliance School, visited students' homes. In a letter he recorded, 'One home I visited the other day [in Nairobi] consisted of one small room, rented for 37s. a month from the city council. In it thirteen people sleep regularly every night. Our boy explained that he waited until they had gone to bed (in bunks up the walls) before doing his prep on some two square feet of table by the light of a hurricane lantern.'

The plans made by Sir Ernest Vasey in 1958–9 for the renascence of the United Kenya Club were realised in 1961–2 with the construction of the new three-storey club buildings which comprised 26 bedrooms in addition to traditional club accommodation. It was opened by the governor, Sir Patrick Renison, in August 1962. Membership increased and the club began to prosper. The Wednesday lunch-time talks continued. Oginga Odinga and Tom Mboya, among others, spoke on the need for Europeans to treat African adults with more courtesy and respect, and in March 1961 Mboya argued for the release of Jomo Kenyatta from detention. Kenyatta was a speaker in November 1961. His speech, at a time when freedom of expression was restricted, was one of his earliest declarations that 'the takeover of land from colonial owners was not his aim'.

Nan Barratt, the teacher, noticed no changes in attitudes among people in Naivasha and Nairobi as Uhuru approached, although the Africans were happy to be getting their independence. A few of the uninformed believed 'All this will be mine, and I think they tried to infiltrate [European establishments]. Then they found that it wasn't to their liking, and they were quite happy doing their own thing, like everybody else.'

In bursts of enthusiasm some African politicians had suggested that after Uhuru everybody would have a car and plenty of money. 'And,' one was quoted as promising, 'you won't have to drive on the left-hand side of the road, you can drive wherever you like.' In the immediate pre-Uhuru euphoria the African staff of a major civil engineering contractor put the names of the European female staff in a hat and drew for who would have whom. One of the cleaners told Kathleen Walker he had won her 'for after independence'. It was a sincere 'draw' on the part of the participants, not frivolity. 'But there was no hostility after independence from Africans,' she added.

An issue which had to be addressed was the poor state of 'linguistic communications' between the different African states and, indeed, within them. There was much talk of achieving a United States of Africa, and Tom Mboya was a keen leader in pan-African matters. He noted that Tanganyika had introduced Swahili as an official language with English in the national assembly. He recognized, however, that much remained to be done to make Swahili an effective language throughout eastern Africa. He knew, too, that 'India had tried to develop one language of its own to replace English, but failed'. Kenya followed Tanganyika's lead.

Perceptions of Kenyatta changed as independence approached. When Reginald Maudling first went to Nairobi as colonial secretary in 1961 Kenyatta was regarded almost universally by the European population in Kenya and by many of his colleagues in the government as an evil and dangerous man. Such was the antipathy to him, said Maudling, 'that I avoided at that time being photographed shaking his hand, for to do so would have made my task infinitely more difficult. Yet he became leader of his country and the horrors that had been predicted, both for the Europeans and for the minority African tribes and parties, did not materialize. He proved a wise and tolerant leader of his people.' Douglas Walker, whose principal role in the Kenya police had been the registration and control of fire-arms owned by Europeans – a role which brought him in contact with most of the community – revised his view of Kenyatta. He approached a meeting with him 'with temerity, but he couldn't have been more pleasant'. Walker had been instructed to give him lessons in armed self-defence and use of the pistol. He was surprised that Kenyatta insisted that the only firearm he would use was what was known as a ladies' handbag pistol. 'He didn't like a big bulky thing'. He had an office with a very deep carpet, and in the course of a lesson on how to use the lightweight pistol, one of the bullets rolled off the desk onto the carpet. 'He looked terrified. He thought one bullet would blow the room up.' Was he was a leader 'to darkness and death?' Walker found it difficult to believe that Kenyatta had had involvement with Mau Mau.

Opinions varied on his suitability for leadership of the country. There were, in administrator Frank Wilson's view, more able men than Kenyatta in terms of education and intellectual ability, but Kenyatta had the status within the tribe. And Murray-Brown, in his sympathetic but objective and perceptive biography of Kenyatta, suggests that he had not shown himself to be notably effective either as a party leader or as a government minister, and there were some who questioned his future usefulness. It was argued that his struggle and 'supposed drinking habits . . . had exhausted his powers and

362

brought him near to senility'. Reginald Maudling's retrospective view of Kenyatta was that he valued his contact with Britain and the west and the traditional western concepts of democracy. 'Would there had been more like him. But what I think pointed to me the contrast most clearly was when I returned to Kenya briefly in a private capacity in 1965 and attended an agricultural show. At the dinner of the farmers, a great occasion for the European community of Kenya, the first toast proposed, and enthusiastically received, was not that of the Queen, but of Mzee, the grand old man'.

Low and Smith provide a more distant, objective and academic analysis of Kenyatta's leadership achievement. By 1963 he had, they write, produced a government 'which was in many ways more securely based than had been in power when he had returned to Kenya . . . seventeen years before'. It had, they argued, 'secured the independence from Britain which the Europeans had once dreamed of for their 'white man's country'. It had been voted into power by an overwhelming majority of the adult population of the country. It had at its disposal an administration more highly qualified and more powerful in relation to the population than had ever been the lot of any British ex-colonial territory since India'.

'Independence now' had been the slogan since before the 1960 Lancaster House conference. Uhuru arrived on the Thursday 12th December 1963, and the celebrations extended over two or three days; longer for some. Some, perhaps many, of the European and Asian settlers had left before Independence Day, and many more departed well before hand-over. Some went south to Rhodesia and to South Africa, some to Australia and New Zealand and others, like the Seys, to Britain. But a significant number stayed. These included European farmers who had fought a hard, sometimes dirty, fight against Mau Mau. They had made Kenya their home and the Africans made them welcome.

Final preparations for 'the big day' were made during the first part of December. Kenyatta had set aside £400,000 for independence celebrations, and each sub-location in Tigani, where Field Marshal Musa Mwariama and his freedom fighters were disposed, contributed 4,000s to purchase 24 sewing machines to make uniforms for the men.

Only weeks before independence, Carey Francis, who had since 1960 been pessimistic about Uhuru, wrote in a letter: 'It could not be madder. It could, however, be far nastier; so far there has been nothing nasty, at all . . . But the exodus of Europeans grows apace, and without their help for sometime yet I prophesy a serious fall in standards and it could be chaos.' However, he attended an official party at Government House just before independence, at which he met 'scores of old Alliance School boys . . . most of them in high positions . . . most determined to make a go of the new Kenya'. Francis stayed on but died, literally, teaching in 1965. Reference is made earlier to the seven former Alliance School boys who acted as his pall-bearers, and were African members of the government or held high political office. Oginga Odinga was one bearer, and he was demonstrably affected by Francis' death. In his autobiography he paid tribute to Francis, his principal at Maseno school, who had taught and fostered him, subsidized his education and thrashed him four 'kibokos' (strokes with a hippopotamus-hide whip) when he took paraffin from the school without permission. Different people mourned in different ways.

Before Independence Day Nellie Grant had heard the Kenya national anthem for the first time, on the wireless. She had waited for something 'garish, blatant and cheap, but the most beautiful melody came over, restained, sad, with the sadness and mystery of deep down Africa in it'. She spent the 'history-making week' on the farm, where 'it couldn't have been quieter or duller'. Her retainers 'all got Wed. and Thurs. off on full pay'. The weather was 'grey, almost weeping clouds all the time [and] . . . cold, cold but the farm people couldn't have been sweeter or better behaved'. Independence Day 'started off Xmas-like on the lawn with jumble', after which she 'whacked out individual bags to each head of family containing meat, suet, sugar, tea according to the size of family, also four gallons of milk, twentyfive bottles of beer, fifty oranges and prizes for the sports'. The afternoon was completely quiet, she wrote – 'sleeping off beer, I expect'.

Lady Pamela Scott was not invited to any of the official celebrations, and midnight found her in bed at Deloraine. When a big cheer came from the nearby African village, a tame hyrax on the roof began to screech 'as though he was celebrating too'. She had no doubts that she wanted to become a Kenyan citizen and was one of the earliest European to take up citizenship. Her papers were signed by Daniel arap Moi, who was to succeed Jomo Kenyatta as president.

K.P. Shah embraced the independence celebrations. Shah had

come to Kenya from India in 1941, aged 19. A self-taught businessman he had become an active and enthusiastic politician, writing letters to the press and joining the relevant associations before becoming a member of LEGCO in 1961. He was a delegate at the 1962 Lancaster House conference. An ardent Kenyan, he stayed on.

Up in Nanyuki, Ngoro Ole Leputalai, a Masai who had acted as tracker for the Kenya Regiment, went along to see them changing the flag, but after Uhuru nothing else changed. 'It was as if nothing had happened . . . The tribes came together but soon split up again'.

Game Warden Peter Jenkins saw even less of the independence celebrations than Leputalai. He was one of 'three of us [Europeans] . . . sitting in the bush in Tsavo'. All their staff had been given the day off. Jenkins told his colleagues, 'Well, we'll be lucky if we are here in two years' time'. But they stayed on far beyond two years.

Harry Thuku, whose early 'kipandi protests' together with other 'subversive' activities in the 1920s led to his arrest and imprisonment, spent the day on his farm planting out new coffee trees. He was one of the first to carry the torch for Kenyatta, but his contribution to the cause was remembered by very few. He had embraced Christianity and enjoyed a happy marriage.

Meteorologist Dr Hugh Sansom and his wife Susan celebrated in Nairobi. His five-year diary for Tuesday 10th December records, 'After work drive family in and through town to see lights and Uhuru decorations'. On Wednesday 11th it read, 'To Stadium for Flag Raising Ceremony'. (There is little space in a five-year diary). His diary recognised '*the* day' with block capital letters, thus showing unusual enthusiasm. Thursday 12th reads, 'INDEPENDENCE DAY to bed 3am – Patch [their cat] having kittens! Get up 8am and watch ceremonies on TV. Rest pm'. His wife Susan, 30 years on, could 'still remember the evening, listening to, not watching, the raising of the Kenyan flag on the day of Uhuru – I still remember it as quite a thrilling moment in my life to listen to this – thrilling, exciting. Because I had always been pro-independence, I felt it must come. It was a crazy situation, the British tiny minority ruling the majority'. The Sansoms stayed on, and Hugh's diary reflects very little change in the pattern of the family's lifestyle after independence.

It was a good time for the criminal classes. A Nellie Grant letter reported, 'There were nearly three hundred stock thefts during the three days'.

An 'enormous cocktail party' was given in the parliament buildings as part of the independence celebrations. Michael Blundell and Barbara Castle were two of many invited to it. The latter teased Blundell that he would soon be back in politics. He told her that farming was his 'first love' and said his intention was to return to it and to his business affairs. He stayed on, but stayed out of politics.

Fenner Brockway (later elevated to the peerage) attended the party with his wife, where she met his 'other' family – the Koinanges. 'I introduced Edith,' Brockway wrote, 'to my five Kenya wives, widows of ex-chief Koinange, who were allocated to me when I was made his blood brother . . . As always, "son" Mbiyu greeted me as Dad. He was now a minister.' The Brockways spoke, too, with Tom Mboya whose ability 'as a builder of trade unionism in Kenya' Brockway had always admired. Now, Brockway remarked, 'he suddenly became warm and genial'.

Former governor Baring declined an invitation, but Queen's Counsel D.N. Pritt, who had represented Kenyatta and the other top leaders at their trial, attended. All interests, 'sides', colours and creeds attended the celebrations in Nairobi or at one of the many other gatherings.

Kenya was the 34th state in Africa to achieve independence. Some people taking part in the formalities had considerable experience to draw on. The Queen was represented by the Duke of Edinburgh. Much was made of his tongue-in-cheek question to Mzee Jomo Kenyatta as he was about to hand over power: 'Do you want to change your mind?'

For Kenyatta the 12th December was 'the happiest day of my life . . . the greatest day in Kenya's history'. Typically, the now leaders of emerging republics spent some time as trouble-makers or terrorists and graduated as political prisoners. Kenyatta's course ran true to form, but his speech contained no recriminations. He urged his audience to pull together. 'Harambee!' ['Work together!'] he called, and they responded with enthusiasm.

Oginga Odinga's description of the ceremony which marked the end of 68 years of colonial rule includes notes of regret. He refers to 'Nairobi's independence arena plunged into darkness [at midnight] while the Union Jack was hauled down [and] at one minute after midnight, in full flood lighting, our black, red, green and white flag of Independent Kenya was hoisted to the standard to the shouts of the people'. His regret was that 'Kenyatta's own speech inexplicably made no mention of the people who had laid down their lives in the struggle, the fighters in the forests and the camps who had been in danger in Kenya of becoming the forgotten men of the freedom fight because it suits the ambitions of the self-seeking politicians to divert our people from the real freedom aims of our people'. Most politicians, wrote Odinga, 'have not been as foolish as to openly denounce the forest fighters but rather have they connived at letting this period sink into forgetfulness.'

Field Marshal Musa Mwariama's post-Independence Day experience provides a case which illustrates the validity of Odinga's reservations. Independence Day saw Mwariama's men in convoy from Limuru to Meru, and then to Nyeri where the function of laying down arms was held. 'You should,' recounted Mwariama, 'have seen the happiness on their faces, their singing told a story of the end of an era and the beginning of a new one.' The celebrations at Ruringu stadium in Nyeri were, for him, memorable. There were speeches, parades and feasting. The ex-fighters and their thousands of admirers camped at the stadium for six days. They consumed at least 30 bulls, some 7,000 loaves and an unknown quantity of drinks, until it all ran out and people had to go home. But few had homes to go to, and they were at a loose end.

Mwariama and his fellow fighters had subsisted for too long in the forest. It would take time before they would be able to re-adjust to living in 'polite society'. He and the leading fighters went to Nairobi at the end of the sixth day to see the new government. They were placed in 'transit' camps while 'the government was working on how [they] would be helped', but in February there was 'an incident' and Mwariama was arrested. He does not state the nature of the incident, but he was sentenced by magistrate Mr J.R. McReady (now working for the Republic of Kenya) to serve five years and three months, and he was taken to Kamiti maximum security prison, to which there is reference in earlier chapters.

General Muthoni Kirima's return to society had something in common with Mwariama's. She had been told by Kenyatta that she would be picked up from Nyeri on 12th December for night ceremonies in Nairobi. Most of the freedom fighters would celebrate at Ruingu, but Kirima was for Nairobi. In the event she appears to have been met by the defence minister, Dr Munyua Waiyaki, at

Ruringu. She makes no further mention of Nairobi, but her future was bleak. She 'had thought that all those people who had left the forest first, those who had been in detention and other places would have come to celebrate with us'. But, she continues, 'I was wrong, because after one week I was brought some poisoned soda'.

When the ceremonies were over the freedom fighters were told to go home, but the government had made no provision for them. Kirima scratched an itinerant living collecting ivory from the forest and carrying it on her 'shoulders and back, to take to where public transport was available. Most of the time,' she wrote, 'I would go hungry'. She sold it to the government for 'a mere 12s per kilo'. The government sold it on at 400s per kilo.

The day after independence, teacher Nan Barratt and some friends went into Nairobi. 'There was,' she recalled, 'nothing but happiness, joy and jubilation' in the crowds. This applied to all members of the community: 'everybody was there; it was a big day'.

Several days before independence biology teacher Enid Dawson and two members of staff had taken a small group of senior African school girls down to the coast for a marine biology course. She speculated that virtually all of them would never have seen the sea before, let alone known anything about it. They stayed at a beach bar courtesy of Ian Pritchard, who had been involved in the pseudo-gangs against the Mau Mau. 'We had,' she recalled, 'been there a week, and we got to this day which should be extraordinarily significant in the lives of these girls. But they were singularly unimpressed. It was much more impressive to them to be at the coast than to face this idea of independence. One or two were thrilled but not the majority. 'I said to the girls, "What are we going to do to celebrate?" One of them said, "Well, lets just sit on the beach after supper and sing hymns. Our thanksgiving to God." This is,' commented Dawson, 'a mission-based school, remember.'

Ocean Sports, 'the little beach bar, had quite a few Europeans, and after the girls had had their supper we trooped down on the beach. In front of the European beach bar there was, suddenly, a group of Africans sitting on the beach. And the girls sang. African girls can sing magnificently . . . and singing hymns in English. They sang for maybe twenty, thirty minutes and quietly finished. And that was it'. Almost 30 years later, recalling Independence Day, an acquaintance remarked to Dawson, 'I was down at Ocean Sports and the most symbolic thing happened, a group of African girls sang hymns. It was as if a new era had started.'

From the British standpoint the transfer of power went smoothly. Reginald Maudling, who as colonial secretary had played no small part in bringing independence about, was well pleased with events, although Kenya was a relatively small part of his political career. In his autobiography he opined that 'Kenya eventually came to independence in an atmosphere of which Britain could be proud. Of all the countries we have governed in Africa I think Kenya in many ways has been closest to the British heart, and the British tradition . . . What a change there had been, and in what a short time!'

And Duncan Sandys remarked shortly after the handover: 'If every commonwealth statesman was as wise, as co-operative and as helpful as Jomo Kenyatta, there would be no problems in the commonwealth.'

Above: A light-hearted moment from the second Lancaster House conference, Michael Blundell showing Ronald Ngala how to deal with Secretary of State Reginald Maudling.

Below: Reginal Maudling opens the conference in February 1962.

Epilogue
Questions, Hypotheses, Assessments

"The blood was just for nothing." (Henry Muoria)

An aim of this book has been to give a fair and balanced account of the people involved and their part in the unfolding story. There remain, however, questions to be asked, hypotheses to be tested and assessments to be made.

QUESTIONS

What caused the Mau Mau uprising?

The Kikuyu people undoubtedly sought more land to support their increasing population; the black Africans resented rule by Britain and domination by white settlers; landless Kikuyu peasants were envious of prosperous members of their own tribe who had held land before the British arrived; and African soldiers who had travelled abroad during the war had seen enough of the green grass of the outside world to make them feel deprived. But was there a single root cause?

In an early independent study, *The Myth of Mau Mau*, Rosberg and Nottingham considered the crucial turning point in colonial nationalism to be the rejection by the protest movement or political parties of the legitimacy of the colonial system. At this point, they suggest, there occurred a marked shift from a limited civil liberties ideology to demands for the acquisition of political power and, ultimately, a monopoly of coercive powers. Mau Mau unquestionably used coercive powers.

Was Mau Mau a tribal or a national movement?

This leads one to seek a definition of 'tribe'. The *Concise Oxford Dictionary* (9th ed.) refers, first, to 'a group of (esp. primitive) families or communities, linked by social, economic, religious or blood ties and usually having a common culture and dialect and a recognized leader', but in a study of Mau Mau made some 25 years after the events Lonsdale suggests that tribes 'are not actual social organizations: rather, they are states of mind'. He goes further and concludes that

371

'tribes, like nations – and they are alike in most respects other than in their lack of a state – are changing moral arenas of political debate' All that said, Kenyan Africans consulted during research for this book have no difficulty identifying characteristics which separate, say, Luo from Kikuyu and Kikuyu from Masai, even if the differences between Kikuyu, Embu and Meru might be less distinct.

L.S.B. Leakey traces the leaders of Mau Mau through the Kikuyu Central Association (KCA) and the Kenya African Union (KAU), finding that 'in Kikuyu country at least, most of the people leading the local branches of the KAU [were] the same people who were formerly prominent in the councils of the KCA'. He observes that 'the vast majority of the Kikuyu regard the Mau Mau Association as nothing more than the old Kikuyu Central Association', an impression supported by the fact that 'there is a remarkable similarity between the wording of the oath that was formerly taken by the KCA . . . [which later became] the new Mau Mau oath'.

There were, then, national links through the (Kenyan) KAU and (Kikuyu) KCA, but the evidence is that virtually all Mau Mau activity was contained in 'Kikuyuland' and was carried out almost exclusively by Kikuyu (which includes Meru and Embu) tribespeople. And Rosberg and Nottingham concluded that, 'organizationally, nationalism remained fragmented, dominated by tribal parocialism'. Few of those present at the time, from all sections of the population, would doubt that Mau Mau was predominantly a Kikuyu movement.

Was Jomo Kenyatta the 'manager' of Mau Mau?
At the trial in November 1952 the first charge against the five defendants was that of 'management of an unlawful society . . . known as Mau Mau between 12th August 1950 and 21st October 1952'. Bildad Kaggia admitted his involvement but at the same time stated that Kenyatta was never a member of Mau Mau central committee. Indeed, he records Kenyatta's surprise when confronted with members of the committee, and his various statements disassociating himself from the society. There was evidence of plans to assassinate him for his condemnation of Mau Mau at public meetings. Several people who knew him well make much of his rejection of violence. It was reported, later, that the director of prosecutions himself believed that Kenyatta was not the leader of Mau Mau. Certainly, even before he was released, and after independence had been achieved, Kenyatta

played down the role of Mau Mau in the independence cause and increasingly isolated himself from it. Oginga Odinga's regret at the way in which Kenyatta disparaged the contribution of Mau Mau is well recorded.

Kenyatta himself had no doubt about his stance. In his autobiography *Suffering without Bitterness – the Founding of the Kenya Nation*, published in 1968 and written in the third person singular, he wrote that 'far from being a catalyst of disaster, Kenyatta was an implacable opponent of lawlessness and violence. By his words, and by his very presence, he stood unyieldingly for nationalist demands, to be secured by the forces of peace'. He provides many independent sources which dissociated him from Mau Mau, and he includes the text of his speeches given at the KAU meetings at Nyeri on 26th July 1852 to some 50,000 people and at Kiambu on 24th August that year to an audience of a similar size.

The British administration disregarded his words as insincere, but Kenyatta insists that he meant what the words said – that the 'disease in Kikuyuland . . . which some people seem to call Mau Mau [was] causing harm' to the people; that 'by demanding freedom', KAU did not intend 'to oust the other races when it achieve[d] freedom'; that the African should 'rule himself in a peaceful way . . . by the hard work of the African'; and that they 'must be faithful and responsible' and 'love each other, and love other races as well'.

It would be simple to dismiss Kenyatta's book on the grounds that it was written for political advantages, but it is difficult to see what he stood to gain in 1968 by denying his contribution to a movement still regarded by many as the principal cause of Kenya's independence. Indeed, having won independence, he might have achieved even more glory among the Kenyan people as their military leader from imperialism. In the event he distanced himself from Mau Mau and all its works. But, in the words of the Indian barrister T. R. Johar, who represented many Mau Mau detainees at their trials, 'the fact is that people who were Mau Mau regarded him as their leader'.

Did the Lari Massacre have a significant affect on the advancement of the Mau Mau cause?

There is ample evidence that the massacre lost Mau Mau support in the international press, accelerating deployment against them of 'loyal' forces such as the home guard and the tribal police who were paid by, and generally supported, the British administration. It brought home the reality of civil war to native troops and gave settlers evidence of the justice of their cause: 'Remember Lari!'

It was the atrocity which caused the greatest number of casualties to 'loyal' Kikuyu. After it, Mau Mau leaders, as students of the war suggest, were perhaps determined that such a foray should not recur. The incident during which Sid Moscoff, an NCO in the Kenya Regiment, was urged by a Catholic missionary to let justice be done and hand over his Mau Mau prisoners to loyal Kikuyu for summary execution, illustrates an hardening of attitudes for which the massacre at Lari was almost certainly a catalyst.

Did Mau Mau achieve its goals?

Robert Edgerton, an American writer highly critical of colonialism, suggests that it did not. 'The leaders of Mau Mau had hoped,' he wrote, 'that their rebellion would become an irresistible force for freedom spreading throughout Kenya. Not only did it not unite the African peoples of Kenya; it even failed to unite the Kikuyu. Instead, it led Kenya's largest tribe into a bitter and bloody civil war.'

He concluded that by 1956 most of Kenya's Africans had repudiated Mau Mau, that the 'rebellion' was over, its goals unmet, its legacy uncertain. And in response to the question, 'Do you think all that bloodshed made very much difference to the outcome?' Henry Muoria, a veteran campaigner for African independence was adamant: 'No, it didn't; the blood was just for nothing.'

Did the Mau Mau uprising accelerate independence?

Most people interviewed, of all races, believed it did. Others, however, observed that both Uganda and Tanganyika, the other members of the East African trinity, obtained independence before Kenya without recourse to violence. On the other hand, Uganda and Tanganyika did not have such an influential and vociferous European population as Kenya – a population keen to retain its superior standing.

There can be little doubt that the British government would, in the second half of the 1950s, have been most reluctant to embark on another military engagement in Kenya and that memories of Mau Mau concentrated minds in Westminster. But by that time Mau Mau had been defeated, and the early wind of change was beginning to blow the 'front' from forest to LEGCO and Lancaster House.

Why did Westminster withdraw its support from the settlers?

Perhaps the question should be, why did Westminster support them for as long as it did? They had made a major contribution to the Kenyan economy, but as imperialism became ever more unacceptable in the western world, the empire became an embarrassing political liability rather than an economic asset. The European settlers became expendable and Westminster withdrew its support.

Many outside observers might feel the British government dealt very shabbily with the white settlers. The settlers were an important factor in the government's economic equation in the early days of settlement, and as late as the second half of the 1950s new British families were being encouraged by the government to settle in Kenya. They were encouraged at a time when some second generation settlers were leaving Kenya rather than continue to face a civil unrest to which they could see no certain end. Established settlers served Britain faithfully during the Second World War at front and on farm, and made a significant contribution to the economic development of Kenya. Then, when colonialism became unfashionable, they were dumped, not by a Labour government – which would not have surprised the generally politically Conservative settlers – but by their 'own kind', by a Conservative government.

Blundell was in much closer contact with changing British attitudes in Westminster than the average settler in Kenya, but even he was surprised and disappointed, as the 1950s drew to a close, to hear a former Bow Group Tory MP say over a dinner table, 'What do I care about the fucking settlers; let them bloody well look after themselves.' Certainly, few of them were looked after adequately by their country. Most received inadequate compensation for the loss of their farms and for the disruption (even the dissolution) of their lives.

HYPOTHESES

It is interesting to speculate on what might have occurred had events not taken the paths they did . . .

Assume that Europeans had not colonized Africa

How would Africa in general and Kenya in particular have developed? Lamb remarks that 'the ancient Mali Empire stretched over what is now nine countries', from which, he suggests, 'it is reasonable to assume that Africa would have formed viable regional entities' had European powers not intervened. Such 'empires' would, he adds, 'have reduced tribalism – though not without bloodshed'. Africa in time 'would have been led by legitimate presidents or monarchs. A sense of nationalism would have followed'. He gives no evidence to suggest that the people who made up the tribes which were 'reduced' – with bloodshed – would have fared better under 'legitimate' black presidents from other tribes than did the black tribespeople under European rulers, but events in the republics formed when European colonists withdrew in the 1960s indicate that they would not.

Earlier African history suggests that the primary interest of African natives was not in ruling others but in acquiring their land or stock for their own use. The Kikuyu acquisition of land from the Ndorobo provides but one example. In East Africa the weak were overcome by the strong, and in the aftermath of tribal forays the conquered males perished, and women, if they did not share the fate of their men-folk, were absorbed into the dominant tribe. In West Africa it was the more powerful, enterprising and better organized tribes which managed the collection and exportation of their weaker neighbours for transportation to the Americas for slavery. In East Africa, at the end of the 19th century, it was the Somalis and Ethiopians north of Kenya who put pressure on Kenya's borders in order to find new pastures for their livestock and local natives for export as slaves for the Middle Eastern markets. And reference is made elsewhere in this chapter to the fact that the countries which were never colonized were those which were the most backward and undeveloped in the continent. There is nothing to indicate that tribes colonized by other tribes fared better than those colonized by most European powers. Indeed, generally they fared far worse, and many of the post-colonial African republics in the second half of the 20th century descended into corruption, anarchy and genocide.

Lamb suggests that even without colonialism 'Africa would have been no more isolated from Western influence than is, say, Asia.' The missionaries would have come, he writes 'followed by businessmen from London, New York and Tokyo seeking markets and resources. Africans would still have gone off to Europe and the United States to be educated and returned home to understand their continent's problems'. So they might, but to do so their countries would have had to reach a state of development which could offer something of value to the businessmen and support the cost of overseas education. There is little historical evidence to indicate that incoming commercial undertakings would have provided a more rosy future for the Kenyan 'common man' than did the colonial administration under the British government.

Assume that Mau Mau rebellion would have been averted had Jomo Kenyatta been acknowledged as the African leader by the British before Mau Mau took root
Before he returned to Kenya from Britain he had been closely connected with the establishment and management of the Pan African Federation, and he had written a number of pamphlets on the future of the protectorates in general and of Kenya in particular. In 1946 he attended a meeting in Manchester of the Pan African Conference which 'made some considerable impact on [his] thinking'. He became convinced that 'it was no longer enough to struggle in piecemeal fashion for the removal of grievances or to secure the separate – still less the tribal – ingredients of human and political justice'. He decided that 'the paramount design must be to unite all the people of Kenya, and that the purpose must be nothing short of independence'. He had heard much talk in Manchester 'on the necessity for violence as a tool in winning independence . . . and on the whole motif of an end justifying any means'. He took into 'dispassionate account' the 'possible effect of this attitude on the progress of Kenya towards the kind of sovereignty to the accompaniment of, rather than at the price of, gathering and widely 'shared prosperity'. He knew that he, himself, 'could be obdurate' and he did not underestimate the tactical worth of controlled gestures of some militancy.

'But,' Kenyatta wrote of himself, 'basically he found violence – the "solution" to many challenges so glibly advanced by more barren minds – to be personally and even intellectually repugnant. Above all, he believed that to sow the wind of crude and unalloyed violence at that time, in Kenya, would reap the whirlwind of crushing repression in riposte; that it would simply – apart from ethics and moralities – never work; that it would not just perpetuate but magnify the miseries of the people.' Idealistic and pragmatic conclusions! Kenyatta 'made no lavish promises [and] right from the early days of his task as KAU President . . . he spoke to the people in terms of hard work and the rule of law'. He eschewed idleness, accepted that freedom would 'not come falling from Heaven' and spoke to his people, 'getting rid of our reputation for robbery and theft'.

Between 1948 and 1951, writes Kenyatta, there was the first emergence of a feeling in Kenya that 'we are all in this together', built on the efforts of such men as Gichuru and Koinange who were at that time better known than Kenyatta. Official British records of his words at public meetings refer to his calls for national unity rather than subversion and to his proclamation that 'violence and thuggery could only delay Kenya's independence'. James Gichuru stood down from presidency of KAU so that Kenyatta might succeed him as the latter was in most, possibly all, respects the most popular and best qualified potential African leader.

It seems, therefore, reasonable to suggest that had Kenyatta been acknowledged by the British administration as the African leader, Mau Mau (which Kenyatta asserted had 'spoiled the country') would not have taken root.

Assume that the Hola Massacre had not occurred
Hola was for 1959 what Lari had been for 1953, but the roles of African and European were reversed. Hola is a story of incompetence rather than calculated brutality, but brutality was certainly in evidence. Even the initial attempt to gloss over the incident demonstrates ludicrous ineptitude. Nevertheless 11 detainees were killed at a time when attempts were being made to bring together black and white Africans – no matter that they were killed by black African wardens, who were under orders from, and control of, British officers.

The outcome was that the prime minister, Harold Macmillan, decided that he had to take a hand in the affair, and Enoch Powell made a damning speech in the Commons which was, when he died almost 40 years later, still regarded as a master speech by one of the most eloquent speakers the House had heard. Lennox-Boyd, the colonial secretary, and Baring, the governor, both offered their resignations and Baring later referred to the incident as being seen as one of the major blights on Britain's colonial reputation.

The affair gave rise to two government inquiries and two major debates in the House of Commons, and it almost caused the resignation of a minister of state and the governor of Kenya. It may be argued that few, if any, other systems of colonial government would have reacted with so much concern to the deaths of 11 notoriously recalcitrant, 'hardcore' African detainees in a remote camp in Africa. But that does not excuse the killing, neither does the fact that the deaths were caused, not by systematic brutality by European prison officers but by frightened, inadequately supervised African wardens who lost control of a situation. The Hola Massacre occurred only one year before Macmillan's 'wind of change' speech. There is no evidence that it was a direct cause of change in British colonial policy, and Blundell observed that at only one of the meetings in England at which he spoke had the issue been raised by the 'ordinary listener' who was interested in East Africa. Nevertheless, Blundell was no doubt near the mark when he suggested that the affair had in an indefinable way increased the moral unease which was always present in the minds of many people in Great Britain over the whole colonial issue as the 1950s gave way to the 1960s.

Assume that the European farmers had followed Michael Blundell's lead

Blundell was among the first of the European farmers to appreciate that the supremacy which they had experienced and enjoyed until the late 1940s and early 1950s would, within a decade or two, come to an end. He was aware of the proposals which Macmillan had made in 1942 to buy out the European farmers as a cheaper alternative to racial conflict in post-war Kenya (Macmillan was a shrewd politician). He was aware, too, of Labour's proposals for a constitutional conference in 1953 which all races would attend and at which political changes would be discussed. Only the declaration of emergency in 1952 had halted the conference and Blundell knew, as did many other settlers, that Labour were not supporters of their cause.

Then, in December 1954, Blundell was undoubtedly impressed by Winston Churchill's pronouncements during his private interview with him in London. Churchill had made much of the need for negotiation with Mau Mau, to secure co-operation and cease 'the slaughter'. He referred to 'a terrible situation which was getting Great Britain into very bad odour in the world'. He regretted that Britain, 'the home of culture, magnanimity of thought, with all the traditions of our country and democracy, should be in a situation of using power against these people'. Churchill had congratulated Blundell on all he was doing, told him he was on the right path and assured him that he had his support. Blundell was, then, aware of the way the wind was blowing in Westminster, even as the European settlers were fighting off Mau Mau attacks on their farms.

Four years later, in May 1959, Blundell had a further private interview with another prime minister in the same room as his meeting with Churchill. This time it was Harold Macmillan, who spoke of adopting a liberal policy of evolution to draw the emerging African moderates to their administration's side. He confirmed that Britain could not support a policy which did not offer moral conviction, and told Blundell that a small committee of intimate advisers had been set up to produce 'principles of Conservative policy in Africa, and especially in the multiracial states'. Macmillan invited Blundell's views on policy, but he was 'rather astringent about the worries of the Kenya settlers', which he considered be no more or less than those of Britain. At that time the possibility of nuclear warfare was uppermost in Macmillan's mind.

Less than a year after his meeting with Macmillan, Blundell was in the thick of the 1960 Lancaster House conference. With his knowledge of Westminster's current colonial policy in mind, he was able to negotiate for what he believed to be the best that the European settlers might be able to achieve, and he was, to a considerable extent, successful. Unfortunately for both Blundell and the settlers, their aspirations and his realization of what was achievable had little in common and the settlers felt betrayed. Their feelings were displayed when one threw the '30 pieces of silver' at his feet as he arrived at Nairobi airport after the Lancaster House conference. It was an unkind cut, and in later years all but a few die-hard European settlers realized the exceptional quality of his leadership. One who served with him on LEGCO and in other connections over a period of years was the Earl of Portsmouth. He acknowledged that Blundell's whole political life was 'an act of courage . . . which earned him little enough in thanks from his fellow Europeans or his many African friends'. Nevertheless, Portsmouth never wavered in his faith that Blundell was the one 'big man' to help the transformation of colonial rule to self-government.

With the benefit of hindsight it appears that the fate of the European settlers was determined in the second half of the 1950s, by which time the breeze of change was gathering strength until, in

1960, Macmillan confirmed that the breeze was a wind which would blow away imperialism in Africa. It seems unlikely that whatever the European settlers had done would have made much difference to the final outcome. The African politicians had sensed the wind's change of direction before the local Europeans had, and in the final stages of the political game they manipulated Westminster, Whitehall and international pressure groups more craftily than the settlers.

ASSESSMENT

> *For when the One Great Scorer comes*
> *To write against your name,*
> *He marks – not what you won or lost –*
> *But how you played the game.*
> (Grantland Rice)

How did the participants play the game?

By what rules and by whose and by what standards should any assessment be made?

Social and political standards changed almost beyond recognition in the second half of the 20th century. Not until the 1960s, when in the USA the likes of Martin Luther King led protest movements against racial segregation, did white Europeans and North Americans take integration seriously and did the doors of many restaurants, hotels and equal employment opportunities begin to open to blacks. One such door was that to the House of Lords. In 1969 that most exclusive club included in its number the former celebrated black cricketer Sir Learie Constantine. Miscegenation, which had been unacceptable to the vast majority of both blacks and whites, became acceptable, almost fashionable.

Capital punishment was not abolished in Britain until 1965, and corporal punishment of prisoners in custody continued until the 1970s. Caning persisted in British state schools until the 1980s and was not outlawed in private schools until 1998. It seems sensible to assess the behaviour of nations, tribes and people by their own standards and the standards of their time.

In the second half of the 19th century European powers had regarded it as beneficial for both themselves and for advancement of the subject peoples to establish new colonies in Africa, and the USA

381

colonized the Philippines and Hawaii. In the closing decade or two, by which time the United States was well established as an independent nation rather than part of the British empire, it completed the virtual extinction of the native Americans as the incomers pushed west across the continent. Not until the end of the Second World War did western Europe and the USA start burying their imperialism: racial equality still had some way to go. The following assessments are, then, made by the standards of the time and applying the rules which pertained in western Europe and the USA.

Between tribe and tribe

Towards the end of the 19th century the Ndorobo people were living on the plains north of the swampy area which was to be developed by the British government and named Nairobi. Over a period of years Kikuyu settlers moved to the plains. The Kikuyu tribe were a more numerous, more advanced, better organized and more powerful farming people who needed more land to accommodate their successful and growing population. They may well, as Kenyatta claims, have bought the land from the primitive, hunter-gatherer Ndorobo according to Kikuyu property law, but the Ndorobo, like the native Americans at the coming of the Europeans, occupied rather than owned land, and they almost certainly had small understanding of the implications of the transactions to which they were party. Later, European settlers discovered that many of the Kikuyu people they encountered regarded the Ndorobo as wild animals rather than human beings, and had little or no compunction about killing them, particularly if they hunted on or gathered from land which the Kikuyu now regarded as their land. So it was that the Ndorobo retreated west, disappeared or married into the incomers' society. By the time the European settlers arrived, the Kikuyu had only recently taken possession of the fertile 'highlands' where the Ndorobo had until recently roamed. The Kikuyu had won the game, but they set the rules and the playing field had been tilted in their favour. The winner took all.

Rule Britannia

Now the British joined in. They played the Africans by European rules which were drafted to comply with European standards of the time. They came to advance commerce, Christianity and civilization (to use Dr. Livingstone's words), and to protect the natives from Arab slave traders. Britain also provided protection from other European powers and from invasion by their neighbours, particularly from the Somali. One of the first challenges Kenyatta had to face in 1963 as Kenya approached independence was the threat of invasion across its northern borders by the Somali Republic.

The first European rule was that 'might is right', but other rules worked to the advantage of the 'protected' natives. The 'might is right' rule had, indeed, applied from earliest times and was accepted in the western World until the Second World War had demonstrated the risk people ran when ruled by a 'mighty' dictator such as Hitler. And might, east of the 'iron curtain', continued to be all that mattered. During the debate in correspondence conducted between 1942 and 1945 by Margery Perham and Elspeth Huxley on what should be the future of Kenya, Huxley wrote as the intelligent daughter of settlers and Perham as an academic liberal opposed to colonialism generally. Huxley referred to the present native Africans in Kenya as being, themselves, 'immigrants of an earlier date' and suggested that the European settler in Kenya had as much right to occupation as the Europeans in North America and Australia. Indeed, if duration of occupancy is used as a measure of ownership, farmers such as Lipscombe, who arrived in the 1920s, had stronger rights than some of the Kikuyu who had acquired land from the Ndorobo at much the same time as the Europeans arrived.

How well and how fairly did the British imperialist colonizers play the game?

In his autobiography, the former governor Sir Philip Mitchell wrote of British colonization in East Africa, 'Never in history has a colonizing enterprise been carried out with such humanity and justice and such effective protection of the native inhabitants, in many cases recent colonists themselves, as part of the great tribal migrations, and of their liberties and rights, including land rights.' But he would write something like that, wouldn't he? It would be foolish to expect an objective answer from a British source, so one must look elsewhere.

In 1955 John Gunther, an American referred to later by a fellow American, David Lamb, as 'no supporter of colonialism as an institution', published *Inside Africa*, 'an attempt to describe all of

Africa . . . in a single volume', to use Gunther's own words. His work has provided 960 pages of reasonably objective reference for many subsequent writers. In *The Africans*, published in 1984, Lamb followed in Gunther's footsteps. His book is far less detailed, less objective and more anti-imperialist than Gunther's, but together Gunther and Lamb provide a basis for comparison of the performance of the European colonizers of Africa – Britain, France, Belgium, Portugal and Spain.

France ruled the greatest territory (4 million square miles, compared with Britain's 2 million square miles), but the population ruled by Britain, at 62.4 million, was significantly more than the 44.2 million ruled by France. Indeed, the African population ruled by Britain was almost as numerous as the sum of those ruled by the other four powers put together (France 44.2, Belgium 12.0, Portugal 9.5 and Spain 1.5 million).

The European powers adopted different approaches to governance. The French tried to open the doors of French culture and civilization to the Africans in their charge. They were taught French in the schools, and in theory the African was 'a citizen of France with privileges and duties more or less equal to those of a French citizen in Rouen or Bordeaux'. Gunther places emphasis on the words 'in theory'.

The British operated 'indirect rule' under which the Africans were administered 'through the mechanism of native chiefs'. Africans were encouraged to retain their own languages, and administrators were required to learn the local native tongue. 'Great Britain is,' wrote Gunther in 1954, 'the only colonial power that maintains an avowed official policy, the ultimate objective of which is to train Africans for complete self-government within the commonwealth.' He quotes the British government's policy statement in 1923, made by the colonial secretary, the Duke of Devonshire, 'than whom', wrote Gunther, 'no one could have been more Tory'. The colonial secretary stated, Gunther said, that 'primarily Kenya is an African territory [and that] the interests of the African natives must be paramount and that if and when those interests and the interests of the immigrant races [i.e. the British and Indian] should conflict, the former [i.e. the African] should prevail'. Reference to this policy is made earlier in this book.

As for the other European powers, Gunther noted that the Belgians gave their African subjects no voting rights but that they provided them with economic opportunities. The Portuguese treated their colonies as provinces of Portugal, Gunther found, and the Africans were 'years behind those in most of the rest of Africa. Portuguese Africa still has forced labour'. He suggested that Spain had a presence in, rather than governance of, its African territories. In Gunther's opinion the benefits the colonial system brought to Africa were 'incontestable . . . even if it brought abuses, too'. He concedes that 'perhaps much of what the white man did was selfish, since it was for the benefit of the white communities themselves; nevertheless the record stands for itself. The Europeans may have ravaged a continent, but they also opened it up to civilization. Colonialism made to-day's nationalism possible, and opened the way to democracy. The Europeans abolished slavery and ended tribal warfare. They created communications; improved the standard of living; developed natural resources; introduced scientific agriculture; fought to control malaria and other diseases; established public health controls; and gave natives who were only an inch away from barbarism a stable administration and a regime based in theory at least on justice and law (The white man's law, of course.) Most important, they brought Christianity and western education'.

An elderly Sudanese, when asked what British rule had meant to him, stated quite simply: 'For the first thirty years of my life [before British rule] I never knew if I would return home safely; the last thirty years I have known peace and security'. Thirty years later, in post-colonial Africa, Lamb found that 'almost every president [was] the product of a missionary education' and that many remained 'closely associated with the church'. He listed eight states, of which Kenya was one. He regarded as 'something of a miracle' statistics derived from research carried out by a Dr. Barrett (another American) that every year six million Africans were 'added to the Christian rolls', which indicated that 'by the year 2000 the continent would have the greatest concentration of Christians in the world'. Lamb did not question the statistics. His opinion was, however, that no matter how valuable the church had been, it had traditionally acted as a tool of the white establishment. His opinion, in that respect, differs from that held by Elliot Kendall, chair of the Methodist church in East Africa (1957–67), who refers to African converts 'who split from the establishment and set up their own independent churches' and to others whose Christian education, 'not only in Kenya but elsewhere [produced] a nationalist movement'. It was, he said, 'the Gospel itself which sets people free and gives them dignity . . . And then they see their lack of freedom and struggle for it.' The missionaries' dilemma was that they had to press forward with educating the African, knowing all the time that in the end education would 'undermine the colonial regime'. In 1952–3 Gunther had met many Africans, 'particularly on the east coast, who conceded frankly that they were not remotely ready for full self-government as yet'. But he found that nationalist Africans felt they must start somewhere, sometime, and that they would 'much prefer to have bad government of their own than good government by a white outsider'. Their plea was that expressed by Henry Muoria: 'Let us rule ourselves badly rather than have other people ruling us well.'

Lamb admitted that Liberia and Ethiopia, the two black African countries that were never colonized, remained 'among the most backward on the continent', and that officials there often admitted that 'they missed the material benefit of colonialism'. Nevertheless, he considered that the European imperialists' 'cruellest legacy' was that it left the Africans with 'a lingering inferiority complex [and] a confused sense of identity'. In addition to this (if one accepts Lamb's opinion), the retiring European powers each left different legacies. France had governed though a policy of assimilation or 'cultural imperialism', its rule being direct, authoritarian and centralized, with limited powers invested in appointed chiefs. They left behind 'trained leaders', wrote Lamb, who were 'imbued with the culture of France'. The British left behind 'a superior infrastructure: better roads, schools and communications, a more efficient civil service'.

Gunther concluded that, all in all, British rule was best. 'If,' he wrote, 'I were an African I would rather live in a British territory than any other. The British do not give as much economic opportunity in some realms as the Belgians, and perhaps not as much political and racial equality as the French in Black Africa, but the average African in British territory has more copious access to the two things Africans need most – education and justice.' As we have seen, he regarded Britain as the only colonial power that set out to train Africans for self-government. That said, Gunther believed that in the early 1950s Africa's single common denominator was the desire to get rid of colonial rule. In addition Africans sought development and education, removal of the colour bar, greater equality and nationalism.

By the end of 1963, when Kenya ceased being a colony, only 14 of the 46 former European colonies in African had not obtained independence. Seven were British, five Portuguese, one Spanish and another (South West Africa) was a disputed territory. Of those who were now independent, six had gained independence in the 1950s, seventeen in 1960 and the remaining eight in the years down to 1963. Kenya's British neighbours, Tanganyika and Uganda, became independent in 1961 and 1962 respectively, leaving Kenya as the last of the trio.

Natives and incomers
How did the people living and working in Kenya during its transition from colony to nation 'play the game'?

The most significant difference between Kenya and its immediate, comparable neighbours, Tanganyika (Tanzania) and Uganda, was the significant number of Kenya's European settlers, the majority of whom were British. In post-war Kenya white settlement was, Elspeth Huxley argued, not 'a disturbing and distracting addition', but 'part and parcel of the whole Kenya set up, built into the very foundation of the colony'. As a voice at the foundation, Oginga Odinga associated the whites with five main things: inoculations, tax collections, European expectations that the Luo would wear clothes, orders for villagers to take part in road construction works and children's attendance at school. The last mentioned was the cause of Odinga's rise from village-boy to prominent leader of his country – a leader whose death was recorded in the day's most prominent obituary in the *Daily Telegraph* long after Kenya had ceased to be everyday news.

Perham, staunch liberal and advocate of independence for the black African, wrote that she realized that 95 per cent or even 99 per cent of European settlers were 'decent, kindly, even highly intelligent and public spirited, many of them retired servants of the Crown', but she argued that in the 1940s the settlers' position in Kenya seemed almost morally untenable for the present and, in all probability, physically untenable in the future. She would not, she said, advise a friend to put himself and his children into such a position, in which the relationship between Europeans and Africans would always change in the African's favour. Huxley, the daughter of settlers, acknowledged that most Europeans were not there to raise standards for the Africans: their motives were largely self-centered,

387

and she agreed with Perham when she wrote, 'It would, I think, be the first time in history that a ruling minority had actively helped a subject people to undermine their own supremacy,' adding that she would be delighted if such a state of affairs came to pass in Kenya. Nevertheless, to paraphrase Huxley, the settlers, by their presence, provided initiative, enterprise, direction and capital. By Western standards they took land which by itself had little intrinsic worth, and from their products and the markets they discovered that they added value to the land. They cleared, fertilized, fenced against game; ploughed and irrigated; imported and improved stock; and developed rail, roads and transport generally. They suffered heartbreak in cultivation, crop failures, cattle diseases, game damage, locusts, drought, unreliable labour and fluctuating or non-existent markets.

Huxley maintained that in Europe and America one could find 'more injustice and inequality, much more real poverty and suffering and man-made misery, and certainly more squalor . . . than you ever could in Kenya'. The natives' standard of living was 'what the people themselves made of it, it was what they had known for thousands of years and . . . it was steadily rising'. She did not, however, justify acceptance of the status quo, and she made suggestions to improve equality and understanding.

Earlier chapters contain examples of inconsiderate, occasionally cruel behaviour by European settlers towards their African employees, but these were the exceptions. Visits to European farms in Kenya in the 1990s revealed numerous examples of Africans who had worked in the same 'European' farm continuously since the 1940s and 1950s albeit, in some instances, with periods spent in detention camps. At the time of the 1990s visits there were many African-owned farms which offered alternative employment, but the African employees had not moved from white to brown or black employers.

The other Europeans in close proximity with the native Africans were the administrators. The earlier colonial years, before those covered in this book, provide examples of district officers treating Africans, whose welfare they were intended to safeguard, in ways that left something to be desired. In the post-Second World War period, however, there are few causes for complaint and many for praise.

During the Mau Mau 'war' there were undoubtedly atrocities committed by both white and black participants. Both sides admit to excesses but, remarkably, neither – and particularly the Africans –

seem to hold grudges. Kikuyu workers who were detained and interrogated, occasionally harshly, returned to their former occupations almost without looking back, and European employers readily accepted their return. It was as if the war had been a rough game that, now being over, left people to pick things up where they had left off. The relatively small number which took to the forest after Dedan Kimathi's capture, emerging from time to time for forays into farms to cause mayhem and replenish their food stocks, lacked co-ordinated purpose.

During the year or two before Uhuru they were constantly criticized by Kenyatta, who warned them that such behaviour would not be tolerated when Kenya became a republic. They were a nuisance to farmers of all colours and an embarrassment to both white and black governments in turn, but they were not a serious threat to people or to the stability of the country.

Scram from Kenya?

When the time came, Tom Mboya did *not* tell the European settler 'Your time is past . . . Scram from [Kenya]'. In the closing years of British rule in the country, Mzee Jomo Kenyatta's message was 'Stay'. He left them in no doubt that they would be welcomed, and he was as good as his word.

Postscript

Ultimately Kenyatta won the game and Kenya gained independence, but he was magnanimous and pragmatic in victory. He appreciated the benefits of keeping British personnel in the upper echelons of the Administration, and many British staff were encouraged to stay on. That many members of the police force and the justiciary were the same Europeans after independence as before suggests that, despite the allegations of brutality and injustice occasionally levelled at the colonial power, there had been more right than wrong. Earlier pages contain a report of a conversation some years after independence, when the former governor Evelyn Baring visited Kenyatta in his presidential office. Baring remarked that he had signed Kenyatta's detention order while sitting at the desk which Kenyatta now occupied. Kenyatta's reply was that, in Baring's shoes at that time, he would have done the same, adding 'and I've signed a good few detention orders on it myself'.

The transition of power had meant 'under (almost) new management', but 'business as usual'. His presidency was not, however, all sweetness and light. There were political assassinations, the best known of which was that of Tom Mboya, who was gunned down in a Nairobi street. There were, too, political divisions which were not infrequently resolved by the detention of the dissidents. Nevertheless, Kenyatta became a respected and admired leader, who made Kenya the epitome of successful post-colonial states, particularly in the earlier years of his presidency, and he remained on close terms with the people from whom he had acquired his country's independence.

Readers will draw their own conclusions.

Footnotes and References

Page numbers are followed by words from the text which are linked to the relevant footnote and/or reference: see Sources section, page 414.

Chapter 1: Colonial Days

3   BRITAIN'S SLICES (Patterson 1934:10).

ARAB AND PORTUGUESE (Harman 1986:13).

'LIVINGSTONE I PRESUME' (London Missionaries Society 1880:271-2).

RELIABLE FIGURES (Davidson 1980:27, 284 and 95, Harman 1986:7-8, 15).

EXPLORERS WERE (Pakenham 1991:286-8).

PRIZE FOR EUROPEAN (Pakenham 1991:291).

TYRANNICAL KINGS (Pakenham 1991 301).

4   PROTECTING TRADE (Huxley 1968:32).

IT WAS ARGUED (Barnett 1972:24-8).

SOME ADVANTAGES (Oliver and Sanderson 1985:101).

THE LAND THEY (Rosberg & Nottingham 1966:2-3).

APPEARED UNOCCUPIED Two principal sources have been used in this chapter, particularly in reference to the Kikuyu: Jomo Kenyatta's magnum opus *Facing Mount Kenya,* first published in 1938 in England while he was in virtual exile, and Louis Leakey's *The Southern Kikuyu before 1903,* written in Kenya also in 1938. Kenyatta drew on his own recollections of Kikuyu oral history while Leakey, the Kenya-born son of a missionary, a Kikuyu elder and an archaeologist and anthropologist fluent in Kikuyu, collected and edited contributions from a number of Kikuyu elders and relied on his own research. Both accounts are remarkably similar and are concerned with the Kikuyu prior to British colonisation. References for these two works are not noted separately, but Kenyatta 1979 pp. 1–25, 68, 132–4, 194–5, 208–11 and 234–66 and Leakey 1977 pp. 1–17, 87–9 and 128–9 refer. References by other authors are shown in the usual way.

5   SHY NDOROBO (Huxley 1960:96). Huxley conversation with Tengetcha.

NOMADIC PEOPLE (Huxley 1962:229).

SEEMED ALMOST IDYLLIC (Huxley 1960:65-6, 1953:113).

COMMISSIONER SIR ARTHUR (Trzebinski 1985:53-4). Trzebinski's text provides the most detailed description in regard to the white settlers.

6   POLYMATH, POLYGLOT (Huxley 1968:75-6).

OF LATER GOVERNORS (Mitchell 1954); (Bewes 1953:22-3).

LORD DELAMERE WAS (Huxley 1968:8, Trzebinski 1985:25–7). Huxley was Delamere's biographer.

A STEADY FLOW (Huxley 1964:57,:86, 233, 1990:86).

7   THREE COUPLES MADE (Trzebinski 1985:14–24, 39–43, 104).

MADE THEIR FORTUNE (Lipscomb 1949:19; Blundell 1994:13).

AT LOGGERHEADS (Trzebinski 1985:144).

SETTLERS' CONVICTION (Huxley 1990:95, Roberts 1986:659, (Blundell 1964:21).

8   POLICY WAS DETERMINED (Barnett 1972:67-8).
    GOVERNMENT WHITE PAPER (Huxley and Perham 1994:25).
    WITH THE TENURE (Watkins 1995:211).
    FEELINGS OF VULNERABILITY (Huxley 1962:16, 75).
9   MUTUALLY HAPPY RELATIONSHIPS (Huxley 1984:104, 126).
    FACT WHICH SPEAKS (Huxley 1984:108-11).
    FUNDAMENTAL DIFFERENCE (Huxley 1962:46–7).
    BLACK/WHITE RELATIONSHIPS (Kirshon 1989:424-622).
10 INDIANS ARRIVED (Low and Smith 1976:469-72, 78).
    MIGHT BE SAID (Pandit 1994:PC, Perham 1976:228-9, Johar 1993:PC).
11 THE GRANT FAMILY (Huxley 1984).
12 ADVICE ON EDUCATION (Roberts 1986:53, 681).
    DELAMERE'S CONTRIBUTION TO (Huxley and Perham 1944:206).
    CHRISTIAN CAREY FRANCIS (Greaves 1969:1, 189, 195, 86).
13 ONE EUROPEAN MISSIONARY (Roberts 1986:696, Perham 1976:24).
    FOR SOME AFRICAN (Mitchell 1954:43).
14 OF LANDLESS KIKUYU (Corfield 1960:296).
    FOR THE FUTURE (Horne 1988:148-9, Blundell 1964:186-90).
    INVASION OF BRITAIN (Horne 1988:147-8).
16 THE OUTSIDE WORLD (Blundell 1964:50-9; Kaggia 1975:26-50).

Chapter 2: Room for More White People

17 BECOMING UNFASHIONABLE (Crowder 1984:28-49) *The Cambridge History of Africa*, and quoting Taylor.
    YEARS SAW PROSPERITY (Pandit 1993:PC; Mitchell 1954:230); Jaynti Pandit established the first building society for all races in East Africa.
    NAIROBI AFRICANS LIVED (Chenevix Trench 1993:200).
18 FARM IN AFRICA (Roberts 1986:112).
    IS AMPLE ROOM (APSB 1945:70) Agricultural Production and Settlement Board, *Kenya Settlement Handbook*.
    AS PARADISE (Huxley & Perham 1944:29). A dialogue between Huxley and Perham during which Perham adopts the liberal's and Huxley the colonist's daughter's stance published during the war as a series of letters written over a period of years.
19 SUITABLE EX-SERVICEMEN (APSB 1945:76).
    PURE EUROPEAN DESCENT (Blundell 1964:61-4) Nellie Grant, too (Huxley 1984;162); Among the incomers (Stapleton 1956:7-15, 25-30).
20 OTHER ARRIVALS WERE (Whittall 1956:80-1).
    PEOPLE LIKE J R LIPSCOMB (Lipscomb 1949:15,36,41).
21 AS A TRIBE (Kariuki 1963:14).
    SHE WAS WIDOWED (Huxley 1984:176)
    THE RELATIONSHIP BETWEEN (Oliver & Sanderson 1985:685).
    FIRST IS PROVIDED (Campbell 1986:36 and van der Post 1952:51-2).
22 AGITATION, FRENZY (Mitchell 1954:217); Mitchell joined the ranks of the settler-farmers when he retired from governorship in 1952 and settled in Kenya.

MISSIONARY AT HEART (Greaves 1969:81).
EXPLAINS HOW (Blundell 1964:73-4).
23   MASS PUBLIC (Blundel 1964:79-80).
FEELING AROUSED (van der Post 1952:56).
IDENTITY CARD CONTROVERSY (Blundell 1964:81).
24   POST-WAR YEARS SAW (Dawson J and R 1995:PC).
25   METHOD OF RECRUITING (Watkins 1993:131).
POST-WAR RECRUITS WERE (Cumber IWMDSR).
26   MOST OBVIOUS METHOD (Greaves 1969:82-8).
27   RELEASE CHILDREN TO (Wilson IWMDSR Chenevix Trench 1994:82, 211).
SOIL CONSERVATION SHOULD (Corfield 1960:20).
28   MOST APPROPRIATE WAY (Chenevix Trench 1993:207-9).
29   DISTRICT OFFICERS' RECORDS (Wilson IWMDSR).
BEHIND HER PARENTS (Baralon 1992:PC).
30   ONE EUROPEAN'S ATTITUDE (Odinga 1967:56-8)
SEGREGATION ON BUSES (Muoria R 1992:PC).
WITH URBAN AFRICANS (Chenevix Trench 1993:201).
31   FROM KIPLING'S POEM (Winkler 1996:1–5).
WIDENING THEIR HORIZONS (Johar 1992:PC).
IT WAS APARTHEID (Milner 1987).
PROSPECT OF EATING (Watkins 1993:122-5, 167, 225).
32   WAS NOT RESTRICTED (Campbell 1986:6).
THE LAST WORD (Delf 1961:46).
33   MISUNDERSTANDING AND (Corfield 1960:22).
FOR DISSEMINATING INFORMATION (Berman & Lonsdale 1992:414–5, Muoria
1992:PC, Milner 1987).
34   OF BLACK PEOPLE (Corfield 1960:79).
SEEN ANOTHER WORLD (Barkas, Campbell-Clause, Carnally, Carver,
Dawson, Murray 1994:PC, Kariuki 1963:11, Huxley & P erham 1944:29).

Chapter 3: Kenyatta Returns

35   THE PEOPLE WERE (Odinga 1967:98)
WRITTEN ABOUT KENYATTA (Kenyatta 1979:XV-XVII)
NO MARKED INTELLIGENCE (Murray-Brown 1972). Probably the most
dispassionate and thorough biographer of Kenyatta, he is the source of
this brief review, unless otherwise stated.
37   NOT VERY FAR (Delf 1961:96, 70).
38   HIS CRITIQUE OF (Kenyatta 1979:XI).
SHE DESCRIBES HIM (Huxley 1984:125).
39   WHO KNEW HIM (Gavaghan 1995;PC).
HE WAS HAPPIER (Delf 1961:156).
FIRST TO LEAVE (Wachanga 1975:XIII-IV).
ON THEIR SIDE (Presley 1992:118-9).
40   WAS NOT LONG (Milner 1987).
A REPORT DATED (Corfield 1960:50).
A GENERAL STRIKE (Chenevix-Trench 1993:209).

KENYATTA WAS REPORTED (Corfield 1960:67).
41   THERE IS EVIDENCE (KNA MAA 8/8 quoted by Edgerton 1989 211).
      KAGGIA WAS BORN (Kaggia 1975:55-78).
      HE FELL OUT (Odinga 1967:73-5).
42   TRADE UNION MOVEMENT (Wachanga 1975:XXII–V).
      BY NO MEANS (Chenevix-Trench 1993:279).
43   WITHOUT WISHING (Corfield 1960:66-7, 296-7).
      THE KIKUYU VIEW (Wachanga 1975:4-5).
44   TRAGEDY FOR KIKUYU (Berman & Lonsdale 1992:418).
      NO RECORD OF (Mitchell 1954:273-6).
45   ON ONE SUCH (Cumber IWMDSR).
      THE ISSUE WAS (Chenevix-Trench 1993:209).
      THE IRONY WAS (Watkins 1995:135, 154).
46   EARLY IMPRESSIONS OF (Cumber IWMDSR).
      NELLIE GRANT'S LETTER (Huxley 1984:165).
      KENYATTA WAS IMPRESSING (Chenevix-Trench 1993:210–11).
      UPLANDS BACON FACTORY (Chenevix-Trench 1993:209–10, Thiongo 1981:93).
47   A VIEW ENDORSED (Pandit 1993:PC).
      STRIKE CUM RIOT (Wilson IWMDSR).
      CHIEFS ALSO (Corfield 160:31, 68-71).
48   ISSUE OF PROSCRIBING (Murray-Brown 1972:218-29).
      WAS THE BEGINNING (Delf 1961:151).
      KENYATTA HAD WRITTEN - (Kenyatta 1979:223-5).
49   KIKUYU WOMEN RECALLED (Presley 1992:118).
      THE NEW OATHS (Odinga 1967:96-7).
      BY THE EARTH (Kenyatta 1979:223-5).
      ADMINISTERED EN MASSE (Odinga 1979:96-7).
      VERY STRONG RUMOUR (Corfield 1960:72).

Chapter 4: Growth of Mau Mau

51   FREEDOM FIGHT BEGAN (Singh 1981).
      GOVERNOR THEREFORE (Blundell 1964:74).
      DEVELOP THEIR POWER (Odinga 1967 98, 107-8).
      REMARKABLE AND MODERATE (Chenevix Trench 1993:202-3).
52   ALL YOU NEED (Blundell 1994:85).
      WHERE GROGAN SPOKE (Huxley 1984:170). This is the Grogan who was
      sent down from Cambridge for keeping a goat in his room, the disciple
      of Rhodes who walked the length of Africa carrying a Union Jack.
      WHICH INCLUDED PART (Blundell 1994:73, 84).
      THE FIRST OCCASION (Scott P 1991:161).
53   ALMOST FASCIST (Llewelyn 1994:PC).
      AND TO BED (Stapleton 1956:147-8).
      STATE ITS POLICY (Corfield 1960:26, 75).
      THINGS HEATED UP (Delf 1961:156).
54   MAU MAU OATHING CEREMONY (Chenevix Trench 1993:203).
      FORT HALL REPORTED (Corfield 1960:78-9).

A KIKUYU LOYAL (Milner 1987, Corfield 1960:77).
THE NAME MAU MAU (Kaggia 1975:115). Coded warning for uma uma, Corfield 1960:297; Olenguruone connection, Wachanga 1975:18, similar to Kaggia Kariuki 1963:24, derived from 'muhima', Swahili for important.)

55   SOCIETY WITHOUT A NAME (Milner 1987).
ALL KIKUYU CHRONICLERS (Huxley 1960:236–7).
THE OATH HELPED (Muoria 1992:PC)..

56   SMALL TRADERS AND (Crowder 1984:171).
BOYCOTT INDIAN TRADERS (Corfield 1960:79).
AN INDIAN RETURNING (Pandit 1993:PC).
ASIAN DID NOT (Wilson:IWMDSR).
AFRICAN/ASIAN RELATIONSHIPS (*East African Standard*, January 1948).
FORT HALL'S REPORT (Corfield 1960:79).

57   BY ANOTHER WARNING (Cocker:1989:6 Corfield 1960:80–1).
THE OLD RELIGION (Meinhertzhagen 1983:106).
SUFFICIENT CONCRETE EVIDENCE (Corfield 1960:82).
THERE WERE REPORTS (Corfield 1960:82–3).

58   NEAR MAU SUMMIT (Robotham 1994:160-1).
TOOK UP RHODORA (Seys 1993:21, 31, 36–8).
ON AFRICAN FARMS (Chenevix Trench 1993:177–8).
EVICTION OF KIKUYU (Corfield 1960:82).

59   CONFERENCE OF KAU (Corfield 1960:55).
HIS 1949 REPORT (Corfield 1960:83).
AN AMERICAN, RESIDENT (Winkler 1996:5).

60   NANDI EX-SOLDIERS PEGGED (Huxley 1960:56).
TWO GO-AHEAD CHIEFS (Chenevix Trench 1993:207).
HIS FIRST OATHING (Barnett & Njama 1966:56–9). Barnett makes much of his role as assistant to Njama and writing up Njama's account of his experiences in the field, Njama being the author. The fee for oathing appears to vary from place to place. 60, 62.5 and, below, 80 shillings are mentioned. Monthly wage for a farm labourer was 12 to 14 shillings.

64   KIAMBU SUBMITTED (Edgerton 1989:19).
OF MANY TRIALS (Corfield 1960:84–5, 84–90, 100, 299–300).

65   TAKEN NO ACTION (Chenevix Trench 1993:221).

66   IN PARALLEL WITH (Corfield 1960:88-91).
OATH-TAKING CONTINUED (Corfield 1960:91–2, 99–100, Chenevix Trench 1993:220).

67   FOCUSED ON RAISING (Corfield 1960:55, 83–4).
DETACHED OBSERVER'S VIEW (Sansom 1994:PC).
THE AUTHORITIES DECIDED (Corfield 1960:89).

68   INTEREST OF WESTMINSTER (Castle 1993:259).
NOT A COMMUNIST (Murray-Brown 1972:164).
HIS ONLY SIN (Delf 1961:159).
THAT RACIAL SEPARATION (Brockway 1963:55).
MOMENT OF EMBARRASSMENT (Castle 1993:260, Brockway 1963:62).
GOVERNOR WAS ON (Brockway 1963:57–8).

69   GOODWILL GARDEN PARTY (Brockway 58–62).

WATCHED BROCKWAY EMERGE (Blundell 1964:96).
70   WITHIN A WEEK (Corfield 1960:102).
     MUCH IN COMMON (Winkler 1996:5).
     MODEST, ALMOST COVERT (Corfield 1960:94–5, 101).
71   EARLY SETTLER'S DAUGHTER (Scott J 1992:PC).
     AT MAU SUMMIT (Robothan 1994:PC).
     SEYS AT RHODORA (1993:63–116).
73   REPORTS OF 'NJUKU' (Corfield 1960:97–8).
     CHIEF NDERI (Corfield 1960:97–9).
     TOO MANY FARMERS (Edgerton 1989:31).
     CORFIELD HISTORICAL SURVEY (Corfield 1960:100–1).

Chapter 5: More Militant and Impatient

75   MILITANT AND IMPATIENT (Odinga 1967:111–2).
     FARMERS WERE DIVIDED (Chenevix Trench 1993:217–9, Blundell 1964:83–7).
76   ON 12TH JANUARY (Corfield 1960:87–8, 103).
77   NEED TO BE (Kaggia 1975:67–8).
     A ROUTINE MATTER (Stapleton 1956:199–201).
     AT TOM AGGETTS' (Corfield 1960:106).
78   IN BRITAIN, THE (Castle 1993:261).
     GRIFFITHS VISITED KENYA (Blundell 1964:270 and 94:94).
     MITCHELL'S DIARY RECALLS (Mitchell1954:229–30).
     KENYATTA HAD A (Corfield 1960:106, Blundell 1953:95).
79   A MASTER FROM (Greaves 1969:100).
     SUBVERSION AND LAWLESSNESS (CORFIELD 1960:88).
     FOR MANY YEARS (KAGGIA 1975:79–80).
     THREE PUBLIC MEETINGS (Corfield 1960:103–111).
80   IN ADDITION TO (Corfield 1960:113–4).
81   END OF OCTOBER (Corfield 1960:113–5).
     EUROPEAN FARMERS WERE (Terry, Carver, Dawson, Jenkins 1994:PC at individual structured meetings).
     A POWER STRUGGLE (Kaggia 1975:80–2). Kaggia's close connection may have distorted his view of Kenyatta's involvement. Mbotela was not Kikuyu.
     SECURITY WORKING COMMITTEE (Corfield 1960:115–7).
82   APPARENTLY RELAXED ATTITUDE (Chenevix Trench 1993:223).
     ANNUAL REPORT WAS (Chenevix Trench 223).
     THE FACTS WERE (Corfield 1960:121–3, Mitchell 229-30).
83   ENCOURAGING YEAR FOR (Winkler 1996:5–6).
     MADE AN IMPRESSION Blundell 1964;73).
     'MUSICAL CHAIRS' TIME (Chenevix Trench 1993:224–5, Blundell 1964:94).
84   FACED WITH (Chenevix Trench 1993:225).
     NO REAL TEETH (Blundell 1964:91).
     BUGGERS QUIET (Chenevix Trench 1993:225).
85   INVOLVED IN BURNING (Chenvix Trench 1993:221).
     OUTBREAKS OF ARSON (Corfield 1960: 20, 123–6). Corfield's 'History'

provides a major source of information about the activities of theAdministration and its relationship with European settlers in this chapter (Chenevix Trench 1993:226).

SHE PASSED THROUGH (Scott J 1992:PC).

NEVER BOTHERED (Johar 1993:PC).

CONSTRUCTION BEGAN (Winkler 1996:6).

86   AS A MEMBER (Kaggia 1975:95–6).

ATTENDED THE MEETING (Corfield 1960:104, 128–36).

89   STAMP IT OUT (Pickering 1957:140).

DID NOT PANIC (Chenevix Trench 1993:199).

THE LAND ISSUE (Kaggia 1975:114–5).

90   THE NEW GOVERNOR (Douglas-Home 1978:216).

GERRICK WAS CHARGED (Edgerton 1989:35).

WAS MADE LEADER (Blundell 1964:89).

DOWN IN HISTORY (Chenevix Trench 1993:221, 225, 227).

BLUNDELL WROTE THAT (1964:96).

91   ON HIS RETIREMENT (Douglas-Home 1978:217–8).

EARL OF PORTSMOUTH'S (Portsmouth 1965:284).

MUCH WAS HAPPENING (Odinga 1967:100–1).

92   KAGGIA WAS BUILDING (Kaggia 1975:99–103).

OF CIVIL DISOBEDIENCE (Kaggia 1975:96–111).

THEY ALSO OPERATED (Crossman 1954:88).

93   TAXI DRIVERS WERE (Kaggia 1975:110–1).

MAU MAU WAS (Kaggia 107–13, 89–92, 30).

WAS INCREASING (Corfield 1960:137).

KIKUYU DOMESTIC STAFF (Carnally 1994;PC).

BLUNDELL, NOW LEADER (Blundell 1964:91–4, Corfield 1960:139–40).

94   CORFIELD REPORTED (Corfield 1960:140–1).

95   DIFFICULTIES ARISING FROM (Chenevix Trench 1993, 224–5, Corfield 1960:162).

96   THE NEXT MONTH (Corfield 1960:141–2).

Chapter 6: Mass Meetings and Murder

97   PEOPLE IN ATTENDANCE (Barnett and Njama 1966:73, Corfield 1960:137).

EXCELLENT AND BALANCED (160:138).

98   LAND AND FREEDOM (Barnett and Njama 1966:73, 77–8).

SONGS AND CHORUSES (Rosberg and Nottingham 1966:260).

THERE IS LITTLE (Wachanga 1975:14).

99   PASS CODED MESSAGES (Cumber IWMDSR).

BEST PLATFORMS KENYATTA (Corfield 1960:138, 301–8). Corfield draws on several sources in his report which provide the core of this incident.

101   DEVOTED SEVEN PAGES (Barnett and Njama 1966:73–7, 80).

AN AUTHORIZED MEETING (Corfield 1960:142–3, 148–9).

POLICE WERE DRAFTED (Chenevix Trench 1993:288–9).

CALL FOR EMERGENCY (Blundell 1964:93–5).

104   SPECIAL INTELLIGENCE REPORT (Chenevix Trench 1993:226).

DIFFERENCE OF OPINION (Chenevix Trench 1993:226).

TWO MEETINGS WERE (Corfield 1960:144–50).
INTELLIGENCE NOW ARRIVED (Corfield 1960:309–10).
105 HIGH LEVEL MEETING (Corfield 1960:132–4, 145–52).
106 CATHOLIC AND PROTESTANT (Edgerton 1989:62).
REBELLION DID NOT (Corfield 1960:152–3).
THE GOVERNMENT PLANNED (Kaggia 1975:113–4).
107 NOW WORK TOGETHER (Corfield 1960:152–3).
THIS DENUNCIATION (Edgerton 1989:63).
THE CLOSING SPEAKER (*East African Standard* 26 August 1952).
INTELLIGENCE SUMMARY (Corfield 1960:152–3).
108 MAU MAU CENTRAL COMMITTEE (Kaggia 1975:113–4).
THE NATIONAL LEADER (Kaggia 1975:113–4).
DENOUNCED MAU MAU (Edgerton 1989:56, Muoria 1992:PC).
MORE REMOTE FARMS (Seys 1993:157).
NUMBER OF VERNACULAR (Kaggia 1975:82–5).
109 LEGISLATION REQUESTING (Corfield 1960:153).
EIGHT MURDERS WERE (Corfield 1960:153, Chenvix Trench 1993:231).
IN THE WAKE (KNA, paper 19 September 1952, Nairobi).
110 WHILE CONFIDENTIAL REASSURANCES (Corfield 1960:155–6).
111 FOUR EMINENT MEMBERS (KNA, paper 19 September 1952, Nairobi).
MAU MAU WITH KAU (Corfield 1960:156–7).
AN APPRECIATION STATEMENT (Corfield 1960:156–7).
112 INTERREGNUM WAS COMING (Douglas-Home 1978:216–224).
113 WHO MET POTTER (Brockway 1963:102, 127-8).
MODERN BRITISH GOVERNOR (Blundell 1964:98).
FAMILY TIES (Scott P 1991:168).
HAD BEEN BORN (Douglas-Home 1978:15–20,29–31,40, 81, 97, 169).
114 WAS MURDERED (Corfield 1960:138, 157–8, Barnett and Njama 1966:127, Murray-Brown 1972:253, Edgerton 1989:65–6, Douglas-Home 1978:231).
115 IMPORTANT TOOL (Chenevix Trench 1993:220).
WARUHIU'S MURDER (Douglas-Home 1978:226–7, Corfield 1960:158).
116 WERE ATTACKED (Stoneham 1953:51–5).
LONG AND BALANCED (Huxley 1984:178–9).
SENT A TELEGRAM (Douglas-Home 1978:228–9).
117 LAW AND ORDER (Corfield 1960:158–90).
KIKUYU WERE ARRESTED (The gunman and driver later withdrew their confessions).
TAKING SPECIAL PRECAUTIONS (Seys 1993:160).
118 SENT IN RESPONSE (Blaxland 1971:270-1).
KAGGIA WAS WARNED (Kaggia 1975:116-7).
LEADER OGINGA ODINGA (Odinga 1967:103).
119 SIGNED THE PROCLAMATION (Kaggia 1975:119).
EX-SENIOR CHIEF (Corfield 1960:159).
DO HONESTLY THINK (Huxley 1984:179–80).
IMPLICATIONS OF MAU (Carver J, Campbell-Clause J F, Dawson J:1994:PC, Robathan 1994:179, Stapleton 1956:192).
YOUNG GAME WARDEN (Jenkins 1994:PC).

120   LIVING IN NAIROBI (Sansom 1994:diary).
     MAN IN NAIROBI (Mitton 1994:PC).

Chapter 7: State of Emergency

121   COMMONLY KNOWN AS (Blundell 1964:107).
     UNIQUE REGIMENT (Coulson 1994:PC).
122   OFTEN BROKE (Campbell 1986:1).
     TO DISBAND (Blundell 1964:132).
     CALL CAME (Campbell 1986:50).
     NOT A SHOT Williams 1956:51–2).
     STREETS WERE DESERTED (Kaggia 1975:120).
     FAILED TO MAINTAIN (Blundell 1964:107).
     LEAST, SUCCESSFUL (Odinga 1967:115)..
123   THEY WERE DISPERSED (Kaggia 1975:119–20).
     MORNING SERVICE (Sansom H 1965:diary).
     CHURCHES AT (Mboya 1963:21–2)..
124   POWERFUL PEOPLE (Wachanga 1975:11, 25–30).
     DURING THE YEAR (Buttery 1995:PC).
     EUROPEAN FARMS (Seys 1993:160–1).
     GENERATION SETTLER (Dawson 1994:PC)..
125   A FEW DAYS (Huxley 1984:180).
     LYTTLETON'S FIRST (Lyttleton 1962:398).
     OUT OF JOINT (Blundell 1964:114-5).
     NOTHING TO ENDEAR (Brockway 1955:128–9).
126   IMPRESSED BY BARING (Lyttleton 1962:398–401).
     WHICH FOUND HIM (Blundell 1964:100–1)..
127   BIOGRAPHER SUGGESTS (Douglas-Home 1978:232, 250).
128   THEIR ARRIVAL (Blundell 1964:108).
     HAD BEEN HOT (Brockway 1955:118–21).
     DEAL OF DAMAGE (Seys 1993:161–3).
129   HALES SOCKS BECAME (Cumber IWM DSR).
130   AFTER THEIR VISIT (Brockway 1955:120–43, 1963:103).
131   GOOD WITH BROCKWAY (Blundell 1964:108). A sequel to the Brockway and
     Hale visit was the acquittal of ex-Senior Chief Koinange who had been
     arrested on the 20th October on a charge of giving false evidence in
     connection with the assassination of Chief Waruhiu. Hale and Dingle
     Foot secured his acquittal but he was rearrested as he left court and was
     held in detention for six years. He was an old man and became ill. He
     was released shortly before his death. He had been Brockway's host
     during his visit to Kenya in 1950 and Brockway visited him in prison.
     Brockway wrote that 'this was one of the most unforgivable things
     I have ever known. I find it difficult to think kindly of the Governor and
     the Colonial Secretary who ordered the ex-Chief's detention.'
     SOCIAL LIFE WAS (Huxley 1984:180, Barnett and Njama 1966:130–4).
132   WITH THE POLICE (Williams 1956:197, Coulson 1994:PC).
133   AFTER THE DECLARATION (Blundell 1964:109).

HEAD OF MI5 (Clayton 1984:33, Douglas-Home 1978:230–1).
TWO POLICE FORCES (Douglas-Home 1978:232).
134 KAR DURING (Coles IWM.DSR)..
135 DETERRENT TO MAU MAU (Clayton 1984:14–5).
SIEGE OF THE (Blundell 1964:111).
RECRUIT TWO DOROBO (Huxley 1984:181–2).
MURDERED IN NAIROBI (Kaggia 1975:82, Corfield 1960:266).
AN INDIAN SHOPKEEPER (Edgerton 1989:71, 111)..
136 WERE EMERGING (Seys 1993:164–6).
WAS NOT REALLY (Huxley 1984:183–4).
MORE BRAZEN (Wachanga 1975:15, 17).
COLONIAL SECRETARY ANNOUNCED (Morgan J 1963:183)..
137 GLOOMY. FOR NELLIE (Huxley 1984:184–5).
STILL TEACHING (Njama 1966:136).
WITH A MISSIONARY (Greaves 1969:112).
CLOSING MONTHS (Blundell 1964: 115–6, 130–1).
138 NOT ENJOYING LIFE (Barnett and Njama 1966:136–7).
KENYA'S MIDDLE (Pandit 1993:PC, Blundell 1964:112)..
139 INDIANS OPENLY (Edgerton 1989:226).
IN THE FIGHT (Shah 1992:13).
FOUND IT DIFFICULT (Douglas-Home 1978:246).
THE TRIAL OF (Rosberg and Nottingham 1966:281)..
140 AGAINST THE PRISONERS (Kaggia 1975:121–2).
DESCRIBED THE COURT (Wilson IWM:DSR 1988).
HAD AMPLE TIME (Kaggia 1975:123–4).
141 FOR FIVE YEARS (Chenevix Trench 1993:235).
FAR FROM SMOOTH (Kaggia 1975:126–9).
WERE TRUMPED UP (Milner 1987).
WILSON, HIMSELF (IWM DSR 1988).
TRANSCRIPT OF (Douglas-Home 1978:243–7).
142 AFTER THE TRIAL (Kaggia 1975:136).
FURTHER APPEALS (Kaggia 1975:13).
BARING'S BIOGRAPHER (Douglas-Home 1978:247–8)..
143 MANAGING MAU MAU? (Delf 1961:156).
HIS COUNSEL SAID (Milner 1987).
REFUSAL TO MODERATE (Kaggia 1975: 113–4).
KENYATTA HIMSELF (Kariuki 1963:2).
MUORIA WHO (Muoria 1992:PC).
MET KENYATTA (Johar 1993:PC).
HIMSELF BELIEVED (Milner 1987)..
144 BARING VISITED (Chenevix Trench 1993:236).
DILEMMA EUROPEAN (Huxley 1984:185).
WASN'T VERY PLEASANT (Stapleton 1956:218).
WERE VERY STRICT (Scott J 1992: PC).
POST-WAR FARMER (Thompson 1994:PC)..
145 AT TIMAU (Llewelyn 1994:PC).
A FEW MILES (Murray 1994:PC).

Footnotes and references

LOST THEIR YOUNG (Campbell-Clause 1994:PC).
PICKERINGS WERE (Pckering 1957:203–4).
DELORAINE AT NJORA (Scott P 1991:169–70)..

146 SECURITY BEING (Bewes 1953:10).
CAREFUL SECURITY (Williams 1956:87–8).
SERVANT KARANJA (Huxley 1984:185–6).
RETURNING TO NAIROBI (Bewes 1953:71:2).
TACKLED THE HOTEL (Blundell 1964:128).

147 BARING OPENED (Winkler 1996:6).
HIS WIFE SUSAN NOTICED (Sansoms 1993:PC).
PICK ITSELF UP (Odinga 1967:115–6)..

148 THE BRITISH PEOPLE (Seys 1993:169–70).
A MILITARY PRESENCE (Clayton 1984:5–6, Majdelany 1962:129–30).
HARDENED HEARTS AGAINST (Williams 1956:89–90).

149 ROUGH, TOUGH DIAMOND (Scott J 1992:PC).
LOCAL PAPER WRITTEN (Mercer 1988:740).
RECORDED IN DETAIL (Blundell 1964:138, 124).

150 JABBED CIGARETTE (Gunther 1955:338).

151 READING THUCIDYDES (Douglas-Home 1978:236:7).
PERFECT COMPOSURE (Blundell 1964:124–7).
SERVANTS OUTNUMBERED (Williams 1956:90, Blundell 1964:127).
BLUNDELL SINGLE-HANDED (Gunther 1955:338).
CHARACTER OF (Gunther 1955:336).

152 CONTINUED TO DETERIORATE (Blundell 1964:120–3).
NOSTALGIC TALK (Evans 1994:PC).
WHOSE OPINION (Williams 1956:56–7).
FOR RESOLUTION OF (Stapleton 1956:219)..

153 ATTACKS WERE DIRECTED (Scott J 1992:PC).
SIMPLE CORRELATION (Aggett 1994:PC).
FORCES WERE ACTIVE (Odinga 1967:129).

154 MORE POSITIVE STEPS (Blundell 1964:120).
EIGHT DAYS AFTER (Blundell 1964:117-23).
GRASS ROOTS LEVEL (Huxley 1984:187).
SELDOM HAVE I (Gunther 1955:319, 327, 342).

155 TIME TO READ (Huxley 1984:187).
MOVEMENTS OF KIKUYU (Huxley 1984:186–7).
IT APPEARS HOWEVER (Pickering 1957:143).
LIVING CONDITIONS (Huxley 1984:188).

156 IN THE ASCENDANCY (Blundell 1964: 132).
TO THE FORESTS (Barnett and Njama 1966:137).
40 YEARS' HINDSIGHT (Blundell 1994:97).

157 ECONOMIC CHANGES (Crowder 1984:438).
A GOVERNMENT STOOGE (Wachanga 1975:60).
APPEARS TO BE (Furedi 1990:122).
ROOT AND SYMBOL (Rosberg and Nottingham 1966:290).
FOURTH AND SIXTH (Blundell 1994:97–100).

158 WITNESSED THE AFTERMATH (Cumber IWM DSR).

159 AN NCO IN (Campbell 1986:77–8).
   MASSACRE AS SUCCESSFUL (Barnett and Njama 1960:137–8).
160 ONLY WHITE SOLDIERS (Wachanga 1975:60).
   OF ALL COLOURS (Berman and Lonsdale 1992:453–4).
   FEELING OF RESPECT (Edgerton 1989:78).
   DASH AND PRECISION (Seys 1993:176–7
   FIRST-CLASS RAID (Williams 1956:103).
   MOST IMPORTANT (Wachanga 1975:57–8).
161 ACCOUNT OF THE ATTACK (Njama 1960:137).
   THE RAID REFERS (Edgerton 1989:78).
   LARI AND ON NAIVASHA (Wachanga 1975:59).
   MUCH CRITICISM FELL (Blundell 1964:188).
   NO MEANS WELL (Scott J 1992:PC).
   BETWEEN THE SECURITY (Pickering 1957:206–7).
162 PROBLEMS AND CONCERNS (Blundell 1964 120–1).
   AS 'VERY DANGEROUS' (Seys 1993:177–8).
   'WHAT NO GOVERNOR?' (Douglas-Home 1978:245).

Chapter 8: Civil War

163 BEWES BY NOW (Bewes 1953:64, Greaves 1969:112-3).
   ON THE OTHER (Presley 1992;120,129–33).
164 LIVED IN DEFENSIBLE (Wilson IWM DSR).
   WAS VILLAGIZATION (Blundell 1964:170).
   LOCAL HOME GUARD (Coles IEWM DSR).
   A FEW WEEKS (Blundell 1964:170).
   PUFFS OF SMOKE (Barnett and Njama 1966:188).
165 AN IMMEDIATE IMPROVEMENT (Blundell 1964:170).
   'ONE-MILE STRIP' (Cumber IWM DSR).
   COULD BE SHOT (Campbell 1986:53, Wilson IWM DSR).
   FIRST CLOSE CONTACT (Huxley 1984:190–1).
   REGIMENTS ARRIVED (Blaxland 1971:273).
p166 EXTREMELY DIFFICULT (Barnett and Njama 1966:145–6).
   MILITARY PATROLLING (Blaxland 1971:274–6).
   THEIR OWN BRAND (Scott J 1993:PC).
167 THE IMAGINATION (Scott J private report May 1969, *Daily Express* 20 April 1953, *Daily Telegraph*, PC).
   PUBLISHED ITS ACCOUNT (Campbell 1986:53).
   SERIES OF MEETINGS (Blundell 1964:137).
168 BRITISH FORCES WERE (Blaxland 1971:276, 279–81).
169 KEEP A TALLY (Campbell 1986:94, Coulson 1994:PC).
   LESS THAN CONVINCED (Seys 1993:177).
   ROYAL CELEBRATION (Mitchell 1954:269–70).
   NEWSPAPER REPORTS (Huxley 1984:191).
   BLUFF AND DOUBLE (Barnett and Njama 1966:40).
170 ADVANTAGE OF LIAISON (Wachanga 1975:60–1).
171 FEW NATIONAL SERVICEMEN (Barnett and Njama 1966:220).

REGIMENT PROVIDED (Blundell 1964:130–2).
AN ODD BUNCH (Campbell 1986:100).
AS A REGULAR (Campbell 1986:51).
172 FOR HIS ASKARIS (Ferguson IWM DSR).
HAD SERVED (Coles IWM DSR).
OPERATION SCHEMOZZLE (Cumber IWM DSR).
173 A GROUSE DRIVE (Huxley 1984:195–6).
RELATIVE POPULARITY (Lyttleton 1962:405).
ON THE 11TH JUNE (PRO:WO 71/1218).
175 MORNING IN JUNE (Seys 1993:181).
STAFF OFFICER KARARI (Barnett and Njama 1966:208–9).
ARRIVED IN NAIROBI (Blaxland 1971:277).
AS DEPUTY GOVERNOR (Douglas-Home 1978:245).
ERSKINE'S APPOINTMENT (Blundell 1964:163, Douglas-Home 1978:241).
176 TEMPO OF OFFENSIVE (Blaxland 1971:277–8).
SCORE OF KILLS (Clayton 1984:38–9).
LONG TO ASSESS (Douglas-Home 1978:243).
BRITISH FORCES COMPRISED (Edgerton 1989:85–7).
177 HAD AGAINST THEM (Barnett and Njama 1966:195–7, 203–5, 215–7).
178 SUCCESSFUL NIGHT ATTACK (Blaxland 1971:278–9).
PUPIL OF CAREY (Greaves 1969:112).
'KILLS' SHOULD NOT (Blaxland 1971:281:2).
179 THE ONLY VICTIMS (Huxley 1984:192).
THE LONG PADDOCK (Pickering 1957:190).
THE MURDER OF (Huxley 1984:192).
CONTENDING WITH MAU (Huxley 1984:192.
SETTLERS WERE QUICKLY (Stapleton 1956:204, 192, 104, 207).
180 EMERGENCY HAD LITTLE (Scott P 1991:169–71).
181 WORK-FORCE AWAY (Scott J 1992:PC).
LIGHTER MOMENTS (Carnally 1994:PC).
182 WACHANGA WRITES (Wachanga 1975:*x,xi*).
FROM HIS BIOGRAPHY (Barnett and Njama 1966:248, 278, 281, 292, 314).
184 UP IN TIMAU (Murray I 1994:PC).
FOREST TO ESCAPE (Barnett and Njama 1966:273–81).
DID THEIR BEST (Barnett and Njama 1966:184-9, 194–5).
185 MAU MAU COURTS (Barnett and Njama 1966:192–4, 208, 270. Loyalty to a cause was always difficult to ascertain. Many British members of the Administration believed that 80% or more of the Home Guard were sympathisers or had taken the Mau Mau oaths. (Cumber IWM DSR).
RELATIVELY TRIVIAL (Wachanga 1975:vii, 24, 27, and Barnett and Njama 1966:187-8).
INCREASING DIFFICULTY (Barnett and Njama 1966:201, 209–10, 271-3).
186 KEEP THEIR FEET (Wachira 1994:PC).
MWATHA MEETING (Barnett and Njama 1966:227–67, 284, 297–300, 305–7).
187 POLITICAL RATHER THAN (Odinga 1967:118).
189 WACHANGA FORMED (Wachanga 1975:60–65).
CLOSING MONTHS (Barnett and Njama 1966:314-26).

TROOPS CONTINUED (Blaxland 1971:279–80).
ERSKINE WROTE (Douglas-Home 1978:243).
190   SANSOM'S HOME GUARD (Sansoms, H & S 1993:PC).
191   THEN A TEENAGER (Baralon 1992:PC).
      RUTH, LATER WIFE (Muoria R 1992:PC).
      DEVELOPED DEFENSIBLE (Blundell 1964:133).
      VISIT TO FORT (Huxley 1984:195).
192   RANGE OF VIEWS (Blundell 1964:148–9, 116).
193   COULD BE EXPLOITED (Johar 1993:PC).
      SETTLERS BECAME (Stapleton 1956:207).
      BRUTALITY OF MASSACRES (Blundell 1964:191–2).
      ON BOTH SIDES (Odinga 1967:121).
      COLOURED THEIR ACCOUNTS (Njagi 1993:51–2, MacLauchlan IWM DSR).
      EUROPEANS WHO SERVED (Johar 1993:PC).
194   AMPLE EVIDENCE OF (Edgerton 1989:112, 161–2).
195   the court martial of Captain Griffiths documents are to be found at PRO,
      WO71/1218.
197   AS 'AN EMBITTERED Clayton 1976:41–3).
      FIRST COMPANY COMMANDER (MacLaughlan IWM DSR).
198   ATTEMPTS TO KILL (Liddle IWM DSR).
      BECAME INCREASINGLY ISOLATED Dawson J 1994:PC).
      WANTED NO TRUCK (Terry 1994:PC).
      ENDORSING TERRY'S OBSERVATION (Seys 1993).
201   SAW THE CONFLICT (Maclaughlan IWM DSR).
      A DILEMMA OF (Cossar 1994:PC)..
199   RICHARD CROSSMAN MP (Crossman 1954:88).
      NO SHORTAGE OF EVIDENCE (Bewes 1953;56, Murray 1994:PC, Scott P
      1991:171, Johar 1993:PC).
      MORE SANGUINE (Scott P 1991:171, Murray 1994:PC, Campbell 1986:105)..
200   GLIMMER OF RECONCILITATION (Bewes 1953:64, Huxley 1984 195).
203   END OF THE YEAR (Edgerton 1989:87, Blaxland 1971:279–83).
      TIME FOR REVIEW (Stapleton 1956:209).
201   HAD ALWAYS EXPRESSED (Greaves 1969:110–25).

Chapter 9: The Decline and Fall of Mau Mau

205   BASED UPON ALL (Barnett and Njama 1966:331).
206   FIVE AIMS WERE (ditto 329,335, 339–40).
207   THE 'PRESENT CONDITION' (Leakey 1954:1–12).
208   SURVEY BEEN MADE (Scott J PC, *Sunday Graphic*, Reuter).
209   ONE SUCCESS FOR (Chenevix Trench 1994:263).
210   BY THEIR PARLIAMENT (Barnett and Njama 1966:350–1).
      A WEEK OR TWO (ditto 234–5, 381).
      TO DESTROY MAU MAU (Ferguson IWM DSR, Coles IWM DSR, Liddle
      IWMDSR, Lamb 1984:166).
211   PERENNIAL RIFT BETWEEN (Douglas-Home 1978:242-4, Mitchell 1954:222-3).
212   BALANCE OF LIBERALISM (Blundell 1964:146-9, 215-7).

213   METAPHORICALLY 'BASHED' (Johar 1994:PC).
      MEMBER A.B PATEL (Seidenberg 1983:128–30).
      CASTLE OBSERVED (Castle 1993:268).
      MIDDLE OF THE ROAD (Seidenberg 1983:128–34).
214   COMMON PARLANCE (Blundell 1964:146-59, 215–6).
      'IT IS USELESS (Whittall 1956:129).
215   'POLITICAL' AFRICANS (Mboya 1963:117–8).
      THEME OF THE DAY (Odinga 1967:137–8).
216   HAD A COMMITMENT (Blundell 1964:148).
      MORE THAN ALTRUISM (ditto 64, 148–53, 211).
217   OPPOSITE THE RIGHT (Seys 1993:252).
      MOST IMPORTANT (Blundell 1964:156–7).
      BEEN GREAT PRESSURE (Douglas-Home 1978:261).
218   POLITICAL SHOCK ABSORBER (Blundell 1964:162–5).
219   UNDER SEPARATE COMMANDS (ditto 187–8).
      TO BE EXPANDED (ditto 187–8).
220   GREAT REPUTATION (Douglas-Home 1978:253).
221   WAS WELL AWARE (Douglas-Home 1978:251–5).
      SNOOPERS WERE RESENTED (Evans 1994:PC).
      MOST OF WHOM (Blundell 1964:177).
222   A RECRUITING DRIVE (Walker 1995:PC).
      WITH DIFFERENT SKILLS (Wilson IWM DSR).
223   MAU MAU INFLUENCE SPREADING (Blundell 1964:171).
      REPORTS OF KAMBA (Chenevix Trench 1994:260–5).
      CONTINUED TO RECRUIT (Wachanga 1975:83–4).
      REMOVAL OF 30,000 (Blundell 1964:166–7).
225   100,000 BEING (Odinga 1967:118–9).
      MAU MAU CAMPS (Barnett and Njama 1966:208).
      EUROPEANS HAD (Stapleton 1956:208).
      HUGH SANSOM'S DIARY (Sansom H:PC and diary).
      INTENSIFICATION OF (Blundell 1964:116–9).
      FOR THE SOLDIER (Liddle IWM DSR, MacLachlan IWM DSR).
226   PERAMBULATIONS AMONG (Barnett and Njama 1966:382–3).
      IN THE ABERDARE (Cole IWM DSR, Liddle IWM DSR).
      HIMSELF ALMOST CAPTURED (Barnett and Njama 1966:366–9).
228   A WOMAN FIGHTER (Njagi 1993:103–13).
230   ERSKINE'S STRATEGY (Kitson 1960:foreword).
231   HAD BEEN RUMOURS (Barnett and Njama 1966:41, 436–7, 441).
      BARING NOTED (Blundell 1964:107).
      WHITE VERSUS BLACK (Barnett and Njama 1966:237–8)..
      EVERYONE OPPOSED (ditto 436–8).
232   PRIVATE CONVERSATION (Blundell 1964:108–10).
      DISAPPEARING EMPIRES (Mercer 1988:744–65).

Chapter 10: War Brings Nothing About

233   SCREENING BEGAN IN (Chenevix Trench 1994:258–9).
234   A POST-WAR FARMER (Thompson 1994:PC).

VIEW AT THE (Kitson 1960:2, 7, 8, 21, 29, 45–6, 51).

235 INCIDENT INVOLVING THEFT (Grant R 1995:PC)..
236 WOMEN DETAINEES BEGAN (Presley 1992:144–6).
UNDERTOOK SCREENING (KNA).
SOME ABUSES (Chenevix Trench 1994:258–60).
INSTRUCTED BY GENERAL 1994:PC).
237 LOADS OF DETAINEES (Gavaghan 1995:PC).
SANSOM'S DIARY (Sansom diary and 1994:PC).
INTELLIGENCE WAS COLLECTED (Campbell 1986:59).
238 NOT ENTIRELY AGREE (Kitson 1960:95).
GATHERU EXPLAINED (Huxley 1990:166–7).
JUST WALK BACK (Blundell 1964:195).
SENSE OF SMELL (Campbell 1986:57).
239 CARRIED OUT AT NIGHT (Edgerton 1989:139).
CONVERSATION IN KIKUYU (Kitson 1960:72–8, 148, 207).
AMBIVALENCE OF THE KIKUYU (ditto:205–6).
240 TRAINING COUNTER TERRORISTS (ditto:126–7).
NOT SLOW TO USE (ditto:92–4, 194).
241 WAR COUNCIL'S (Blundell 1964:194).
242 PARALLEL WITH FIGHTING (Barnett and Njama 1966:436–8).
AFTER TALKING (ditto:350–3)..
243 BEEN SETTLER (Douglas-Home 1978:259).
SETTLERS WANTED (Blundell 1964:190–1).
CHINA WAS (Majdalany 1962:194–202).
13TH MARCH (Barnett and Njama 1966:459–65).
245 SECOND TEAM (Wachanga 1975:105–23).
HIGHER RANKS (Barnett and Njama 1966:267–71).
WERE BEDEVILLED (Barnett and Njama 1966:472–6, Wachanga 1975:123).
246 SURRENDER TERMS (Wachanga 1975:105–35, Njagi 1993:59, 83–4, 103–113).
DECLINING SUPPORT (Barnett and Njama 1966:443–54).
247 THE BIG LEADERS (ditto:476–87).
THIN ON THE GROUND (Blundell 1964:192).
HUNT FOR KIMATHI (Njagi 1993:81–2).
248 WHO HAD PURSUED (Henderson 1958:22–43).
249 AFTER KIMATHI'S CAPTURE (ditto).
LETTERS TO HER (Huxley 1984:191–221).
253 WHEN THE FIGHT (Leakey 1954:V, 4–5).
RIGHT HE WAS (Huxley 1984:207–8).
DESCRIBED THE MURDER (Wachanga 1975:43).
LIKE MOST OF (Huxley 1984:207).
IN THE ATTITUDE (Scott J 1992:PC).
254 BENEFIT OF RESOURCES (Seys 1993:211–50).
255 STRIKES IN MOMBASA (Mboya 1963:39–41)..
CIVILIANS WERE (Edgerton 1989:96–7).
256 CLUB DECLINED DESPITE (Winkler 1996:6–8).
A STRESSFUL TIME (Odinga 1967:133–4).
WAS NOT LAVISH (Douglas-Home 1978:301–2).

257 HOUSE GUESTS (Seys 1993:258).
WITH 14 STAFF (Huxley 1984:221).
AN AGRARIAN REVOLUTION (Douglas-Home 1978:258–9).
ILLUSTRATE THE SCOPE (Chenevix Trench 1994:268–71).
LAND CONSOLIDATION (Douglas-Home 1978:264).
258 WERE TWO PRISONS (Watkins 1993:182–7).
260 DESCRIBES THE ROUTINE (Kaggia 1975:139–43).
261 HIGHLY CRITICAL OF (Edgerton 1989:236).
PUTS AN EARLIER DATE (Barnett and Njama 1966:491).
BLUNDELL ATTRIBUTES (Blundell 1964:106).
AN APPROPRIATE POINT (Edgerton 1989:106, 242).

Chapter 11: Politics and Convergence

263 BALANCE OF POLITICAL (Singh 1981:233–4).
OF BRITISH DEFEAT (MacMillan 1971:379).
264 POSTSCRIPT TO MAU (Ngugi wa thiong'o & Mugo 1976:*viii*).
265 REFERRED TO HIM (Douglas-Home 1978:278–9).
266 SPEECHES REFLECTED (ditto 278–85).
AMONG THE FIRST (Blundell 1964:219, 235–9).
267 OF EIGHT AFRICANS (Odinga 1967:141–9).
268 REPRESENTATION ON LEGCO (ditto 150).
ISSUED A PRESS (Mboya 1963 119).
AFTER THEIR ELECTION (Blundell 1964:219–20).
269 ON THE OTHER (Odinga 1967:151–2).
WHOS WHO IN (Segal 1961:220).
DEMANDS FOR MORE SEATS (Odinga 967:152–3).
ENGLAND IN AUGUST (Mboya 1963:120–2).
FOR REPRESENTATION (ditto 122).
270 FAILED TO ACHIEVE (Blundell 1964:241–3).
SIGNIFICANT INTERNATIONAL (Mboya 1963:13–4, 61–3, 80 Odinga 1967:158–61).
271 VERY FEW ISSUES (Blundell 1964:244–5, Odinga 1967:158-63, 166–7).
DILEMMA WHICH (Macmillan 1971:413).
SETTLERS MAY HAVE (Blundell 1964:65).
OF THAT YEAR (Odinga 1967:163–71).
272 POLICIES THE GROUP (Blundell 1964:250–3,263–4).
273 46 MEMBERS (Odinga 1967:164-5, Mboya 1963:107–8).
MULTI-RACIAL BUT (Odinga 1967:164–5,170).
THE KENYA INDIANS (Seidenburg 1983:134–148).
275 BEEN A CHANGE (Fisher 1973:144).
DINNER AT THE HOUSE (Blundell 1964:254–5, 61–6).
276 LATE IN 1959 (Huxley 1960:210–2,249, 254).
OLD CONSERVATIVE IDEAS (Blundell 1964;205).
277 POLITICAL AND AGRARIAN (Hill 1991:29–30).
LIKENED JOMO (Huxley 1960:239–65).
'TRANSFORMATION' CREATED (Odinga 1967:67–8, 134–5).
AFTER A PERIOD (Huxley 1960:99, 104, 110–1, 119, 186, 207).

278 AN OBJECTIVE PERSPECTIVE (Wood 1960:45–56).
280 FIRST SIGHT APPEAR (Campbell 1986:135–6).
WAS NOT LIFTED (Sansom H&S 1994:PC).
LED THE WAY (Dawson I 1994 PC).
281 COMPLETED HER TEACHER (Barrett 1994:PC).
STRETCHING THEIR LEGS (Pickering 1957:223).
RAILWAY ENGINEER'S (Baralon 1992:PC).
282 BUILDING SOCIETY MOVEMENT (Pandit 1993:PC).
UNITED KENYA CLUB (Blundell 1964:76, Winkler 1996:8–9).
EUROPEAN FARMERS (Pickering 1957:222–4).
283 MAKE NO REFERENCE (Huxley 1984:222–33).
284 WELL-ORDERED LIFE (Seys 1993:262-95).
LLEWELYNS IN TIMAU (Llewelyn 1994:PC).
285 DESPITE PLEAS FOR   The imprisonment of Kenyatta and other senior leaders in Lokitaung and their release is covered by Watkins 1993:156–9, 187–95 as a member of the Administration; by Kaggia 1975: 145-59, providing a prisoner's view; by Kenyatta's biographer Murray-Brown 1972 291–6 and 372; Cossar 1994:PC; and Kenya Intelligence Committee Monthly Appreciation PRO CO1–848 Dec 1958.

Chapter 12: From Detention to Reconciliation

289 THEIR DETENTION (Njagi 1993:70).
290 BULL PEN OF HUMANITY (Gavaghan 1945:12-4).
ADVERTISEMENT IN ENGLAND (Image T IWM DSR).
291 14,000 (MAINLY AFRICAN) (Clayton 1976:18).
TREATMENT OF DETAINEES (Barnett and Njama 1966:209).
BADLY INJURED DETAINEES (Dowson and Gavaghan 1996:PC).
MORAL RE-ARMAMENT (Huxley 1984:196–7). Gavaghan 1995:PC).
292 SUCCESSFUL SCREENERS (Blundell 1964:198–9).
293 REFERENCES IN EARLIER (Kariuki 1963:46–142).
296 WROTE THE FOREWORD (ditto *xi*-45).
OFFICER IN CHARGE (Gavaghan 1999:216–20).
297 MOSTLY NON-KIKUYU (Chenevix Trench 1993:275–6, 287).
WE ARE TRUSTEES (Gavaghan 1995:PC).
TIME GAVAGHAN BECAME (Milner 1987).
298 MINIMAL COMPELLING FORCE (Gavaghan 1995:PC).
FOUR 'PIPELINE CAMPS' (Gavaghan 1995:104, 121).
299 WERE NOT CONVERTED (Gavaghan 2003:PC).
THE WOMEN DETAINEES (Presley 1992:139).
RECONCILIATION WHICH (Odhiambo 2003:191–226).
300 CAMP BECAME KNOWN (Blundell 1964:256).
IN ANOTHER CAMP (Image T IWM DSR).
303 SUSPENDED FROM DUTY (Douglas-Home 1978:293–4).
MOST BLATANT COVER-UP (Castle 1993:289).
304 MACMILLAN'S DIARY (MacMillan 1971:733).
IN A REAL JAM (Douglas-Home 1978:174).

OFFERED HIS RESIGNATION (MacMillan 1971:734–5).

PART PLAYED BY (Douglas-Home 1978:294–7).

306 HIS PROSECUTION WAS (Chenevix Trench 1993:278).

REASON FOR HASTENING (Douglas-Home 1978:294–7).

OFFERED THEIR RESIGNATIONS (MacMillan 1971:735).

CLOSE-RUN THING (Douglas-Home 1977:299).

311 THE POLITICAL WORLD (Blundell 1964:256).

307 PUBLIC MEETINGS BANNED (Odinga 1967:162).

MBOYA WAS PLEASED (Mboya 1963:126).

CHANGING THE NAME (Kariuki 1963:158).

18 YEARS AFTER (Douglas-Home 1977:298).

PREDICTIONS THAT (Chenevix Trench 1993:277, 287).

312 PROBABLY JUSTIFIED (Wilson IWM DSR).

308 30 YEARS LATER (Murray G 1994:PC).

IN THE FOREST (Njagi 1993:68–9).

IN THE AFTERMATH (Furner 1994:PC).

ULTRA-HARDCORE MAU MAU (Blundell 1964:256).

309 WITH WHITE SOLDIERS (Njagi 1993:68-73).

THEY HAD WALKED (Odinga 1967:164).

EVE OF HIS (Douglas-Home 1978:305–7).

COMPLEX HUMAN PERSONALITIES (Blundell 1964:99–102).

A DEVOUT CHRISTIAN (Scott P 1971:168).

GRUNT/FOGHORN (Douglas-Home 1978:303).

310 SEEM TO UNDERSTAND (Mboya 1963:130).

BEEN ACCUSED (Douglas-Home 1978:305–7).

WROTE HIS BIOGRAPHER (Fisher 1973:141–5).

311 POOLE, A EUROPEAN (ditto 151).

IMPERIALISTS WERE EXPERIENCING (Bogonko 1980, quoted by Edgerton 1989:204).

WERE YEARS (Edgerton 1989:212).

Chapter 13: Conferences and Speeches

313 ROCK-SOLID HEADMASTER (Greaves 1964:166).

KNOW HOW FIRM (Blundell 1964:258-60).

ODINGA, THAT SHREWD (Odinga 1967:173–5.

314 'LOYALISTS AND (Mboya 1963:81).

STRANGER TO WESTMINSTER (Blundell 1964:267).

TIME HAD COME (Odinga 1967:177–8, Fisher 1973:147).

MACLEOD'S MESSAGE (Odinga 1967:176–8).

315 ON A DRAMATIC NOTE (Blundell 1964:268).

PREPARED SPEECH (Odinga 1967:177, Mboya 1963:115-6).

Fisher 1973:145–7).

316 END OF THE FIRST (Blundell 1964:269–73, Mboya 1963:116).

BILL OF RIGHTS (Odinga 1967:178–9, Mboya 1963:115–6).

AFTER SOME FIVE (Fisher 1973:147).

CONVEYED HIS PROPOSALS (Mboya 1963:115–6).

317 EVE OF LEAVING (ditto 128).
PLEASED WITH THE (Blundell:1964:275–6).
AFRICAN GROUP'S EXPRESSION (Odinga 1967:178).
HAD PRESENTED HIS (Blundell 1964:272–3).
BRIDGE BETWEEN WHITE (Fisher 1973:148).
DECEITFUL AND EVASIVE (Blundell 120-2, Fisher 1973:148).

318 MACMILLAN'S DIARY (Macmillan 1972:165).
NUMBER OF 'SIDE' (Odinga 1967:179, 196, Mboya 1963:127).
REASON TO REMEMBER (Blundell 1964:122, 283–4).

319 NOT ALL EUROPEANS (Portsmouth 1965:295).

320 CONFERENCE WAS (Fisher 1982:236).
MIGHT BE FOREGIVEN (Blundell 1964:277–9).

321 RESIGNED AS SPEAKER (Blundell 1994:122).
BRIGGS WROTE IN (Edgerton 1989:208).
BITTER FRUITS OF (Dawson J, Carver, Terry 1994:PC).
WORKING FOR A MISSIONARY (Cossar 1994:PC).
FAMILY AT RHODORA (Seys 1993:309).
THOUGHT WAS GIVEN (Murray G and I 1994:PC).

322 PARTICULARLY THE OLDER (Carver, McCall, Terry 1994:PC).
GOOD OR BAD (Greaves 1969:168).
TWO AFRICAN PARTIES (Mboya 1963:83–5).
SETTLERS ALSO PREFERRED (Cumber IWM DSR).
PEOPLE WHO LED (Mboya 1963:83–5, Segal 1961:347, Odinga 1967:193–4).
REGARDLESS OF TRIBAL (Blundell 1994:118).

323 AFTER THEIR FORMATION (Odinga 1967:215).
AFTER JANUARY 1960 (Edgerton 1989:213).
30 YEARS AFTER (Blundell 1994:119).
WAS IMPRESSED BY (Cumber IWM DSR).
HEADED A POLITICAL (Blundell 1964:284).

324 SEYS FAMILY BELIEVED (Seys 1993:298–9).
ASIAN FRONT (Seidenberg 1983 – a comprehensive study of roles and relationships).

325 AND IN OCTOBER (Mboya 1963:162).
WORK OF REGISTERING (Walker D 1994:PC).
OF THE FEW (Odinga 1967:251).
LIBERAL COMMENTATOR (Wood 1960:57–8).
CONTINUED THEIR ACTIVITIES (Seidenberg 1983:151–63, Shah 1996:PC).

326 GROUPS WHICH BLOSSOMED (Odinga 1967:194–5).
IN THE EVENT (Blundell (1964:286).
DISTRICT OFFICER'S WIFE (Buttery 1995:PC).
APPEALS WERE DISMISSED (Fisher 1973:151).
BITTERNESS AROSE BETWEEN (Blundell 1964:286).
CALLED A PRESS CONFERENCE (Fisher 1973:150).

327 VIRTUALLY ALL EUROPEANS (ditto).
GREAT EVENT HERE (Seys 1993:301–2).
JOSTLING FOR PLACE (Odinga 1967:200).

328 NOT ALONE IN (ditto 197).

FORM A GOVERNMENT (ditto).
IMMEDIATE RELEASE OF (Shah papers and PC).
NOTHING TO SAY (Odinga 1967:199).
SEATS ON LEGCO (Blundell 1994:211–2, 123,1964:289–93).

330   BENEFIT OF HINDSIGHT (Mboya 1963:131–2).
LACK OF CONFIDENCE (Odinga 1967:199–205).

331   FORMED A GOVERNMENT (Blundell 1964:294).
PROCEEDED TO NEGOTIATE (Chenevix Trench 1993:290).
BUT MACLEOD SUGGESTED (Fisher 1973:151).
CHAMBER TO COUNTRYSIDE (Edgeton 1989:214).
STILL IN DETENTION (Kaggia 1975:168).

332   FOUND THE POLICIES (Odinga 1967:207–8).
AGREED THAT UNITY (Kaggia 1975:168–70).
PROSPECT OF FRICTION (Odinga 1967:206–8).
DIFFICULT TO ASSESS (ditto 213).
NUMBER OF EUROPEAN (Blundell 1994:130).

333   THE POLITICAL LEADERS (Odinga 1967:215–7).
IN TWO STAGES (Fisher 1973:150).
HILL STATION (Murray-Brown 1972:304–5).

334   THE LARGEST CROWD (Odinga 1967:218).
BUSINESSMAN CUM POLITICIAN (Shah 1996:PC).
MADE THE JOURNEY (Blundell 1964:296–7).

335   OFFICE AT KIAMBU (Blundell 1994:131).
TIME THE BBC (Murray-Brown 304–7).
FROM DETENTION (Odinga 1967:219–21).
QUOTED PAGE 170 (Seys 1993:319).

336   COST HIM LEADERSHIP (Fisher 1973:198).
6,000 EUROPEANS LEFT (Odinga 1967:206, Edgerton 1989:213).
HAD TAKEN UP (Maudling 1978:92-3).
MEMBERS INCLUDED (Blundell 1964:300–1).

337   ONLY POSSIBLE TACTIC (Maudling 1978:93).
KADU CAMP (Blundell 1964:301).
IN NO DOUBT (Odinga 1967;223–8).

338   LONG AND HARD (Maudling 1978:93).
CONTINUALLY DUCKING (Blundell 1964:301–2).
VIRTUALLY NO PROGRESS (Odinga 1967:224, 228).

339   REACHED AGREEMENT (Maudling 1978:93).
VIRTUAL ULTIMATUM (Odinga 1967:230).
PROBLEM REMAINED (Maudling 1978:93–4).
FOR THE VETO (Odinga 1967:230–1).

340   ON A COURSE (Maudling 1978:85).
FEDERAL TYPE (Blundell 1964:303).
NOW PRIVATE SECRETARY (Cumber IWM DSR).
MAUDLING VISITED NAIROBI (Maudling 1978:94–5).
BECAME THE ORDER (Buijtenhuijs 1971:49).
ISSUE OF CITIZENSHIP (Mboya 1963:109–11).

341   VERY FEW REFERENCES (Murray-Brown 1972:310).

REVIEWING THE ELECTIONS (Odinga 1967:facing 1).
342 WOMEN'S CONTRIBUTIONS (Mboya 1963:160).
APPOINTED PRIME MINISTER (Low and Smith 1976:150–3).
PERIOD OF COALITION (Odinga 1967:232–49).
DICTATORIAL AND DIFFICULT (Blundell 1964:288-9).
REGIONALISM AS CONCEIVED (Mboya 1963:83–5).
343 CAME THE SPEECH (Huxley 1990:180–1).
ALREADY COMMITTED (Murray G 1994:PC).
WONDERFUL THING (Evans and Carver 1994:PC). Remarkably, Kenyatta's speech which did so much to give confidence to white settlers, and was the factor which led many to stay, is not mentioned in *Suffering Without Bitterness*, Kenyatta's collection of speeches made during the colony's closing years.
344 APPREHENSIONS OF EUROPEAN (Blundell 1994:130–1).
'INFLUENTIAL INDIAN' NOTICED (Delf 1961:161).
AFRICAN AUDIENCE (Huxley 1990:181–2).
ENTIRELY ALTRUISTIC (Low and Smith 1972:154).
NATION-WIDE TOUR (Odinga 1967:232, Dawson 1994:PC).
OBSERVED THE EMERGENCE (Watkins 1993:212).
IMPERIALIST, RUDYARD KIPLING (Mboya 1963:114).

Chapter 14: From Colony to Nation

345 OFFICERS TRAINED AFRICANS (Chenevix Trench 1993:294).
TRY SOMETHING NEW (Gavaghan 1996:PC).
346 SUITABLE AND CAPABLE (Wilson IWM DSR).
FIRST FOUR AFRICANS (Chenevix Trench).
347 SIGNIFICANT BODY (Cumber IWM DSR).
MADE A DISTINCTION (Blundell 1964:293, 194:127).
THE OTHER HAND (Gavaghan 1995:151).
SPEED OF TRANSFER (Walker D 1994:PC).
348 FOR PEACEFUL HANDOVER (Campbell 1986:86).
WROTE AN EDITORIAL (Fisher 1982).
PROVISION WAS MADE (Nottidge & Goldsack 1966:1–42).
349 75 PER CENT WAS SOLD (Storrar 1997:PC).
350 HOUSE IN ENGLAND (Llewelyn T 1994:PC).
ONE OF THE BEST (Robathan 1995:PC).
McCALL FELT STRONGLY (McCall 1994:PC).
BY THE VALUER (Robathan 1995:PC).
VIEWS OF UNDERVALUATION (Campbell-Claus, McCall 1994:PC).
RESISTED THE PRINCIPLE (Blundell 1964:239–40).
351 FAMILY HAD FARMED (Scott P 1991:181–2).
A MAJOR ACHIEVEMENT (Blundell 1964:205).
WITH THE ARRIVAL (Seys 1993:294–6).
352 INCREASED IN HORROR (Huxley 1984:238).
ALMOST 50 YEARS (ditto 234–61).
356 FROM THE SEYS (Seys 1993:294–328).

357 THAN THE DROUGHT (Scott P 1991:179–83).
ONE OF SEVERAL (Dawson J 1994:PC).
358 MWARIAMA'S OUTLAW LIFE (Njagi 1993:74–84).
SURVIVING FEMALE (ditto 112–6).
359 REMOTE FROM MAU MAU (Chenevix Trench 1993:293–4).
FUTURE WERE DIVIDED (Sansom S 1994:PC).
BARRATT WAS POSTED (Barratt 1994:PC).
ENGINEER'S DAUGHTER (Baralon 1993:PC).
360 OUTLAW RACIAL (Odinga 1967:245).
COLOUR AND CREED (Edgerton 1989:212).
TRIED TO WRIGGLE (Odinga 1967:246).
ADAPTABLE AND INDUSTRIOUS (Pandit 1993:PC).
AS INDEPENDENCE APPROACHED (Johar 1993:PC).
CONDITIONS FOR AFRICANS (Greaves 1969:173–4).
361 UNITED KENYA CLUB (Winkler 1996:10–2).
NO CHANGES IN (Barratt 1994:PC).
BURSTS OF ENTHUSIASM (Walker D 1995:PC).
PRE-UHURU EUPHORIA (Walker K 1995:PC).
PAN-AFRICAN MATTERS (Mboya 1963:220–2)..
362 CHANGED AS INDEPENDENCE (Maudling 1978:85).
WHOSE PRINCIPAL ROLE (Walker D 1995:PC).
ON HIS SUITABILITY (Wilson IWM DSR).
IN HIS SYMPATHETIC (Murray-Brown 1972:308).
363 VALUED HIS CONTACT (Maudling 1978:85).
MORE DISTANT, OBJECTIVE (Low and Smith 1976:154).
THE BIG DAY (Njagi 1993:74).
PESSIMISTIC ABOUT UHURU (Greaves 1969170–1).
364 DIED, LITERALLY (Odinga 1967:*xi*, 32–4, 36–8, Greaves 1969:195).
KENYA NATIONAL ANTHEM (Huxley 1984:260–1).
NOT INVITED TO (Scott 1991:184).
365 FROM INDIA IN 1941 (Shah 1996:PC).
ACTED AS TRACKER (Leputalai 1994:PC).
SAW EVEN LESS (Jenkins 1994:PC).
'SUBVERSIVE' ACTIVITIES (Murray-Brown 1972:310).
CELEBRATED IN NAIROBI (Sansom S 1994:PC).
30 YEARS ON (Sansom S 1994:PC).
THE CRIMINAL CLASSES (Huxley 1984:261).
366 ENORMOUS COCKTAIL (Blundell 1994:155).
TO THE PEERAGE (Brockway 1977:218–9).
HAPPIEST DAY (Murray-Brown 1972:209–10).
68 YEARS (Odinga 1967:253–4).
367 POST-INDEPENDENCE (Njagi 1993:74–85).
RETURN TO SOCIETY (ditto 116–20).
368 WENT INTO NAIROBI (Barratt N 1994:PC).
DAYS BEFORE INDEPENDENCE (Dawson E 1994:PC).
369 TRANSFER OF POWER (Maudling 1978:85).
376 STATESMAN WAS AS WISE (Fisher 1973:150).

Sources

Written sources consulted include published works and private papers located in libraries such as the Kenya National Archive (KNA) and in private collections. Personal communications (PC), other than written, were generally made during pre-arranged interviews and were audio taped. The Imperial War Museum, Department of Sound Records (IWM DSR) audio tapes and televised programmes have been used and are listed. Sources are listed below in alphabetical order, with author/contributor, date, title and publisher. (Definite and indefinite articles are not noted.) The first name of joint authors determines the item's position in the list.

Agricultural Production & Settlement Board (APSB), 1945, *Kenya Settlement Handbook*.
Aggett C, 1994, PC, Rumuruti, Kenya
Archer J, 1969, *African Firebrand, Kenyatta of Kenya*, Julian Messner, NY
Ayittey GBN, *Africa Betrayed*, St Martins Press
Barnett C, 1972, *Collapse of British power*, Eyre Methuen
Baralon J, 1992, PC, Lewes, England
Barkas R, 1994, PC, Nanyuki, Kenya
Barnett D & Njama Karari, 1966, *Mau Mau from Within*, Macgibbon & Kee,
Barratt N, 1994, PC, Gilgil, Kenya
Bennett G & Rosberg CG, 1961, *Kenya Elections, 1960–1*, OUP
Benuzzi F, 1989, *No Picnic on Mount Kenya*, Patrick Stephens
Berman B, 1990, *Control and Crisis in Colonial Kenya*, James Currey
Berman B and Lonsdale J, 1992, *Unhappy Valley*, James Currey
Best N, 1979, *Happy Valley*, Secker & Warburg
Bewes TF, 1953, *Kenya Conflict, Mau Mau and the Christian Witness*,
    Highway Press, London
Blaxland G, 1971, *Regiments Depart*, William Kimber
Blixen K, 1985, *Out of Africa*, Century Publishing
Blundell M, 1964, *So Rough a Wind*, Weidenfeld & Nicolson, London
  Ditto, 1994, *Love Affair with the Sun*, Kenway, Nairobi
Bolton K *ed.*, 1962, *Lion and the Lily*, Geoffrey Bles
Brockway F, 1955, *African Journeys*, Gollanz
  Ditto, 1963, *Outside the Right*, Allen and Unwin
  Ditto, 1977, *Towards Tomorrow*, Granada
Brown M, 1989, *Where Giants Trod*, Quitter Press
Buittenhuijs R, 1973, *Mau Mau, Twenty Years After*, The Hague
Buttery M, 1995, PC, Lewes, England
Campbell G, 1986, *Charging Buffalo – a History of the Kenya Regiment*,
    Leo Cooper/Secker & Warburg
Campbell-Clause JF, 1994, PC, Naivasha, Kenya
Carey Jones NS, 1965, 'Decolonisation of the White Highlands of Kenya',
    RGS Journal Vol 131 part 2
Carnally M, 1994, PC, Naivasha, Kenya
Carothers JC, 1955, 'Psychology of Mau Mau', private report
Carver John and Jane, 1994, PC, Nyeri, Kenya

Sources

Castle B, 1993, *Fighting All the Way*, Macmillan, London

Churchill W, 1908, *My African Journey*, Holland Press

Chenevix Trench A, 1964, *Desert's Dusty Face*, William Morrow, NY
  Ditto, 1983, *Men Who Ruled Kenya*, Radcliffe Press, London

Clayton A, 1984, *Counter-insurgency in Kenya 1952–60*, Nairobi, Transafrica, Sunflower Press

Cocker M, 1989, *Richard Meinhertzhagen – Soldier, Scientist and Spy*, Secker & Warburg

Coles G, 1988, IWM DSR 100 90/2

Colonial Office, 1959, 'Record of proceedings into deaths of Mau Mau detainees at Hola Camp, Kenya', CMND 795, HMSO
  Ditto, 1959, Documents relating to the above
  Ditto, 1960, 'Kenya Independence Conference, Constitution and Coastal Strip', CMND 2156 Oct 1963

Cook A, 1973, *America*, BBC

Corfield FD, 1960, *Origins and Growth of Mau Mau*, CMND 1030, HMSO.

Cossar J, 1994, PC, Madehurst, Arundel, England

Coulson T, 1994, PC, Gilgil, Kenya

Cranworth Lord, 1919, *Profit and Sport in British East Africa*, Macmillan

Crossman RHS, 1953, Report on Mau Mau, *New Statesman and Nation*, 23 Jan

Crowder M, *ed.*, 1984, Cambridge history of Africa (CHA) 1940–75, CUP

Cumber J, 1988, IWM DSR 10187/6

Dane F, 1994, PC, Lasham, England

Davidson B, 1980, *African Slave Trade*, Atlantic, Little, Brown

Dawson E and J, 1994, PC, Nanyuki, Kenya

Delf G, 1961, *Jomo Kenyatta, Towards Truth About*, Gollanz
  Ditto, *Asians in Africa*, OUP

Dick A, 1894, Unpublished letters, Dawson E, Nanuki, Kenya

Douglas-Home C, 1978, *Evelyn Baring; The Last Proconsul*, Collins, London

East Africa Women's League (EAWL) Bulletin.

EAWL 1962, *They Made It Their Home*

Edgerton R, 1989, *Mau Mau – an African Crucible*, Collier Macmillan, London and Free Press, NY

Edwards M, 1995 *Accidental Country*, private papers

Eliot Sir Chas, 1905, *East African Protectorate*, Arnold

Evans J, 1994, PC, Rumuruti, Kenya

Farson N, 1949, *Last Chance in Africa*, Gollanz

Ferguson IA, 1988, IWM DSR 10064/2

Fisher N, 1973, *Iain Macleod*, Deutsch
  Ditto, 1982, *Harold Macmillan*, Weidenfeld and Nicolson

Fox J, 1982, *White Mischief*, Jonathan Cape

Furedi F, 1990, *Mau Mau War in Perspective*, Heinemann Kenya, Nairobi

Furner W, 1997, PC, London

Gavagham TJF, 1995, *Corridors of Wire*, private publication
  Ditto, 1995, PC, London
  Ditto, 1999, *Of Lions and Dung Beetles*, Arthur H Stockwell, Ilfracombe, Devon

Gicherii JN, 1994, PC, Mweiga, Kenya

Grant R, 1994, PC, London
Greaves LB, 1969, *Carey Francis of Kenya*, Rex Collings
Gregory JR, 1946, *Under the Sun*, English Press, Kenya
Gunther J, 1955, Inside Africa, Hamish Hamilton
Hackett G, 2003, PC, Sinai
Harman N, 1986, *Bwana Stokesi and his African Conquests*, Jonathan Cape
Henderson I, 1958, *Hunt for Kimathi*, Hamish Hamilton
Hill MJD, 1991, *Harambee Movement in Kenya*, PhD thesis, Athlone Press, London
Hopcraft M, 1994, PC, Naivasha, Kenya
Horne A, 1988, *Macmillan (1894–1956)*, Macmillan
Ditto, 1989, *Macmillan (1957–86)*, Macmillan
Huxley E, 1939, *Red Strangers*
Ditto, 1948, *Settlers of Kenya*, Longmans, Green & Co
Ditto, 1948, *Sorcerer's Apprentice*, Chatto and Windus
Ditto, 1953, *White Man's Country, vol 2 (1914–31)*, Chatto and Windus
Ditto, 1954, *Thing to Love*
Ditto, 1957, *No Easy Way*, East African Standard
Ditto, 1960, *New Earth – an Experiment in Colonialism*, Chatto and Windus
Ditto, *Flame Trees of Thika*, 1962, Penguin
Ditto, 1964, *Mottled Lizard*, Reprint Society
Ditto, 1964, *Forks and Hope*, Chatto and Windus
Ditto, 1968, *White Man's Country, vol 1 (1870–1914)*, Chatto and Windus
Ditto, 1984, *Nellie: Letters from Africa*, Weidenfeld and Nicholson
Ditto, 1987, *Out in the Midday Sun*, Penguin
Ditto, 1990, *Nine Faces of Kenya*, Harvill, Harper Collins
Huxley E and Perham M, 1944, *Race and Politics in Kenya*, (with 1955 re-assessment)
Image DM, 1988, IWM DSR 12205/3
Image TJ, 1988, IWM DSR/12204/3
Ingham K, 1965, *History of East Africa*, Longman
Jenkins P, 1994, PC, Lewa Downs, Kenya
Johar TR, 1993, PC, Leicester, England
Kaggia B, 1975, *Roots of Freedom*, East Africa Publishing House
Kariuki JM, 1964, *Mau Mau Detainee*, London
Kenya Ministry of Information and Broadcasting (KMIB), undated 1980s-1990s?, *Kenya, The Land of Contrast*
Kenya National Archive, Nairobi (KNA)
Kenyatta J, 1945, *Kenya, Land of Conflict*, Panaf
Ditto, 1968, *Suffering Without Bitterness*, East African Publishing House
Ditto, 1970, *The Challenge of Nationhood – Speeches and Writings*, London
Ditto, 1979 (reprint), *Facing Mount Kenya*, Heinemann, London
Kirkman WP, 1966, *Unscrambling an Empire*, Chatto & Windus
Kirshon JW *ed.*, 1989, *Chronicle of America*, Longman
Kitson FE, 1960, *Gangs and Counter-gangs*, Barrie and Rockliffe
Lamb D, 1984, *Africans*, Vintage Books, NY
Lamb G, 1974, *Peasant Politics*, Davison

Leakey LSB, 1936, *Kenya, Contrasts and Problems*, Methuen
Ditto, 1952, *Mau Mau and the Kikuyu*
Ditto, 1954, *Defeating Mau Mau*, London
Ditto, 1977, *Southern Kikuyu Before 1903*, Academic Press, London and NY
Leputalai Ngoro Ole, 1994, PC, Nanyuki, Kenya
Leys N, 1924, *Kenya*, Hogarth
Liddle AL, 1988, IWM DSR 10091/4
Lipscombe JF, 1949, *From the Beginning*, Nakuru Press
Llewelyn T, 1994, PC, Timau, Kenya
Llewelyn-Davies M (producer/director), 1993, 'Memories and Dreams', Allegra Production for BBC
London Missionary Society, 1880, *Life of David Livingstone*, Hodder and Stoughton
Lovell MS, 1987, *Straight on Till Morning*, Arena
Lovatt Smith [*see* Smith D Lovatt]
Low DA and Smith A *editors*, 1976, *History of East Africa* vol 3, Clarendon Press
Lyttelton O, 1962, *Memoirs of Lord Chandos*, Bodley Head, London
Maciel M, 1985, *Bwana Karani*, Merlin Books, Braunton, Devon
McCall G&J, 1994, PC, Gilgil, Kenya
McGregor RW, 1927, *Kenya from Within*, Allen & Unwin
MacLachlan S, 1988, IWM DSR 10010/3
Macmillan H, 1971, *Autobiography*, Vol. 4: *Riding the Storm 1956–59*, Macmillan
Ditto, vol. 5: *Pointing the way 1959–61*, Macmillan
Majdalany F, 1962, *State of Emergency*, Longmans, London
Markham B, 1984, *West with the Night*, Virago
Maudling R, 1978, *Memoirs*, Sidgwick and Jackson
Mboya T, 1963, *Freedom and After*, London
Ditto, 1993, *Challenge of Nationhood*, East African Educational Publishing Ltd
Meinhertzhagen R, 1983, *Kenya Diary* (1902–6), Eland Books
Mercer D, *ed.*, 1988, *Chronicle of the Twentieth Century*, Longman
Milner JE (producer), 1987, 'No Easy Walk', Acacia for Channel 4 TV
Mitchell Sir P, 1947, *Agrarian Problems in Kenya*, Nairobi Govt. Press
Mitchell P, 1954, *African Afterthoughts*, Hutchinson
Mitton B, 1994, PC, Ukunda, Kenya
Morgan J, 1981, *Backbench Diaries of Richard Crossman*, Hamish Hamilton
Morgan WTW, 1963, 'White Highlands of Kenya', *RGSJ* Vol 129 part 2
Mungai N, 1967, *Independent Nations of Africa*, private
Muoria HM, 1992, PC, London, England
Murray G&I, 1994, PC, Timau, Kenya
Ngugi J, 1966, *Weep Not, Child*, Heinemann
Ngugi wa Thiong'o & Mugo MG, 1976, *Trial of Dedan Kimathi*, EAE, Nairobi
Ngugi wa Thiong'o, 1977, *Petals of Blood*, Heinemann
Ditto, 1981, *Detained, a writer's prison diary*, EAE, Nairobi
Njagi D, 1993, *Last Mau Mau Field Marshals*, Ngwataniro Self Help Group, Nairobi
Nottidge CPR & Goldsack JR, 1966, 'Million Acre Settlement Scheme 1962–66', Department of Settlement, Republic of Kenya
Ochieng WR *ed.*, 1989, *Modern History of Kenya 1895–1980*, Evans Bros.

Odhiambo ESA & Lonsdale J, 2003, *Mau Mau & Nationhood*, James Currey,
  Oxford, EAEP, Nairobi, Ohio UP
Odinga O, 1967, *Not Yet Uruhu*, Heinemann
Ogot BA, 1981, *Historical Dictionary of Kenya*, Scarecrow Press
Oliver R and Sanderson GN, 1985, *Cambridge History of Africa 1870–1905*
Pakenham T, 1991, *Scramble for Africa*, Weidenfeld & Nicolson
Pandit J, 1993, PC, Hove, England
Patel K, 1994, PC, Naivasha, Kenya
Patterson JH, 1934, *Man Eaters of Tsavo*, Macmillan
Perham M, 1976, *East African Journal (1929–30)*, Faber & Faber
Pickering E, 1957, *When the Windows were Opened*, Geoffrey Bles, London
Poer-Trench J, 1994, PC, Kenya
Portsmouth The Earl of, 1965, *Knot of Roots*, Geoffrey Bles, London
Presley CA, 1992, *Kikuyu Women, the Mau Mau Rebellion and Social Change in
  Kenya*, West View Press, Oxford
Robathan D, 1994, *Those Were the Days, memoirs of Kenya 1933–65*, private
Roberts AD ed, 1986, *Cambridge History of Africa (CHA) 1905–40*, CUP
Roberts G ed., 1954, *Mau Mau in Kenya*, Hutchinson & Co, London
Rosberg EG & Nottingham J, 1966, *Myth of Mau Mau*, Hoover
Russell A, 1999, *Big Men, Little People*, Macmillan
Sansom H, 1965, *Diary of life in Kenya*, private
Sansom H & S, 1994, PC, Tunbridge Wells, England
Scott J, 1992, PC, London
Scott P, 1991, *Nice Place to Live*, Michael Russell, Norwich
Segal R, 1961, *Political Life in Africa*, Stevens & Sons, London
Seidenberg D, 1983, *Uhuru and the Kenya Indians*, Heritage Bookshop Ltd,
  Nairobi, Kenya
Seth S, 1993, PC, Leicester, England
Shah KP, 1996, PC, London
Shah M, 1981, *Vision for Uhuru*, private
Shaylor C&E, 1994. PC, Lasham, England
Singh C, 1981, *Uhuru Chronicle, 16 year book*, Newspread International,
  Nairobi
Slater M. 1955, *Trial of Jomo Kenyatta*, Secker & Warburg
Smith D Lovatt ed., 2002, *History of the Kikuyu Guard*, private
Smith Mackenzie, circa 1900, Smith Mackenzie & Co, private draft for paper
Stapleton JW, 1956, *Gate Hangs Well*, Hammond, Hammond & Co
Stoneham CT, 1953, *Mau Mau*, Museum Press
Storrar A, 1997, PC, Lodsworth, Sussex
Stratton A, 1964, *Great Red Island*, Chas. Scribner and Sons, NY
Terry R, 1994, PC, Gilgil, Kenya
Thiong'o [*see* Ngugi wa Thiong'o]
Thompson A, 1994, PC, Timau, Kenya
Throup D, 1988, *Economic and Social Origins of Mau Mau*, Currey
Thurston A, 1991, 'Guide to archives and manuscripts relating to Kenya and
  East Africa in the UK', Hans Zall
Trevelyan GM, 1964, *English Social History*, Pelican

Sources

Trzebinski E, 1985, *Kenya Pioneers*, Heinemann
Valery A, 1991, *Talking About the War*, Isis, Oxford
Van de Post L, 1952, *Venture Into the Interior*, Hogarth
Wachanga HK, 1975, *Sword of Kirinyaga*, Kenya Literature Bureau
Wachira PM, 1994, PC, Mweiga, Kenya
Walker D & K, 1992, PC, Worcester Park, England
Watkins E, 1993, *Jomo's Jailer*, Mulberry Books, Calais
  Ditto, 1995, *Oscar from Africa*, Radcliffe
Waugh, 1979, *Diaries of Evelyn Waugh*, Penguin Books
Whittall EW, 1956, *Dimbilil, the story of a Kenya farm*, Arthur Barker, London
Williams H, 1956, *Paradise Precarious*, Welcome Press, Nairobi
Williamson J, 1984, *The Crucible of Race*, OUP
Wilson FR, 1988, IWM DSR/10257/3
Winkler AM, 1996, *History of the United Kenya Club*, private
Wood S, 1960, *Kenya, the Tensions of Progress*, OUP

Acknowledgements

The Sources section lists people and bodies who contributed in various ways. The author's debt to them is obvious and is gratefully acknowledged. Further acknowledgements and thanks are due to the following:

My wife, Maureen, who contributed to many interviews with 'people involved' in Kenya and Britain, eliciting responses which would not otherwise have come to light and which add colour and other perspectives. She subsequently coped with the gestation of *Scram!* over the years.

My son Christopher, who suggested contributors and, with Carl Nye and others, managed the initial processing of the words.

Those people who would probably prefer not to be named but who have read and commented on various aspects of the book.

The wonderful librarians, archivists and others in Lewes Library, the Kenya National Archive, the Imperial War Museum, and the *East African Standard,* together with others who have produced material both in response to my enquiries and, not infrequently, on their own initiative.

Terry and members of the family and friends who have provided expert assistance and material and provided links.

David Arscott, my editor and publisher at Pomegranate Press, who has gone far above and beyond the call of duty in the closing stages of the book's production – and that was before we compiled the index!

Index

*Numbers in **bold** refer to illustrations. Kenya has a long oral tradition, and the names of people and places appear in an often bewildering variety of transliterations in the written sources. An attempt has been made to adopt those most commonly and authoritatively used.*